高等职业教育"十三五"规划教材

扫码1元看本书课件

● 国际贸易专业系列

国际贸易实务

（双语）

主编◎孙国忠　曹　兰

GUOJI MAOYI

SHIWU

北京师范大学出版集团
BEIJING NORMAL UNIVERSITY PUBLISHING GROUP
北京师范大学出版社

图书在版编目（CIP）数据

国际贸易实务：双语／孙国忠，曹兰主编. -- 2 版. -- 北京：北京师范大学出版社，2018.12

（高等职业教育"十三五"规划教材. 国际贸易专业系列）

ISBN 978-7-303-24401-0

Ⅰ. ①国… Ⅱ. ①孙… ②曹… Ⅲ. ①国际贸易-贸易实务-双语教学-高等职业教育-教材 Ⅳ. ①F740.4

中国版本图书馆 CIP 数据核字(2018)第 284654 号

营 销 中 心 电 话	010-62978190　62979006
北师大出版社科技与经管分社	www.jswsbook.com
电 子 信 箱	jswsbook@163.com

出版发行：北京师范大学出版社　www.bnup.com
　　　　　北京市海淀区新街口外大街 19 号
　　　　　邮政编码：100875

印　　刷：三河市东兴印刷有限公司
经　　销：全国新华书店
开　　本：787 mm×1092 mm　1/16
印　　张：23
字　　数：580 千字
版　　次：2018 年 12 月第 2 版
印　　次：2018 年 12 月第 2 次印刷
定　　价：45.80 元

策划编辑：沈　炜　张自然	责任编辑：沈　炜　张自然
美术编辑：刘　超	装帧设计：高　霞
责任校对：李　菌	责任印制：孙文凯　赵非非

内容提要

　　本书是配合实施任务驱动型教学改革而编写的一本双语教材，分为国际贸易实务中文和国际贸易实务英文两部分，以提高国际贸易专业学生的英语水平和英语专业学生国际贸易职业能力为核心，以一名大学毕业生到外贸公司开始从事国际贸易业务入手，详细阐述了贸易前的准备、合同的磋商和订立、出口合同的履行、进口合同的履行、争议的处理等业务操作。每个任务中都包含任务描述与分析、相关知识、任务实施与心得等部分，开篇前均列明了知识要点和技能要点，便于学习者有针对性地学习。在每章的末尾，精心设计了知识拓展、课堂训练和业务技能训练。每个情境后都配以综合训练。

　　本教程可作为高职院校、应用型本科院校相关专业的国际贸易实务操作教程，也可作为外贸行业各类培训辅导教材，以及相关专业学生或外贸业务人员的参考资料。

前　　言

对外贸易作为拉动我国经济增长的主要动力之一，它的可持续发展直接关系到我国的经济发展态势，而这一切需要大量的国际贸易方面的复合型人才。目前国际贸易从业人员素质参差不齐，高校国际贸易人才培养与社会实际需求有所脱节。

《国际贸易实务》作为国际贸易专业的核心课程之一，在培养高素质的国际贸易应用型、技能型人才上起着重要作用。从事国际贸易工作，英语是第一外语工具，用人单位也大都从国际贸易和英语这两大类专业中招聘人才。为了更有效地加速培养国际贸易实用型紧缺人才，以适应国际市场竞争的迫切需要，为克服英语专业学生国际贸易技能的欠缺和国际贸易专业学生英语水平的低下，我们根据国家最新颁布的有关法律、法规，并结合国际贸易惯例，按照任务驱动型教学需要特意编写本双语教材，希望对国际贸易专业、商务英语专业以及其他相关专业学生提高国际贸易技能和英语水平有所帮助。

本教材遵循国际贸易业务的一般程序，以一位大学生毕业后到常州常信外贸公司从事外贸业务为主线贯穿教材，精心设计了 5 个情境和 17 个任务，把国际贸易业务能力巧妙地设计在各个任务中。每个任务都包含任务描述与分析、相关知识、任务实施与心得等部分，开篇前均列明了知识要点和技能要点，便于学习者明确任务，有针对性地学习。在介绍知识时，突出其实用性，并在其中穿插案例分析、相关网站链接等，引导学习者思考并寻找解决问题的方法，培养其自主学习的能力，精心设计了知识拓展、课堂训练和业务技能训练，并配以综合训练，旨在强化训练学习者掌握贸易前的准备、业务洽谈、合同的磋商和订立、仓储运输、投保、商检、报关、制单、合同的履行、业务善后与争议的处理等技能，满足就业上岗的需要。

附录部分给出了常用经贸术语及缩略语速查表。本教材内容体系、编写方式、实务训练安排等方面均有较大的创新，重点突出国际贸易实务专业英语能力和业务实际操作技能，深入浅出，通俗易懂；语言简练，实用性强，可读性高，符合高职院校课堂教学和实践技能训练的要求，可作为中、高职院校学生、应用型本科院校国际贸易实务操作教程，也可以作为外贸行业各类培训教材，以及相关专业学生或外贸业务人员的参考资料。

本教材由孙国忠、曹兰负责设计总体框架并制定编写大纲，中文部分由孙国忠(任务1、任务6、任务7、任务9、任务10、任务14、任务15、综合训练)、张成伟(任务2)、曹兰(任务3)、江波(任务4、任务8)、杨育文(任务5、任务17)、祁美琴(任务11)、杨华(任务12)、赵茵(任务13)及王迪(任务16)共同编写，最后由孙国忠统稿和定稿。英语部分由张成伟(任务1、任务2、任务17)、曹兰(任务3至任务9)、孙国忠(任务10、任务14、任务15)、祁美琴(任务11)、孙秀峰(任务12)、赵茵(任务13)、王迪(任务16)共同编写，最后由曹兰负责统稿、定稿工作。

本教材充分体现了校企合作的成果，在深化教学改革的过程中，与国内一些外贸企业进行了合作，能够把目前一线国际贸易的实践做法吸收进教材中。深圳市晶诚高科技有限公司的孙秀峰先生、马瑞丽动力系统(上海)有限公司的祁美琴参与了教材编写。常州锐臻国际贸易有限公司的郑隽一先生、常州市天宁对外贸易有限公司的姚臻先生、贾毅先生在本教材在编写过程中提供了很好的建议和部分案例。本书的编写也得益于众多国际贸易专家、学者的著作，以及北京师范大学出版社编辑对编者的指导与帮助。在此特别表示感谢。

由于时间仓促，书中不妥之处在所难免，恳请读者批评指正。

编者

目　录

情境 3　出口合同的履行

情境 4　进口合同的履行

情境 5　业务善后

CONTENTS

Workshop 3 Fulfillment of an Export Contract

Workshop 4 Fulfillment of an Import Contract

Workshop 5 Settlement of Disputes and Claims

情境 1　贸易准备

任务 1
熟悉对外贸易政策及措施

知识要点

1. 国际贸易相关概念
2. 对外贸易政策的类型
3. 关税壁垒和非关税壁垒
4. 国际贸易的特点及发展趋势

技能要点

- 查找我国对外贸易政策措施的变动内容
- 了解相关贸易伙伴国家的对外贸易政策措施的变动情况，查找具体内容

1.1　任务描述与分析

1. 任务描述

2010 年 7 月，孙大伟(David Sun)从南京某高等职业技术学院毕业后，到常州常信外贸有限公司(以下简称常信公司)工作。该公司自 1985 年成立以来，一直致力于纺织品服装、复合地板和电子产品的出口。公司法人代表陈哲安排他到出口部工作，跟资深外贸业务员陈明先生熟悉国际贸易业务，首先让孙大伟了解我国近年的对外贸易政策、措施以及国际贸易的大环境。

常州常信外贸有限公司

江苏常州鸣新路 25 号

电话：0086-519-86338171

传真：0086-519-86338176

电子邮箱：czdavid@126.com

2. 任务分析

常信公司长期出口竞争力强的服装、复合地板、电子产品等优势产品，进口我们所需要的面料、木材等。

国际贸易业务是在不同国家(地区)间开展贸易，具有很强的涉外性和综合性，具体涉及国际贸易理论与政策、国际贸易法律与惯例、国际结算、国际金融、国际运输与保险等诸多方面的理论与实际操作。所以开始从事国际贸易业务工作，一定要学习好国际贸易相关理论与实务，掌握开展国际贸易业务所必须具备的理论知识与技能。

国际贸易业务受国家宏观经济政策的影响很大，所以从事国际贸易工作一定要了解我国和贸易伙伴所在国的对外贸易政策、措施，熟悉相应的国际惯例和贸易规则。

1.2　相关知识

1.2.1　国际贸易的基本概念

1. 国际贸易与对外贸易

国际贸易也称"世界贸易"，是指国际间的商品和劳务的交换。它由各国(地区)的对外贸易构成，是世界各国对外贸易的总和。

对外贸易是从一个国家的角度来看它与其他各国家(地区)之间的商品和劳务的交换。一些海岛国家，如英国、日本等，常把对外贸易称为海外贸易。

2. 进口贸易与出口贸易

国际贸易由进口和出口两部分组成。对输入商品或劳务的国家(地区)来说，是进口；对输出商品或劳务的国家(地区)来说，是出口。

如果出口国与进口国之间进行的贸易买卖，其货物运输必须要通过第三国的国境，对第三国来说，就构成了该国的过境贸易。

一个国家对于某种商品往往既有出口又有进口，在一定时期内(假定一年)出口大于进口,为净出口;相反,即为净进口。

3. 对外贸易值与国际贸易值

对外贸易值是以货币表示的贸易金额。一定时期内一国从国外进口的商品的全部价值,称为进口总额;一定时期内一国向国外出口的商品的全部价值,称为出口总额。两者相加为进出口总额,它是反映一个国家对外贸易规模的重要指标。联合国编制和发表的世界各国对外贸易值的统计资料是以美元表示的。

把世界上所有国家的进口总额或出口总额用同一种货币换算后加在一起,即得世界进口总额或世界出口总额。由于各国一般都以 FOB(装运港船上交货)价计算出口额,按 CIF(成本加保险费、运费)价计算进口额。因此世界出口总额略小于世界进口总额。从国际贸易来看,一国的出口就是另一国的进口,如果把各国进出口值相加作为国际贸易总值就是重复计算。因此,通常所说的国际贸易值就是世界出口总额。

4. 有形贸易与无形贸易

有形贸易是指贸易双方所进行交易的商品是可以看得见的有形实物。无形贸易是指劳务或其他非实物商品的进出口交易。《联合国国际贸易标准分类》把国际贸易商品共分为十大类,即:食品及主要供食用的活动物(0);饮料及烟类(1);燃料以外的非食用粗原料(2);矿物燃料、润滑油及有关原料(3);动植物油脂及油脂(4);未列名化学品及有关产品(5);主要按原料分类的制成品(6);机械及运输设备(7);杂项制品(8);没有分类的其他商品(9)。

有形贸易的金额显示在一国的海关统计上;无形贸易的金额一般不反映在海关统计上,但显示在该国的国际收支表上。

5. 贸易顺差与贸易逆差

贸易差额是一国在一定时期内(如一年、半年、一季、一月)出口总值与进口总值之间的差额。

当出口总值与进口总值相等时,称为"贸易平衡"。当出口总值大于进口总值时,出现贸易盈余,称"贸易顺差"或"出超"。当进口总值大于出口总值时,出现贸易赤字,称"贸易逆差"或"入超"。通常,贸易顺差以正数表示,贸易逆差以负数表示。

知识链接

中国海关数据统计:2010 年中国进出口总值为 29 727 亿美元,其中:出口 15 779 亿美元,进口 13 948 亿美元,贸易顺差 1 831 亿美元。

6. 直接贸易、间接贸易与转口贸易

直接贸易是指商品生产国与商品消费国直接买卖商品的行为。间接贸易是指商品生产国与商品消费国不直接买卖商品,而是通过第三国进行买卖商品的行为。对生产国而言,是间接出口;对消费国而言,是间接进口;对第三国而言,就是转口贸易。

7. 国际贸易商品结构与国际贸易地理方向

国际贸易商品结构是指一定时期内各大类商品或某种商品在整个国际贸易中的构成。国际贸易商品结构可以反映出一国或世界的经济发展水平、产业结构状况、科技发展水平等。

国际贸易地理方向又称国际贸易地区分布,是表明世界各洲、各国或各个区域集团在国际贸易中所占的地位。观察和研究不同时期的国际贸易地理方向,对于掌握市场行情的发展变化,认识世界各国间的经济交换关系及密切程度,开拓国外市场,具有重要意义。中国 2009 年进出口总额排序的前三大贸易伙伴为欧盟、美国和日本。

8. 对外贸易依存度

对外贸易依存度是指一国对外贸易额在该国国民生产总值中所占比重。这是衡量一国国民经济对进出口贸易的依赖程度的一个指标。由于各国经济发展的水平不同,对外贸易政策的差异,国内市场的大小不同,导致各国的对外贸易依存度有较大的差异。

1.2.2 对外贸易政策

对外贸易政策的目的是为了保护本国市场,扩大本国产品出口,促进本国产业结构的改善,积累资本,维护本国对外的政治、经济利益。

不同国家或同一国家的不同时期的对外贸易政策会不断变化。随着世界经济和贸易的发展,目前世界各国或多或少采取自由贸易和保护贸易这两种既相互对立又相互并存的对外贸易政策。

1. 自由贸易政策

自由贸易政策在历史上多为经济强盛的国家所采用。采取该政策的国家取消对进出口货物贸易、服务贸易和与贸易有关的投资上的限制和障碍,取消对它们的各项特权和优惠,使其在国内外市场上自由竞争。

近年来,在经济全球化深入发展的同时,区域经济一体化迅猛发展,以自由贸易区为主要形式的区域贸易不断涌现。世界主要国家和区域集团均加快发展自由贸易区,在全球范围内掀起了一股新的自由贸易浪潮。我国顺应这一新形势,稳步推进自由贸易区建设,取得了很大进展。

2. 保护贸易政策

保护贸易政策是指国家设置各种障碍,利用各种限制进口的措施,来保护本国市场免受外国货物、服务、技术与投资的竞争,并对本国的出口给予优惠和补贴。

1.2.3 对外贸易措施

实施对外贸易措施的目的往往是为了奖出限入,也就是鼓励和帮助本国商品出口而限制外国商品进口。此外,各国还实施出于某些特殊目的出口限制措施。对外贸易措施主要有关税措施和非关税措施两大类。

1. 关税壁垒

关税壁垒又称为关税措施,是指国家通过对进口商品征收高额关税,增加商品成本,达到限制进口目的的措施。

进口税主要可分为最惠国税和普通税两种。最惠国税率比普通税率低,二者税率差幅往往很大。

按差别待遇和特定的实施情况分类,除正常进口税以外,还有进口附加税、优惠关税和惩罚关税、报复关税等。

(1)进口附加税

进口附加税是对进口商品除征收一般关税外,再加征额外的关税。进口附加税主要有反贴补税、反倾销税、差价税三种。

(2)优惠关税

优惠关税是指对从某些国家或地区进口的全部商品或部分商品,给予特别优惠的低关税或免税待遇。但它不适用于从非优惠国家或地区进口的商品。普遍优惠制是比较常用的优惠关税之一。

普遍优惠制是发达国家对从发展中国家或地区输入的商品,特别是制成品和半制成品,给予普遍的、非歧视性的和非互惠的关税优惠待遇。

> 网站链接:可以登录中国海关网查询具体商品的相关进出口税率、增值税率、消费税率和监管条件等,网址为:http://www.customs.gov.cn/publish/portal0/tab9409/。

2. 非关税壁垒

非关税壁垒是指除关税以外的一切限制进口的各种措施。第二次世界大战后,许多国家加入关贸总协定,各国的关税水平都有不同程度的降低,关税的贸易保护作用减弱,限制进口的各种非关税壁垒措施则日益被广泛应用。

非关税壁垒具有更大的灵活性、针对性、隐蔽性和歧视性,更能达到限制进口的目的。非关税壁垒措施名目繁多,现仅就几种重要的措施阐述如下。

(1)进口配额制

进口配额制是非关税壁垒最常见的形式,是一国政府在一定时期以内,对某些商品的进口数量或金额所加的直接限制。配额可以按照国家分配,也可以不按照国家规定一个总的配额。在规定的期限内,配额以内的货物可以进口,超过配额不准进口,或者征收更高的关税、附加税或罚款后才能进口。

(2)"自动"出口配额制

"自动"出口配额制是出口国家或地区在进口国的要求或压力下,自愿规定某一时期内某些商品对该国的出口限制,在限度的配额内自行控制出口,超过配额即禁止出口。"自动"出口配额制有非协定的"自动"出口配额制和协定的"自动"出口配额制。

(3)进口许可证制

进口许可证制是进口国家规定某些商品进口必须事先领取许可证,才可进口,否则一律不准进口。通过发放进口许可证,进口国可以对进口商品的种类、数量、来源、价格和进口时机等加以直接的控制。

(4)新贸易壁垒

新贸易壁垒措施是以技术壁垒为核心,包括环境壁垒、绿色贸易壁垒和社会壁垒在内的,所有阻碍国际贸易自由进行的新型非关税壁垒。

其他还有外汇管制、海关估价制、进出口国家垄断、歧视性政府采购政策、进口最低限价和禁止进口、进口押金制等非关税壁垒。

3. 出口鼓励措施

许多国家在利用关税和非关税措施限制进口的同时,往往还采取各种鼓励措施扩大商品的出口。鼓励出口措施有许多,主要介绍以下几种。

(1)出口信贷

出口信贷是一个国家的银行为了鼓励商品出口,加强商品的竞争能力,对本国出口商或国外进口商提供的贷款。它是一国出口厂商利用本国银行的贷款扩大商品出口，特别是金额较大、期限较长的成套设备、船舶出口的一种重要手段。

出口信贷按借贷关系可以分为卖方信贷和买方信贷。

（2）出口补贴

出口补贴是一国政府为了降低出口商品的价格，加强其在国外市场上的竞争能力，在出口某种商品时，给予出口厂商的现金补贴（直接补贴）或财政上的优惠待遇（间接补贴），诸如减免税收，降低运费等。

（3）商品倾销

商品倾销是出口企业以低于国内市场的价格，甚至低于商品生产成本的价格，在国外市场抛售商品，打击竞争者以占领市场的行为。

商品倾销通常被认为是不公平竞争，会损害进口国的利益，因而进口国会对倾销商品征收反倾销税等。

（4）外汇倾销

外汇倾销是出口企业利用本国货币贬值的机会，争夺国外市场的特殊手段。当一国货币贬值后，出口商品以外国货币表示的价格降低，提高了该商品的竞争能力；而且货币贬值后，货币贬值国家进口商品的价格随之上涨，削弱了进口商品的竞争力。因此，货币贬值起到了促进出口和限制进口的双重作用。

（5）其他措施

有些国家还实行一些促进出口的行政组织措施，如：设立专门组织，研究与制定出口战略；建立商业情报网，加强商业情报的服务工作；组织贸易中心和贸易展览会；组织出口商的评奖活动等。

此外，在一些实行外汇管制的国家，政府实行外汇留成（分红）和出口奖励制度；利用官方援助或贷款，推动商品出口。

4. 出口管制措施

为了达到一定的政治、军事和经济目的以及履行联合国的某些决议，一些国家对一些商品，特别是战略物资与先进技术实行出口管制或禁止出口，这就是出口管制。

1.3　任务实施与心得

 任务实施

通过政府部门的网站了解国家外贸政策和措施

"国事、家事、天下事，事事关心。"孙大伟养成关注各国经济贸易政策和措施的良好习惯，每天关注以下主要网站，及时查找相关的贸易政策、措施的内容。

中华人民共和国商务部 http：//www. mofcom. gov. cn

国家质量监督检验检疫总局 http：//www. aqsiq. gov. cn

中华人民共和国海关总署 http：//www. customs. gov. cn

国家外汇管理局 http：//www. safe. gov. cn

国家税务总局 http：//www.chinatax.gov.cn

美国商务部 http：//www.commerce.gov/

日本经济产业省 http：//www.meti.go.jp/english/index.html

香港贸易发展局 http：//www.hktdc.com/

澳门经济局 http：//www.economia.gov.mo/index.jsp

新加坡国际企业发展局 http：//www.iesingapore.gov.sg/wps/portal/CN

任务实施心得

《国际贸易实务》是一本专门研究国际间商品交换的具体过程的教材，对外贸从业人员今后从事国际贸易业务起着关键的作用。学习者要学好国际贸易理论和实务，在学习时以完成国际贸易的基本业务来学习必要的理论和方法，在完成业务过程中掌握技能。在学习时，主要把握以下几点：

(1)理论联系实际，重视国际惯例的学习

在学习时，要以国际贸易基本原理和国家对外方针政策为指导，力求做到理论与实践、政策与业务有效地结合起来，不断提高分析与解决实际问题的能力。

在学习过程中，结合我国国情来研究国际上一些通行的惯例和普遍实行的原则，加速同国际市场的真正接轨。如国际商会等国际组织制定的《国际贸易术语解释通则》、《托收统一规则》、《跟单信用证统一惯例》等。

(2)注重案例分析和实训

国际贸易实务是一门实践性很强的应用学科。在每个任务完成后，要重视实例分析和课后的实训操作练习，并利用课余时间到校外参观、实习，以增加感性知识，加强基本技能的训练，注重自身动手能力的培养。

(3)提高外语能力，加强其他课程知识的整合

对于外贸从业人员而言，外语能力尤其重要，用外语与外商交流、谈判以及收发外贸函电、制作外贸单证。如果外语掌握不好，就很难胜任工作，甚至会影响业务的顺利进行。因此，学习者必须强化外语学习，切实提高外语口语和听力水平。

1.4 知识拓展

1. 外汇核销

出口收汇核销制度是外汇局对出口单位的出口货物实施跟踪监管直到货款收回进行核销的一种事后监督制度。其目的是为了督促企业安全及时收汇。

在实际出口业务中，核销工作需要遵循以下几个步骤：

(1)领单

出口单位在开展出口业务前到外汇管理局领取出口收汇核销单(以下简称"核销单")，当场在每张核销单的"出口单位"栏内填写单位名称或者加盖单位名称章。出口单位填写的核销单应与出口货物报关单上记载的有关内容一致。

(2)报关

出口单位持在有效期内、加盖出口单位公章的核销单和相关单据办理报关手续。

(3)海关退回核销单

海关退回核销单并出具的贴有防伪标签、加盖海关"验讫章"的出口报关单。

（4）核销

出口单位凭核销单、银行出具的"出口收汇核销专用联"到外汇管理局办理出口收汇核销。外汇管理局审核相关单证，核销完毕。

2. 出口退税

出口退税是指对出口商品已征收的国内税部分或全部退还给出口商的一种措施。出口退税主要通过退还出口货物的国内已纳税款来平衡国内产品的税收负担，使本国产品以不含税成本进入国际市场，与国外产品在同等条件下进行竞争，从而增强竞争能力，扩大出口创汇。

我国从 1985 年开始实行出口退税政策，此后，对出口产品的出口退税经过多次调整。

根据现行税制规定，我国出口货物退（免）税的税种是流转税范围内的增值税、消费税两个税种。

办理出口退税应该附送以下材料：报关单、出口销售发票、进货发票、收汇通知书（结汇水单）、产品征税证明、出口收汇已核销证明以及与出口退税有关的其他材料。

> 网站链接：出口退税率查询 http：//www.chinatax.gov.cn/n480462/n481069/n481099/index.html

1.5　业务技能训练

1.5.1　课堂训练

1. 谈谈你对国际贸易实务课程的认识；国际贸易实务课程与其他课程之间是一种什么样的关系；在今后的学习中你将如何学习这门课程。

2. 查找目前我国对哪些产品征收出口税。了解当前我国产品在国外遭遇反倾销的状况。

3. 目前的外贸形势对本地区出口产品的影响有哪些？为此，我国采取了哪些鼓励出口的措施？

4. 学生上网查询最近中国进出口商品的金额、国别（地区）、商品大类情况以及贸易差额。

1.5.2　实训操作

1. 常州天信外贸有限公司是我国最大的男衬衫生产出口公司之一，公司生产各种档次、规格的男衬衫，产品全部出口到欧美等国，与众多国外用户建立长期良好的合作关系。请查找 2007—2010 年我国对男衬衫出口政策方面的变化。上国家税务总局出口退税率查询网 http：//202.108.90.146/guoshui/web/listArticle1.jsp 查找男衬衫、牛仔布的出口退税率是多少？

2. 江苏天地木业有限公司是我国最大的木地板生产出口基地之一，公司生产各种档次、规格的复合地板，产品全部出口到世界各国，与众多国外用户建立长期良好的合作关系。请在国家税务总局出口退税率查询网 http：//202.108.90.146/guoshui/web/listArti-

cle1.jsp 查找复合地板的出口退税率是多少？

3. 每位学生给自己起个英文名字，适应外商称呼上习惯，计算机选用英文 OFFICE 操作系统，使用全英文界面，注册一个 HOTMAIL 或者 YAHOO.COM 电子邮件信箱，方便客户联系你。

每位学生参考常信公司拟成立一个从事进出口业务的公司，在熟悉国家相关政策的基础上，初步选定自己公司出口产品的大类。

附：部分产品资料

①男式睡裤 MEN'S DORM PANT

海关编码：62034290，20PCS PER CARTON，COLOR：HEALTHER GREY FABRIC，CONTENT：100% COTTON

毛重：13.000 千克/CARTON，净重：11.000 千克/CARTON，体积：0.14300 立方米/CARTON，国内采购参考价：RMB55/PC，国外销售参考价：USD11.74/PC

②女式牛仔裤 WOMEN'S WHISHERED BOTTCUT JEAN

海关编码 62046200，20PCS PER CARTON，COLOR：LIGHT SANDBLAST，FABRIC，CONTENT：100% COTTON

毛重：15.000 千克/CARTON，净重：13.000 千克/CARTON，体积：0.14300 立方米/CARTON

国内采购参考价：RMB68.50/PC，国外销售参考价：USD14.20/PC

③强化地板 LAMINATED FLOORING

海关编码：4411131900（thickness：小于等于 8mm）4411141900（thickness：大于等于 12mm）

毛重：19 800 千克/CONTAINER，净重：19 600 千克/CONTAINER，体积：25 立方米/CONTAINER

国内采购参考价：8mm RMB 60－70/SQM；12mm RMB 100－120/SQM

国外销售参考价：8mm FOB Shanghai USD 4.5/SQM；12mm FOB Shanghai USD 6.5/SQM

④黄鸭玩具 YELLOW DUCK

海关编码：95034100 ，48PCS PER CARTON 10INCH

毛重：8.000 千克/CARTON，净重：6.000 千克/CARTON，体积：0.16400 立方米/CARTON

国内参考价：RMB5.80/PC，国外参考价：USD1.20/PC

⑤圣诞老人玩具 SANTA CLAUS

海关编码：95034100，64PCS PER CARTON

毛重：12.000 千克/CARTON，净重：10.000 千克/CARTON，体积：0.16400 立方米/CARTON

国内参考价：RMB11.50/PC，国外参考价：USD2.50/PC

⑥蘑菇罐头 CANNED MUSHROOMS (CHAMPIGNONS)

海关编码：20039010，6TINS PER CARTON 2840GRAMS NET WEIGHT

毛重：18.744 千克/CARTON，净重：17.040 千克/CARTON，体积：0.02280 立方

米/CARTON

国内参考价：RMB52.50/CARTON，国外参考价：USD10.10/CARTON

⑦什锦蔬菜罐头 CANNED MIXED VEGETABLES

海关编码：20059090，24TINS PER CARTON 425GRAMS NET WEIGHT

毛重：11.220 千克/CARTON，净重：10.200 千克/CARTON，体积：0.01425 立方米/CARTON

国内参考价：RMB30.17/CARTON，国外参考价：USD5.82/CARTON

任务 2
掌握国际贸易业务流程

知识要点

1. 国际贸易业务的基本流程
2. 贸易磋商的环节
3. 发盘、接受的构成条件

技能要点

- 掌握外贸公司的主要业务流程，熟悉公司的产品和客户
- 熟悉询盘、发盘、还盘和接受等函电的写作

2.1　任务描述与分析

1. 任务描述

　　一周后，孙大伟已经大致熟悉我国近年的对外贸易政策、措施，重点了解了最近相关产品出口退税税率的变化情况。在这期间，陈明先生把上月刚出口到美国洛杉矶的一笔 8 000 条裤子的业务流程都教了孙大伟，同时把该笔业务所有单据的副本也给了孙大伟让他熟悉。

　　7 月 10 日，陈先生转给孙大伟一份法国公司有关求购服装信息的 E-mail，请他与对方建立业务联系并给对方发盘，并让他开始独立完成和该法国公司的出口服装业务。下面是法国公司的地址和联系方式。

GOLDEN MOUNTAIN TRADING CO.，LTD
ROOM 1618 BUILDING G
NO. 36 THE FIRST LYON STREET，
PARIS，FRANCE
TEL.：0019-33-44-55 FAX：0019-33-44-56
E-MAIL：paul@hotmail.com

2. 任务分析

　　从事国际贸易业务的人员，必须熟练掌握国际贸易业务的流程，以确保国际贸易的顺利开展。国际贸易具有不同于国内贸易的特点，其交易过程、交易条件、贸易习惯及所涉及的法律问题，都远比国内贸易复杂，进出口双方只有按照正确的国际贸易流程进行实务操作，才能确保在将来获得预期的利润，任何一个程序中的偏差或失误都可能导致巨大的损失。

　　国际贸易业务具有线长、面广，中间环节多，受外在因素的影响大，变化快，涉及的法律复杂，交易成本较大，风险较高等特点。

2.2　相关知识

　　在国际贸易实际业务中，不同的交易、不同的贸易条件，其业务环节也不尽相同。在具体工作方面，各个环节又常先后交叉进行，或者出现齐头并进的情形。但是，无论是出口贸易，还是进口贸易，就它们的基本业务程序而言，主要包括交易前的准备、国际贸易合同的磋商订立以及合同的履行三个阶段。具体国际贸易业务流程如图 2-1 所示。

2.2.1　交易前的准备工作

　　交易前的准备是整个国际贸易程序中的第一个环节，也是整个交易的基础。国际贸易交易前的准备主要包括国际市场调研、寻找客户及与客户建立业务关系三方面内容。

1. 国际市场调研

　　国际市场调研是为了获得与贸易有关的各种信息，通过对信息的分析，得出国际市场

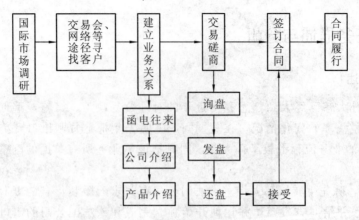

图 2-1　国际贸易业务流程

行情特点，判定贸易的可行性并进而制订贸易计划。国际市场调研主要在于客户调研。

客户调研在于了解欲与之建立贸易关系的国外客户的基本情况，包括它的历史、资金规模、经营范围、组织情况、信誉等级等总体状况，还包括它与世界各地(包括我国)其他客户开展对外经济贸易的历史和现状。只有对国外客户有了一定的了解，才可以与之建立贸易联系。在我国对外贸易实际业务中，常有因对对方情况不熟悉，匆忙与之进行交易而造成重大损失的事件发生。因此在交易磋商之前，一定要对国外客户的资金和信誉状况有十足的把握，不可急于求成。

2. 寻找客户

外贸企业在国际市场调研的基础上，一般必须对自己的企业进行市场定位并寻找客户。在国际贸易业务中，每个企业都会使出浑身解数来寻找客户。外贸企业寻找客户的方法很多，可以简单地概括为第三方介绍、媒体寻找、传统的交易会寻找三类。

网站链接：很实用的 16 种寻找客户的方法

http://info.jctrans.com/zxzx/jszd/sjxw/20061128356494.shtml

3. 建立业务关系

企业通过各种渠道找到国外客户，在对客户资信情况进行调查后，然后选择客户并与之建立业务联系。

国际贸易中，买卖双方业务关系的建立，往往是由交易一方通过主动向对方写信、发传真或 E-mail 等形式开展，有时也会通过正式的谈判建立。建立业务关系的函件一般包括下列内容：

1)信息来源。即如何取得对方的资料，如通过他人介绍、网上信息等。

2)言明去函目的。如扩大交易范围、建立长期业务关系等。

3)本公司情况。包括公司性质、业务范围、宗旨及公司经营优势等。

4)产品介绍。分两种情况，一是明确对方需求，此时宜选取某类特定产品，进行具体的推荐；二是不明确对方需求，此时宜对企业产品整体情况作笼统介绍(最好附上商品目录、报价单或另寄样品供对方参考)。

5)激励性结尾。即希望对方给予回应或采取行动。

2.2.2　交易磋商

国际贸易的磋商形式主要包括口头谈判和书面谈判两种。口头谈判主要是在谈判桌上的面对面谈判和双方通过语音通信手段进行的交易磋商。书面谈判主要是通过信件、电报、传真等通信方式来洽谈交易。书面洽谈正成为日常交易磋商最常用的方式。

一般来说，口头谈判和书面谈判都可以分为询盘、发盘、还盘和接受四个环节。其中发盘和接受是达成交易、订立合同必不可少的环节。

1. 询盘

询盘是指交易的一方有意出售或者购买某种商品而向对方发出的关于买卖该商品的有关交易条件的意思表示。实践中，询盘一般是向不特定的相对方发出，其内容可以包括一项或多项交易条件。

根据发出主体的不同，将询盘分为两种：买方发出的询盘是买方询盘，由卖方发出的询盘是卖方询盘。

例1：意购中号 T 恤 1 500 打，请报最低价及最早装运期。（买方询盘）

例2：能够提供 T 恤 2 000 打。（卖方询盘）

2. 发盘

发盘亦称报价，在法律上称之为"要约"，是买卖双方中的一方向特定的对方提出各项交易条件，并愿意按这些条件达成交易、订立合同的一种意思表示。《联合国国际货物销售合同公约》（以下简称《公约》）认为，"向一个或一个以上特定的人提出的订立合同的建议，如果内容十分确定并且表明发盘人在得到接受时将承受约束的意思表示，即构成发盘"。

在实际业务操作中，发盘多为卖方发出，称之为售货发盘；如果是买方发出，则可称为购货发盘或递盘。

（1）发盘的构成条件

依据《公约》的规定，要构成一项有效的发盘，必须同时具备以下四项要件。

1）发盘的相对方为一个或一个以上特定的人。

2）发盘的内容十分确定。

3）表明发盘人将受其约束。

4）传达到受盘人。

（2）发盘的有效期

发盘的有效期是指可供受盘人对发盘是否做出接受的时间限制。在发盘的有效期内，发盘人要受发盘的约束，不得随意撤销，超过有效期，发盘人就不再受其约束。故受盘人的接受必须在发盘的有效期内做出，超期接受无效。在实际业务中，发盘有效期的规定通常有以下三种方法：

1）明确规定发盘的有效期，规定最迟接受的期限或规定一段接受的时间。该种情况下的发盘自其送到受盘人时生效，到规定的有效期结束时终止。

例如：发盘……限 3 月 20 日复到。

发盘 7 日内复有效。

2）未明确规定发盘有效期。该种发盘并非永久有效，根据《公约》第十八条的规定，受盘人在这种情况下必须在合理时间内做出接受的意思表示，否则接受无效。但是，对"合理时间"的解释各国法律有所差异，难以做出明确统一的解释。因此，为了避免产生纠纷，尽量避免使用该种规定方法。

3)口头发盘。依《公约》规定，采用口头发盘的，除发盘人发盘时另有声明外，受盘人只能当场表示接受才有效。

（3）发盘的撤回与撤销

发盘在一定情形下可以撤回和撤销，具体如表2-1所示。

表 2-1 发盘的撤回与撤销的比较

	发盘的撤回	发盘的撤销
概念	发盘人在其发盘送达受盘人以前，将该项发盘取消的行为	发盘人将已经送达受盘人的发盘取消的行为
《公约》的规定	发盘在未被送达受盘人之前，如果发盘人改变主意，可以将其撤回，但发盘人必须将撤回通知于发盘送达之前或与发盘同时送达受盘人	已经被受盘人收到的发盘，如果撤销通知在受盘人发出接受通知前到达受盘人，可以撤销
不得撤回或撤销的情形	在实践中，由于贸易双方多用传真和电子邮件等比较快捷的方式进行发盘，撤回基本上无法实现	发盘是以规定有效期或以其他方式表明不可撤销的；受盘人有理由信赖该发盘是不可撤销的，并已根据该信赖采取了行动

（4）发盘的终止

发盘的终止也称为发盘的失效，是指已经生效的发盘失去法律效力。发盘的终止对于发盘人来说，他不再受该发盘约束，对受盘人来说，他也失去了接受该发盘的权利。

在实践中，引起发盘终止的事由主要有以下几种。

1)受盘人做出还盘或拒绝的意思表示。

2)发盘人依法撤销发盘。

3)发盘的有效期届满或发盘虽未规定有效期，但已经超过了合理时间，发盘人仍未收到受盘人的答复。

4)因发生了某些特定情况而依法失效。如发盘人在发盘被接受前丧失了行为能力或被正式宣告破产；发盘人因违法而被取消经营权；发盘中的商品被政府宣布为禁止进出口的；发盘中特定的标的物灭失等。

3. 还盘

受盘人在接到发盘后，不能完全同意发盘的内容，为了进一步进行交易的磋商，对发盘提出修改意见，用口头或书面形式表示出来，就构成还盘。

还盘的形式并不固定，有的明确使用"还盘"字样，有的仅在内容中表示出对发盘的修改。还盘是对发盘的拒绝，还盘一经做出，原发盘即失去效力，发盘人也不再受其约束，该还盘即成为一个新的发盘。

例1：你方10月8日的发盘，如果改为付款交单，我们就可以接受。

例2：我们认为你方的发盘要价过高，我们很难接受。

4. 接受

法律上将接受称为"承诺"，指交易的一方在接到对方的发盘或还盘后，以声明或行为的方式向对方表示同意。接受和发盘一样，既属于商业行为，也属于法律行为。《公约》对接受作了明确的规定。

例：我方接受"红星"牌手套 2 000 打，每打 HK＄3. 50 CIF LONDON，七月底前装运，不可撤销即期信用证支付。

（1）接受的构成条件

根据《公约》的解释，构成有效的接受要具备以下四项要件。

1）接受必须由受盘人做出。

2）受盘人表示接受，要采取声明的方式即以口头或书面的声明向发盘人明确表示出来。另外，还可以用行为表示接受。

3）接受的内容要与发盘的内容相符。

4）接受的通知要在发盘的有效期内送达发盘人才能生效。

（2）接受内容的变更

接受必须是同意发盘所列的全部交易条件。如果受盘人在接受时附加了某一项或几项条件，对发盘做出了变更。这种对发盘内容有所变更的接受是还盘的一种形式，不能构成真正有效的接受。

（3）接受的撤回

根据《公约》规定，接受可以撤回，但撤回通知必须于接受生效之前或与接受通知同时到达发盘人为限。接受不得撤销，因为接受生效后，合同已经成立，如果要撤销接受，在实质上已属毁约行为，问题的性质就大相径庭了。

（4）逾期接受

晚于发盘人规定的有效期送达的接受称为逾期接受。逾期接受不具法律效力。但《公约》第 21 条规定，逾期接受在下列两种情况下仍具有法律效力。

1）如果发盘人毫不迟延地用口头或书面的形式将认可逾期接受的意思通知受盘人。

2）如果载有逾期接受的信件或其他书面文件表明，它在传递正常的情况下是能够及时送达发盘人的，那么这项逾期接受仍然具有接受的效力，除非发盘人毫不迟延地用口头或书面方式通知受盘人，明确表示该发盘已经失效。

2. 2. 3　合同的签订与履行

经过交易磋商后，如果就某项交易的基本条件达成一致意见，双方一般会以书面形式将该一致意见记录下来，并各自签署盖章，这就是签订合同。合同是后续贸易业务施行的基础和依据，因此，在签订合同过程中必须谨慎。合同签订后，双方就进入履行合同的阶段。

1. 出口合同的履行

出口合同履行，指出口人按照合同的规定履行交货义务直至收回货款的整个过程。出口合同履行是目前我国外贸企业出口工作最重要的阶段。采用 CIF 术语按信用证支付方式成交的出口合同，履行程序一般包括备货、催证、审证、改证、租船订舱、报关、报验、保险、装船和制单结汇等步骤。

2. 进口合同的履行

进口合同履行,指进口人按照合同规定的义务履行付款义务直至提取货物的整个过程。它是进口工作的最后阶段,应该注意货款和货物的流转进程,同时必须重视货物的验收工作,保证交易商品物有所值。在贸易术语的选择上,出于整体利益的考虑,应尽可能采用 FOB 术语,在支付方式的选择上也要慎重对待,争取采用对进口方有利的方式付款。但目前在实践中,多为 L/C 方式。进口合同履行程序一般包括开立信用证、租船订舱和催装、保险、审单和付汇、报关和接货、验收和拨交、进口索赔等环节。

2.3　任务实施与心得

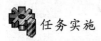 任务实施

孙大伟写了一封建立业务关系的函电给对方,并请对方就具体产品进行询价。

DEAR SIRS,

WE LEARNED FROM THE INTERNET THAT YOU ARE ONE OF THE MAJOR EXPORTERS OF TEXTILES AND GARMENTS IN YOUR COUNTRY. WE ARE WRITING TO ENTER INTO BUSINESS RELATIONS WITH YOU ON THE BASIS OF MUTUAL BENEFITS AND COMMON INTERESTS.

OUR CORPORATION IS A STATE-OWNED FOREIGN TRADE ORGANIZATION, DEALING IN THE IMPORT AND EXPORT OF TEXTILES AND GARMENTS. OUR PRODUCT IS OF FASHIONABLE DESIGN, COMFORTABLE FEELING AND HIGH QUALITY, WHICH ENJOYS HIGH REPUTATION BOTH IN AMERICA AND ASIA.

AS REQUESTED, ENCLOSED IS OUR LATEST CATALOGUE. IF YOU HAVE SPECIAL REQUIREMENTS, PLEASE INFORM US.

LOOKING FORWARD TO YOUR PROMPT REPLY.

YOURS FAITHFULLY

DAVID SUN

(SIGNATURE)

任务实施心得

寻找客户对外贸业务员来说至关重要,但这是一个长期的过程。找到潜在的客户,建立业务关系仅仅是外贸业务的第一步,然后进入艰苦的询盘、发盘和还盘等磋商阶段。

发盘、还盘和接受是建立在对产品的成本核算以及对产品市场行情的把握上的。出口商品交易的实施过程,包括货源采购、出运报关、运交买方三个基本阶段,其间产生的成本、费用是构成出口商品价格的最主要因素。出口商品对外发盘,需根据出口成本、国际市场价格和经营意图等多方面综合考虑。因发盘时有些费用尚未真正发生,即使已发生的费用,具体分摊也要经过一段时间,因此成本在拟订价格时很难准确地确定,只能进行估算。

2.4 知识拓展

1. 包销

包销也称为独家经销，指出口人（委托人）通过协议把某一种商品或某一类商品在某一个地区和期限内的经营权给予国外某个客户或公司的贸易做法。

出口人与包销商之间的关系是买卖关系，包销商赚取的是货物的进价与销价之间的差价。包销商从出口企业处购进货物后，自行销售、自负盈亏，承担货价涨落及库存积压的风险。

2. 代理

代理是指出口商（委托人）授权国外代理人向其他中间商或用户，代表出口商本人销售其产品的一种贸易方式。

代理人与委托人之间的关系属于委托代理关系。代理人在代理业务中，只是代表委托人进行交易，他本身并不作为合同的一方参与交易。代理人不管交易的盈亏，只收取佣金。

根据出口商赋予代理商的特许经营权限，代理分为总代理、独家代理、佣金代理三种类型。

3. 寄售

寄售是指委托人（货主）先将货物运往寄售地，委托国外一个代销人（受委托人），按照寄售协议规定的条件，由代销人代替货主进行销售。

代销人不负担风险与费用，一般不需垫付资金，多销多得。寄售对代销人有利，适用于比较难以销售的产品。

4. 招标与投标

招标与投标常在国家政府机构、公用事业单位或国际经济组织在采购大批物资、大型器材设备或援建项目中广泛采用。

招标是指招标人发出招标公告或招标单，提出准备买进商品的品种、数量和有关交易条件，邀请投标人在规定的时间、地点，按照一定的程序进行投标，然后招标人择优取标，达成商品交易的一种方式。

投标是指投标人应招标人的邀请，根据招标公告或招标单的规定条件，在规定的时间内向招标人递盘的行为。

5. 拍卖

通过拍卖进行交易的商品大都是品质规格复杂、难以标准化的，或是难以久存的，或是习惯上采用拍卖方式进行交易的商品。如茶叶、烟叶、兔毛、皮毛、木材、水貂皮、澳洲羊毛、古玩、艺术品等。

拍卖是一种单批实物的现货交易。拍卖后卖方或拍卖举办人对货物的品质一般不负赔偿责任。按质论价、优质优价的特点在拍卖中表现得尤为突出，故对卖方较为有利，往往可以使卖方获得较高的价格。

6. 展卖与加工贸易

展卖是出口商通过参加或举办展览会、展销会、博览会及其他交易会形式，将自己的商品展示给客户，从而进行销售的方式。

加工贸易是一种加工再出口业务。它把加工和扩大出口，收取工缴费收入结合起来。目前的主要做法有来料加工、进料加工、来件装配等。

2.5　业务技能训练

2.5.1　课堂训练

1. 简述国际贸易实际业务程序。简述出口合同的履行程序。

2. 构成发盘和接受的有效条件有哪些？分组讨论，以实际业务举例说明。

3. 案例分析题

(1)我国某出口公司与美商洽谈一宗交易，我方于 2008 年 6 月 7 日以电报发盘，规定 6 月 12 日前复到有效。美商在 6 月 10 日以电报表示接受。我方 14 日收到该项复电。业务员因其为逾期接受，应属无效，未予理睬，将该货又售另一客户。事后美商坚持合同已成立，要我方发货。你认为合同是否成立？我方是否应交货并阐述理由。

(2)我国某外贸公司于 6 月 1 日向美国进口商发出电传，发盘供应一批瓷器 1 000 件并列明"牢固木箱包装"。美国进口商收到我方电传后立即复电表示接受并要求用新木箱装运。我方收到复电后立即着手备货，准备于 7 月份装船，两周后，美国进口商来电称："由于你方对新木箱包装要求未做确认表示，所以双方合同没有成立。"而我方认为合同已经成立，为此双方发生了争执，试分析美国进口商的理由能否成立。

(3)A 向 B 发盘"蝴蝶牌缝纫机 JA－1 型 3 000 架木箱装每架 62 美元 CFRC2％科威特 10 月装即期信用证限 6 日复到此地。"B 于 9 月 5 日回电："你 3 日电如 62 美元 CFRC3％ D/P 即期接受。"A 对此未予答复，问双方合同是否成立？为什么？

2.5.2　实训操作

1. 2010 年 9 月 15 日，常州天信外贸有限公司从国外一个老客户处得知加拿大客户 JAMES BROWN&SONS(以下简称 J. B. S 公司)要求订购型号 MS691、MS862 的男衬衫。现在请你写一函电给 J. B. S 公司，以建立业务合作关系。

常州天信外贸有限公司
CHANGZHOU TIANXIN IMPORT & EXPORT CORP.
Room 2601，Changzhou International Trade Center
801 Yan Ling Road(w)，Changzhou，Jiangsu 213001
TEL：＋86 519 86338175
FAX：＋86 519 86338177

JAMES BROWN&SONS.
♯304－310 JaJa Street，Toronto，Canada
TEL：(1)7709910
FAX：(1)7701100

2. 2010 年 10 月 25 日，江苏天地木业有限公司收到美国现代公司的要求订购木地板的传真，现在请你回传真，说明天给他们具体报价。

江苏天地木业有限公司

JIANGSU TIANDI WOOD CO.，LTD

CUIBEI VILLAGE，HENGLIN TOWN，WUJIN DISTRICT，CHANGZHOU，JIANGSU

TEL：0086-519-88507666

FAX：0086-519-88507777

MODEN TRADE，INC.

66750 VOSE ST. NORTH HOLLYWOOD，CA 91605 USA

TEL：215/880-9066

FAX：816/232-0388

3. 在熟悉国际贸易业务流程的基础上，每位学生对照自己公司的出口产品，完成以下操作。

(1)在中国制造网(http：//cn. made-in-china. com/)等相关网站上寻找供应商，进行询价比较，取得产品的国内价格信息。

(2) 熟悉常用的著名 B2B 网站，在 http：//www1. tradekey. com/、http：//www. ec21. com/或者到针对某个国际市场的贸易平台如：新加坡贸易网 http：//tradelink. com. sg/、非常活跃的印度市场 http：//www. trade-india. com 等相关网站上寻找国外客户，发出建立业务关系函，最好在成本核算的基础上发盘。

(备注：如果短时间内不能联系到国外客户，那请学生成立模拟的国外进口公司，请出口公司与其他学生的进口公司开展业务。)

(3)对收集到的客户资料和供应商资料进行整理。

4. 学生登录一些知名的外贸论坛的网站 http：//bbs. fobshanghai. com/、http：//bbs. tradehr. com/、http：//bbs. globalimporter. net/，学习外贸的实际操作经验，吸取别人的经验和教训，然后分组交流心得。

综合训练一

1. 业务背景

2010 年 9 月 4 日，常州永盛进出口公司(CHANGZHOU YONGSHENG IMPORT & EXPORT CORP. 88. YANLING ROAD, CHANGZHOU，JIANGSU，CHINA)收到新加坡一新客户 RAFFLES TRADING CO. LTD. 来函，对永盛进出口公司在网上发布的"黑牡丹"牌牛仔布感兴趣。

2. 训练任务

根据相关背景及资料，以永盛进出口公司业务员身份，向客户发出建立业务关系函，内容包括向客户寄送样品、介绍"黑牡丹"牌牛仔布、邀请客户来参观等。

查找我国的牛仔布出口退税率以及进出口关税情况，对客户进行资信调查。

3. 相关资料

(1)客户名称、地址：

RAFFLES TRADING CO. LTD.

69 INTERNATIONAL TRADE PLAZA

ORCHARD ROAD，SINGAPORE

客户电话：(065)6402588

传真：(065)6403688

客户开户银行及账号：中国银行新加坡分行（BANK OF CHINA，SINGAPORE），03063288

（2）商品信息

货名及货号："黑牡丹"牌牛仔布、0866；

规格：坯布经纬纱30支×36支，每英寸经纬密度72×69，克重400GSM，每匹幅宽150cm，长42码；

包装：捆(布)，每捆5匹，体积：150CM(L)×60CM(W)×40CM(H)，毛重：80千克，净重：77千克。

情境 2　合同的磋商与订立

任务 3

订立合同的标的条款

知识要点

1. 表示商品品质的方法
2. 运输标志的组成
3. 溢短装条款的内容
4. 常用的计重方法

技能要点

- 选择合适的方法来表示商品的质量
- 能够计算集装箱内所装货物的数量
- 能够正确确定溢短装数量和运输标志
- 正确订立出口合同的品质、数量、包装条款

3.1　任务描述与分析

1. 任务描述

常信公司已经和法国 GOLDEN MOUNTAIN TRADING CO.，LTD 建立了业务关系，法国公司有意购买中国服装与玩具等日用消费品，第一笔订单希望先从服装开始。

常信公司的服装出口一般采用纸箱包装，主要有均色均码和混色混码两种包袋方式，通常是以一只 40 英尺的集装箱所装货物的数量为最低订货数量来进行出口报价的。由于是第一次和常信公司开展业务，法国 GOLDEN MOUNTAIN TRADING CO.，LTD 的试订单为一只 20 英尺的集装箱的服装，如果销售不错，以后再加大进口量。

孙大伟已经和法国公司的 Pual 就具体业务磋商了一段时间，并且初步选定出口一批女式风衣到法国。现在就具体出口服装的名称和品质、包装展开细致的讨论，准备拟订合同的品名与品质、数量、包装条款。

2. 任务分析

商品的名称和品质、数量、包装是国际货物买卖当事人双方首先需要商定的交易条件，也是国际货物买卖合同中的重要条款。

《公约》规定，卖方交付的货物必须与合同所规定的名称、质量、数量相符。如果卖方交货不符合约定的名称规定、品质条件，买方有权要求损害赔偿，也可以要求修理或交付替代物，甚至拒收货物和撤销合同。如卖方交货数量大于约定的数量，买方可以拒收多交的部分，也可以收取多交部分中的一部分或全部，但应按合同价格付款。如卖方交货数量少于约定的数量，卖方应在规定的交货期届满前补交，但不得使买方遭受不合理的不便和承担不合理的开支，而且买方有保留索赔的权利。如果卖方交付的货物未按约定的条件包装，或者货物的包装与行业习惯不符，买方有权拒收货物。

在货物买卖合同中，品质条款一般包括商品的品名、规格、等级、品牌、标准以及交付货物的品质依据等。数量条款主要包括成交商品的具体数量、计量单位。按重量计算商品，还须明确计算重量的方法。对于一些以个数计量的货物，一般还在数量条款中加订溢短装条款。包装条款主要包括包装材料、包装方式、包装规格、包装标志、包装费用和每件包装中所含物品的数量或重量等内容。

3.2　相关知识

3.2.1　商品的名称

买卖双方在磋商和签订进出口合同时，一定要明确、具体地订明商品的名称，并尽可能使用国际上通用的名称，避免履约的麻烦。

1. 商品的名称与 HS 编码

我国目前实施的商品分类，全部采用了《商品名称编码协调制度》（HS）目录中对商品的分类原则、结构和全部商品名称，将商品分为 22 类 98 章。因此，在国际贸易对外成交采用商品名称时，应与 HS 规定的品名相对应。

2. 商品名称条款的内容

合同中的品名条款一般比较简单，多在"商品名称"或"品名"的标题下，列明交易双方成交商品的名称。有时为了省略，也可不加标题，只在合同的开头部分，列明交易双方同意买卖某种商品的文句。

规定品名条款时，应注意以下事项：

1)商品的名称必须能够切实反映商品的实际情况，是卖方能够提供而且是买方所需要的商品，避免空泛、笼统的规定，不必要的描述性的词句不应列入。

2)商品的名称要尽可能使用国际上通行的名称；商品的名称在《协调制度》中能够准确归类。

3)对某些商品还应注意选择合适的品名，以利于减低关税，方便进出口和节省运费开支。

3.2.2　商品的品质

商品质量的好坏，不仅关系到商品价格的高低，而且还影响商品的销路和信誉。有些国家规定，凡品质不符合其法令法规规定的，一律不准进口。提高商品品质，使之适应外国政府的法律要求，符合安全卫生标准，是突破其保护壁垒、扩大出口的有效途径之一。

在国际货物买卖中，商品种类纷繁复杂，规定商品品质的方法也多种多样。归纳起来，主要有以下两大类。

1. 以样品表示商品的品质

样品通常是从一批商品中抽出来或由生产部门设计、加工出来的，足以反映和代表整批商品品质的少量实物。凡以样品表示商品品质并以此作为交货依据的称为凭样品买卖。

在国际贸易中，按提供者的不同，可分为卖方样品、买方样品和对等样品三种，如表3-1所示。

表3-1　样品的分类

	卖方样品	买方样品	对等样品
定义	由卖方提供的样品	由买方提供的样品	卖方根据买方来样仿制或从现有货物中选择品质相近的样品提交买方确认，这种样品称对等样品
凭样品成交	凡凭卖方样品作为交货品质依据者，称为凭卖方样品买卖	按买方提供的样品成交，称为凭买方样品买卖。在我国称为"来样成交"或"来样制作"	在实际业务中，谨慎的卖方往往不愿意承接按买方来样交货的业务，以免交货品质与买方样品不符而招致买方索赔甚至退货的危险
合同条款的规定	在买卖合同中应该订明："品质以卖方样品为准"	在买卖合同中应该订明："品质以买方样品为准"	实际上是用卖方样品取代了买方样品，使卖方在交货时取得主动
交货商品的要求	卖方所交整批货物的品质，必须与其提供的样品相同	卖方所交整批货物的品质，必须与买方样品相同	卖方所交整批货物的品质，必须与对等样品相同

　　凭卖方样品买卖时，卖方提供的样品叫原样或标准样品，送交买方时，应留存一份或数份同样的样品，这种样品叫复样。复样以备将来组织生产、交货或处理质量纠纷时作核对之用。卖方应在原样和留存的复样上编制相同的号码，注明样品提交买方的具体日期，以便日后联系、洽谈交易时参考。留存的复样应妥善保管，以保证样品品质的稳定。

　　在确认按买方样品成交之前，卖方必须充分考虑按来样制作特定产品所需的原材料供应、加工技术、设备和生产安排的可行性，以确保日后得以正确履约。还需防止侵犯第三者工业产权，应在合同中明确规定：如果发生由买方来样引起侵犯第三者工业产权的事情，概由买方负责，与卖方无关。

> **注意：参考样品**
>
> 　　有时买卖双方为了发展贸易关系和增进彼此对对方商品的了解，往往采用互相寄送样品的做法。这种以介绍商品为目的而寄出的样品，最好标明"仅供参考"（For Reference Only）字样，以免与标准样品混淆。在寄送"参考样品"的情况下，如买卖合同中没有订明交货品质以该项样品为准，而是约定了其他方法来表示品质，这就不是凭样品买卖，这种样品对交易双方均无约束力。

　　作为样品，一般都反映其所代表的商品的整体品质。但也有一些样品，它们只被用作反映某些商品的一个或几个方面的部分品质，而不反映全部品质。例如，色样只表示商品的颜色，花样款式样品只表示商品的花样款式。至于该商品的其他品质内容，则采用文字说明来表示。

　　凭样品买卖时，卖方交货品质必须与样品完全一致。否则，买方有权提出索赔甚至拒收货物。因此，凭样品买卖容易产生品质纠纷，只能酌情采用；凡是能用科学的指标表示商品品质时，不宜采用凭样品买卖。如对品质无绝对把握，应在合同中作出灵活规定，如规定：品质与样品近似。

　　用样品表示商品品质，一般适用于不能用科学方法来表示品质或在色、香、味或造型方面有特殊要求的商品，主要是一部分工艺品、服装、轻工产品和土特产品等。

2. 用文字说明表示商品的品质

　　在国际货物买卖中，大多数商品采用文字说明来规定其品质。具体有以下六种方式，如表 3-2 所示。

表 3-2　文字说明表示商品品质的分类

	注意事项	示例	适用商品
凭规格买卖	将主要指标订入合同，如成分、含量、纯度、大小、粗细等，不宜罗列过多次要指标	中国东北大豆：水分（最高）14%，含油量（最低）18%，杂质（最高）1%，不完善粒（最高）7%	大多数商品
凭等级买卖	商品的等级指同一类商品根据其品质的差异划分为不同的级别和档次，从而产生品质优劣的若干等级。等级一般用重、中、轻；甲、乙、丙；特级、一级、二级、三级等表示	中国绿茶　特珍眉特级　货号 41022	有明确等级的商品，如矿产品等

续表

	注意事项	示例	适用商品
凭标准买卖	采用凭标准买卖时,应尽量采用国际通行标准,以扩大出口;在援用标准时,应注明版本年份,以避免引起争议,如 GB 17323-1988	利福平 英国药典 1993年版	有通用标准的商品
凭商标或品牌买卖	如果一种品牌的商品同时有许多种不同型号或规格,为了明确起见,就必须在规定品牌的同时,明确规定型号或规格;在采用买方定牌交易情况下,卖方应对涉及的知识产权问题作出规定	Model:KV-2553TC 索尼牌彩电	在国际上久负盛名的名牌产品
凭产地名称买卖	产地必须能够反映商品的品质,在国际市场上享有盛誉	四川榨菜	在品质方面具有其他产区商品所不具有的独特风格和特色
凭说明书或图样买卖	买方为了维护自身利益,往往要求在合同中订立卖方品质保证条款和技术服务条款;说明书或图样成为合同的一部分	品质和技术数据必须与卖方所提供的产品说明书严格相符	机器、仪表、大型设备、交通工具等技术密集型商品

凭等级买卖,在列明等级的同时,最好同时规定每一等级的具体规格。例如我国出口的钨砂,主要根据其三氧化钨和含锡量的不同,分为特级、一级、二级三种,如表 3-3 所示。

表 3-3　我国出口钨砂的等级标准

	三氧化钨(最低)(%)	锡(最高)(%)	砷(最高)(%)	硫(最高)(%)
特级	70	0.2	0.2	0.8
一级	65	0.2	0.2	0.8
二级	65	1.5	0.2	0.8

在国际贸易中,有些特殊商品既无法用文字概括其品质,又没有品质完全相同的样品以作为交易的品质依据,如珠宝、字画等,对于这些商品,买卖双方只能看货成交。

看货成交又称凭现货买卖,即根据现有商品的实际品质买卖。具体做法:在货物存放地卖方向买方展示货物,买方或其代理人逐一验看,如果满意,即与卖方达成交易。只要卖方交付的货物是验看的商品,买方就不能对品质提出异议。这种做法多见于寄售、拍卖、展卖等贸易业务中。

3.2.3　计量单位和度量衡制度

商品的数量是通过一定的度量衡单位来表示的。了解度量衡制度,熟悉各种计量单位的特定含义和计量方法,是国际贸易人员必须具备的技能。

1. 常用的计量单位

在不同的计量方式下,通常采用的计量单位名称及适用的商品,具体如表 3-4 所示。

表 3-4 常用计量单位

	常用计量单位	适用商品	具体商品举例
重量	公吨、长吨、短吨，千克、磅、盎司、克拉	农产品、矿产品以及部分工业制成品	羊毛、棉花、谷物、矿产品、油类、药品等
个数	只、件，打、双，台、套、架、辆、头。有些商品也可按箱、包、桶、袋	一般日用工业品、轻工业品以及一部分土特产品	文具、玩具、成衣、车辆、活牲畜等
长度	米、英尺、码、厘米	纺织品，绳索、电线、电缆	
面积	平方米、平方英尺、平方码、平方厘米	皮制商品、塑料制品、地毯、玻璃	塑料地板、皮革、铁丝网等
体积	立方米、立方英尺、立方码、立方英寸	化学气体、天然气和木材	
容积	公升、加仑、蒲式耳	酒类、油类商品、谷物类，以及部分流体、气体产品	小麦、玉米、汽油、酒精、啤酒等

2. 常用度量衡制度

在国际货物买卖中，除了使用的计量单位、计量方法不同以外，各国使用的度量衡制度也不相同。目前国际贸易中通常使用的度量衡制度有四种：

1）公制：主要在东欧、拉美、东南亚、非洲等国采用。

2）英制：主要在英国、新西兰、澳大利亚等国采用。

3）美制：主要在北美国家采用。

4）国际单位制：国际标准计量组织制定，在许多国家采用。

不同的度量衡制度下，同一计量单位表示的实际数量有时会有很大差异。例如，表 3-5 为吨在不同的度量衡制度下所代表的实际数量。所以，了解和熟悉不同的度量衡制度关系到货物的计量单位是否符合进口国有关计量单位使用习惯和法律规定等问题。

表 3-5 公吨、长吨、短吨含量

	千克	磅
公制——公吨	1 000	2 204.60
英制——长吨	1 016	2 240
美制——短吨	907.20	2 000

3.2.4 重量的计算方法

在国际货物买卖中，多数商品是按重量计量的。计算重量的方法主要有以下几种。

1. 毛重

毛重（Gross Weight，简写为 Gr. Wt. 或 GW.）是指商品本身的重量加皮重，即商品连同包装的重量。这种计量方法一般适用于低值产品。

2. 净重

净重（Net Weight，简写为 Nt. Wt. 或 NW.）指商品本身的重量，即从毛重中减去皮重。在国际货物买卖中，按重量计算的商品大多采用以净重计算。

有些单位价值不高的农产品或其他商品有时采用"以毛作净"的办法计重。例如，大米、大豆等农产品，用麻袋包装以毛作净，即以毛重作为计算价格和交付货物的计量基础。

由于这种计重方法直接关系到价格的计算，因此，在销售上述产品时，不仅在规定数量时，需表明"以毛作净"，在规定价格时，也应该加注此条款，如：核桃100公吨，每公吨300美元，单层麻袋包装，以毛作净。

3. 其他计算重量的方法

公量是用科学方法除去商品的实际水分，再加上标准水分所得的重量，适用于吸湿性较强的商品，如羊毛、生丝、棉花等。公量的计算方法是

$$公量＝干净重＋标准含水量$$
$$＝实际重量×(1＋标准回潮率)÷(1＋实际回潮率)$$

理论重量指从商品的件数推算出商品的重量，适用于按固定规格生产或买卖的商品，其每件重量也大致相同。如马口铁、钢板、铝锭等。

法定重量是纯商品的重量加上直接接触商品的包装材料，如内包装的重量。而除去包装重量所表示出来的纯商品的重量，则是实物净重，又称净净重。这两种重量是海关征收货物从量税的基础。

在国际货物买卖合同中，如果货物按重量计量和计价，而没有具体规定采用何种方法计算重量和价格时，根据国际惯例应按净重计量和计价。

3.2.5 商品包装的种类

根据包装在流通过程中的不同作用，可分为运输包装和销售包装两种类型。

1. 运输包装

运输包装是指为满足货物装卸、储存、运输要求而进行的包装，又称大包装、外包装。它具有保障产品安全，方便储运装卸，加速交接、点验等作用。

运输包装可分为单件运输包装和集合运输包装两种。

(1)单件运输包装

货物在运输过程中作为一个计件单位的包装称作单件运输包装。单件运输包装按包装的造型和使用的材料不同又有以下几种的形式，如表3-6所示。

表3-6 常见单件运输包装

包装种类	适用商品	具体形式
箱	适用于不能紧压的货物	木箱、板条箱、纸箱、瓦楞纸箱、漏孔箱
桶	适用于液体、半液体以及粉状、粒状货物	木桶、铁桶、塑料桶
袋	适用于粉状、颗粒状和块状的农产品及化学原料等	麻袋、布袋、纸袋、塑料袋等
包	适用于羊毛、棉花、生丝、布匹等可以紧压打包的商品	包、捆

此外，还有筐、捆、坛、罐、缸、瓶等包装。

（2）集合运输包装

集合运输包装是指由若干单件运输包装组合而成的一件大包装，以便使用相应的运输工具及其他设施，大大提高装卸效率，减轻劳动强度，降低运输成本，减少商品损耗，促进商品装运现代化的实现。

常见的集合运输包装有集装箱、集装包（袋）、托盘三种方式。

2. 销售包装

销售包装是以促进销售为主要目的，随商品进入零售市场直接与消费者见面的包装，又称内包装。

（1）销售包装的装潢和文字说明

销售包装的装潢应突出商品的特性，能够吸引消费者，同时还应该考虑进口国的风俗习惯和对颜色、图形、数字的爱好和禁忌，对不同的国家采用不同的图案和色彩。

销售包装的文字说明或粘贴、悬挂的商品标签、吊牌等，应注意有关国家的标签管理条例的规定。例如，日本政府规定，凡销往该国的药品，除必须说明成分和服用方法外，还要说明其功能，否则，就不准进口。此外，有的国家明文规定所有进口商品的文字说明必须使用本国文字或几种文字。如加拿大政府规定，销往该国的药品，必须同时使用英、法两种文字说明。使用外文说明注意词义的正确表达。

（2）条形码标志

条形码是一种产品代码，由一组粗细间隔不等的平行线条及其相应的数字组成。它可以表示商品的许多信息，通过光电扫描输入电脑，从而判断出某件商品的生产国、制造商、品名规格、价格等一系列产品信息。

目前得到国际公认用于商品包装的条形码主要有两种，即 UPC 条形码和 EAN 条形码。图 3-1 是某物品的条形码标志。

图 3-1　物品条码标志

3.2.6　包装标志

包装标志指在运输包装上书写、压印、绘制的图形、数字和文字等，其目的是为了在装卸、运输和保管过程中，便于识别货物，防止错发错运，保护商品和人员的安全等。包装标志主要有运输标志、指示性标志和警告性标志三种。此外，通常在包装上还有重量体积标志、原产地标志等。

1. 运输标志

运输标志又称唛头，通常由一个简单的几何图形和一些字母、数字及简单的文字组成。其主要作用为识别货物，防止错发错运。

国际标准化组织建议运输标志应包括以下四项内容。

1)收货人或买方名称的英文缩写字母或简称。例如 ABC CO.。

2)参考号。如合同号码、订单号码和发票号码等;例如 SC9750。

3)目的地。货物运送的最终目的地或目的港的名称,一般不能用简称或代号,如有重名,还应加列国名,如需转船或转运,则应加列"转运"字样和转运地名称。例如:London Via Hong Kong。

4)件数号码。本批每件货物的顺序号和该批货物的总件数。

在货物付运时,货主都要对每件货物按顺序编号,主要用来说明一批货物的总包装件数、本件货物的号码或整批货物与本件货物的关系。如果标志为 Nos.:1/100,表明整批货物共有 100 件,本件为第一件。如果包装件数待定,也可表示为"C/Nos:1/Up"。这种表示方法在客户订单或来往函电中常常见到。

下面是一则运输标志:

ABC CO.	收货人名称
SC9750	合同号码
LONDON Via HONG KONG	目的港和中转港
Nos. 1/100	件号(顺序号和总件数)

有时候,运输标志还要加上一些图形标志,例如把数字和字母写在三角形、菱形、正方形中。此时,不仅要把数字和字母刷在包装上,还要在外面按要求刷制三角形、菱形、正方形等图形。

2. 指示性标志

指示性标志是对某些易碎、易损、易变质的商品,在装卸、运输和保管过程中需要注意的事项,用简单、醒目的图形和文字在包装上标出,以提醒有关人员在操作时注意。常见的有"此端向上"、"小心轻放"、"保持干燥"、"禁止翻滚"、"勿用手钩"等。图 3-2 是一些指示性标志示意图。

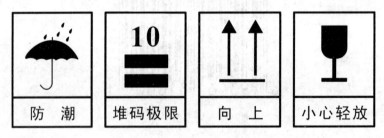

图 3-2   指示性标志

3. 警告性标志

警告性标志又称危险品标志,是针对易燃、易爆、有毒或具有放射性的货物,在外包装上以醒目的图形和文字标明危险性质以警示有关人员在货物的运输、保管和装卸过程中,根据货物的性质,采取相应的防护措施,以保护人身安全和运输物资的安全。

在我国危险货物的运输包装上,要同时标明我国颁布的《危险货物包装标志》和海事协商组织规定的《国际海运危险品标志》两套危险品标志,以防货到国外港口时不准靠岸卸货而造成不必要的损失。

在运输危险品时一定要按照有关规定在包装上的明显部位刷制警告性标志,要注意颜色必须牢固、醒目，并防止脱落、褪色。

4. 重量体积标志和原产地标志

重量体积标志是指在运输包装上标明包装的毛重、净重和体积，以方便运输、装卸。

另外，一般在内外包装上均注明产地，作为商品说明的一个重要内容。商品产地是海关统计和征税的重要依据。

3.3 任务实施与心得

 任务实施

（1）双方经过一段时间的交流，对彼此的业务产品互相有了一定了解，法国公司准备先进口一批女式风衣，孙大伟于 2010 年 8 月 15 日给 Paul 寄送了样品，样品编号为 LJ566。对方收到样品后，对质量进行了仔细检查，认可产品的质量。于是，双方在合同中约定的品质条款如下：

LADIES COAT，women，with bronze-colored buttons，2 pockets at side，like original sample NO. LJ566 sent on AUG.，15，2010.

（2）一个 20 英尺的集装箱的体积大概是 25 立方米，每个纸箱尺寸 $50 \times 40 \times 80$，体积为 0.16 立方米。$25 \div 0.16 = 156$ 箱，每箱装 8 件，因此服装总数量为 1 248 件。为避免实际装箱时有误差，因此订立溢短装 5% 的幅度可以接受。

孙大伟就服装的数量和 Pual 取得了一致，在合同中签订数量条款如下：

QUANTITY：1 248pcs，5% more or less at seller's option.

（3）双方同意决定包装采用混色混码，8 件装一只纸箱，第一次发一个 20 英尺的集装箱的货物。双方在合同中约定的包装条款如下：

8pcs per carton，assorted color and size，per pc in polybag.

W×H×L：$50 \times 40 \times 80$.

SHIPPING MARK：FTC

　　　　　　　　CZCX080180

　　　　　　　　MARSEILLES

　　　　　　　　NO.1/UP

 任务实施心得

（1）针对不同的商品，正确选用表示品质的方法，品质条款要有科学性和合理性

一般来说，凡能用科学指标来说明商品品质的，可适用于凭规格、等级、标准买卖；品质稳定、具有一定特色的名优产品，可适用于凭商标或牌号、产地买卖；某些结构、性能复杂的机械产品，则适用于凭说明书买卖；难以规格化、标准化的商品，则适用于凭样品买卖。凭样品买卖时，应列明样品的编号、寄送日期，有时还要加列交货品质与样品"大致相符"等说明。

凡可用一种方式表示品质的，就不要采用两种或两种以上的方式，订得过于烦琐只会增加生产和交货的困难。在规定品质条款时，用词要简单、具体、明确，切忌使用"大

约"、"左右"、"合理误差"等含糊的字眼，避免引起纠纷。

(2)在包装条款中要具体规定使用的包装材料和包装方式，明确包装费用和运输标志

如果由买方提供包装或包装物料，应明确规定买方提供包装或包装物料的时间，以及由于包装或包装物料未能及时提供而影响发运时买卖双方所负的责任。还应明确填充物料及加固条件等。

按国际贸易惯例，运输标志一般由卖方决定，并无必要在合同中作具体规定。但如果买方要求指定时，就需要在合同中具体规定运输标志的式样和内容；如果合同规定由买方另行指定，应规定买方通知卖方运输标志的最后期限，过时则卖方可自行决定。

包装费用一般包括在货价之中，不另计收。在进口国外商品时，尤其是包装技术较强的商品，最好在单价条款后注明"包括包装费用"，以免事后发生纠纷。

(3)明确度量衡制度，避免误解，合理确定成交商品的数量，制定溢短装条款

在数量条款中，对计量单位的规定，应该明确采用的度量衡制度，如以"吨"计量时，要订明是长吨、短吨还是公吨。对一些机械产品的螺纹，还要明确是英制还是公制。

根据装载工具确定每次成交的具体数量，节省运输成本。如果采用集装箱运输，成交的商品数量一般应该正好满足集装箱整箱装运的需要，最大限度利用装载空间。如果数量太多或太少，采用拼箱装运，运费就昂贵了许多。

溢短装条款是指买卖双方在数量条款中约定一个机动幅度，允许卖方交货数量可以在一定范围内灵活掌握。只要卖方交货数量在该机动幅度之内，就属于按合同规定交货，买方不能以交货数量不符为由拒收或提出索赔。溢短装条款主要包括数量机动幅度、机动幅度的选择权以及溢短装部分的作价方法。机动幅度一般为 3%～5%；机动幅度选择权一般为负责租船订舱的一方。

(4)UCP600 有关数量的增减幅度规定

凡"约"、"大概"或类似的词语，用于信用证金额、数量和单价时，应解释为有关金额、数量或单价不超过 10% 的增减幅度。

在信用证未以包装单位件数或货物自身件数的方式规定货物数量时，货物数量允许有5% 的增减幅度，只要总支取金额不超过信用证金额。

其他商品品质条款举例：

例 1：茶具·品质与 5 月 16 日航空邮递的样品 CT78 一致

例 2：1515A 型多梭箱织机，详细规格如所附文字说明与图样

例 3：9971 中国绿茶 特珍一级 货号 9307

例 4：盐酸四环素糖衣片 250 毫克，按 1980 年版英国药典规定

例 5：白籼米 碎粒(最高)25%

　　　杂质(最高)0.25%

　　　水分(最高)15%

其他数量条款举例：

例 1：东北红小豆，100 公吨，单层新麻袋装，每袋约 100 千克，以毛作净

例 2：500 公吨，上下 5%，由卖方决定

例 3：数量 1 000 公吨，为适应船舱容量需要，卖方有权多装或少装 5%，超过或不足部分按合同价格计算

例 4：试订购 1 000 打烟火，500 箱蚊香

其他包装条款举例：

例 1：木箱装，每箱 50 千克，净重

例 2：包装：纸箱装，每箱 60 听，每听 1 000 片

例 3：每件装 1 塑料袋，半打为 1 盒，10 打装 1 木箱

例 4：纸箱装，每箱 4 盒，每盒约 9 磅，每颗水果涂蜡，包纸

例 5：每台装 1 个出口纸箱，810 只纸箱装 1 只 40 英尺集装箱运送

3.4 知识拓展

1. 常见的表示品质一定灵活性的两种方法

（1）品质机动幅度

品质机动幅度是指对特定品质指标在一定幅度内可以机动。具体方法有规定范围、极限和上下差异三种。品质机动幅度主要适用于初级产品，以及某些工业制成品的品质指标。

（2）品质公差

品质公差指国际上公认的产品品质的误差，即允许卖方的交货品质可高于或低于一定品质规格的误差。这一方法主要适用于工业制成品。

2. 中性包装与定牌生产

（1）中性包装

中性包装是指在商品上和内外包装上既不标明生产国别、地名和厂商名称，也不标明商标或牌号的包装。采用中性包装是为了打破某些进口国家或地区的关税壁垒和非关税壁垒，或者为适应交易的特殊性（如转口贸易等）。它是出口厂商加强对外竞争和扩大出口的一种手段。

（2）定牌

定牌是指卖方按买方要求在其出售的商品或包装上标明买方指定的商标或品牌。目的是利用买方的经营能力、商业信誉和品牌声誉，以提高售价和扩大出口。

在我国具体有以下几种做法：

1）在定牌生产的商品和/或包装上，只用外商所指定的商标或牌号，而不标明生产国别和出口厂商名称，这属于采用定牌中性包装的做法。

2）在定牌生产的商品和/或包装上，标明我国的商标或牌号，同时也加注国外商号名称或表示其商号的标记。

3）在定牌生产的商品和/或包装上，在采用买方所指定的商标或牌号的同时，在其商标或牌号下标示"中国制造"字样。

3.5 业务技能训练

3.5.1 课堂训练

1. 简述规定商品品质条款应注意的问题。

2. 为什么在某些商品的买卖合同中要规定品质机动幅度条款和溢短装条款?

3. 如果包装由买方提供,签订合同包装条款时应该注意什么问题?刷制运输包装标志时应注意的问题有哪些?

4. 学生讨论如何确定商品的数量,合同数量除了集装箱的容积外,还受哪些因素的影响?

5. 如果短装后,卖方可以补交短少的数量吗?讨论在什么条件下,卖方补交短少的数量,就不算违反合同约定。

6. 案例分析题

(1)我国某出口公司向外商出口一批苹果。合同及对方开来的信用证上均写的是三级品,但卖方交货时才发现三级苹果库存告罄,于是该出口公司改以二级品交货,并在发票上加注:"二级苹果仍按三级计价不另收费"。请问:卖方这种做法是否妥当?为什么?

(2)朝鲜一家进出口公司与常州自行车厂洽谈业务,准备从我国进口"金狮"牌自行车6 800辆。但要求我方改用"捷安特"牌商标,在包装上不得注明"Made in China"字样。请问:我方是否可以接受?在处理此项业务时,应注意什么问题?

(3)我国某出口公司对外出口一批罐头,合同规定数量为454克×24听纸箱1 000箱。我方根据库存情况,实际出口454克×48听纸箱装500箱。外商以我方包装不符为由拒收货物。问:外商拒收是否有理,为什么?

(4)国内某公司出口至俄罗斯一批黄豆,合同的数量条款规定:每袋净重100千克,共1 000袋,合计100公吨。货抵俄罗斯后,经检验,黄豆每袋净重96千克,1 000袋合计96公吨。适值黄豆价格下跌,俄罗斯客户以单货不符为由提出降价5%的要求,否则拒收。请问买方的要求是否合理,为什么?

(5)国内某粮油进出口公司从国外进口小麦,合同数量500万公吨,允许溢短装10%,而外商装船时共装了600万吨,对多装的50万吨,我方应如何处理?

3.5.2　实训操作

1. 常州天信外贸有限公司于2010年10月5日寄送两种型号MS691、MS862的男衬衫给加拿大客户JAMES BROWN&SONS,样品编号分别为08091、08092,对方接到样品后后,同意按卖方样品成交。请你拟订具体的品名和品质条款。

MS691、MS862的男衬衫包装为:一件一个塑料袋,10件一个纸箱,均色均码,纸箱尺寸为:80cm×40cm×50cm。请你拟订具体的包装条款,并设计一个唛头。

商定MS691、MS862的男衬衫一共出一个40英尺集装箱的货物,两种型号的衬衫数量相等,假设40英尺集装箱能够装58CBM货物。请你拟订具体的数量条款。

2. 江苏天地木业有限公司寄送5个规格的复合地板给美国现代公司,现代公司对M567,M695这两个型号的地板比较中意,决定购买这两种型号的地板,具体要求为M567,胡桃木1 215mm×195mm×8.3mm,25g OVERLAYER,WHITE HDF,以及M695,苹果木1 220mm×200mm×8.8mm,35g OVERLAYER,请你拟订具体的品名和品质条款。

M567,M695这两个型号的地板的包装为:8块地板一个纸箱,尺寸为:1 220mm×200mm×70mm,毛重:15kg,净重:14.5kg,请你拟订具体的包装条款,并设计一个唛头。

江苏天地木业有限公司与现代公司商定 M567，M695 这两个型号的地板分别出一个 40 英尺集装箱的货物，假设 40 英尺集装箱能够装 58CBM、21MT 的货物。请你拟订具体的数量条款。

3. 每位学生就自己公司和客户洽谈的出口产品，准备出口 1 个 40 英尺集装箱的货物，就出口产品的包装材料、数量和运输标志等包装情况进行磋商。订立合同的品名和品质、数量、包装条款。

任务 4
订立合同的价格条款

知识要点

1. 贸易术语的概念和作用
2. 主要贸易术语中买卖双方的权利和义务

技能要点

- 正确选用恰当的贸易术语，明确买卖双方的权利和义务
- 进行不同贸易术语之间的价格转换
- 制定出口合同的价格条款

4.1 任务描述与分析

1. 任务描述

孙大伟向附近几家合作多次的供应商询价，得知该批出口的女风衣采购成本为每件人民币 160 元左右，包含 17% 的增值税，出口退税率为 11%，公司的定额费率为 5%，预期利润率为 10%。

孙大伟现在准备和对方谈价格的相关事项，订立合同的价格条款，此时该商品的面料价格不断上涨，美元对人民币汇率不断走低。

2. 任务分析

国际贸易的商品价格包括总价和单价两项基本内容。单价由计价货币、贸易术语、计量单位、单位价格金额四个部分组成，还经常包括佣金和折扣等。

价格是国际贸易的核心，是买卖双方争议的焦点，直接关系到买卖双方的经济利益。

在对外贸易中，我国外贸企业在与国外客户磋商和订约时，应考虑各种影响因素，不同的价格往往意味着不同的质量、数量、包装等。除了按照国际市场价格水平，结合经营意图和国别地区政策确定价格外，还应正确选择计价货币，适当地选用贸易术语，列明作价方法，必要时，还须规定价格调整条款。同时，对佣金和折扣应视交易的具体情况，正确地加以运用和规定。

4.2 相关知识

4.2.1 贸易术语概述

1. 贸易术语的含义与作用

贸易术语又称价格术语、贸易条件，是进出口商品价格的一个重要组成部分。它是指用一个简短的概念或三个英文字母的缩写来表明商品的价格构成，说明买卖双方货物交接过程中有关手续、费用和风险的责任划分等问题的专门用语。

在报价中使用贸易术语，明确了双方在货物交接方面各自应承担的责任、费用和风险，说明了商品的价格构成，从而简化了交易磋商的手续，缩短了成交时间，也有利于船公司、保险公司和银行等其他有关机构开展业务活动。

2.《2000 年国际贸易术语解释通则》

为避免各国在对贸易术语解释上出现分歧和引起争议，一些国际组织和商业团体分别就某些贸易术语做出统一的解释与规定。这些规则在国际上被广泛采用，因而成为一般的国际贸易惯例。

国际商会(ICC)制定的《国际贸易术语解释通则》(以下简称《通则》)是目前国际贸易中使用最为广泛和普遍的贸易术语惯例。1999 年国际商会再次修订并公布了《2000 年国际贸易术语解释通则》(以下简称《2000 年通则》)，并于 2000 年 1 月 1 日起生效。

(1)《2000 年通则》的适用范围

《2000 年通则》只限于销售合同当事人的权利、义务中与已售货物(指"有形的"货物，不包括无形货物,如电脑软件)交货有关的事项,不涉及违约的后果以及某些情况的免责等。这些问题必须通过买卖合同中其他条款和适用的法律来解决。

(2)《2000年通则》的结构

《2000年通则》将13种贸易术语划分为下列四组:第一组为E组,卖方仅在自己的地点为买方备妥货物;第二组为F组,卖方需将货物交至买方指定的承运人;第三组为C组,卖方须订立运输合同,但对货物灭失或损坏的风险以及装船和起运后发生意外所发生的额外费用,卖方不承担责任;第四组为D组,卖方须承担把货物交至目的地国所需的全部费用和风险。表4-1为《2000年通则》13种贸易术语列表。

表4-1　INCOTERMS 2000

组别	术语缩写	术语英文名称	术语中文名称
E组起运(实际交货)	EXW	Ex Works	工厂交货
F组主运费未付 (象征性交货)	FCA	Free Carrier	货交承运人
	FAS	Free Alongside Ship	装运港船边交货
	FOB	Free On Board	装运港船上交货
C组主运费已付 (象征性交货)	CFR	Cost and Freight	成本加运费
	CIF	Cost, Insurance and Freight	成本加保险费、运费
	CPT	Carriage Paid to	运费付至
	CIP	Carriage and Insurance Paid to	运费、保险费付至
D组到达 (实际交货)	DAF	Delivered at Frontier	边境交货
	DES	Delivered Ex Ship	目的港船上交货
	DEQ	Delivered Ex Quay	目的港码头交货
	DDU	Delivered Duty Unpaid	未完税交货
	DDP	Delivered Duty Paid	完税后交货

(3)使用《2000年通则》应注意的问题

通则不是法律,不具有强制性。有关贸易术语的国际贸易惯例建立在当事人"意思自治"的基础上,故当事人选用何种贸易术语及其所采用的术语受何种惯例管辖,完全根据自愿的原则来确定。如果合同的当事人在签订销售合同时,希望引用《2000年通则》,为避免引起不必要的纠纷,应在合同中规定:按《2000年通则》的规定办理。例如:"CIF New York INCOTERMS 2000"或在合同中注明:"This contract is governed by INCO-TERMS 2000"。

4.2.2　装运港交货的三种常用贸易术语

1. FOB

Free On Board(…named port of shipment)装运港船上交货(⋯⋯指定装运港)是指卖方负责在合同规定的装运期内,在指定的装运港将货物装上买方指定的船上,并负担货物装船时越过船舷为止的一切费用和风险。

该术语仅适用于海运或内河运输。根据《2000 年通则》的解释，现将 FOB 术语下，买卖双方各自应承担的责任、费用和风险如表 4-2 所示。

按 FOB 术语订立合同，并按各自承担的义务履行合同时，还须注意以下问题。

(1)"装上船"的要求和风险划分界限

卖方及时将货物装上船，是 FOB 术语的要求。按照《2000 年通则》的规定，FOB 合同的卖方必须及时在装运港将货物"交至船上"或"装上船"，其交货点为船舷。而买卖双方风险的划分是以货物"越过船舷为界"，即货物装船之前的风险，包括装船时货物跌落海中所造成的损失，均由卖方承担，货物装船后，包括在运输途中所发生的损失，均由买方承担。

表 4-2 FOB 术语下买卖双方各自应承担的责任、费用和风险

当事人 义务	卖 方	买 方
责任、费用、风险	①取得出口报关所需的各种证件，并负责办理出口报关手续，承担出口报关费用和出口应交纳的一切税捐 ②在合同规定的时间或期限内，在指定装运港按照习惯方式将与合同规定相符的货物装上买方指定的船只，并及时通知买方 ③提交商业发票和证明货物已交至船上的运输单据，或具有同等效力的电子单证 ④承担货物在指定装运港越过船舷前的一切费用和风险	①取得进口报关所需的各种证件，并负责办理进口报关手续以及必要时经另一国过境的海关手续，承担进口报关费用、进口关税及需经另一国过境时所应交纳的一切税捐 ②负责租船订舱，将船名及装船日期及时通知卖方，在合同规定的时间到达装运港接运货物，以及自办货物运输保险 ③接受与合同规定相符的货物和单据，并按照合同规定支付货款 ④承担货物在指定装运港越过船舷后的一切费用和风险，包括运费、保险费等

(2)船货衔接问题

在 FOB 合同中，买方负责租船订舱，并将船名、装船地点和装船时间通知卖方，而卖方负责在合同规定的期限和装运港将货物装上买方指定的船只。因此，在 FOB 合同中，买卖双方对船货衔接事项，除了应在合同中作出明确规定外，在订约后尚需加强联系，密切配合，防止船货脱节。

(3)美国等美洲国家对 FOB 的特殊解释

《1941 年美国对外贸易定义修订本》将 FOB 分为六种，其中只有第五种"装运港船上交货"(FOB Vessel named port of shipment)与《2000 年通则》解释的 FOB 相近，但该术语的出口报关的责任在买方而不在卖方。因此，我国在与美国、加拿大等拉美国家洽谈进口贸易使用 FOB 方式成交时，一定要注意在 FOB 和装运港名称之间加上"Vessel"(船)字样，还应明确由对方(卖方)负责办理出口报关手续。

2. CIF

Cost，Insurance and Freight(…named port of destination)成本加保险费、运费(……指定目的港)是指卖方负责租船或订舱，在合同规定的期限内将货物装上船只，办理货物

运输保险，负责支付将货物运到指定目的港所需的运费和保险费，并承担货物装上船以前的一切费用和风险。这里的运费，仅指按照惯常航线航行的正常运费，不包括运输途中发生的任何额外费用。

该术语只适用于海运或内河运输。根据《2000年通则》的解释，按照 CIF 术语达成的合同，买卖双方各自应承担的责任、费用和风险如表4-3所示。

表 4-3   CIF 术语下买卖双方各自应承担的责任、费用和风险

当事人 义务	卖 方	买 方
责任、费用、风险	①取得出口报关所需的各种证件，并负责办理出口报关手续，承担出口报关费用和出口应交纳的一切税捐 ②按通常条件订立运输合同，在合同规定的时间，在装运港将与合同规定相符的货物装上船只，并及时通知买方，按 CIF 金额的110%办理货物运输保险，承担货物运至指定目的港的正常运费及保险费 ③提交商业发票和证明货物已交至船上的运输单据以及保险单，或具有同等效力的电子单证 ④承担货物在指定装运港越过船舷前的一切费用和风险	①取得进口报关所需的各种证件，并负责办理进口报关手续以及必要时经另一国过境的海关手续，承担进口报关费用、进口关税及需经另一国过境时所应交纳的一切税捐 ②接受与合同规定相符的货物和单据，并按照合同规定支付货款 ③承担货物在指定装运港越过船舷后的一切费用(从装运港到目的港的运费和保险费除外)和风险

采用 CIF 术语成交时，应注意以下问题：

(1)CIF 合同属于"装运合同"

CIF 及其他 C 组术语(CFR、CPT、CIP)与 F 组术语(FCA、FAS、FOB)一样，卖方在装运地完成交货义务，采用这些术语订立的买卖合同均属"装运合同"性质。卖方按合同规定在装运地将货物交付装运后，对货物可能发生的任何风险不再承担责任。

(2)保险险别与保险金额

在 CIF 术语下，卖方负责办理投保，支付保险费。投保险别和保险金额应事先在合同中约定，以免事后引起纠纷。

如果合同没有确定什么险别，《2000年通则》规定卖方只需投保最低的险别，但在买方要求时，并由买方承担费用的情况下，可加保战争险、罢工险、暴乱和民变险，保险金额则最少应为合同金额的110%，同时须以合同货币投保。

(3)租船订舱

采用 CIF 术语成交，卖方的基本义务之一是租船订舱，办理从装运港到目的港的运输事项。除非双方另有约定，对于买方事后提出的关于限制装运船舶的国籍、船型、船龄、船级以及指定装载某班轮公司的船只等要求，卖方均有权拒绝接受。

(4)象征性交货

从交货方式看，CIF 是一种典型的象征性交货。所谓象征性交货，是针对实际交货而言的。前者是指卖方只要按期在约定地点完成装运，并向买方提交合同规定的包括物权凭

证在内的有关单证，就算完成了交货义务，而无需保证到货。后者则是指卖方要在规定的时间和地点将符合合同规定的货物交给买方或其指定人，而不能以交单代替交货。

CIF 交易实际上是一种单据的买卖，装运单据在 CIF 交易中有着特别重要的意义。

3. CFR

Cost and Freight(… named port of destination)成本加运费(……指定目的港)是指在装运港货物越过船舷卖方即完成交货，卖方必须支付将货物运至指定的目的港所需的费用和运费。但交货后货物灭失或损坏的风险，以及由于各种事件造成的任何额外费用，由卖方转移到买方。

CFR 是介于 FOB 和 CIF 术语之间的一种术语。与 FOB 相比，卖方除承担 FOB 术语的义务外，还需负责安排运输，支付将货物运往指定目的港的正常运费。与 CIF 相比，CFR 合同的卖方不负责办理投保手续和支付保险费，不提供保险单，除此之外，两者关于买卖双方责任的划分基本上相同。

按 CFR 术语成交，需要特别注意的是装船通知问题。在 CFR 合同中，由卖方安排运输，买方办理货运保险，如果卖方不及时发出装船通知，则买方就无法及时办理货运保险，甚至有可能出现漏保货运险的情况。因此，卖方装船后务必及时向买方发出装船通知；否则，卖方应承担货物在途中的风险和损失。

在进口业务中，按 CFR 条件成交时，鉴于由外商安排装运，由我方负责保险，故应选择资信好的客户成交，并对船舶提出适当要求，以防外商与船方勾结，出具假提单，租用不适航的船舶，或伪造品质证书与产地证明。若出现这类情况，会使我方蒙受不应有的损失。

FOB、CFR 和 CIF 三种贸易术语，买卖双方在货物交接方式、交货地点和风险划分的界限方面是完全相同的，它们的区别，主要是买卖双方承担的运输、保险责任和费用方面有所不同，具体如表 4-4 所示。

表 4-4 FOB、CFR、CIF 术语的异同点

相同点	适用的运输方式相同：水上运输
	风险划分的界限相同：装运港船舷；卖方承担的风险：FOB＝CFR＝CIF
	交货地点相同：出口国装运港
	交货形式相同：都是象征性交货，都叫"单据买卖"
	办理进出口手续的责任人相同：出口手续卖方办理、进口手续买方办理
不同点	就卖方承担的责任和费用而言不同：CIF＞CFR＞FOB
	以装运港船舷为界，FOB 还需扶一把(以获得清洁提单)、CFR 还需送一程(租船订仓支付通常运费)、CIF 还需保一段(按最低责任保险险别投保)

4. 贸易术语的变形

班轮运输的装卸费用包含在班轮运费中。程租船运输，由于船方一般不负担装卸船费用，为了避免在此问题上引起纠纷，买卖双方须事先明确装卸货费用由谁负担，便产生了贸易术语的变形。

(1)装船费用的负担及 FOB 术语变形

FOB 术语下，为了明确程租船运输时装船费用由何方负担，买卖双方往往在 FOB 术语后加列附加条件，从而形成 FOB 术语的变形。它们主要有：FOB 班轮条件、FOB 吊钩下交货、FOB 包括理舱费、FOB 包括平舱费、FOB 包括理舱费和平舱费。

(2)卸货费用的负担以及 CIF 术语变形

CIF、CFR 术语，在装运港的装船费应由卖方负担，依靠 CIF、CFR 术语的变形来明确卸货费用由谁来负担。CIF、CFR 术语的变形相同。

CIF 术语变形主要有：CIF 班轮条件、CIF 卸到岸上、CIF 吊钩交货、CIF 舱底交货。

4.2.3 向承运人交货的三种贸易术语

向承运人交货的贸易术语有三种，它们分别是 FCA、CPT 和 CIP。这三种贸易术语适用于包括多式联运在内的任何运输方式。它们都属于象征性交货，都以"货交承运人"作为风险划分的界限。

在《2000 年通则》中，对"承运人"作出了具体规定。"承运人"是指在运输合同中，通过铁路、公路、空运、海运、内河运输或上述运输的联合运输方式承担履行运输或承担办理运输业务的任何人。

1. FCA

Free Carrier(…named place)货交承运人(……指定地点)。在采用这一贸易术语时，买方必须自负费用订立从指定地点装运货物的运输合同并及时通知卖方有关承运人的名称和交货的时间。卖方必须在合同规定的期限内，在指定的地点将货物交给买方指定的承运人，并及时给予买方关于货物已交承运人监管的通知，负责办理出口手续，并承担货交承运人之前的一切风险和费用。

根据《2000 年通则》的解释，按照 FCA 术语达成的合同，买卖双方各自应承担的责任、费用和风险如表 4-5 所示。

表 4-5　FCA 术语下买卖双方各自应承担的责任、费用和风险

当事人 义务	卖　方	买　方
责任、费用、风险	①取得出口报关所需的各种证件，并负责办理出口报关手续，承担出口报关费用和出口应交纳的一切税捐 ②在合同规定的时间或期限内，并按约定方式或当地习惯方式，在指定地点将与合同规定相符的货物交由买方指定的承运人监管，并及时通知买方 ③提交有关货运单证，或具有同等效力的电子单证 ④承担货物在指定地点交由承运人监管以前的一切费用和风险	①取得进口报关所需的各种证件，并负责办理进口报关手续以及必要时经另一国过境的海关手续，承担进口报关费用、进口关税及需经另一国过境时所应交纳的一切税捐 ②指定承运人，订立从指定地点承运货物的运输合同，并通知卖方，以及自办货物运输保险 ③接受与合同规定相符的货物和单据，并按照合同规定支付货款 ④承担货物在指定地点交由承运人监管以后的一切费用和风险

2. CIP

Carriage and Insurance Paid to(…named place of destination)运费、保险费付至(……

指定目的地）。在采用这一贸易术语时，卖方自负费用订立将货物运至指定目的地的运输合同，自负费用办理货物运输保险，在约定地点、规定日期或期限内，将货物交给第一承运人监管，负责办理出口手续，并承担货物交第一承运人以前的一切费用和风险。

根据《2000 年通则》的解释，按照 CIP 术语达成的合同，买卖双方各自应承担的责任、费用和风险如表 4-6 所示。

CIP 术语与 CIF 术语的基本模式相似，它们的价格构成中都包括了通常的运费和约定的保险费，而且按这两种术语成交的合同都属于"装运合同"，都是卖方凭单交货，买方凭单付款。

表 4-6　CIP 术语下买卖双方各自应承担的责任、费用和风险

当事人 义务	卖　方	买　方
责任、费用、风险	①取得出口报关所需的各种证件，并负责办理出口报关手续，承担出口报关费用和出口应交纳的一切税捐 ②按通常条件订立运输合同，在合同规定的时间或期限内，在指定地点将与合同规定相符的货物交给第一承运人监管，并及时通知买方，按 CIP 金额的 110% 及时办理货物运输保险，承担货物运至指定目的地的正常运费及保险费 ③提交商业发票和证明货物已交至船上的运输单据以及保险单，或具有同等效力的电子单证 ④承担货物在指定地点交由承运人监管以前的一切费用和风险	①取得进口报关所需的各种证件，并负责办理进口报关手续以及必要时经另一国过境的海关手续，承担进口报关费用、进口关税及需经另一国过境时所应交纳的一切税捐 ②接受与合同规定相符的货物和单据，并按照合同规定支付货款 ③承担货物在指定地点交由承运人监管以后的一切费用和风险

3. CPT

Carriage Paid to（…named place of destination）运费付至（……指定目的地）。在采用这一贸易术语时，卖方自负费用订立将货物运至指定目的地的运输合同，在约定地点、规定日期或期限内，将货物交给第一承运人监管，负责办理出口手续，并承担货物交第一承运人以前的一切费用和风险。

买方在上述指定地向承运人收取货物，除支付货款外，并需支付除运费以外的有关货物在运输途中直至到达目的地为止的一切费用和卸货费用以及进口税捐，还须承担货物已交由第一承运人保管后的一切风险。

CPT 术语下，买卖双方之间的责任和费用划分介于 FCA 和 CIP 术语之间。

综上所述，FCA、CPT 和 CIP 三种术语都适用于包括多式联运在内的任何运输方式，卖方的交货地点和风险划分界限也是完全相同的，而且以这三种术语达成的合同也都属于装运合同。它们之间的区别，主要在于买卖双方在办理运输、保险责任和支付运费、保险费方面有所不同。

4. FCA、CPT、CIP 与 FOB、CFR、CIF 的比较

FCA、CPT 和 CIP 三种术语是分别从 FOB、CFR、CIF 三种传统术语发展起来的，这两类术语之间有以下三个共同点：

1）都是象征性交货，相应的买卖合同为装运合同。

2）均由出口方负责出口报关，进口方负责进口报关。

3）买卖双方所承担的运输、保险责任互相对应。即 FCA 和 FOB 一样，由买方办理运输；CPT 和 CFR 一样，由卖方办理运输；而 CIP 和 CIF 一样，由卖方承担办理运输和保险的责任。

这两类贸易术语的主要不同点在于：

1）适合的运输方式不同。FCA、CPT 和 CIP 适合于各种运输方式，包括多式联运，其承运人可以是船公司、铁路局、航空公司，也可以是安排多式联运的联合运输经营人；而 FOB、CFR 和 CIF 只适合于海运和内河运输，其承运人一般只限于船公司。

2）风险划分点不同。FCA、CPT、CIP 方式中，买卖双方风险和费用的责任划分以"货交承运人"为界，FOB、CFR、CIF 术语下，风险和费用的划分点则以"船舷"为界。

3）装卸费用负担不同。FCA、CPT、CIP 均由承运人负责装卸，因而不存在需要使用贸易术语变形的问题，而 FOB、CFR、CIF 这三种术语通过贸易术语变形来规定装卸费用。

4）运输单据不同。在 FOB、CFR、CIF 术语下，卖方一般应向买方提交已装船清洁提单。而在 FCA、CPT、CIP 术语下，卖方提交的运输单据则视不同的运输方式而定。如在海运和内河运输方式下，卖方应提供可转让的提单，有时也可提供不可转让的海运单和内河运单；如在铁路、公路、航空运输或多式联运方式下，则应分别提供铁路运单、公路运单、航空运单或多式联运单据。

所以，除了风险点不同之外，可以把 FCA、CPT、CIP 看成是 FOB、CFR、CIF 方式从海运向各种运输方式的延伸。

4.2.4　其他几种贸易术语

1. EXW

Ex Work(…named place)工厂交货(……指定地点)。在采用这一贸易术语时，卖方在其所在地(如工场、工厂或仓库等)将备妥的货物交付买方，以履行其交货义务。按此贸易术语成交，卖方既不承担将货物装上买方备妥的运输工具，也不负责办理货物出口清关手续。除另有约定外，买方应承担自卖方的所在地受领货物时起的全部费用和风险。因此，EXW 术语是卖方承担责任、费用和风险最小的一种贸易术语。该术语适用于各种运输方式。

2. FAS

Free Alongside Ship(…named port of shipment)装运港船边交货(……指定装运港)。在采用这一贸易术语时，卖方把货物运到指定的装运港船边，即履行其交货义务。买卖双方负担的风险和费用均以船边为界。该术语仅适用于海运或内河运输。

3. 目的地交货的贸易术语

目的地交货的贸易术语共有五种，即《2000 年通则》中的 D 组术语：DAF(Delivered

At Frontier)、DES（Delivered Ex Ship）、DEQ（Delivered Ex Quay）、DDU（Delivered Duty Unpaid）、DDP（Delivered Duty Paid）。

按照 D 组术语成交的合同称到达合同（Arrival Contract），这是 D 组术语与前面各组术语的最大区别。D 组术语条件下，卖方所承担的风险要大于前面各组。

《2000 年通则》中，13 种贸易术语各自特点如表 4-7 所示。

表 4-7　《2000 年通则》13 种贸易术语对照表

标准代码	交货地点	责任		费用		风险划分界限	出口报关责任与费用	进口报关责任与费用	适用的运输方式
		办理租船订舱	办理保险	支付运费	支付保险费				
EXW	商品产地	买方	买方	买方	买方	买方受领货物起	买方	买方	任何运输方式
FCA	出口国内地、港口	买方	买方	买方	买方	货交承运人处置时起	卖方	买方	任何运输方式
FAS	装运港（出口国）	买方	买方	买方	买方	货交船边后	卖方	买方	海运和内河运输
FOB	装运港（出口国）	买方	买方	买方	买方	货物越过装运港船舷	卖方	买方	海运和内河运输
CFR	装运港（出口国）	卖方	买方	卖方	买方	货物越过装运港船舷	卖方	买方	海运和内河运输
CIF	装运港（出口国）	卖方	卖方	卖方	卖方	货物越过装运港船舷	卖方	买方	海运和内河运输
CPT	出口国内地、港口	卖方	买方	卖方	买方	货交承运人处置时起	卖方	买方	任何运输方式
CIP	出口国内地、港口	卖方	卖方	卖方	卖方	货交承运人处置时起	卖方	买方	任何运输方式
DAF	两国边境指定地点	卖方	卖方	卖方	卖方	货物交买方处置时起	卖方	买方	任何运输方式
DES	目的港船上	卖方	卖方	卖方	卖方	货物交买方处置时起	卖方	买方	海运和内河运输
DEQ	目的港码头上	卖方	卖方	卖方	卖方	货物交买方处置时起	卖方	买方	海运和内河运输
DDU	进口国指定目的地	卖方	卖方	卖方	卖方	货物交买方处置时起	卖方	买方	任何运输方式
DDP	进口国指定目的地	卖方	卖方	卖方	卖方	货物交买方处置时起	卖方	卖方	任何运输方式

4.2.5　国际贸易术语解释通则®2010

为适应国际贸易的快速发展和国际贸易实践的变化，国际商会对《2000 年国际贸易术语解释通则》进行了修订。国际贸易术语解释通则®2010 于 2011 年 1 月 1 日起生效。它考虑了无关税区的不断扩大，商业交易中电子信息使用的增加，货物运输中对安全问题的进一步关注以及运输方式的变化。

国际贸易术语解释通则®2010 包含 11 个术语，删除了原来的 DAF、DES、DEQ 和 DDU。他把术语分为特征鲜明的两大类：

第一类包括适用于任何运输方式或多种运输方式的七个术语：EXW(工厂交货)、FCA（货交承运人）、CPT(运费付至)、CIP(运费、保险费付至)、DAT(运输终端交货)、DAP(目的地交货)、DDP(完税后交货)。

第二类的 FAS(船边交货)、FOB(船上交货)、CFR（成本加运费）、CIF(成本、保险费加运费)四个术语的交货地点和将货物交至买方的地点都是港口，因此被称为"适用于海运及内河水运的术语"。其中后三个术语省略了以船舷作为交货点的表述，取而代之的是货物至于"船上"时构成交货。这样的规定更符合当今商业现实，且能避免那种已经过时的风险在一条假想垂直线上摇摆不定的情形出现。

此外，国际贸易术语解释通则®2010 对国际和国内货物买卖合同均可适用。

4.2.6　商品的价格核算

1. 价格核算

在对外报价、制定价格条款前，要注意加强成本预算，以提高经济效益。进行成本预算的指标主要有出口商品换汇成本(换汇率)、出口商品盈亏率、出口创汇率三种。

商品的价格构成可以分为三个部分，即成本、费用和利润。

商品成本是在采购成本中扣除出口退税后的成本，即实际采购成本；费用可分为"国内费用"(如包装费用、存储及处理费用、国内运费、检验及证明书费用、装货费用、出口捐税、邮电费及银行手续费、预计损失、垫款利息、业务费用等)和"国外费用"(视贸易术语不同，可能是海运或陆运、空运费和运输保险费。除此之外，还有可能是支付给中间商的佣金等)；利润即出口公司的预期利润。

> FOB 价＝进货成本价＋国内费用＋净利润
>
> CFR 价＝进货成本价＋国内费用＋国外运费＋净利润
>
> CIF 价＝进货成本价＋国内费用＋国外运费＋国外保险费＋净利润

FOB 价换算为其他价：

> CFR 价＝FOB 价＋国外运费
>
> CIF 价＝(FOB 价＋国外运费)/[1－(1＋投保加成率)×保险费率]

CFR 价换算为其他价：

> FOB 价＝CFR 价－国外运费
>
> CIF 价＝CFR 价/(1－(1＋投保加成率)×保险费率)

CIF 价换算为其他价：

$$FOB\ 价＝CIF\ 价×[1－(1＋投保加成率)×保险费率]－国外运费$$
$$CFR\ 价＝CIF\ 价×[1－(1＋投保加成率)×保险费率]$$

FCA、CPT 和 CIP 三种贸易术语的价格构成和价格换算关系，与 FOB、CFR 和 CIF 相类似。

2. 佣金和折扣

(1)佣金

在国际贸易中，有些交易是通过中间代理商进行的。因中间商介绍生意或代买代卖而需收取一定的酬金，此项酬金叫佣金。包含佣金的价格称为含佣价，不含佣金则为净价。

在商品价格中包括佣金时，通常应以文字来说明。例如："每公吨 200 美元 CIF 旧金山，包括 2％佣金。"也可在贸易术语上加注佣金的缩写英文字母 C 和佣金的百分比来表示。例如："每公吨 200 美元 CIFC2％旧金山"。商品价格中所包含的佣金，还可以用绝对数来表示。例如："每公吨付佣金 25 美元"。

佣金的规定应合理，其比率一般掌握在 1％至 5％，不宜过高。

常见的公式如下：

$$佣金额＝含佣价×佣金率$$
$$净价＝含佣价×(1－佣金率)$$
$$含佣价＝净价÷(1－佣金率)$$

(2)折扣

折扣是指卖方按原价给予买方一定百分比的减让，即在价格上给予适当的优惠。国际贸易中使用的折扣，名目很多，除一般折扣外，还有为扩大销售而使用的数量折扣，为实现某种特殊目的而给予的特别折扣以及年终折扣等。

在国际贸易中，折扣通常在合同价格条款中用文字明确表示出来。例如："CIF 伦敦每公吨 200 美元，折扣 3％"。此例也可这样表示："CIF 伦敦每公吨 200 美元，减 3％折扣"。此外，折扣也可以用绝对数来表示。例如："每公吨折扣 6 美元"。

4.3　任务实施与心得

 **任务实施**

(1)选择合适的贸易术语

业务员孙大伟考虑到，虽然运费由于原油价格的变动不断变化，但由我方办理运输和保险较能控制货物的出运，故选择使用"CIF MARSEILLES"的贸易术语。

(2)进行商品的价格核算与报价

孙大伟对商品价格进行核算，采购成本为每件 160 元，包含 17％的增值税，出口退税率为 11％，定额费率为 5％，上海到马赛港的 20'FCL 运费换算为人民币 9 380 元，公司如按客户要求加一成投保一切险和战争险，费率为 0.8％和 0.02％，公司的预期利润率为 10％，CIF 术语下的人民币报价如下：

$$CIF＝实际成本＋定额费用＋运费＋保险费＋利润$$
$$＝160－160÷(1＋17％)×11％＋160×5％＋9\ 380÷1\ 248＋CIF×$$

$$110\% \times 0.82\% + CIF \times 10\%$$

CIF＝180.11 元/件，以美元和人民币汇率为 6.47 计算：

$$CIF＝180.11/6.47＝27.84 \text{ 美元/件}$$

在磋商过程中，进口商要求 3％的佣金，业务员孙大伟以 CIF 马赛港每件 27.80 美元的净价，核算含佣价：

$$\text{含佣价＝净价}/(1-\text{佣金率})＝27.84/(1-3\%)＝28.70 \text{ 美元}$$

（3）制定价格条款

孙大伟经过价格核算，考虑到交货期较近，虽然存在美元贬值和原材料价格上涨因素，但并未制定价格调整条款和外汇保值条款，只是适当抬高价格，并和对方磋商，签订以下价格条款：

单价：每件 28.70 美元 CIF 马赛港含 3％佣金

总值：35 817.60 美元

Unit Price：USD28.70 PER PIECE CIF MARSEILLES including 3％ Commission

Total Value：USD 35 817.60(Say U. S. Dollars Thirty Five Thousand Eight Hundred and Seventeen and Cents Sixty Only)

其他价格条款参考示例：

（1）净价条款

单价：每公吨 120 美元 CIF 曼谷

总值：13 000 美元

（2）含佣价条款

单价：每箱 15 英镑 FOB 广州含 2％佣金

总值：14 350 英镑

（3）含折扣单价条款

单价：每码 100 美元 FOB 上海减 2％折扣

（4）固定价格条款

单价：每公吨 235 美元 CIF 纽约包含佣金 2％。合同成立后，不得调整价格

任务实施心得

订立合同价格条款的难点在于事先进行准确的价格核算，并多方考虑各种价格影响因素。为了使价格条款的规定明确合理，必须注意下列事项。

（1）根据经营意图和实际情况，选用适当的贸易术语

目前在国际贸易中，较多使用象征性交货的术语，即以装运港或装运地交货的方式成交。在出口贸易中，争取按 CIF 或 CIP 方式成交，进口贸易中，争取使用 FOB 或 FCA 术语。采用货到付款或托收等商业信用的收款方式出口时，尽量避免采用 FOB 或 CFR 术语。

（2）正确书写单价中涉及的计量单位、装卸地名称

注意价格条款与合同中其他条款的相关内容一致，如计量单位、装卸地名称等。

对于贸易术语，要注意术语中所涉地点与贸易术语相适应，如：F 组术语所涉地点为装运地，C 组术语所涉地点为卸货地；FOB、CFR、CIF 术语所涉地点为港口，FCA、

CPT、CIP 术语所涉地点可以是港口，也可以是机场等。

（3）考虑各种影响价格的因素，合理确定商品的单价，防止作价偏高或偏低

如交货品质和数量约定有一定的机动幅度，则对机动部分的作价也应一并规定；如包装材料和包装费另行计价时，对其计价办法也应一并规定；对港口拥挤费、选择费等特殊费用，如果由对方负担的，也须在价格条款中订明。

4.4 知识拓展

1.《1932 年华沙—牛津规则》和《1941 年美国对外贸易定义修订本》

除了《2000 年通则》，目前国际上影响较大的有关贸易术语的惯例还有以下两种：

国际法协会专门为解释 CIF 合同而制定的《1932 年华沙—牛津规则》。

美国九个商业团体制定的《1941 年美国对外贸易定义修订本》。该惯例共包括 6 种贸易术语，它们是：产地交货；在运输工具上交货；在运输工具旁交货；成本加运费；成本加保险费、运费；目的港码头交货。

2. 选择合适的计价货币，规避汇率风险

进出口业务中，常用的计价货币有：美元（US $ 或 USD）；英镑（£ 或 GBP）；欧元（EUR）；加拿大元（CAN $ 或 CAD）；港元（HK $ 或 HKD）；日元（J¥ 或 JPY）；瑞士法郎（SF 或 CHF）等。

在出口业务中，一般应尽可能争取多使用汇率稳定且有升值趋势的货币，即所谓"硬币"。在进口业务中，一般应尽可能争取多使用汇率有下降趋势的"软币"。此外，也还可采用其他的方式，如：压低进口价格或提高出口价格，软硬币结合使用，采取远期外汇交易、择期交易、掉期交易等来防止风险。

网站链接：世界各国货币即时汇率查询网：http://www.xe.com/ucc/full.shtml

4.5 业务技能训练

4.5.1 课堂训练

1. 简述 FOB、CIF、CFR 主要异同（风险划分点、费用划分点、运保费）。

2. 简述 CIF 贸易术语买卖双方的主要义务。

3. 计算题

（1）我方对外出口某商品，CFRC3% 价为 1 500 美元，现在外商要求改报 CFRC 5% 价。在保持我方净收入不变的前提下，应如何报价？

（2）设我方出口某商品，FOB 价为 10 000 美元，该批货物的运费为 2 000 美元，投保一切险加战争险，两者保险费率合计为 1.5%，加成 20% 投保。请计算 CIF 价格。

4. 填写下表。

国际贸易术语买卖双方责任和费用一览表

组别	术语	交货地点	风险划分	责任		税费			
				租船订舱	投保	运费	保费	出口税	进口税
E组	EXW								
F组	FCA								
	FAS								
	FOB								
C组	CFR								
	CIF								
	CPT								
	CIP								
D组	DAF								
	DES								
	DEQ								
	DDU								
	DDP								

5. 分析下列我方出口单价的写法是否正确？为什么？

每码 3.50 元 CIF HONGKONG　　　每件 580 日元 FOB SHANGHAI

每打 5.80 元 CIF NEW YORK　　　每吨 100 美元 FOB TOKYO

每箱 100 FOB TOKYO　　　每公吨 200 美元 FOB 新港

每打 30 英镑 CFR 英国　　　每箱 CIF 伦敦 50.50 元

每台 300 马克 CIF 上海　　　每辆 40 美元 CFR 新加坡

每吨 1 000 美元 FOB LONDON

6. 案例分析题

(1)我方从泰国 A 公司进口一批大米，签订"CFR 上海"合同，货轮在台湾海峡附近沉没。A 公司未及时向我方发出装船通知，我方未办理投保，无法向保险公司索赔。故我方要求对方承担责任，但泰国 A 公司以货物离港，风险已经转移给我方为由拒绝承担责任。问：泰国 A 公司的行为是否合理，究竟由谁承担责任？为什么？

(2)某公司以 CIF 鹿特丹与外商成交一批货物，按发票金额 110% 投保一切险及战争险。买卖合同中的支付条款规定为"Payment by L/C"。国外来证条款中有如下文句"Payment under this credit will be made by us only after arrival of goods at Rotterdam."(该证项下的款项的货到鹿特丹后由我行支付)。受益人在审证时未发现，因此，未请对方修改。我方外贸公司在交单结汇时，议付行也未提出异议。不幸的是 60% 货物在途中被大火烧毁，船到目的港后开证行拒付全部货款。问：1)开证行拒付是否合理？为什么？2)本案有何教训可以吸取？

4.5.2 实训操作

1. 常州天信外贸有限公司与加拿大客户 JAMES BROWN&SONS，商定 MS691、MS862 的男衬衫一共出一个 40 英尺集装箱的货物。请你拟订具体的价格条款。

货号：　　　　　　　含税采购成本（每件）

MS691（男衬衫）　　　　120 元人民币

MS862（男衬衫）　　　　100 元人民币

每个 40 英尺 FCL 出口运费为 4 400 美元。

其他信息如下：

出口退税率：15%，增值税：17%；

国内费用：出口包装费 15 元/纸箱，仓储费 5 元/纸箱；

一个 40 英尺集装箱的其他国内费用为：国内运杂费 400 元，商检费 550 元，报关费 50 元，港口费 600 元，其他费用 1 400 元。

保险：按发票金额加成 10% 投保一切险和战争险，费率为分别为 0.6% 和 0.3%。

预期利润：报价的 10%，付款方式是即期信用证。

2. 江苏天地木业有限公司对 M567，M695 地板进行报价。

货号：　　　　　含税采购成本（每件）

M567　　　　　40 元人民币/M²

M695　　　　　52 元人民币/M²

每个 40 英尺 FCL 出口运费为 4 400 美元。

其他信息如下：

出口退税率：13%，增值税：17%；

公司费用为采购净成本的 5%，利润为报价的 8%。

3. 每位学生就出口产品，询问供应商的进货价格，查找该产品的出口退税率，假设公司利润率为 5%，费用率为 10%，请进行成本核算，对外报价，并订立合同的价格条款。

任务 5
订立合同的运输条款

ℹ️ **知识要点**

　　1. 装运港、目的港

　　2. 分批、转运

✊ **技能要点**

　　• 能够根据具体情况，选用合适的运输方式

　　• 能够订立出口合同的装运条款

5.1　任务描述与分析

1. 任务描述

常信公司和法国公司商定出口一个 20 英尺集装箱的服装，孙大伟正和 Paul 商量如何拟订合同中的装运条款，考虑采用何种运输方式。

2. 任务分析

国际货物运输不同于国内运输，它具有线长面广、中间环节多、情况复杂多变和风险大等特点，需要经过买卖双方的配合和合理安排才能实现。

装运条款包括装运时间、装运港和目的港、分批装运和转船以及装运通知和装运单据等内容。为了顺利完成国际货物运输任务，必须选择合适的运输方式，订好进出口合同中的装运条款，才能够在履行合同时不出差错，减少双方在运输方面的纠纷。

5.2　相关知识

5.2.1　国际货物运输方式

在国际货物运输中，涉及的运输方式很多，主要有海洋运输、铁路运输、航空运输、邮政运输、国际多式联运、集装箱运输等。下面主要介绍海洋运输和集装箱运输。

1. 海洋运输

海洋运输是利用货船在国内外港口之间通过一定的航线和航区进行货物运输的一种运输方式。目前，其运量在国际货物运输总量中占 80% 以上。根据船舶经营方式不同，海洋运输方式可以分为班轮运输和租船运输。

（1）班轮运输

班轮运输指按固定的航线和事先公布的时间表航行，沿途停靠若干固定的港口，并按事先公布的费率收取运费的运输方式。班轮运输成为国际海运中的主要运输方式之一，深受货主欢迎。

班轮运输具有以下特点。

1）"四固定"。班轮公司根据固定的航行时间表，在固定的航线上航行，在固定的挂靠港口停靠，并以相对固定的费率向托运人收取运费。

2）"一负责"。承运人负责配载和装卸货物，并承担相应的费用；因此，班轮运输不计算装卸时间、滞期费和速遣费。装卸费用包括在运费内，实际上由支付运费的一方承担。

（2）租船运输

租船运输是指租船人向船东租赁船舶用于运输货物的业务。在国际海运业务中，根据船舶的经营方式不同，租船运输主要可以分为定程租船和定期租船。

在定程租船合同中，运费按所承运的货物数量计算，与航程所用的时间无关；出租人承担了时间风险，为促使承租人尽快完成装卸作业，以便出租人尽早完成约定的航程，以便投入下一航次，赚取更多的运费，出租人在租船合同中约定了滞期费和速遣费。出租人对在规定的时间内提前完成装卸作业的承租人给予的奖金，称为速遣费；出租人对未能在规定的时间内完成装卸作业的承租人给予的罚款，称为滞期费。速遣费一般是滞期费的一半。

2. 集装箱运输

集装箱运输是以集装箱作为运输单位进行货物运输的一种现代化运输方式。它可适用于海洋运输、铁路运输、公路运输、内河运输和国际多式联运等。目前，集装箱海运已成为国际主要班轮航线上占有支配地位的运输方式。

国际上主要使用的是 20 英尺(TEU)和 40 英尺(FEU)集装箱。

集装箱运输有整箱货(FCL)和拼箱货(LCL)之分。整箱货由发货人在工厂或仓库进行装箱，货物装箱后直接交集装箱堆场等待装运，到达目的地后，收货人可直接从目的地的集装箱堆场提走货柜。拼箱货是指货量不足一整箱，需由承运人在集装箱货运站负责将不同发货人的货物拼装在一个集装箱内，货到目的地后，由承运人拆箱后分拨给各收货人。

集装箱的交接方式应在运输单据上予以说明。通用的集装箱的交接方式如表 5-1 所示。

表 5-1　集装箱的交接方式

货物交接方式	装箱人	拆箱人	交接地点	表达方式
整箱交整箱接(FCL/FCL)	货方	货方	门到门、场到场门到场、场到门	Door to Door, CY to CY, Door to CY, CY to Door
拼箱交拆箱接(LCL/LCL)	承运人	承运人	站到站	CFS to CFS
整箱交拆箱接(FCL/LCL)	货方	承运人	门到站场到站	Door to CFS, CY to CFS
拼箱交整箱接(LCL/FCL)	承运人	货方	站到门站到场	CFS to Door, CFS to CY

注："门"(Door)指发货人、收货人工厂或仓库；"场"(CY)指港口的集装箱堆场；"站"(CFS)指港口的集装箱货运站。

3. 其他运输方式

(1)铁路运输

铁路运输与其他运输方式相比较，具有运量大、速度快、不受气候条件的影响，运输准时、使用方便等特点，还具有占地少、能耗低、事故少、污染少等优势。

国际铁路联运，发货人由始发站托运，使用一份铁路运单，铁路方面根据运单将货物运往终点站交给收货人。在由一国铁路向另一国铁路移交货物时，不需收、发货人参加，亚欧各国按国际条约承担国际铁路联运的义务。

(2)航空运输

航空运输是一种现代化的运输方式，具有运送迅速、节省包装和储存费用、不受地面条件限制等许多优点。但航空运费一般较高。通常只有急需物资、精密仪器、鲜活商品、季节性强和贵重商品适合采用航空运输的方式。

航空运输有班机运输、包机运输、集中托运、航空快递业务四种。其中航空快递业务是一种最为快捷的运输方式，特别适合于各种急需物品和文件资料的运输。

航空快递业务是由快递公司与航空公司合作，向货主提供的快递服务，其业务包括：由快速公司派专人从发货人处提取货物后以最快航班将货物出运，飞抵目的地后，由专人接机提货，办妥进关手续后直接送达收货人，称为"桌到桌运输"。

> 网站链接：世界著名的快递运输公司的网址
> FedEx：http：//www.fedex.com/cn/
> DHL：http：//www.cn.dhl.com/
> UPS：http：//www.ups.com/asia/cn/chsindex.html
> TNT：http：//www.tnt.com/country/zh_cn.html
> EMS：http：//www.ems.com.cn/

（3）邮政运输

邮政运输是一种较简便的运输方式。邮政运输具有手续简便、费用低的优点，一般适用于运输量轻（不超过 20 千克）和体积小（长度不得超过 1 米）的样品、药品、机器零件和零星贵重物品的运输。国际邮件可分为函件和包裹两大类。

（4）国际多式联运

《联合国国际货物多式联运公约》对国际多式联运所下的定义是："国际多式联运是指按照多式联运合同，以至少两种不同的运输方式，由多式联运经营人把货物从一国境内接运货物的地点运至另一国境内指定交货物的地点。"根据此项定义，可知国际多式联运具有如下特点：

1）多种方式。即必须有国际间两种或两种以上不同运输方式的联合运输。

2）一份合同。即一份多式联运合同，合同中明确规定多式联运经营人和托运人之间的权利、义务、责任和豁免。

3）一份单据。即全程仅使用一份包括全程的多式联运单据。

4）一个费率。即全程只有一个运费率，其中包括全程各段运费的总和、经营管理费用和合理利润。

5）一人负责。即多式联运经营人对全程运输负总的责任。

国际多式联运简化了手续，减少了中间环节，加快了货运速度，降低了运输成本，提高了货运质量，是实现"门到门"运输的有效途径。

5.2.2　装运时间

在 FOB、CIF、CFR 贸易术语下，一般卖方在装运港完成交货义务，装运时间和交货时间大体一致。

装运时间是买卖合同中的主要交易条件，延迟装运属根本性违约，买方有权解除合同，并提出索赔；提前装运也属违约，买方可以收取货物，也可以拒绝，但不能解除合同。常见装运时间的规定方法，通常有以下几种：

1）明确规定具体装运时间。可以规定某月或某几个月装运，也可以限定最迟装运时间。

如："3月份装运"，"6月30日前装运"，"不迟于6月30日装运"，"2/3月装运"。

2)规定在收到信用证后若干天内装运。为了防止买方拖延或拒绝开证,卖方还应该进一步规定信用证开抵卖方的最迟期限,以保护自己的利益。

如"收到信用证后 30 天内装运,买方信用证须在 3 月 1 日前抵达卖方"。

3)规定在收到货款后若干天内装运。这种方法表明买方需要预付货款。因此,这对卖方最有利。

5.2.3　装运港和目的港

装运港是指货物起始装运的港口,目的港是指最终卸货的港口。通常装运港由卖方提出,经买方同意后确定,目的港由买方提出,经卖方同意后确定。

确定装运港和目的港应考虑货物的合理流向并贯彻就近装卸的原则,考虑港口的设施、装卸条件等实际情况。

装运港和目的港的规定方法通常有以下几种:

1)在一般情况下,装运港和目的港都规定为一个。例如,装运港:青岛;目的港:伦敦。

2)有时按实际业务的需要,也可分别规定两个或两个以上。例如,装运港:青岛、大连、上海;目的港:伦敦、利物浦。

3)在磋商交易时,如明确规定装运港或目的港有困难,可以采用选择港办法或仅作笼统规定。例:装运港:青岛/大连/上海;目的港:伦敦/利物浦。

5.2.4　分批装运和转船

分批装运和转船直接关系到买卖双方的权益,对卖方而言,允许分批装运和转运比较有利,但对买方而言,除非市场销售需要,一般都不希望分批装运和转运。如果合同中没有明文规定允许分批装运,按照某些国家的合同法,不等于允许分批装运;但《跟单信用证统一惯例》规定,除非信用证另有规定,分批或转船均被允许。有鉴于此,为防止误解,在我国的外贸业务中,应该在合同中对分批装运和转运作出明确具体的规定。

1. 分批装运

分批装运是指一笔成交的货物,分若干批装运。在大宗货物交易中,买卖双方根据交货数量、运输条件和市场售价等因素,可在合同中规定分批装运条款。

在买卖合同中规定分批装运的方法主要有三种:

1)只原则规定允许分批装运,对于分批的具体时间、批次和数量均不作规定。这种做法对卖方比较有利,卖方完全可以根据货源和运输条件,在合同规定的装运期内灵活掌握,可以全数出运不分批,也可以分批出运,每批数量不限。例:"允许分批装运"。

2)规定分若干批装运,而不规定每批装运的数量。

3)在规定分批装运条款时,具体订明每批的时间、批次和数量。这种做法往往是根据买方对货物的使用或销售的需要确定的,对卖方的限制较严。例如:"3 月至 6 月分四批,每月平均装运"。

2. 转船

转船是指货物从装运港到目的港的运输过程中,允许在中途港口换装其他船舶转运至目的港。转运不仅延误时间、增加费用,并可能造成货损货差,因此买方一般不愿转运。

但如果没有直达船或班轮不停靠目的港，卖方必须力争在合同中订立"允许转船"条款。

5.3　任务实施与心得

 任务实施

（1）选择运输方式

结合实际情况，选择采用集装箱的班轮运输，如果不能够及时将货物出运，再采用空运，以跟上货物的销售旺季。

（2）确定装运时间、装运港口等

经查询得知，没有从南京直达马赛的船只，一般可从上海、宁波、大连港出发，且中途极有可能发生中转。因此，在订立运输条款时，应争取把装运港订为中国港口，同时要求允许转运。考虑到上海到马赛的海运时间为 1 个月左右，所以装运时间定为 9 月下旬。

（3）拟订合同中的装运条款

Shipment：from Shanghai China to Marseilis France by sea betweeen 20 Sept.，2010 and 30 Sept.，2010；otherwise to transport from Shanghai China to Marseilis France between 1 Oct.，2010 and 15 Oct.，2010 on seller's account by air. Transshipment is allowed. Partial Shipment is not allowed.

> **其他装运条款举例**
>
> 例 1：5 月底或以前装船，由上海至惠灵顿，允许分批和转船，卖方在装船后两天内发出装运通知。
>
> 例 2：5 月份装船，由伦敦至上海，允许分批，不允许转船，卖方在装运月份前 45 天将备妥货物可供装船的时间通知买方。
>
> 例 3：3/4 月份分两批每月平均装运，由香港转运，1/3 正本提单和一套非议付单证在装船后 3 天内通过敦豪快运送交买方。
>
> 例 4：卖方应以电报通知买方，说明装运数量、发票金额、装运船名、装货港、预定开航日期等，以便买方办理保险。
>
> 例 5：目的港：下列港口之一由买方选择并负担选港附加费。买方应于船舶预期抵达第一个选卸港 5 天前向承运人宣布确定的目的港。

任务实施心得

孙大伟已经完成了合同的运输条款，从中的感悟是：

（1）规定装运时间要具体，并留有余地

规定装运时间应考虑货源和船只的实际情况，对装运期的规定要明确，不要使用诸如迅速装运、立即装运、尽快装运等模糊不清的词语，还要考虑装运期限是否适度、开证日期是否明确合理等。

在出口业务中，有时国外客户对销售季节性强的商品，要求在合同中规定保证货物到达的时间，这种做法会改变合同的性质。在实际业务中，我们一般不能接受。

(2)规定装运港和目的港力求具体明确

对国外装运港或目的港的规定，应力求具体明确，一般都应该是基本港。我国出口合同的目的港或进口合同的装运港一般不使用"欧洲主要港口"或"美国主要港口"之类笼统的规定方法。但出口合同装运港或进口合同目的港规定为中国港口，有利于我方在租船订舱时具有较大的选择权。

不能接受内陆城市为装运港或目的港，避免冬季选用季节性港口，防止因冰冻原因船舶不能够进港。如果没有直达班轮，在合同中应该规定允许转运的条款。避免把正在进行战争或有政治动乱的地方作为装运港或目的港。

(3)重名港口的处理

为防止发生差错，凡重名的港口应明确标明所在国家和方位。世界上重名的港口主要有维多利亚、的黎波里、波特兰、波士顿等。建议养成在港口后加上所在国家或地区名称的习惯。

5.4   知识拓展

UCP600 对分批装运有以下相关规定。

1. 分批装运中一批未按期发运的后果

UCP600 第 32 条规定："如信用证规定在指定的时间段内分期支款或分期发运，任何一期未按信用证规定期限支取或发运时，信用证对该期及以后各期均告失效。"因此，在出口业务中，接受此类条款时，应予慎重对待，以免造成被动。但这种做法可以有利于买方合理安排使用或销售，有利于资金和仓储周转。

2. 不视为分批装运的情形

UCP600 第 31 条 b 款规定："表明使用同一运输工具并经由同次航程运输的数套运输单据在同一次提交时，只要显示相同目的地，将不视为分批发运，即使运输单据上标明的发运日期不同或装卸港、接管地或发送地点不同。如果交单由数套运输单据构成，其中最晚的一个发运日将被视为发运日。含有一套或数套运输单据的交单，如果表明在同一种运输方式下经由数件运输工具运输，即使运输工具在同一天出发运往同一目的地，仍将被视为分批发运。"符合"四同"情形的货物同时到达目的港，在收货人看来与一批装运没有显著差异，对收货人也不会造成明显的不利影响，故不视为分批装运。

5.5   业务技能训练

5.5.1   课堂训练

1. 进出口合同中的装运期有哪些规定办法？合同中的装运港和目的港有哪些规定办法？

2. 为什么买方一般不愿意接受货物的转运？为什么我国出口商品到南太平洋岛国时，都要订立"允许转运"的条款？

3. 讨论有哪些情形不视为分批装运？如何辨别信用证下是否可以分批装运？

4. 案例分析题

(1)我国粮油进出口总公司天津分公司对新加坡出口 5 000 公吨大豆，国外开来信用证规定：不允许分批装运。结果我方在规定的期限内分别在大连港、天津新港各装 2 500 公吨于同一航次的同一船上，提单也注明了不同的装运地和不同的装船日期。请问这是否违约？银行能否议付？

(2)我国对印度尼西亚按 CFR 合同出口一批化肥，合同规定 1～3 月份装运，国外来证也如此，别无其他字样。但我方在租船订舱时发生困难，因出口量大一时租不到足够的舱位，须分三次装运。问在这种情况下，是否需要国外修改信用证的装运条款？

(3)我国向俄罗斯出口茶叶 9 000 箱，合同和信用证均规定"从 7 月份开始，连续每月 3 000 箱"，问：我方于 7 月份装 3 000 箱，8 月份没装，9 月份装 3 000 箱，10 月份装 3 000 箱，可否？

5.5.2　实训操作

1. 常州天信外贸有限公司与加拿大客户 JAMES BROWN & SONS 通过磋商，决定货物从张家港运到加拿大的温哥华，不允许分批，允许转运，时间为 2010 年 10 月上旬。请你拟订具体的运输条款。

2. 江苏天地木业有限公司与现代公司商定，决定货物从宁波港运到美国的旧金山，允许分批，不允许转运，最迟时间为 2010 年 12 月底。请你拟订具体的运输条款。

3. 每位学生就自己公司和客户洽谈的商品出口产品，订立合同的运输条款。

任务 6

订立合同的保险条款

6.1 任务描述与分析

1. 任务描述

常信公司多数情况下出口采用 CIF 术语，进口采用 FOB 术语。现在孙大伟已经和法国 GOLDEN MOUNTAIN TRADING CO.，LTD 就运输条款达成一致，由于采用的是 CIF 术语，应该由卖方办理保险手续。孙大伟开始和 Paul 讨论货物运输保险的相关事项，并订立合同的保险条款。

2. 任务分析

在国际贸易的货物运输等诸多环节中，可能遇到各种风险，造成货物的各种损失，产生一定的费用。为了转嫁货物在运输途中的风险，通常要投保货物运输险。

保险条款是国际货物买卖合同的一个重要组成部分。合同中的保险条款主要是约定投保的险别，确定保险金额等。我们首先掌握不同的投保险别所承保的范围。因为保险公司是按照不同险别所规定的风险、损失和费用来承担赔偿责任的。

6.2 相关知识

6.2.1 海上货物运输保险承保范围

在海运途中，船只和货物可能遭受暴风、巨浪、雷电、海啸、洪水等自然灾害，也会遭遇由于船舶或驳运工具搁浅、触礁、沉没、碰撞、失火、爆炸等意外事故，此外还有偷窃、渗漏、短量、雨淋、提货不着、串味、受热、受潮等一般外来风险和由于军事、政治、国家政策法令以及行政措施等特殊外来原因造成的风险。特殊外来风险主要包括战争、罢工、交货不到以及货物被有关当局拒绝进口或没收等。

被保险货物在海洋运输中由于以上风险所造成的损坏或灭失，称为海损。按货物损失的程度，海损可分为全部损失和部分损失。

1. 全部损失

全部损失简称全损，是指运输中的整批货物或不可分割的一批货物的全部损失。全部损失又可分为实际全损和推定全损两种。

（1）实际全损

实际全损是指被保险货物（保险标的物）全部灭失；或货物毁损后不能复原；或完全丧失原有用途，已不具有任何使用价值；或不能再归被保险人所有等。如货物沉没海底无法打捞，水泥被水浸泡后变质而完全丧失原有用途，货物全部被海盗劫走等。

（2）推定全损

推定全损是指被保险货物受损后完全灭失已不可避免，或修复受损货物的费用将超过货物本身价值，或被保险货物遭受严重损失后，继续运抵目的地的运费将超过残损货物的价值。

2. 部分损失

部分损失是指被保险货物的损失没有达到全部损失的程度。按照造成损失的原因，它又可分为共同海损和单独海损两种。

(1)共同海损

共同海损是指载货船舶在航行途中遭遇灾害、事故，威胁到船、货共同的安全，为了解除这种威胁，维护船货的共同安全，或者使航程得以继续完成，由船方有意识地、合理地采取措施而造成的特殊损失或支出的额外费用。

共同海损是海洋运输过程中经常遇到的损失，但并不是海上发生的灾害事故都构成共同海损。共同海损成立必须具备以下条件：

1)必须确实遭遇危难。共同海损的危险是真实存在不可避免的，而不是主观臆测的。

2)必须是为船、货共同安全而采取的措施。如果只是为了船舶或货物单方面的利益而造成的损失，不能作为共同海损。

3)所支付的费用是额外的，损失是非常性质的。

4)必须是自动地有意识地采取的合理措施。

(2)单独海损

单独海损是指除共同海损以外的部分损失，即由于遭受承保范围内的风险所造成的损失。

共同海损和单独海损均属部分损失，但二者的性质、起因和补偿方法有较大的区别。

1)造成海损的原因不同。单独海损是承保风险所直接导致的损失；共同海损则不是承保风险所直接导致的损失，而是为了解除船、货共同危险有意采取合理措施而造成的损失。

2)损失的承担责任不同。单独海损由受损方自行承担；共同海损要由船舶、货物和运费受益方按照受益大小的比例共同分摊。

3. 费用

遭遇海上货物运输风险，使货物本身受到损毁导致经济损失外，还可能会产生费用方面的损失。保险人对上述费用都负责赔偿，但以总和不超过保险金额为限。

保险公司负责赔偿的海上费用包括施救费用和救助费用。

施救费用是指被保险货物遭受保险责任范围内的灾害事故时，被保险人或其代理人、雇用人员等为防止损失扩大而采取抢救措施所支付的费用。

救助费用是指保险标的遭遇保险责任范围内的灾害事故时，依靠本身的力量无法摆脱困境，由保险人和被保险人以外的第三方采取救助措施，为此支付给第三方的费用。

6.2.2　我国海洋货物运输保险的险别

保险险别是保险人对风险和损失的承保责任范围，是保险人与被保险人履行权利与义务的基础，也是保险人承保责任大小和被保险人缴付保险费多少的依据。

在我国，进出口运输保险最常用的保险条款是"中国保险条款"。该条款是由中国人民保险公司制定，按照不同的运输方式，分为海洋、陆上、航空和邮包保险条款等。

我国的货物运输保险险别按照能否单独投保，可分为基本险和附加险两类。基本险可以单独投保，而附加险不能单独投保，只有在投保某一种基本险的基础上才能加保附加险。

1. 我国海洋运输货物保险的基本险

按照我国现行的《海洋货物运输保险条款》的规定，海洋货物运输保险的基本险别分为平安险、水渍险和一切险三种。投保人可以根据货物的特点、运输路线等情况选择平安险、水渍险和一切险三种险别中的任一种投保。

(1)平安险

平安险英文原意是指单独海损不负责赔偿，原来的承保范围仅限于货物发生的全部损失和共同海损，不包括货物所遭受的单独海损。但是随着国际贸易的发展，其承保范围已经突破了原先的严格限制，现在保险公司对某些单独海损也负责赔偿。

(2)水渍险

水渍险的责任范围，除包括上列平安险的各项责任外，还负责被保险货物由于恶劣气候、雷电、海啸、地震、洪水等自然灾害所造成的部分损失。

因此，水渍险比平安险的责任范围大，保险费率也比平安险高。

(3)一切险

一切险的责任范围除包括平安险和水渍险的所有责任外，还包括货物在运输过程中，因一般外来原因所造成的被保险货物的全部损失或部分损失。如货物被盗窃、钩损、碰损、受潮、受热、淡水雨淋、短量、包装破裂和提货不当等。

从三种基本险别的责任范围来看，平安险范围最小，它对自然灾害造成的全部损失与意外事故造成的全部损失和部分损失负赔偿责任。水渍险的范围责任比平安险的责任范围大，凡因自然灾害与意外事故所造成的全部损失和部分损失，保险公司均负责赔偿。一切险的责任范围是三种基本险别中最大的一种。一切险是平安险和水渍险加一般附加险的总和。

对上述基本险，保险公司还规定有下列除外责任：被保险人的故意行为或过失所造成的损失；属于发货人责任引起的损失；在保险责任开始前，被保险货物已存在的品质不良或数量短差所造成的损失；被保险货物的自然损耗、本质缺陷、特性以及市价跌落、运输延迟所造成的损失和费用；属于海洋运输货物战争险条款和货物运输罢工险条款规定的责任范围和除外责任。

2. 我国海洋运输货物保险的附加险

附加险是对基本险的补充和扩大。在海运保险业中，投保人除了投保货物的上述基本险别外，还可根据货物的特点和实际需要，酌情再选择加保一种或数种附加险。目前，我国海洋运输货物保险条款的附加险有一般附加险和特殊附加险两类。

(1)一般附加险

一般附加险所承保的是由于一般外来风险所造成的全部损失或部分损失。其险别共有下列 11 种：偷窃提货不着险，淡水雨淋险，短量险，混杂、玷污险，渗漏险，碰损、破碎险，串味险，受热、受潮险，钩损险，包装破裂险，锈损险。

一般附加险不能作为一个单独的项目投保，只能在投保平安险或水渍险的基础上，根据货物的特性和需要加保一种或若干种一般附加险。

(2)特殊附加险

特殊附加险是指承保由于军事、政治、国家政策法令以及行政措施等特殊外来原因所引起的风险与损失的险别。中国人民保险公司承保的特殊附加险主要有 8 种：战争险、罢工险、交货不到险、进口关税险、舱面险、拒收险、黄曲霉素险、货物出口到中国香港(包括九龙)或澳门存仓火险责任扩展条款。下面介绍两种常用的特殊附加险:

1)战争险。它是承保战争或类似战争行为等引起保险货物的直接损失,不能单独投保。

2)罢工险。它对被保险货物由于罢工、工人被迫停工或参加工潮、暴动等人员的行动或任何人的恶意行为所造成的直接损失,和上述行动或行为所引起的共同海损的牺牲、分摊和救助费用负责赔偿。

按国际保险业惯例,已投保战争险后另加保罢工险,不另增收保险费,如仅要求加保罢工险,则按战争险费率收费。

3. 保险公司的保险责任的起讫

我国的海洋运输货物保险条款中除了战争险以外的所有险别的保险责任的起讫,均采用国际保险业惯用的"仓至仓条款",即保险公司的保险责任是从被保险货物运离保险单所载明的起运港(地)发货人仓库开始,一直到货物到达保险单所载明的目的港(地)收货人的仓库时为止。当货物一进入收货人仓库,保险责任即告终止。但是,当货物从目的港卸离海轮后满 60 天,不论保险货物有没有进入收货人的仓库,保险责任均告终止。

海洋运输货物战争险的保险责任起讫不采用"仓至仓条款",而是仅限于水上危险或运输工具上的危险,即自货物在起运港装上海轮或驳船时开始,直到目的港卸离海轮或驳船时为止。如果货物不卸离海轮或驳船,则从海轮到达目的港的当日午夜起算满 15 天,保险责任自行终止。如在中途港转船,不论货物是否在当地卸货,保险责任以海轮到达该港或卸货地点的当日午夜起算满 15 天为止,待再装上续运海轮时恢复有效,保险人仍继续负责。

我国的海洋运输货物保险条款中的三种基本险别的索赔时效,自被保险货物在最后卸离海轮后起算,最多不超过两年。

6.2.3 其他货物运输保险

在国际贸易中,不仅海洋运输的货物需要办理保险,陆上运输、航空运输、邮包运输的货物也都需要办理保险。保险公司对不同运输方式的货物都定有相应的专门条款。

陆上运输货物保险的基本险别分为陆运险和陆运一切险两种,航空运输货物保险的基本险别有航空运输险和航空运输一切险两种,邮包运输保险的基本险别包括邮包险和邮包一切险两种。

此外,还有陆上运输冷藏货物险的专门险,以及陆上运输货物战争险(火车)、航空运输货物战争险、邮包运输货物战争险等附加险。

6.3 任务实施与心得

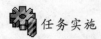
任务实施

现在常信公司的孙大伟经过和对方磋商,签订以下保险条款:

保险由卖方按发票金额的 110% 投保一切险和战争险,以中国人民保险公司 1981 年 1

月 1 日有关海洋运输货物保险条款为准。

Insurance：To be covered by the Seller for 110% of total invoice value against All Risks，War Risks as per and subject to the relevant Ocean Marine Cargo Clause of the People's Insurance Company of China，dated January 1st，1981.

任务实施心得

由于合同中的保险条款与贸易术语有着必然的联系，因此，采用不同的贸易术语，则办理保险手续的责任人也就不一样。

按 FOB、FCA、CFR、CPT 贸易条件签订买卖合同，由买方办理保险手续，并支付保险费。在此情况下，合同中的保险条款比较简单，只须明确保险由买方负责办理。

CIF 合同，需要注意以下事项：

1)明确依据何种保险条款进行投保。通常采用中国人民保险公司 1981 年 1 月 1 日生效的货物运输保险条款。如果国外客户要求按照英国伦敦保险业协会货物保险条款为准，我方也可以接受，根据货物特性和实际需要约定该条款的具体险别。

2)明确投保险别。即根据货物的性质和特点，选择平安险、水渍险或一切险，如需加保一种或几种附加险也应同时写明。

3)规定投保加成率。一般按照发票金额加一成投保，如果买方要求按较高金额投保，而保险公司也同意承保，卖方也可接受，但因此而增加的保险费原则上应由买方承担。如果合同对此未作规定，按《2000 年通则》和《跟单信用证统一惯例》规定，卖方有义务按 CIF 或 CIP 价格的总值另加 10% 作为保险金额。

4)明确保险单据形式。合同中明确注明投保人应提交保险单据的名称(保险单或保险凭证等)。

其他保险条款参考示例：

例 1：保险由买方委托卖方按发票金额的 110% 代为投保水渍险和串味险，保险费由买方负担。以中国人民保险公司 1981 年 1 月 1 日的有关海洋运输货物保险条款为准。

例 2：保险由卖方按发票金额的 120% 投保协会货物条款 A 险，以伦敦保险业协会 1982 年 1 月 1 日货物保险条款为准。

6.4 知识拓展

1. 保险利益

保险人所承保的标的，是保险所要保障的对象。但被保险人(投保人)投保的并不是保险标的本身，而是被保险人对保险标的所具有的利益，这个利益即保险利益。投保人对保险标的不具有保险利益的，保险合同无效。

国际货运保险同其他保险一样，被保险人必须对保险标的具有保险利益。在国际货运中，体现在对保险标的的所有权和所承担的风险责任上。

以 FOB、CFR 方式达成的交易，货物在越过船舷后风险由买方承担。一旦货物发生损失，买方的利益受到损失，所以买方具有保险利益。因此由买方作为被保险人向保险公司投保，保险合同只在货物越过船舷后才生效。货物越过船舷以前，买方不具有保险利益，因此不属于保险人对买方所投保险的承保范围。

以 CIF 方式达成的交易，投保是卖方的合同义务，卖方拥有货物所有权，当然具有保险利益。卖方向保险公司投保，保险合同在货物起运地起运后即生效。

2. 伦敦保险业协会海运货物保险

在国际保险市场上，各国保险组织都制定有自己的保险条款。但最为普遍采用的是英国伦敦保险业协会所制定的"协会货物条款"。现行的伦敦保险业协会的"海运货物保险条款"共有六种险别：协会货物 A 险条款(ICC(A)，以下同)、协会货物 B 险条款、协会货物 C 险条款、协会战争险条款(货物)、协会罢工险条款(货物)、恶意损害险条款。前三者是主险，可单独投保，后三者是附加险，一般不能单独投保。在需要时，战争险、罢工险可独立投保。

以上六种险别中，ICC(A)险相当于中国保险条款中的一切险，其责任范围更为广泛，ICC(B)险大体上相当于水渍险。ICC(C)险相当于平安险，但承保范围较小些。

6.5　业务技能训练

6.5.1　课堂训练

1. 简述构成共同海损的条件。
2. 什么叫共同海损？什么叫单独海损？二者有何区别？
3. 学生讨论在 FOB 、CIF 术语下订立出口合同中的保险条款应注意哪些问题？
4. 案例分析题

(1)有一份 FOB 合同，货物在装船后，卖方向买方发出装船通知，买方向保险公司投保了"仓至仓条款一切险"(All Risks with Warehouse to Warehouse Clause)，但货物在从卖方仓库运往码头的途中，被暴风雨淋湿了 10% 的货物。事后卖方以保险单含有"仓至仓条款"为由，要求保险公司赔偿此项损失，但遭到保险公司拒绝。后来卖方又请求买方以投保人名义凭保险单向保险公司索赔，也遭到保险公司拒绝。试问在上述情况下，保险公司能否拒赔？为什么？

(2)海轮的舱面上装有 1 000 台拖拉机，航行中遇大风浪袭击，450 台拖拉机被卷入海中，海轮严重倾斜，如不立即采取措施，则有翻船的危险，船长下令将余下的 550 台拖拉机全部抛入海中。请问：这 1 000 台拖拉机的损失属于何种性质？

6.5.2　实训操作

1. 常州天信外贸有限公司与加拿大客户 JAMES BROWN&SONS 磋商决定，以发票金额的 120% 投保 ICC(A)险和战争险。请你拟订具体的保险条款。

2. 江苏天地木业有限公司与美国现代公司商定，采用 CFR 术语，买方委托卖方按发票金额的 110% 代为投保水渍险和串味险，保险费由买方负担。以中国人民保险公司 1981 年 1 月 1 日的有关海洋运输货物保险条款为准。请你拟订具体的保险条款。

3. 根据自己公司和外商所磋商的结果，订立合同的保险条款。

任务 7

订立合同的商品检验条款

知识要点

1. 出口商品的检验检疫机构
2. 出口商品检验的时间与地点

技能要点

- 掌握出口合同中检验条款的主要内容和规定方法
- 能够订立出口合同的商品检验条款

7.1　任务描述与分析

1. 任务描述

买卖双方经常会对交货商品的数量、品质等产生纠纷。因此，商品的检验很重要，各方都尽力争取在合同中规定对自己有利的检验方法。

常信公司和法国 GOLDEN MOUNTAIN TRADING CO.，LTD 就其他条款已经达成一致，孙大伟现在准备和对方谈商检的相关事项，订立合同的商品检验检疫条款。

2. 任务分析

能否顺利交货履约，发生问题时能否对外索赔挽回损失，都与商品的检验密切相关。这涉及合同的商品检验条款。

出口合同中的商品检验条款一般包括检验的时间和地点、检验机构、检验证书、复验等相关事项等。不同的检验条款，涉及合同双方的切身利益，在拟订检验条款时应注意该条款的内容与商品品质等其他条款相衔接，不能产生矛盾。

7.2　相关知识

进出口商品检验检疫是指在国际贸易过程中对买卖双方按合同规定成交的商品由商品检验检疫机构对商品的质量、数量、重量、包装、安全、卫生以及装运条件等进行检验，并对涉及人、动物、植物的传染病、病虫害、疫情等进行检疫的工作。

7.2.1　商品检验机构

在国际贸易活动中，进出口商品检验、检疫被简称为商检。商检机构的选择，关系到由谁对商品实施检验并出具有关证书，涉及合同双方的切身利益，需要在合同中加以明确规定。

国际贸易中，商品的检验工作一般都由专业的检验机构负责办理。在国外，检验机构从组织的性质来分，有官方的，有同业公会、协会或民间私人经营的，也有半官方的。检验机构的名称也多种多样，如检验公司、公证行、鉴定公司、实验室或宣誓衡量人等。

根据《中华人民共和国商品检验法》(以下简称《商检法》)的规定，在我国从事进出口商品检验的机构，是国家质量监督检验检疫总局(网站：www.aqsiq.gov.cn)以及所属各地的分支机构。

中国进出口商品检验总公司及其设在各地的分公司根据商检局的指定，也以第三方的身份，办理进出口商品的检验和鉴定业务。

7.2.2　商品检验的时间、地点

确定商品检验的时间和地点，实际上就是确定买卖双方中哪一方行使对货物的检验权的问题。关于合同中检验时间与地点的规定，国际上的常用做法有以下几种。

1. 出口国检验

在出口国检验又可以分为产地检验和装运港检验两种。

（1）产地检验

即在货物离开生产地点（如工厂、农场或矿山）之前，由卖方或其委托的检验机构人员对货物进行检验或验收。卖方承担货物离开产地之前的责任，货物进行检验或验收后，在运输途中出现的品质、数量等方面的风险由买方负责。我国进口重要货物和大型成套设备，一般都在出口国发货前在工厂进行检验或安装、测试。

（2）装运港检验

这种做法又称为"离岸品质、离岸重量"。货物在装运港装运前或装运时，由双方约定的商检机构对货物进行检验后出具的商检证明作为决定商品品质和数量的最后依据。货物运抵目的港后，买方如再对货物进行检验，即使发现问题，也无权再向卖方表示拒收或提出异议和索赔。

2. 目的港检验

这是指货物运抵目的港或目的地卸货后，由双方约定的目的地检验机构验货并出具检验证明作为最后依据，这叫做"到岸品质、到岸数量"。对于技术密集型商品或卸货后不宜拆开包装的商品，也可在买方营业地或最终用户的所在地进行检验。

这种方法对买方有利，对卖方不利，所以也很少采用。

3. 装运港检验，目的港复验

货物在出口国装船前必须进行必要的检验鉴定，但此时出具的装运港检验证明不能作为卖方交货质量和重量的最后依据，只是作为卖方向银行议付货款的一种单据。货物到达目的港后，在双方约定的时间内，买方有权对货物进行复验，复验后若发现货物与合同不符，可根据复验的结果向卖方索赔。

这种做法避免了上述两类方法对卖方或买方单方面有利的矛盾，兼顾了双方权益，比较公平合理，因而在国际贸易中被广泛采用。

7.3　任务实施与心得

任务实施

双方签订以下检验条款：

买卖双方同意以装运港中国出入境检验检疫机构签发的质量检验证书作为信用证项下议付所需单据之一。买方有权对货物的质量进行复验，复验费由买方承担。如发现质量与合同规定不符，买方有权向卖方索赔，并提交经卖方同意的公证机构出具的检验报告。索赔期限为货到目的港（地）180 天内。

任务实施心得

检验条款中的索赔有效期限和复验时间不宜过长，通常视商品性质而言，为货到目的港后 30～180 天不等。其他注意事项主要有：

1）合同的品质条款和包装条款应该明确、具体，否则的话，商品检验便无法进行。

2）明确双方对进出口商品进行检验检疫的机构，以确立其合法性。确定出具的检验检疫证书的名称和份数，以满足不同部门的要求。

3)可以根据业务需要规定检验标准、抽样方法和检验方法。检验标准是指检验机构从事检验工作所遵循的尺度和准则,是评定检验对象是否符合规定要求的准则。一般应按我国的有关标准和抽样方法进行。

4)出口食品和动物产品的卫生检验检疫,一般均按我国标准和有关法令规定办理。如外商提出特殊要求或按国外法规有关标准检验检疫,应要求对方提供有关资料,经出入境检验检疫机构和有关部门研究后,才能接受。

7.4　知识拓展

国际上比较著名的商检机构

国际贸易中的商品检验主要由民间机构承担,民间商检机构具有公证机构的法律地位。比较著名的有:瑞士日内瓦通用鉴定公司、日本海外货物检验株式会社、美国保险人实验室、英国劳合氏公证行、法国船级社以及中国香港天祥公证化验行等。

瑞士日内瓦通用鉴定公司(SGS)成立于 1878 年,总部设在瑞士日内瓦,是世界上最大的从事检验、测试和质量认证服务的公司,在该领域一直是全球的领导者和创新者。SGS 在全球有 1 000 个分支机构和办事处。在中国,SGS 与中国标准技术开发公司于1991年合资成立通标标准技术服务有限公司(http://www.cn.sgs.com/zh/)。

7.5　业务技能训练

7.5.1　课堂训练

1. 在出口贸易中,一般在什么时间和地点检验商品?

2. 简述签订商品检验条款时应注意的问题。

3. 学生讨论下面检验条款的利弊:"装运前买方检验商品质量,以决定商品质量是否符合合同,凭买方签发的质量合格证装运"。

4. 案例分析题

(1)上海某公司对日本出口 100 公吨青菜。合同规定货到目的港后,由日本海事鉴定会进行复验。由于货船航行途中气候的变化,约有 30 箱青菜的颜色变黄。对此,日商由海事鉴定会出具检验报告,并要求我方给予赔偿。请分析我方该如何做?

(2)在一份国外银行开来的信用证中关于商检证书的条款如下:

Inspection certificate in duplicate issued and signed by authorized person of applicant whose signature must comply with that held in our bank's record.

请问:如果你作为出口公司的业务员,这样的条款能接受吗?

7.5.2　实训操作

1. 常州天信外贸有限公司与加拿大客户 JAMES BROWN&SONS,就男式衬衫的检验达成一致:买卖双方同意以装运港中国出入境检验检疫机构签发的质量检验证书作为信用证项下议付所需单据之一,买方有权对货物的质量进行复验,复验费由买方承担。如发现质量与合同规定不符,买方有权向卖方索赔,并提交经卖方同意的公证机构出具的检验报告。请你拟订具体的检验检疫条款。

2. 请你为江苏天地木业有限公司和美国现代公司就某地板出口合同，拟订具体的检验条款。

3. 业务操作：根据自己公司和外商所磋商的结果，订立合同的商品检验检疫条款。

任务 8

订立合同的支付条款

i 知识要点

1. 汇票、本票和支票的内容
2. 汇付和托收的种类、流程、特点
3. 信用证的特点及流程

技能要点

- 正确选择支付方式和支付工具
- 能订立出口合同的支付条款

8.1　任务描述与分析

1. 任务描述

常信公司和法国 GOLDEN MOUNTAIN TRADING CO.，LTD 是第一次接触，洽谈的是第一笔业务，彼此对对方的资信都不太放心。因此孙大伟和 Paul 在商量货款交付方式，确定订立合同的支付条款时，都颇为重视。

2. 任务分析

在国际贸易中，货款的收付是买卖双方的基本权利和义务。货款的收付直接影响双方的资金周转和融通，以及各种金融风险和费用的负担。这是关系到买卖双方利益的问题。

结算方式是支付条款的主要内容，主要有信用证、汇付、托收等方式。订好合同中的支付条款，要选好结算方式，确定好支付时间和地点。在影响不同结算方式利弊优劣的诸因素中，安全是第一要素，其次是占用资金时间的长短。至于办理手续的繁简，银行费用的多少也应给予适当的注意。

8.2　相关知识

8.2.1　结算工具

票据是国际通行的结算工具。国际贸易中使用的票据，主要有汇票、本票和支票，其中以使用汇票为主。

1. 汇票的定义

汇票是由一方向另一方签发的无条件的书面支付命令，要求对方立即或在将来的固定时间或可以确定的时间，支付一定金额给特定的人或其指定的人或持票人。

2. 汇票的种类

汇票的种类很多，根据汇票的当事人、付款期限等方面的不同特征，可以从不同角度对汇票进行分类，如图 8-1 所示。

- 汇票
  - 按是否附有单据
    - 跟单汇票：附有装运单据
    - 光票：不附有装运单据
  - 按付款期限不同
    - 即期汇票：出口商立即收回货款
    - 远期汇票：出口商到期收回货款
  - 按出票人不同
    - 银行汇票：出票人和付款人都是银行
    - 商业汇票：商人或商号为出票人
  - 按承兑人不同
    - 银行承兑汇票：易贴现
    - 商业承兑汇票：不易贴现

图 8-1　汇票的种类

远期汇票的付款时间，有以下几种规定办法：见票后若干天付款；出票后若干天付款；提单签发日后若干天付款；指定日期付款。

国际贸易中经常使用跟单汇票，发货人发货后出具以收货人为付款人的汇票，收取货款；光票经常用于收取货款尾数、佣金或代垫费用，使用较少。银行汇票用于银行汇款；

商业汇票用于收款，常见于信用证和托收业务。

需要说明的是，一张汇票往往可以同时具备几种性质，例如，一张商业汇票可以同时是即期的跟单汇票；一张远期的商业跟单汇票，同时又可以是由银行承兑的汇票。

3. 汇票的当事人

商业汇票的当事人主要有受款人、付款人和出票人。除此之外，还有背书人、承兑人、持票人和善意持票人等。

4. 汇票的使用程序

即期汇票的使用程序为：出票、提示和付款，如图8-2所示。远期汇票的使用程序为：出票、提示、承兑和付款，如图8-3所示。如需转让，还要经过背书手续。汇票遭到拒付时，还要涉及制作拒绝证书和行使追索权等法律问题。

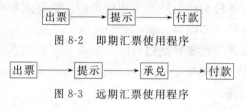

图 8-2　即期汇票使用程序

图 8-3　远期汇票使用程序

（1）出票

出票是指出票人在汇票上填写付款人、付款金额、付款日期和地点以及受款人等项目。汇票经签字后，交付给受款人。出票包括两个动作，一个是缮制汇票并在汇票上签字；另一个是将汇票交付给受款人。

出票时汇票上受款人的抬头有三种写法：

1）限制式抬头。如："Pay A Co. only"或"Pay A Co. Not negotiable"。这种汇票不能转让，只能由抬头人收取货款。

2）指示式抬头。如："Pay A Co. or the order"或"Pay to the order of A Co."。这种汇票经背书后可进行转让。

3）持票人或来人抬头。如："Pay bearer"。这种汇票无须背书即可转让。

（2）提示

提示是指汇票持有人将汇票提交付款人要求承兑或付款的行为。

（3）承兑

承兑是指付款人对远期汇票表示承担到期付款责任的行为，是由付款人在汇票正面写上"承兑"字样，注明承兑日期并由付款人签名交还持有人，有时还加注汇票到期日。付款人对汇票作出承兑，即成为承兑人。承兑人有在远期汇票到期时付款的责任。承兑同样包括两个动作：一是汇票上写明承兑；二是把承兑的汇票交给持有人，或者把承兑通知书交给持有人。

（4）付款

对即期汇票，在持有人提示时，付款人应立即付款；对远期汇票，付款人经过承兑后，在汇票到期日付款。收款人或持有人在收取票款时，应交出汇票，该汇票即成为付款人取得的收据。付款人一般应以汇票载明的货币支付。

（5）背书

背书是转让汇票的一种手续，就是由汇票抬头人在汇票背面签上自己的名字，或再加上受让人(被背书人的名字)，并把汇票交给受让人的行为。经背书后，汇票的收款权利便转移给受让人。汇票可以经过背书不断地转让下去。对于受让人来说，所有以前的背书人及原出票人都是他的"前手"，而对于出让人来说，所有在他让与以后的受让人都是他的"后手"。前手对后手负有担保汇票必然会被承兑或付款的责任。

背书包括两个动作：一是在汇票背面背书；二是交付给被背书人。

(6)拒付

拒付是指当汇票在提示时，遭到付款人拒绝付款或拒绝承兑，或者由于付款人破产、死亡等原因，使付款或承兑实际上成为不可能。

如果汇票经过转让，一旦被拒付，最后的持有人有权向所有的"前手"追索，一直追索到出票人。

持有人为了行使追索权，应及时作成拒付证书。拒付证书是由付款地的法定公证人或其他依法有权作这种证书的机构(例如法院、银行公会等)所作出的付款人拒付的正式文件，凭此可以向其"前手"进行追索的法律依据。

5. 本票

本票是由出票人签发的，保证于见票时或定期或在可以确定的将来的时间，对某人或其指定人或持票人支付一定金额的无条件的书面承诺。

本票可分为商业本票和银行本票。我国《票据法》第七十九条规定，我国只允许开立自出票日起，付款期限不超过 2 个月的银行本票。

在国际贸易结算中使用的大都是银行本票。本票只有两个当事人，本票不需要承兑。

6. 支票

支票是出票人签发的，委托银行或其他金融机构于见票时支付一定金额给特定人或持票人的票据。

支票都是即期的，不需要承兑，本质上是一种无条件的支付命令。支票有三个当事人，付款人一定是银行或其他金融机构。

8.2.2　汇付

汇付是指付款人主动通过银行或其他途径将款项汇交收款人的一种支付方式，它属于顺汇法。

1. 汇付方式的当事人

在汇付业务中，通常有四个当事人：

1)汇款人。汇出款项的人，在进出口交易中通常是进口人。

2)收款人。收取款项的人，在进出口交易中通常是出口人。

3)汇出行。受汇款人的委托，汇出款项的银行，通常是进口地的银行。

4)汇入行。又称解付行，是受汇出行委托解付汇款的银行，通常是出口地的银行。汇入行通常是汇出行在出口商所在地的代理行。

汇款人在委托汇出行办理汇款时，要出具汇款申请书。一旦汇出行接受其汇款申请，就要按申请书中的指示通知汇入行向收款人付款。

2. 汇付方式的种类

根据汇出行向汇入行发出汇款委托的方式，汇付有三种形式。

(1)电汇

汇款人将款项交与汇出行,同时委托汇出行以电报或电传方式指示国外的汇入行将款项解付给收款人。在三种汇付方式中使用最广的是电汇,其交款迅速,但手续费用较高。

(2)信汇

信汇和电汇的区别,在于汇出行向汇入行通过信件方式寄送付款委托书,所以汇款速度比电汇慢。目前大多数银行已不再办理信汇业务。

(3)票汇

票汇是以银行即期汇票为支付工具的一种汇付方式。由汇出行应汇款人的申请,开立以其代理行或分行为付款人,并列明汇款人所指定的收款人名称的银行即期汇票,交由汇款人自行寄给收款人。由收款人凭票向汇票上的付款人(银行)取款。

3. 汇付方式在国际贸易中的应用

汇付方式具有手续简便、费用低廉等优点,但汇付属于商业信用,在进出口双方互不信任的情况下,具有风险大、资金负担不平衡的缺点。

知识链接

当前国际结算中常有"前 T/T"、"后 T/T"的说法。所谓"前 T/T"是指进口人付款在前,出口人发货在后,对进口人风险较大;"后 T/T"则是出口人发货在前,进口人付款在后,对出口人风险较大。在办理货款结算时,"前 T/T"与"后 T/T"常结合使用,如货款的 30%以"前 T/T"预付,其余货款等发货后支付。

汇付方式在国际贸易中多用于贸易从属费用的支付,如运费、保险费、佣金、赔款、定金、利息、货款尾数等。

在实际业务中,汇付可用于预付货款、随订单付现、货到付现、凭单付现、赊账交易(O/A)等做法,进出口商应根据进出口贸易的不同情况做好风险防范工作。

8.2.3   托收

托收是指出口人出具汇票,委托银行向进口人收取货款的一种支付方式,属于逆汇法。托收属于商业信用。

1. 托收方式的当事人

1)委托人。委托银行办理托收业务的人,通常是出口人。

2)托收行。接受出口人委托办理托收业务的银行,通常是出口人所在地银行。

3)代收行。接受托收银行的委托向付款人收款的进口地银行,一般是托收银行的国外分行或代理行。

4)付款人。即汇票的受票人,是应该支付货款的进口人。

除了这四个基本当事人,托收业务中还可能遇到提示行和"需要时的代理"。提示行(Presenting Bank)是向付款人提示单据要求付款的银行,通常由代收行兼任。若代收行与付款人之间没有直接往来,就要委托一家与付款人有往来账户的银行作为提示行。需要时的代理(Principal's Representative in case-of-need)是委托人在付款人所在地指定的代理人,负责在付款人拒付货款时,代委托人办理货物的存仓、保险、转售、运回等事宜,以最大限度地减少委托人的损失。

2. 托收方式的种类

托收可以分为光票托收与跟单托收两大类，如图 8-4 所示。

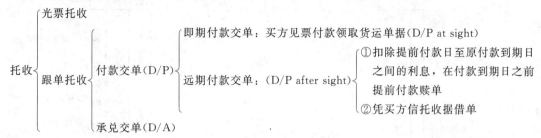

图 8-4　托收方式的种类

光票托收在国际贸易中使用不多，主要用来收取货款尾数、样品费、佣金及其他贸易从属费用；跟单托收是国际贸易中较常见的一种支付方式。卖方开立汇票，连同代表货物所有权的全套货运单据一起交托收行，再转托国外的代收行收货款，只有在进口人付清货款或承兑汇票后，才能把装运单据交给进口人。

跟单托收进一步分为付款交单和承兑交单两种。

（1）付款交单

付款交单是指出口人的交单以进口人的付款为条件。出口人发货后，取得装运单据，委托银行办理托收，并在托收委托书中指示银行，只有在进口人付清货款后，才能把装运单据交给进口人。

按照付款时间的不同，付款交单可以分为即期付款交单和远期付款交单。

1）即期付款交单是指银行提示即期汇票和单据，进口人见票时即应付款，并在付清货款后取得单据。

2）远期付款交单方式在托收委托书中一定要指示银行，只有进口人于汇票到期日付清货款后才能领取货运单据。在采用此方式时，为了鼓励进口方尽快付款，出口方往往要求在托收委托书中加列利息条款。

另外，在远期付款交单条件下，进口方可在付款前凭信托收据（Trust Receipt，T/R）向代收行借单提货，在汇票到期前将票款偿还代收行，换回信托收据。在进口方借单后、付款前，货物所有权属于出口商，若进口商在汇票到期时不能付款，一切责任要由代收行承担。如果代收行是按出口商指示借单，这种做法被称为"付款交单凭信托收据借单（D/PT/R）"，可以帮助进口商及时提货出售，解决其资金周转困难。若进口商品在汇票到期时不能付款，责任由出口商承担。

（2）承兑交单

承兑交单是指出口人的交单以进口人在汇票上承兑为条件。出口人发货后，取得装运单据，委托银行办理托收，并在托收委托书中指示银行，在进口人承兑远期汇票后，即把装运单据交给进口人。

承兑交单只适用于远期汇票的托收。对买方而言；承兑交单是先提货，后付款。买方提货后拒付的话，卖方会遭受很大的损失。因此，承兑交单风险很大，卖方采用时需慎重。图 8-5 为托收方式结算程序。

3. 应用托收方式的注意点

托收属于商业信用，银行办理托收业务时，只是按委托的指示办事，没有检查单据的

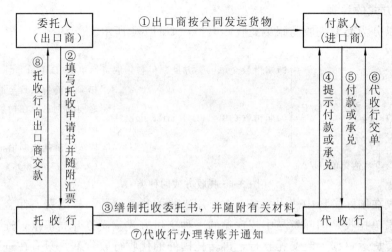

图 8-5   托收方式结算程序

义务，也无承担付款人必然付款的义务。一般而言，托收有利于进口人而不利于出口人。

出口业务中采用托收方式时，应注意下列问题：

1)调查进口商的资信状况和经营作风，正确掌握成交金额。

2)了解进口国家的贸易管制和外汇管制条例，以免进口国不准进口或不准付汇而造成损失。了解进口国托收的商业惯例和习惯做法。

3)出口合同争取以 CIF 条件成交，由出口商办理货运保险或投保出口信用险；如不能采取 CIF 条件成交时，应投保卖方利益险。

4)对托收方式的交易，要建立健全的管理制度，定期检查，及时催收清理，发现问题应迅速采取措施，以避免或减少可能发生的损失。

国际商会为调和各有关当事人的矛盾，以利于商业和金融活动的开展，1995 年颁布了最新的修订本《托收统一规则》(URC522)。它是国际上银行间办理托收业务的最重要的国际惯例。

8.2.4 信用证

1. 信用证的定义

信用证是国际贸易中使用最为广泛的一种结算方式。根据国际商会《跟单信用证统一惯例》的解释，信用证是指由银行(开证行)依照客户(申请人)的要求和指示或自己主动，在符合信用证条款的条件下，凭规定单据向第三者(受益人)或其指定的人进行付款，或承兑和(或)支付受益人开立的汇票，或授权另一银行进行该项付款，或承兑和支付汇票，或授权另一银行议付。

2. 信用证方式的特点

(1)信用证方式属于银行信用

在信用证方式下，开证行承担第一性的付款责任。只要出口人提交了符合信用证条款规定的单据，则无论汇票上的付款人是进口人还是开证行，也无论进口人能否履行其付款责任，开证行都必须对受益人或其指定银行付款。

(2)信用证是一项自足文件，不依附于贸易合同而独立存在

信用证的开立以交易双方间的买卖合同为依据，其各项条款也应与合同条款的规定相一致，但信用证一经开出就成为一项独立的文件。所有的当事人，特别是有关银行，只受信用证条款的约束，而不受合同条款的约束，即开证行不得以任何借口拒绝对符合信用证规定的单据付款或履行其他义务。

(3)信用证业务处理的是单据而不是货物

信用证方式下实行的是凭单付款的原则，只要出口人提交了表面上符合信用证条款规定的单据，就可以得到银行的付款，银行对单据的"形式、完整性、准确性、真实性、伪造或法律效力，以及对单据上所载的或附加的一般及或特殊条件概不负责"。同样，即使货物与合同相符，若单据与信用证规定不符，银行也有权拒绝付款。因此，出口人若要安全、迅速收汇，就必须做到单证一致、单单一致，即"严格相符原则"。

3. 信用证方式的当事人

信用证涉及的当事人较多，主要有开证申请人、开证行、通知行、受益人、议付行和付款行等。有时还会有偿付行、保兑行、受让人等。

4. 信用证的一般业务程序

以议付信用证为例，信用证的一般业务程序如图 8-6 所示：

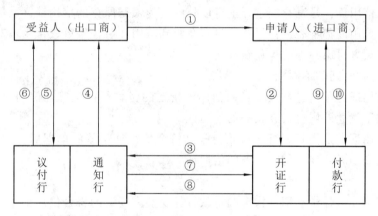

图 8-6　信用证方式结算程序

1)进出口商在合同中规定采用信用证支付方式。

2)开证申请。进口商按买卖合同规定向当地银行提出申请，并交纳一定的押金，要求银行(开证行)开立信用证。

3)开证。开证行根据申请书的要求开出以出口商为受益人的信用证，并将其寄交出口商所在地的分行或代理行(通知行)，请它们将信用证通知或转交受益人。

4)通知。通知行收到信用证后，立即对之进行审核，鉴定信用证表面真实性，核对无误后留存一份副本并将正本信用证交给受益人。

5)受益人审核、修改信用证并交单议付。受益人收到信用证后立即进行审核，如发现有不能接受的内容，应要求对方修改，若对开证行资信有疑虑，可要求申请人通知开证行将其信用证通过另一银行进行保兑。受益人经审核无误或收到信用证修改书后，按规定条件发货，缮制或取得信用证规定的单据，连同信用证正本及修改书一起，在信用证规定的有效期和交单期内，向出口地银行或指定的银行(议付行)办理交单议付。

6)议付行买入单据和/或汇票。议付行审核单据无误后，扣除利息及手续费，有追索权地买入单据和/或汇票。

7)索偿。议付行将单据和/或汇票寄交开证行(或保兑行或开证行指定的银行)索偿。

8)开证行付款。开证行经审核单据无误后，付款给议付行，同时通知开证申请人付款赎单。

9)开证申请人付款赎单。开证申请人审核单据无误后付款，取得单据，凭以向船公司提货。

5. 信用证的种类

(1)根据信用证项下的单据是否附有货运单据划分

1)跟单信用证：是开证行凭跟单汇票或仅凭单据付款的信用证。外贸业务中使用的信用证绝大部分都是跟单信用证。

2)光票信用证：是指开证行仅凭不附单据的汇票付款的信用证。这种信用证一般用于预付货款。

(2)根据信用证是否被保兑划分

1)保兑信用证：是指由开证行以外的另一家银行保兑的信用证。经过保兑后，开证行和保兑行共同承担对信用证受益人的付款义务。保兑信用证一定要注明"保兑"字样。

2)不保兑信用证：是没有经过开证行以外的其他银行保兑的信用证。一般信誉较高的银行所开立的信用证都不需进行保兑。只有在收到信用证后，经审核认为没有保障时再要求加保，以免买方付出额外的保兑费。

(3)根据付款时间的不同划分

1)即期信用证：是指受益人一旦向信用证指定的付款行提交符合信用证条款的单据，开证行或付款行就立即履行付款义务的信用证。

2)远期信用证：是指开证行或付款行收到符合信用证条款的单据后，并不立即付款，而是等到汇票到期时才履行付款义务的信用证。

(4)根据付款方式的不同划分

1)付款信用证：是指信用证指定的付款行凭受益人提交的符合信用证条款的单据付款的信用证。若以后不能向开证行收回款项时，不能向受益人追索。

2)延期付款信用证：属于付款信用证。在该信用证下，受益人不需要开立汇票，只要提供符合信用证条款的单据，付款行就在信用证规定的到期日付款。这种信用证不要求开立汇票，故无法进行贴现。一般在大型设备的交易中，买方为防止卖方将汇票贴现从而逃避对货物的责任，常使用此种信用证。

3)承兑信用证：是指银行将受益人提交的汇票和/或单据审核无误后，承兑汇票并发承兑电，到期后再付款。汇票可以进行贴现。

4)议付信用证：是允许受益人向某一指定银行或任何银行交单议付的信用证。一般在单据相符的条件下，议付银行扣除利息和手续费后买入汇票和/或单据，若以后不能向开证行收回款项时，议付行可向受益人追索款项。议付信用证又分为限制议付信用证和公开议付信用证两种。

除了上述分类外，信用证还有很多种类，如循环信用证、背对背信用证、对开信用证、预支信用证等。

6. 跟单信用证统一惯例

《跟单信用证统一惯例》是全世界公认的非政府商业机构制定的最为成功的国际惯例，《跟单信用证统一惯例(2007 年修订本)》(UCP600)于 2007 年 7 月 1 日正式实施。

8.2.5　支付方式的综合使用

一般而言，信用证结算方式为银行信用，较为安全，但存在费用高、时间长的缺点，同时对业务人员素质要求较高。业务人员只有熟练掌握信用证的审核和信用证下制单，才能安全结汇。汇付和托收均是商业信用。汇付方式较为简便，但在具体应用中要注意资金负担的平衡，通过预付款、单到付款、货到付款等方式的结合，避免风险。托收方式下出口人风险较大，应慎重使用。

交易双方有时将各种支付方式结合在一起，采用综合支付方式，主要有以下几种：

第一，汇付与托收相结合。以汇付方式支付定金，以付款交单的托收方式支付大部分货款。

第二，汇付与信用证相结合。以信用证支付大部分货款，货到目的地经检验计算出确切的货款总额后，以汇付方式支付货款余额。这常见于粮食、矿砂等散装货物的交易。又如，预付定金的买卖，定金部分用汇付支付，其余货款用信用证支付。

第三，汇付与银行保函或备用信用证相结合。常见于大型机械、成套设备的交易。进口方以汇付方式支付定金及每期货款与利息，同时以银行保函或备用信用证对出口方的收款提供保证。

第四，托收与信用证相结合。部分货款以信用证方式收取，部分货款通过托收收取。应注意的是，出口方的全套货运单据随附在托收项下的汇票下，而信用证部分则往往凭出口方开出的光票付款。

第五，托收与银行保函或备用信用证结合。货款以托收方式收取，同时进口方要开出银行保函或备用信用证，为出口方的收款提供保证。

8.3　任务实施与心得

任务实施

在国际贸易中，进出口人应选择恰当的支付工具和支付方式，订立合适的合同支付条款，处理货款的交付。

孙大伟经过和对方磋商，决定采用即期信用证方式结算货款，签订以下支付条款：

The Buyer shall open through BANQUE NATIONAL DE PARIS an Irrevocable sight Letter of Credit to reach the Seller 45 days before the month of shipment, valid for negotiation in China until the 10th day after the month of shipment, but within the validity of the L/C.

其他支付条款举例:

(1)汇付条款

汇付方式通常用于预付货款和赊账交易。为明确责任,防止拖延收付款时间,影响及时发运货物和企业的资金周转,对于使用汇付方式结算货款的交易,在合同中应明确规定汇付时间、具体的汇付方法和金额等。

预付货款

买方应不迟于10月15日将100%的货款经由电汇预付给卖方。

预付货款和货到付款结合

买方同意在本合同签字之日起1个月内将合同总金额的30%的预付款,以电汇方式汇交卖方。其余70%的货款,买方在收到合同所列单据的传真后,于2天内电汇付款。

(2)托收条款

以跟单托收方式结算货款的交易,在合同的支付条款中,须明确规定交单条件和付款、承兑责任以及付款期限等内容。其具体的规定方法,一般可先列明由卖方负责在装运货物后,开立汇票连同货运单据办理托收。

即期付款交单条款

买方应凭卖方开具的即期跟单汇票,于见票时立即付款,付款后交单。

远期付款交单条款

买方对卖方开具的见票后60天付款的跟单汇票,于提示时应立即承兑,并应于汇票到期日付款,付款后交单。

承兑交单条款

买方对卖方开具的见票后60天付款的跟单汇票,于提示时应立即承兑,并应于汇票到期日付款,承兑后交单。

(3)信用证条款

采用信用证方式结算,应在合同支付条款中,明确规定开证时间、开证银行、信用证的受益人、种类、金额、装运期、到期日等。

买方应通过卖方可接受的银行于装运月份前45天开立并送达卖方不可撤销即期信用证,有效期至装运月份后第15天在中国议付。否则,因此不能按规定装运,卖方不负责任,而且有权撤销合同并向买方提出索赔。

买方应通过卖方可接受的银行于装运月份前45天开立并送达卖方不可撤销见票后30天付款的信用证,有效期至装运月份后第15天在中国议付。买方应在信用证内规定:在装运时,如有港口拥挤附加费,由开证人负担,可凭受益人开具的发票和船公司表明实际已付附加费的正本收据,在信用证金额外支付给受益人。

任务实施心得

1. 选择结算方式时需要考虑以下问题

(1)客户信用

对于信用不是很好或对其尚未有充分了解的客户,交易时应选择风险较小的方式,如在出口业务中,一般可采用跟单信用证方式,如有可能也可争取以预付货款方式支付(如前 T/T)。

（2）贸易术语

在使用 CIF、CFR、CIP、CPT 等属于象征性交货或推定交货术语的交易中，就可选择跟单信用证方式。在买方信用较好时，也可采用跟单托收（如 D/P）方式收取货款。但在使用 EXW、DES 等属于实际交货方式术语的交易中，一般不能使用托收。以 FOB、FCA 条件达成的买卖合同，也不宜采用托收方式。

（3）运输单据

如货物通过海上运输或多式联合运输，出口人可通过运输单据控制物权，故可适用于信用证或托收方式结算货款。

如货物通过航空、铁路或邮政运输时，不适宜做托收。即使采用信用证，大多也规定必须以开证行作为运输单据的收货人，以便银行控制货物。

2. 选择合适的结算票据，防范票据风险

一般在信用证和托收方式下，使用商业汇票。在票汇中，常使用银行汇票和银行本票。常见的票据欺诈主要有以下方式：伪造票据、变造票据、"克隆"票据等。

8.4　知识拓展

1. 银行保函

银行保函是指银行应申请人的请求，向受益人开立的一种书面担保凭证，保证在申请人未能按双方协议履行其责任或义务时，承担赔偿责任。

银行保函不仅适用于国际货物的买卖，而且广泛适用于其他国际经济合作领域，如国际工程承包、招标与投标、借贷等。

2. 备用信用证

备用信用证属于银行信用，开证行对受益人保证，在开证申请人未履行其义务时，即由开证行付款。对受益人来说，是备用于开证申请人发生毁约情况时取得补偿的一种方式。

备用信用证使用范围广，广泛适用于国际货物买卖、借贷、工程投标、履约等业务中。开证申请人按期履行合同的义务，受益人就无须要求开证行支付货款或赔款，备用信用证则自动失效。

8.5　业务技能训练

8.5.1　课堂训练

1. 简述信用证与买卖合同的关系。

2. 采用托收时应注意哪些问题？

3. 汇票的一般使用程序如何？汇票的三个当事人一般是谁？

4. 进出口贸易的结算方式有哪些？这几种方式中，哪个对出口商最有利？哪个对出口商最不利？

5. 案例分析题

（1）我国某公司向国外 A 商出口一批货物。A 商按时开来不可撤销即期议付信用证，该证由设在我国境内的外资 B 银行通知并加保兑。我方公司在货物装运后，将全套合格单据送交 B 银行议付，收妥货款。但 B 银行向开证行索偿时，开证行因经营不善已宣布破产。于是，B 银行要求我方公司将议付的货款退还，并建议我方可委托其向 A 商直接索取货款。对此你认为我方公司应如何处理？为什么？

（2）我国某出口商向日本一进口商发盘，其中付款条件为：D/P at sight，对方答复可接受，但付款条件要改为：D/P at 90 days after sight，一般情况下，货物从我国运至日本时间很短。请分析日商为何提出此项条件。

（3）我国某外贸公司与某国 A 商达成一项出口合同，付款条件为 D/P45 天付款。当汇票及所附单据通过托收行寄抵进口地代收行后，A 商及时在汇票上履行了承兑手续。货抵目的港时，由于用货心切，A 商出具信托收据向代收行借得单据，先行提货转售。汇票到期时，A 商因经营不善，失去偿付能力。代收行以汇票付款人拒付为由通知托收行，并建议由我国外贸公司直接向 A 商索取货款。对此，你应如何处理？

8.5.2　实训操作

1. 因常州天信外贸有限公司与加拿大客户 JAMES BROWN&SONS 已有多次合作关系，经过简单磋商，双方确定采用发运前 50％预付款，50％装运后付款的支付方式，请你拟订具体的支付条款。

2. 江苏天地木业有限公司通过与现代公司磋商，双方确定采用 50％即期付款交单，50％即期信用证，请你拟订具体的支付条款。

3. 每位学生就自己公司和客户洽谈，选择好结算方式，订立合同的支付条款。

任务 9
签订出口贸易合同

知识要点

1. 国际贸易合同的形式和内容
2. 《联合国国际货物销售合同公约》的内容

技能要点

· 能够签订出口贸易书面合同

9.1　任务描述与分析

1. 任务描述

常州常信外贸有限公司一般情况下都是采用本公司的销售合同范本，与买方磋商达成一致后，由双方签字盖章后生效。

2010 年 7 月 20 日，经过艰苦的谈判，孙大伟与 Paul 终于就合同的各项条款达成了一致。现在他准备起草一份合同，让老总签字盖章后，传真给对方，让 Paul 会签后回传。

2. 任务分析

经过磋商，买卖双方就货物买卖合同的各项条款达成一致，合同就成立了。然而根据我国贸易实践的习惯，买卖双方还必须签订一定格式的正式书面国际贸易合同。

国际贸易合同是整个国际贸易关系中最为重要的具有法律约束力的文件，是各种进出口业务得以执行的基础和依据。因此要把合同条款订得严密，不要模糊，以防止履行合同时出现纠纷。

9.2　相关知识

9.2.1　进出口合同的形式与作用

在国际贸易实践中，订立合同的形式主要有三种：一种是书面形式；一种是口头形式；一种是以行为表示的。书面合同的形式也不是唯一的，在实践中，有合同、确认书、协议书和订单等形式。其中，销售合同、购货合同和销售确认书、购货确认书和订单、委托订单是最多见的。近年来迅速发展的电子合同，具有与纸质合同相同的法律效力，是纸质合同的替代者。

书面合同的作用一般可归纳为以下三个方面：

1)作为合同成立的证据。在我国现行法律体系中，对口头合同的规定较为模糊，实践过程中，一般都会在口头谈判达成协议后签订书面合同，以避免口说无凭。

2)作为履行合同的依据。双方磋商达成一致意见，签订书面合同后，双方就依照合同享有权利，履行各自的义务。

3)作为合同生效的条件。如果交易双方在发盘或接受时，声明以订立书面合同为准，则只有签订正式的书面合同时，合同才能成立。

9.2.2　进出口合同的内容

目前，进出口合同主要是指书面合同，其内容一般可分为约首、本文和约尾三部分。

约首，即合同的首部，一般包括合同名称、编号、签订日期、地点和签约双方的名称、地址等，有的合同还用序言形式说明定约意图并放在约首。

本文，即合同的主体部分，一般以条款的形式具体列明交易的各项条件，规定双方当事人的权利和义务。通常有品名、品质、数量、包装、价格、支付、运输、保险及争议处理等条款。

约尾，即合同的尾部，一般包括合同的份数、附件及其效力、使用的文字、合同生效的时间、地点及双方当事人（法人代表或其授权人）的签字等。

9.2.3 《联合国国际货物销售合同公约》

《联合国国际货物销售合同公约》是由联合国国际贸易法委员会于 1980 年通过的国际货物买卖统一法，于 1988 年 1 月 1 日起正式生效。

我国在 1986 年 12 月 11 日核准了该《公约》，但其提出了两项保留。一是针对《公约》的第一条第一款 B 项的规定，我国对此作了保留。其意味着对于我国来说，《公约》只适用于营业地位于不同缔约国之间的当事人所订立的货物销售合同。二是针对《公约》第十一条作了保留，导致营业地位于中国的缔约方在缔结国际货物销售合同时必须采用书面形式。

9.3 任务实施与心得

 任务实施

双方签订销售合同如下：

售货合同
SALES CONTRACT

买方：
The Buyers：GOLDEN MOUNTAIN TRADING CO.，LTD
ROOM 1618 BUILDING G
NO. 36 THE FIRST LYON STREET，
PARIS，FRANCE
TEL.：019-33-44-55

合同编号：
Contract NO.：CZCX080180
签订地点：
Signed at：CHANGZHOU，CHINA
签订日期：
Date：JULY 20，2010

卖方：
The Sellers：CHANGZHOU CHANGXIN IMPORT & EXPORT CORP.
NO. 25 MINGXIN RD，CHANGZHOU JIANGSU，CHINA
TEL.：0519-86338171

双方同意按下列条款由卖方售出下列商品：

The Buyers agree to buy and the Sellers agree to sell the following goods on terms and conditions as set forth below：

(1)商品名称、规格及包装 Name of Commodity，Specifications and Packing	(2)数量 Quantity	(3)单价 Unit Price	(4)总值 Total Value
LADIES COAT，woven，with bronze-colored buttons，2 pockets at side，like original sample NO. LJ566 sent on AUG.，15，2010 100% COTTON	1248pcs	USD28.70	CIFC3% MARSEILLES USD35817.60
Total Amount：SAY U. S. DOLLARS THIRTY FIVE THOUSAND EIGHT HUNDRED AND SEVENTEEN AND SIXTY CENTS ONLY			

(Shipment Quantity 5 ％ more or less allowed)S，416 pcs，M，416 pcs，L，416 pcs

Packing：8pcs per carton，assorted color and size，per pc in polybag. W×H×L ：50 ×40×80 cm.

SHIPPING MARK：FTC

       CZCX080180

       MARSEILLES

       NO. 1-UP

(5)装运期限：

Time of Shipment：20 Sept.，2010-30 Sept.，2010 by sea；otherwise 1 Oct.，2010-15 Oct.，2010 on seller's account by air

(6)装运口岸：

Port of Loading：SHANGHAI CHINA

(7)目的口岸：

Port of Destination：MARSEILLES FRANCE

(8)保险：由___卖___方负责，按本合同总值110％投保___一切险和战争险___。

Insurance：To be covered by the ___seller___ for 110％ of the invoice value against All Risks，War Risks as per and subject to the relevant Ocean Marine Cargo Clause of the People's Insurance Company of China，dated January 1st，1981.

(9)付款：

Terms of Payment：The buyer shall open through BANQUE NATIONAL DE PARIS an irrevocable sight letter of credit to reach the seller 45 days before the month of shipment，valid for negotiation in China until the 10th day after the month of shipment，but within the validity of the L/C.

(10)商品检验：买卖双方同意以装运港中国出入境检验检疫机构签发的质量检验证书作为信用证项下议付所需单据之一，买方有权对货物的质量进行复验，复验费由买方承担。如发现质量与合同规定不符，买方有权向卖方索赔，并提交经卖方同意的公证机构出具的检验报告。索赔期限为货到目的港(地)180 天内。

It is mutually agreed that the certificate of quality issued by the China Exit and Entry Inspection and Quarantine Bureau at the port/place of shipment shall be part of the documents to be presented for negotiation under the relevant L/C. The buyers shall have the right to reinspect the quality of the cargo. The reinspection fee shall be borne by the buyers. Should the quality be found not in conformity with that of the contract，the buyers are entitled to lodge with the sellers a claim which should be supported by survey reports issued by a recognized surveyor approved by the sellers. The claim，if any，shall be lodged within 180 days after arrival of the goods at the port of destination.

其他条款：

OTHER TERMS：

信用证内容须严格符合本售货合约的规定，否则修改信用证的费用由买方负担。卖方并不负担因修改信用证而延误装运的责任，并保留因此而发生的一切损失的索赔权。

The contents of the covering Letter of Credit shall be in strict conformity with the stipulations of the Sales Contract. In case of any variation there of necessitating amendment of the L/C, the Buyers shall bear the expenses for effecting the amendment. The Sellers shall not be held responsible for possible delay of shipment resulting from awaiting the amendment of the L/C and reserve the right to claim from the Buyers for the losses resulting therefrom.

卖方（Sellers）：　　　　　　　　　　　　　　买方（Buyers）：

陈哲　　　　　　　　　　　　　　　　　　Paul

任务实施心得

出口贸易合同的双方处于不同国家或地区。因此，在签订出口贸易合同时不仅要熟悉我国的法律，而且要了解对方当事人国家或地区的有关法律以及有关国际惯例等。

在谈判后，我们应重视合同文本的起草，尽量争取起草合同文本，如果做不到这一点，也要与对方共同起草合同文本，然后让对方会签。如果是买方提供的采购合同，我们在签订时必须仔细审核，避免对方加进一些对我不利的条款或遗漏一些对方必须承担义务的条款，以免给以后履行合同带来不必要的麻烦，乃至造成一定的经济损失。

9.4　知识拓展

电子合同的广泛运用

近年来迅速发展的电子合同，具有与纸质合同相同的法律效力，是纸质合同的替代者。电子合同具有纸质合同无法匹敌的优势，能够在电脑中原样归档、检索，提供有用的数据，方便企业查找信息。电子合同还可以导入企业的 ERP 系统，企业在对账、结算、资金控制方面可以获得极大的便利。随着 2004 年我国《电子签名法》的生效，承认电子文件与书面文书具有同等效力，从而使现行的民商事法律同样适用于电子文件。电子合同的应用将越来越广泛。

9.5　业务技能训练

9.5.1　课堂训练

1. 简述书面合同的作用。
2. 学生交流在订立国际贸易书面合同时应注意哪些问题？
3. 案例分析题

我国某公司与外商洽谈进口一批某商品，经往来电传洽谈，已谈妥合同的主要交易条件，但我方在传真中表明交易于签订确认书时生效。事后对方将草拟的合同条款交我方确认，但因有关条款的措辞尚需研究，故我方未及时给对方答复。不久该商品的市场价格下跌，对方电催我方开立信用证，而我方以合同未成立为由拒绝开证。问：我方的做法是否有理？为什么？

9.5.2　实训操作

1. 常州天信外贸有限公司拟就了一份合同，并传真给 J. B. S 公司要求其会签。请你完成具体合同的拟订工作。合同签订时间为 2010 年 8 月 30 日。

2. 江苏天地木业有限公司与现代公司已经就地板交易的各项内容达成一致。请你拟订一份书面合同。

3. 每位学生就自己公司和客户洽谈的各项合同条款，订立完整的书面合同。

综合训练二

1. 业务背景

接综合训练一，新加坡客户接到常州永盛进出口公司去函以及寄送的样品后，确认了样品，于 9 月 10 日来函，要求常州永盛公司报价。经谈判，与新客户达成初笔牛仔布买卖交易。

2. 训练任务

(1) 接到客户 9 月 10 日 E-mail

SAMPLES CONFIRMED. PLEASE OFFER FIRM IT. NO. 0866 4 200 YARDS.

根据以下公司报价要求，2010 年 9 月 12 日向客户发盘(报价)

报价数量：4 200 码；

报价价格：CIF 新加坡每码 2.70 美元；

装运期：2010 年 11 月；

支付方式：不可撤销即期信用证；

保险：一切险加战争险、罢工险。

(2) 9 月 14 日客户回复

YOURS 12TH 4 200 YARDS SHIPMENT NOVEMBER US DOLLARS 2.30 CIFC3 D/P SIGHT PLEASE REPLY SIXTEENTH

请对此进行回复。(日期：2010 年 9 月 16 日)

(3) 客户 9 月 17 日再次还盘

YOURS 16TH QUOTING BEST US DOLLARS 2.40 4 200 YARDS CREDIT 60 DAYS SIGHT

考虑到目前市场竞争特别激烈，又是初次交易，同意将每码价格降低到 2.50 美元、见票 30 天信用证付款，限 19 日前复。请回复客户。

(4) 客户 9 月 20 日同意常州永盛进出口公司条件，请根据双方往来函电缮制出口销售合同。

(5) 寄送合同，要求客户会签和准时开证。

情境 3　出口合同的履行

任务 10
信用证的审核与修改

10.1　任务描述与分析

1. 任务描述

　　2010 年 7 月 20 日合同签订，直到 8 月 10 日还没有接到对方开来的信用证，孙大伟就发 E-mail 询问，请 Pual 早日去银行开出信用证。8 月 15 日中国银行常州分行通知常信公司收到信用证。现业务员孙大伟正在进行审核，以确认信用证各条款是否正确，履行合同时有无问题。

2. 任务分析

　　信用证是银行做出的有条件的付款承诺，银行在规定的期限内凭规定的单据承诺付款。同时，信用证遵循"严格相符原则"，所有单据在表面上必须做到与信用证条款的规定一致，同时各种单据之间也要一致。如果做不到，便不能够安全收汇。做到严格相符的前提是信用证本身正确无误，同时出口方能够做到信用证各项规定要求。

　　因此，出口商作为信用证的受益人必须对信用证的各项条件进行审核，如果信用证与合同或交易要求不符，或者尽管信用证正确，但出口商履行合同时存在困难，无法满足信用证的要求，都应及时提出，让开证人去银行修改信用证。

10.2　相关知识

10.2.1　信用证的内容

　　信用证的内容就是构成信用证基本条款、文句和事项的书面文字，主要有以下几个方面的内容。

　　1）信用证的当事人：包括开证申请人、受益人、开证行、通知行等。

　　2）关于信用证本身的说明：包括信用证的号码、开证日期、地点、有效期及到期地点、信用证金额及货币、信用证性质和种类等内容。

　　3）汇票条款：包括出票人、付款人、汇票期限、金额、出票日期等。

　　4）单据条款：包括受益人应提交的单据种类及份数要求等。

　　5）货物条款：包括货物品名、品质、规格、数量、包装、价格及价格条件、运输唛头等的要求。

　　6）运输条款：包括装运港（地）、目的港（地）、装运期限、分批和转运的规定等。

　　7）费用条款：包括信用证所发生的银行费用由谁承担。

　　8）其他文句：包括开证行负责文句、开证行对议付行的指示文句、特殊条款、附加文句以及遵守《跟单信用证统一惯例》规定的文句等。

10.2.2　信用证的审核

　　信用证是独立于买卖合同之外的一个新契约，采用信用证支付时，出口商对信用证的内容应仔细审核。认真细致地对国外开来的信用证进行审核是关系到出口商是否能够安全及时收取货款的关键。应明确信用证的内容，确保信用证的要求与合同一致，否则，很容易引起后续合同不能履行，或不能顺利收汇。

出口商审核信用证时的主要依据是国内的有关政策和规定、交易双方成交的合同、国际商会的《跟单信用证统一惯例》以及实际业务操作中的情况。审核信用证通常遵循的原则是：信用证条款规定比合同条款严格时，应当作为信用证中存在的问题提出修改（当然，在实际业务中主要是以是否影响出口商安全收汇和顺利履行合同义务为前提）；而当信用证的规定比合同条款宽松时，往往可不要求修改。

1. 信用证审核中常见的问题

（1）信用证的性质

信用证未生效或有限制性生效的条款；信用证为可撤销的；信用证中没有保证付款的责任文句；信用证内漏列适用国际商会 UCP 规则条款；信用证未按合同要求加保兑；信用证密押不符。

按贸易惯例，信用证在送达受益人时即生效，但是有些信用证中有不合理的限制性或保留条款，如买方获得进口许可证后信用证生效，这些需要在审证时注意。

（2）信用证的有效期

没有规定到期日的信用证无效；到期地点在国外；信用证的到期日和装运期有矛盾；装运期、到期日或交单期规定与合同不符；装运期或有效期的规定与交单期矛盾；交单期过短。

（3）信用证当事人

开证申请人公司名称或地址与合同不符；受益人公司名称或地址与合同不符。

（4）金额货币

信用证金额应与合同金额一致，如合同订有溢短装条款，信用证金额也应包括溢短装部分的金额；信用证金额中单价与总值要填写正确；来证所采用的货币应与合同规定一致。

在审核金额时要注意不同价格条件下所产生的费用如运费、保险费由谁负担以及相应的单据是否合理。如采用 FOB 贸易术语，但信用证中要求卖方投保和交付保险单据，或者是要求运费预付等都是不合理的。

（5）汇票

汇票的付款人不是开证行或其指定的付款行，付款期限与合同规定或实际业务要求不相符。

（6）运输

信用证中规定的装运港与目的港、装运期、分批装运和转运等与合同不符；如国外来证晚，无法按期装运，应及时电请国外买方延展装运期限；如信用证规定了分批装运的时间和数量，应注意能否办到；如果信用证对船龄、船籍、船公司或港口等有限制条款，则要考虑能否办到。

注意：

UCP600 第三条规定，"on or about××"表示在所述日期前后各五天内发生，起讫日均包括在内；"to/until/till/from/between ××"用于确定装运期限时，包括所述日期；"before/after ××"不包括所述日期；"from/after ××"用于确定到期日时不包括所述日期。

（7）货物

货物品名规格不符；货物数量不符；货物包装有误；贸易术语错误；使用术语与条款有矛盾；货物单价数量与总金额不吻合；证中援引的合同号码与日期错误；漏列溢短装规定。

（8）单据条款

1）单据的种类与交易条件不相符，如空运方式下要求提供海运提单、FOB 价格条件下要求提供保险单等。

2）单据填制或交付中对受益人较为困难的方面。如果信用证要求提供一些需要特别机构认证的单据或是由一些机构或部门出具的有关文件如许可证、运费收据、检验证明等，要考虑能否提供或能否按时提供。

对来证所需的各种单据应审核有关文字，查看有无特殊要求，我方能否办理。

（9）信用证软条款

软条款是指在不可撤销信用证中出现的某些可能令受益人在无过错情况下蒙受损失的条款。软条款本身并不违背《UCP600》原则，其风险是潜在的，表现形式也多种多样。

知识链接

信用证典型软条款举例

软条款 1：3 份正本提单中，有一份直接寄给开证申请人。我们知道，凭借一份正本提单就可以提货了。这个条款一经执行，就意味着客户可以在银行议付单证前就可径直去提货。信用证受益人面临财货两空的危险。

软条款 2：货物须经开证人检验，出具检验认可报告方可付运，检验报告作为议付单证之一。这个条款的风险在于，假如交货前因市场变化，客户有意毁约，则故意拖延检验，不出具检验报告，导致无法装运和提交检验报告。

软条款的共同特点是让信用证在不同程度丧失执行的独立性和不可撤销性。有了软条款的信用证，客户可以通过各种手段使其在实际执行过程中单方面废止。因此，外贸业务员应该学会识别软条款。诀窍就是牢记两个原则：不能让客户有可能在付款赎单前自行提货；开证以后，所有单证出口商可以单方收集办理，不要依赖客户。

知识链接

软条款的处理

在提高警惕慎重处理的前提下，对有的软条款可酌情考虑接受，或附加其他条款来加以制约，争取既满足客户的需要，又最大限度地降低风险。

比如，进口方是信誉良好的老牌商号，开证行也知名可靠，可以考虑接受"正本提单径交开证人"的条款，在接受的同时，限定提单的收货人为"凭开证行指示"。这样即使客户得到正本提单，也须由银行背书（在提单背面签字盖章，表明执此提单者已经获得银行许可），避免了客户绕开银行私自提货的风险；或修改为"副本提单径交开证申请人"，这样客户可以在提供担保的情况下凭副本提单提货，而所提供的担保也同时保障了受益人的权益。

（10）其他条款

费用条款、索偿途径等条款均应是合理、方便的。

2. 信用证三期之间的关系

信用证中的三期为信用证的有效期、货物的装运期、信用证的交单期。一般情况下信用证的交单期为装运单据签发后 10 天到 15 天，以便在装运货物后有足够的时间办理制单结汇，具体视信用证的规定而定。

UCP600 第十四条规定：正本运输单据必须由受益人或其代表按照相关条款在不迟于装运日后的二十一个公历日内提交，但无论如何不得迟于信用证的到期日。

10.2.3　信用证的修改

1. 受益人通知开证申请人要求修改信用证

改证函电是受益人致信给开证申请人要求其通过开证银行对信用证进行修改的信函，主要表述三个方面的内容：首先是感谢对方及时开来了信用证；之后是逐项列明信用证中的不符点，并告知对方如何修改；最后是希望能早日收到信用证修改书，以便能按时发货。

2. 开证申请人向银行提出修改申请

信用证修改通常在以下几种情况下发生。

(1)出口方(受益人)要求

由于信用证内容与合同不符，或信用证中某些条款受益人无法办到。例如，来证规定货物不允许转运，但实际并无直航船只抵达目的地，也可能是货源或船期等出现问题，要求展期。

(2)进口方(开证申请人)要求修改信用证

一种情况是由于市场销售情况发生变化。例如，需要提前或推后发货，增加或减少货物数量或品种，改变信用证单价、金额等。

另一种情况是进口国某些情况发生变化或国际政治、经济形势变化，使信用证必须修改，才能进口有关货物。如：进口国政策改变，规定进口某些货物必须具备某特定单据等；当战争爆发时，进口商要求增保战争险或改变航运路线等。

(3)开证行工作疏漏，在打字或传递上造成的错误使信用证必须更正。

> **注意：**
> 在提出修改申请时应做到：凡是需要修改的内容，应做到一次性提出，避免多次修改信用证的情况。这样不仅增加双方的费用，而且延误装运期。

3. 原开证行发出信用证修改书并经原通知行传递给受益人

受益人收到信用证修改书后，应注意以下几点：

1)有关信用证修改必须通过原信用证通知行才真实、有效，通过客户直接寄送的修改申请书或修改书复印件无效。

2)收到信用证修改书后，应及时检查修改内容是否符合要求，并视情况表示接受或重新提出修改。

3)对于修改内容要么全部接受，要么全部拒绝。部分接受修改中的内容是无效的。

4)对信用证修改内容的接受或拒绝有两种表示形式：受益人作出接受或拒绝该信用证修改的通知；受益人以行动按照信用证或信用证修改书的内容办事。

5)明确修改费用由谁承担。一般按照责任归属来确定修改费用由谁承担。

10.3　任务实施与心得

 任务实施

(1)催证

为保证出口合同能顺利履行，孙大伟于 8 月 10 日发 E-mail 给 Pual，请他早日去银行开出信用证。

The covering letter of credit is expected to reach here before 15 AUG. , since the stipulated month of shipment is 20 SEPT. -30SEPT. , considering to prepare of the shipment timely, we are looking forward to your immediate covering letter of credit.

(2)审证

法国客户按合同要求，由 BANQUE NATIONAL DE PARIS 银行在 2010 年 8 月 12 日开出了信用证。8 月 15 日中国银行常州分行通知常信公司收到信用证。

MT S700	ISSUE OF	A DOCUMENTARY CREDIT
SEQUENCE OF TOTAL	* 27：	1/1
DOC. CREDIT NUMBER	* 20：	LCH066/08
DATE OF ISSUE	31C：	100812
EXPIRY	* 31C：	DATE 081031 PLACE CHINA
APPLICANT BANK	51A：	BANQUE NATIONAL DE PARIS
	PARIS	FRANCE
APPLICANT	* 50：	GOLDEN MOUNTAIN TRADING CO. , LTD
		ROOM 1618 BUILDING G
		NO. 36 THE FIRST LYON STREET,
		PARIS, FRANCE
		TEL. ：019-33-44-55
BENEFICIARY	* 59：	CHANGZHOU CHANGXIN IMPORT & EXPORT CORP.
		NO. 25 MINGXIN RD,
		CHANGZHOU JIANGSU, CHINA
		TEL. ：0519-86338171
AMOUNT	* 32B：	CURRENCY USD AMOUNT USD35817. 60
AVAILABLE WITH/BY	* 41D：	ANY BANK BY NEGOTIATION

DRAFTS AT   42C：   SIGHT

FOR 100PCT INVOICE VALUE

DRAWEE   42A：   BANQUE NATIONAL DE PARIS

PARIS   FRANCE

PARTIAL SHIPMENTS   43P：   NOT ALLOWED

TRANSSHIPMENT   43T：   ALLOWED

LOADING IN CHARGE   44A：   SHANGHAI CHINA

FOR TRANSPORT TO   44B：   MARSEILLES PORT FRANCE

LATEST DATE OF SHIP 44C：   20 Sept．，2010-30 Sept．，2010 by sea；otherwise 1 Oct．，2010-15 Oct．，2010 on seller's account by air

DESCRIPTION OF GOODS 45A：

LADIES COAT @ USD28．70 PER PIECE CIFC3% MARSEILLES

TOTAL QUANTITY：1248PCS

TOTAL AMOUNT：USD35817．60

DOCUMENTS REQUIRED 46A：

+SIGNED ORIGINAL COMMERCIAL INVOICE IN 6 COPIES INDICATING L/C NO. AND CONTRACT NO. CZCX080180

+3/3 SET OF ORIGINAL CLEAN ON BOARD OCEAN BILLS OF LADING MADE OUT TO ORDER WITH 4 NON-NEGOTABLE COPIES AND BLANK ENDORSED MARKED FREIGHT PREPAID NOTIFYING APPLICANT INDICATING FREIGHT CHARGES

+SIGNED ORIGINAL PACKING LIST/WEIGHT MEMO IN 5 COPIES ISSUED BY BENEFICIARY SHOWING QUANTITY/GROSS AND NET WEIGHT

+SIGNED ORIGINAL CERTIFICATE OF QUALITY IN 5 COPIES ISSUED BY MANUFACTURER.

+2/2 SET OF ORIGINAL INSURANCE POLICY OR CERTIFICATE，ENDORSED IN BLANK WITH 2 COPIES COVERING OCEAN MARINE TRANSPORTATION ALL RISKS AND WAR RISKS FOR 110 PCT INVOICE VALUE SHOWING CLAIMS PAYABLE IN FRANCE IN CURRENCY OF THE DRAFT.

+SIGNED ORIGINAL CERTIFICATE OF ORIGIN IN 5 COPIES.

+SIGNED ORIGINAL CERTIFICATE OF QUANTITY/WEIGHT IN 5 COPIES ISSUED BY MANUFACTURER INDICATING THE ACTUAL SURVEYED QUANTITY/WEIGHT OF SHIPPED GOODS AS WELL AS THE PACKING CONDITION

+SIGNED ORIGINAL QUARANTINE CERTIFICATE FOR WOODEN CASE ISSUED BY AUTHORISED GOVERNMENTAL ORGANIZATION OR DECLARATION OF NO-WOOD PACKAGE STATEMENT ISSUED BY MANUFACTURER

+ONE SET OF EXTRA PHOTOCOPY OF ORIGINAL B/L AND ORIGINAL INVOICE.

ADDITIONAL COND. 47A：

+FOR EACH DOCUMENTARY DISCREPANCY（IES）UNDER THIS CREDIT，A FEE OF USD60.00 WILL BE DEDUCTED FROM THE WHOLE PROCEEDS.

DETAILS OF CHARGES 71B：ALL BANKING CHARGES OUTSIDE THE ISSUING BANK INCLUDING THOSE OF REIMBURSEMENT BANK ARE FOR ACCOUNT OF BENEFICIARY.

PRESENTATION PERIOD 48：DOCUMENTS TO BE PRESENTED WITHIN 10 DAYS AFTER THE ISSUANCE OF THE SHIPPING DOCUMENTS BUT WITHIN THE VALIDITY OF THE CREDIT.

CONFIRMATION *49：WITHOUT

INSTRUCTIONS 78：

+ALL DOCUMENTS TO BE FORWARDED TO BANQUE NATIONAL DE PARIS PARIS，FRANCE IN ONE COVER BY COURIER SERVICE UNLESS OTHERWISE STATED ABOVE.

+WE HEREBY UNDERTAKE THAT UPON RECEIPT OF THE ORIGINAL DOCUMENTS IN COMPLIANCE WITH THE TERMS OF THIS CREDIT.

THE DRAFTS DRAWN UNDER WILL BE DULY HONORED.

+THIS CREDIT IS SUBJECT TO U.C.P. FOR DOCUMENTARY CREDIT，2007 REVISION ICC NO.600

孙大伟根据合同仔细审核信用证，填写表 10-1 信用证分析单。

表 10-1 信用证分析单

证号	LCH066/08	合约号		受益人	CHANGZHOU CHANGXIN IMPORT & EXPORT CORP.		
开证银行	BANQUE NATIONAL DE PARIS PARIS FRANCE	进口商	GOLDEN MOUNTAIN TRADING CO.，LTD	L/C 性质	IRREVOCABLE		
开证日期	AUG.12，2010	索汇方式		起运口岸	SHANGHAI, CHINA	目的地	MARSEILLS PORT FRANCE
金额	USD35 817.60	可否转运	ALLOWED	可否分批	NOT ALLOWED		
汇票付款人	BANQUE NATIONAL DE PARIS PARIS FRANCE	汇票期限	见票＊＊＊＊天期	装运期限	20 Sept.，2010-30 Sept.，2010 by sea；otherwise1Oct. 2010-15 Oct.，2010 on seller's account by air		
提单日后 __10__ 天议付		信用证有效期	NOT LATER THAN OCT.31，2010	唛头			
		到期地点	CHINA				

续表

单证名称	提单	副本提单	商业发票	形式发票	海关发票	装箱单	重量单	尺码单	保险单	产地证	GSP证	贸促会证	许可证	装船通知	投保通知	寄单证明	寄样证明	质量证书	数量/重量证书	木箱检疫证书	非木质包装声明
银行	3	5	6			5	5		2	5									5	5	正本	正本
客户																						

提单	抬头	TO ORDER		保险	险别：ALL RISKS AND WAR RISKS
	通知	APPLICANT			
运费：FREIGHT PREPAID			保额另加 10 %	赔款地点	DESTINATION
背书：BLANK ENDORSED					

现在孙大伟对信用证审核无误后，准备安排货物装运。

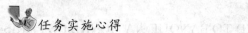 任务实施心得

催证、审证、改证是信用证操作中的重要环节，需要注意以下事项：

1)单据条款、信用证规定的有效期和到期地点是信用证审核中的重点与难点之一，对于来证中要求提供的单据种类、份数、填制方法和签发人等，要进行仔细审核，如发现有不正常规定，特别是软条款，应慎重对待。

2)在信用证方式下事先应在合同中规定来证时间，合同订立后要注意催证。如果不收到信用证就订货，万一对方不开来信用证，就会造成库存积压损失。如果一直等下去，时间晚了给装运带来麻烦，甚至会来不及出运，超过信用证的装运期。

催证函电一般包括：陈述合同规定的开证时间；备货与装运所需时间以及目前的进度；陈述责任，如对方不开证，将视为违约。

3) 改证要注意一定是致函开证申请人，然后由开证申请人请求开证行开来修改证书后，出口人审核修改书正确无误后，才能办理装运。

10.4　知识拓展

SWIFT 信用证

SWIFT 是环球银行金融电讯协会的简称。该组织是一个国际银行同业间非营利性的国际合作组织，专门从事传递各国之间非公开性的国际间的金融电讯业务，其中包括：外汇买卖，证券交易、开立信用证、办理信用证项下的汇票业务和托收等。

SWIFT 信用证具有标准化的统一格式，安全可靠、高速度、低费用、自动加核密押等特点。凡依据国际商会所制定的电讯信用证格式设计，利用 SWIFT 网络系统设计的特殊格式，通过 SWIFT 开立或通知的信用证称为 SWIFT 信用证，也称为"环银电协信用证"。

银行在开立信用证时多采用如表 10-2 所示的 SWIFT MT700 跟单信用证的格式。

表 10-2　**MT700 格式跟单信用证**

M/O	Tag	Field Name	项目名称
M	27	Sequence of Total	报文页次
M	40A	Form of Documentary Credit	跟单信用证格式
M	20	Documentary Credit Number	信用证号码
O	23	Reference to Pre-Advice	预先通知编号
O	31C	Date of Issue	开证日期
M	31D	Date and Place of Expiry	到期日及到期地点
O	51a	Applicant Bank	开证申请人的银行
M	50	Applicant	开证申请人
M	59	Beneficiary	受益人
M	32B	Currency Code，Amount	信用证的货币及金额
O	39A	Percentage Credit Amount Tolerance	信用证金额浮动允许范围
O	39B	Maximum Credit Amount	信用证金额的最高限额
O	39C	Additional Amounts Covered	附加金额
M	41a	Available with … by …	指定的有关银行及信用证的兑付方式
O	42C	Drafts at …	汇票付款期限
O	42a	Drawee	汇票的付款人
O	42M	Mixed Payment Details	混合付款条款
O	42P	Deferred Payment Details	迟期付款条款
O	43P	Partial Shipments	分批装运条款
O	43T	Transshipment	转运条款
O	44A	Loading on Board/Dispatch/Taking in Charge at/form	装船，发运和接受监管的地点
O	44B	For Transportation to …	货物发送的最终目的地
O	44C	Latest Date of Shipment	最迟装运日期
O	44D	Shipment Period	装运期
O	45A	Description of Goods and /or Services	货物/劳务描述
O	46A	Documents Required	单据要求
O	47A	Additional Conditions	附加条款
O	71B	Charges	费用负担
O	48	Period for Presentation	交单期限
M	49	Confirmation Instructions	保兑指示

10.5　业务技能训练

10.5.1　课堂训练

1. 对于信用证中出现的与合同不一致的内容，如果规定比合同宽松，我们应该如何处理？

2. 根据英语部分本任务的例 10-1 的信用证内容填写下列信用证分析单，并回答问题。

信用证分析单

证号			合约号				受益人		
开证银行			进口商				L/C 性质		
开证日期			索汇方式			起运口岸		目的地	
金额			可否转运			可否分批			
汇票付款人			汇票期限		见票____天期		装运期限		
提单日后____天议付			信用证有效期				唛头		
			到期地点						

单证名称	提单	副本提单	商业发票	形式发票	海关发票	装箱单	重量单	尺码单	保险单	产地证	GSP证	贸促会证	许可证	装船通知	投保通知	寄单证明	寄样证明			
银行																				
客户																				

提单	抬头		保险	险别：	
	通知				

运费：		保额另加　　%	赔款地点	
背书：				

问题：如果已装船提单的签发日为 11 月 15 日，则受益人最迟应在几月几日向银行交单？

3. 学生讨论，如何应对信用证中的正本提单寄交开证申请人的问题。

10.5.2　实训操作

1. 常州天信外贸有限公司收到加拿大客户 JAMES BROWN&SONS 开来的 L/C，请你根据有关条件审核信用证并改证。

有关合同重要条款

合同号：010CT9944

卖方：常州天信外贸有限公司

买方：JAMES BROWN&SONS

商品（每件）	规格	数量（件）	CFR 纽约
男衬衫	MS691	2000PCS	USD24.00/PC
	MS862	1500PCS	USD28.00/PC

总额：90 000.00 美元

装运：2010 年 9 月由中国港口运往美国纽约，允许分批

支付方式：不可撤销即期信用证

GREAT EASER BANK, NY 11355 USA

IRREVOCABLE DOCUMENTARY CREDIT

DATE AND PLACE OF EXPIRY：JUNE 1, 2010 AT OUR COUNTER

APPLICANT：JAMES BROWN&SONS.

#304-310 JaJa Street, Toronto, Canada

BENEFICIARY：CHANGZHOU TIANXIN IMPORT & EXPORT CORP.

Room 2601, Changzhou International Trade Center

801 Yan Ling Road(w), Changzhou, Jiangsu 213001

CURRENCY CODE, AMOUNT：USD89000.00 (SAY US DOLLAR EIGHTY - NINE THOUSAND ONLY)

DRAFTS：AT 30DAYS' SIGHT

DRAWEE：JAMES BROWN&SONS

FOR TRANSPORTATION：TO NEW YORK, USA FROM CHINA PORT

LATEST DATE OF SHIPMENT：SEPT. 30, 2010

GOODS：GARMENTS

MS691	2000	USD24.00
MS692	1500	USD26.00

CFR NEW YORK

DOCUMENTS REQUIRED：

——SIGNED COMMERCIAL INVOICE IN TRIPLICATE INDICATING CONTRACT NO. 01 OCT 4499

——FULL SET OF CLEAN SHIPPED ON BOARD OCEAN BILL OF LADING MADE OUT TO ORDER AND BLANK ENDORSED. MARKED FREIGHT PREPAID.

——FULL SET OF INSURANCE POLICY/CERTIFICATE

ADDITIONAL CONDITIONS：

——THE TOTAL AMOUNT OF THE INVOICE MUST BE MENTIONED ON THE CERTIFICATE OF ORIGIN.

——PARTIAL SHIPMENTS PERMITTED BUT TO BE EFFECTED NOT BEFORE SEPT. 30, 2010

THIS IS THE OPERATIVE INSTRUMENT NO MAIL CONFIRMATION WILL FOLLOW.

2. 请你给你的进口商写一封催证的函电。

任务 11

出口货物的准备

知识要点

1. 国内采购合同的格式与具体条款内容
2. 出口货物准备的各项要求

技能要点

- 按照出口合同和供应商谈判，签订购货合同
- 按照出口合同的要求，准备货物，完成货物的包装和唛头的刷制

11.1　任务描述与分析

1. 任务描述

在收到外商询盘后，孙大伟在国内对多家生产女装的厂家进行了联系和询价，当时就是在对女风衣的进货成本有充分的了解的基础上，给法国 GOLDEN MOUNTAIN TRADING CO.，LTD 进行的报价。

常信公司与 GOLDEN MOUNTAIN TRADING CO.，LTD 的出口合同签订后，孙大伟就该批女装与两家供应商进行磋商，准备选择一家进行下单，生产该批出口服装。

2010 年 8 月 15 日孙大伟对法国 GOLDEN MOUNTAIN TRADING CO.，LTD 的信用证审核完毕，没有发现信用证有差错。孙大伟就立即与常州兴隆服装有限公司签订购货合同，落实货源，准备出口货物。

2. 任务分析

合同的双方当事人必须严格履行合同中所规定的各项义务。对于卖方来说，主要是交付与合同规定相符的货物和相关的单据。

除了生产企业自营出口的货物以外，外贸公司出口的货物大多需要在国内采购。这就需要外贸公司的业务员在外销订单落实后，在国内寻找生产厂家，进行询价比较，贸易洽谈，签订采购合同。

常信公司作为一家外贸公司，自身没有生产基地，现在要出口货物，需要找服装厂生产服装出口。孙大伟已经做了许多前期工作，现在进入货物准备阶段。

11.2　相关知识

11.2.1　采购合同的签订

为了保证按时、按质、按量交付约定的货物，在订立出口合同之后，外贸公司必须及时落实货源，与出口货物的生产厂家签订采购合同。采购合同的各项条款必须能够保证出口合同能够顺利履行。

采购合同的品质、包装条款必须和出口合同的品质、包装条款一致，数量可以比出口合同的数量略多一些，确保出口合同的数量不少，交货时间应该比出口合同的装运时间早一些，以便安排装运。

如果在生产工厂交货，就需要外贸公司负责把货物运输到装运港或安排集装箱在工厂进行装柜。此时，该内陆运费就由外贸公司承担。交货地点如果在装运港的仓库，外贸公司就不承担从生产厂到装运港的运费。

采购合同的价格一般应该充分考虑各种因素，确保公司的利润。采购合同的支付条款一般也应该考虑到出口合同的支付条款，这样可以少占用外贸公司的资金。

11.2.2　出口货物的准备

备货工作主要包括按合同和信用证的规定督促货物生产加工或仓储部门组织货源，核实货物的加工、整理、包装和刷唛情况，对应交的货物进行验收和清点。在备货工作中，应做好下列工作：

第一，确保发运货物的时间。为了保证按时交货，应根据合同和信用证对装运期的规定，并结合船期安排，做好供货工作，使船货衔接好，以防止出现"船等货"或"货等船"的情况。

第二，核对货物的品质和规格。交付货物的品质和规格，必须符合约定的要求。如果不符，应进行筛选、加工和整理，直至达到要求为准。

第三，货物的数量要留有余地。必须按约定数量备货，而且应留有余地，以备必要时作为调换之用。如约定可以溢短装一定数量时，则应考虑满足溢装部分的需要。

第四，货物的包装以及包装数量不能够有错。按约定的条件包装，核实包装是否适应长途运输和保护商品的要求。如发现包装不良或有破损，应及时修整或调换。

第五，要核对唛头及标志。在包装的明显部位，应按约定的唛头式样刷制唛头，对包装上的其他各种标志是否符合要求，也应注意。

11.3　任务实施与心得

任务实施

（1）寻找供应商

常州是中国纺织服装名城之一，有大量的服装厂。孙大伟最终选择了常州兴隆服装有限公司作为生产商。因为该厂一直和常信公司合作良好，这次在价格上也给予了一定的优惠。

（2）签订购销合同

常信公司与常州兴隆服装有限公司签订了购销合同如下，要求常州兴隆服装有限公司按时高质量完成女风衣的生产。

购 销 合 同 书

供方（甲方）：常州兴隆服装有限公司　　　　合同编号：CZCX2010096005

需方（乙方）：常州常信外贸有限公司　　　　签订地点：常州

　　　　　　　　　　　　　　　　　　　　签订时间：2010 年 08 月 18 日

经供、需双方平等协商，达成产品买卖合同如下，以兹共同遵守：

第一条：产品名称、规格、数量、单价、总价、生产时间和货款：

产品名称	规格型号	数量	单价(元)	总金额(元)
女风衣	棕色和灰色	小号、中号、大号各 416 件	160 元/件	199 680.00 元

总金额：人民币计壹拾玖万玖仟陆百捌拾元整。

第二条：付款方式：合同签订后乙方支付甲方定作定金：玖万元整。余款在交货后 30 天内付清。

第三条：交货期限及地点：甲方在 2010 年 9 月 20 日前，把货物直接送到上海需方指定的仓库。

第四条：验收方法、标准和期限：乙方在收到货物后即对货物进行检验，若货物质量、重量与合同约定不符的，应在收到货物后七日内以书面形式告知甲方，在约定期限内没有提出质量、重量疑议的，视为质量、重量符合要求。

第五条：包装标准、包装物：另附。

第六条：合同的执行：甲、乙双方不得随时变更或解除合同，任何一方解除合同导致对方损失，应当按所有的损失赔偿责任，包括对方预期利益损失。本合同在履行过程中发生的争议，由双方当事人协商解决；也可由当地工商行政管理部门调解；协商或调解不成的，提交仲裁委员会。

第七条：本合同一式两份，双方各执一份。本合同自签字盖章之日起生效。此合同涂改无效，传真件有效。

供　　　方	需　　　方
甲方(章)：常州兴隆服装有限公司	乙方(章)：常州常信外贸有限公司
住址：武进区西湖路 217 号	住址：
法定代表人：	法定代表人：陈哲
委托代理人：郑书鸣	委托代理人：孙大伟
电话：0519-86338170	电话：0519-86338171
传真：0519-86338177	传真：0519-86338176
开户银行：中行武进支行	开户银行：中行常州分行
账号：	账号：

（3）检查货物的质量、数量、包装

根据合同的交货时间，孙大伟几乎每天和常州兴隆服装有限公司保持联系，跟进生产进度。如果生产进度出现问题，及时采取合理措施，保证产品的正常交货。

对产品的质量加以控制，确保产品质量和寄送的样品质量一致，检查产品包装的唛头是否正确。

按照合同要求混色混码进行商品的包装。

任务实施心得

生产厂家生产货物的数量、质量以及包装等，直接涉及外贸公司对外履行合同的状况。

选择合作良好的供应商至关重要，因为只有得到供应商的通力协作，才能够完成该笔货物的出口，也只有这样，将来才能与国外客户的业务越做越大。

把外销合同转化为与供应商的购销合同，合同条款要吻合，注意在合同的数量、交货时间等上适当留有一些余地。注意要求供应商提供增值税发票，否则不能够得到出口退税。

购销合同签订后的工作中心是与供应商及时沟通，进行跟单管理，尤其是对质量和生产进度的跟踪尤为重要。因为许多时候，供应商会出现不能够按时交货的情况，产品质量也常常不能够达到外商的要求。

生产厂家在合同签订后，需要将合同转化为生产通知单，下发到具体车间。在转化时，需要将外商联系资料以及价格等机密隐去，产品规格、型号、数量、包装、出货时间等具体要求应该明确，不能够模糊，并且要落实分解，逐一与生产部门衔接好。

11.4　知识拓展

1. 生产进度落后时的对策

在出口合同的履行过程中，经常会遇到生产厂家不能够按时交货的问题。生产厂家会由于种种原因造成生产进度落后，外贸公司的跟单员应该及时掌握工厂的生产进度，一旦发现工厂有生产进度落后的情况，应该及时与工厂分析原因，采取切实可行的措施，以保证按时完成出口货物的生产。

如果时间允许的话，增加人员和机器设备。如果增加机器设备来不及，可延长员工的工作时间，增加临时工，将单班制改成双班制或三班制。

妥善处理生产异常事务，确保机器正常运转，改进生产管理方法，以此提高效率。

将一些合适的订单给其他车间生产，或者进行外发加工。调整生产计划，将其他生产向后推，腾出人力和机器来生产该批货物。

如果采用了一切方法，还不能够按时完成对外出货，应该由业务员及时与外商协调，明确告知生产进度延误，协商适当延迟交货期。

2. 供应商的选择

供应商选择的基本准则是"Q. C. D. S"原则，即质量、成本、交付与服务并重的原则。

1)质量：质量因素是最重要的，首先要确认供应商是否建立有一套稳定有效的质量保证体系，然后确认供应商是否具有生产所需特定产品的设备和工艺能力。

2)成本与价格：要对所涉及的产品进行成本分析，并通过双赢的价格谈判实现成本节约。过低的价格只能取得低劣的产品。

3)交付：要确定供应商是否拥有足够的生产能力，人力资源是否充足，有没有扩大产能的潜力。

4)服务：供应商的售前、售后服务的记录也非常重要。

11.5　业务技能训练

11.5.1　课堂训练

1. 购销合同和外销合同的关系是什么？如何处理两个合同中货物的数量、价格、交货时间等问题？

2. 订立购销合同应该注意什么问题？

3. 寻找供应商的途径有哪些？如何处理好和供应商的关系。

4. 讨论在出口货物的生产过程中，会出现哪些问题？应该如何解决？

11.5.2　实训操作

1. 常州天信外贸有限公司在签订完合同后，由出口部业务员与工厂进行联系，并于当日传真购货合同到生产工厂——常州天信服装有些公司。请你拟订具体的购货合同。

2. 江苏天地木业有限公司与现代公司签订完合同后，给车间下了生产通知单。请你拟订具体的生产通知单。

3. 每位学生就自己公司和外商洽谈签订的合同，在国内寻找供应商，磋商订立购货合同。

任务 12
出口货物的报检和报关

🛈 知识要点

  1. 出口报检程序

  2. 出口货物报关程序

  3. 出口税费的计算

✊ 技能要点

- 能够填制出境货物报检单
- 能够办理一般出口货物的报关手续
- 能够正确填制出口货物报关单

12.1　任务描述与分析

1. 任务描述

2010 年 9 月 10 日，常信公司向常州兴隆服装有限公司采购的女风衣已经生产完成 80%。因为风衣属于法定检验商品，现在孙大伟向商检局办理相应的报检手续。因为信用证中需要常信公司提供质量检验证书，孙大伟去商检局时一并办理。

货物办妥商品检验后，常信公司进行了货物的托运，开船日期为 2010 年 9 月 25 日，孙大伟正抓紧时间准备报关单，办理相应的出口报关手续，否则就会延误装运。

2. 任务分析

出口商品的报检和报关是国际贸易业务流程中的重要环节。根据我国进出口商品检验检疫的有关规定，凡被列入国家法定检验检疫范围的商品，最迟应于报关或出境装运前 10 天，向货物所在地检验检疫机构申请报检；由内地运往口岸出口的货物在产地办理预检，合格后方可运往口岸办理出境货物的查验换证手续，只有取得检验检疫局出具的货物通关放行单，海关才放行。

在实际业务中，买卖双方往往根据有关国家的法律和法规和贸易习惯，在合同、信用证中订明卖方应向买方提供所需的检验证书。一般由商品检验检疫机构按合同、信用证中的具体要求出具检验证书。

《中华人民共和国海关法》规定："进出境运输工具、货物、物品，必须通过设立海关的地点进境或出境。"

孙大伟应该准备一系列文件资料和出口报关单一起，在开船 24 小时前向海关报关。只有海关审核无误，确定放行后，货物才能够装运出口。

12.2　相关知识

12.2.1　出境货物报检单的填制

出境货物检验检疫主要包括报检、检验检疫、检验检疫处理、签证放行等主要步骤。

根据备案登记制及报检员证制，报检单位首次报检时须先办理备案登记手续，取得报检单位代码。报检人员取得报检员证，凭证报检。代理报检的，须向检验检疫机构提供报检委托书。

出口单位在报检时需要填制出境货物报检单，报检单的格式由出入境检验检疫局统一制定，申报单位按要求填制。

出境报检单必须按照所申报的货物内容填写，填写内容必须与所附单据相符，填写必须完整、准确、真实，不得涂改。

申请人在填单时应按要求翔实填写，所列项目应填写完整、准确、清晰，不得涂改。出境货物报检单的填制规范具体见表 12-1。

表 12-1　出境货物报检单的填制规范

栏　目	填　制　规　范
1. 报检单位(加盖公章)	在检验检疫机构登记注册的单位全称及代码,可用"报检专用章"
2. 编号	由出入境检验检疫机构人员填写
3. 报检单位登记号	报检单位在检验检疫机构的登记号或注册号(指代理报检单位)
4. 联系人	报检员或代理报检员
5. 电话	报检员或代理报检员电话
6. 报检日期	检验检疫机构实际受理报检的日期
7. 发货人	预报检时可填生产单位名称;出口报检时,可填外贸合同中的卖方或信用证受益人。如需要出具英文证书的,填写中英文
8. 收货人	预报检时,可填出口公司名称;出口报检时可填外贸合同中的买方。如需要出具英文证书的,填写中英文
9. 货物名称	按外贸合同、信用证填写
10. H. S. 编码	按海关商品分类目录填写 8 位或 10 位编码
11. 产地	货物的真实生产地
12. 数量/重量	按实际数量/重量填写。重量一般以净重填写,如填写毛重,或以毛重作净重则需注明
13. 货物总值	按本批货物合同或发票上所列总值填写(以美元计),如同一报检单报多批货物,需列明每批货物的总值(注:如申报货物总值与国内、国际市场价格有较大差异,检验检疫机构保留核价权力)
14. 包装种类及数量	按实际包装类别和数量填写。指本批货物运输包装的件数及种类,应注明材质。如:500 纸箱
15. 运输工具名称号码	预报检时可不填,出口报检时应填船名、车号、航班号码。报检时,未能确定运输工具编号的,可只填写运输工具类别
16. 贸易方式	填写货物实际贸易方式:如一般贸易、三来一补、边境贸易、进料加工、其他贸易
17. 货物存放地点	指本批货物存放的地点
18. 合同号	预报检时,可填国内购销合同号;出口报检时,填外贸合同号
19. 信用证号	预报检时,可不填。出口报检时以信用证结汇的,填信用证号;不是以信用证方式结汇的,须注明结汇方式
20. 用途	按照货物的实际用途填写。指本批货物出境用途,如种用、食用、奶用、观赏或演艺、伴侣、实验、药用、饲用、加工等
21. 发货日期	指出口装运日期,预报检时可不填
22. 输往国家(地区)	按外贸合同填写。指贸易合同中买方(进口方)所在国家或地区,或合同注明的最终输往国家

续表

栏　目	填　制　规　范
23. 许可证审批号	对国家出入境检验检疫局已实施《出口商品质量许可证制度目录》内的出口货物和其他已实行许可制度、审批制度管理的货物,报检时填写安全质量许可证编号或审批单编号
24. 起运地	出口装货口岸。装运本批货物离境的交通工具的起运口岸/地区城市名称
25. 到达口岸	国外到达口岸。指装运本批货物的交通工具最终抵达目的地停靠的口岸名称
26. 生产单位注册号	生产/加工本批货物的单位在检验检疫机构的卫生注册登记编号
27. 集装箱规格、数量和号码	按实际填写。指装载本批货物的集装箱规格(如 40 英尺、20 英尺等)以及分别对应的数量和集装箱号码全称。若集装箱太多,可用附单形式填报
28. 合同/信用证订立的检验检疫条款或特殊要求	按合同/信用证要求填写。指贸易合同或信用证中贸易双方对本批货物特别约定而订立的质量、卫生等条款和报检单位对本批出境货物的检验检疫的其他特别要求
29. 标记及号码	按出境货物的实际标记及号码(唛头)填写,如没有标记,填写 N/M,标记填写不下时可用附页填报
30. 随附单据	按实际提供单据,在对应的栏内打"√"
31. 需要证单名称	按需要检验检疫机构出具的证单,在对应的栏内打"√",并应注明所需证单的正副本的数量
32. 检验检疫费	必须由检验检疫机构有关工作人员填写
33. 报检人郑重声明	必须由报检员或代理报检员手签
34. 领取证单	由领证人填写实际领证日期并签名

12.2.2　检验证书

1. 检验证书的种类

检验检疫机构对进出口商品进行检验检疫或鉴定后,根据不同的检验结果或鉴定项目签发的各种证书,统称为检验证书。

目前,我国检验检疫机构签发的检验证书主要有品质检验证书、重量或数量检验证书、熏蒸检验证书、价值检验证书、兽医检验证书、卫生检验证书、消毒检验证书、温度检验证书、残损检验证书、货载衡量检验证书等。

2. 检验证书的作用

一般来说,国际贸易中,商品检验证书有如下作用:

1)作为证明卖方所交货物的品质、重量、包装以及卫生条件等是否符合合同规定的依据。

2)作为买方对商品提出异议、拒收货物、要求索赔、解决争议的凭证。

3)作为卖方向银行议付货款的单据之一。

4)作为海关通关验放的有效证件。

5)作为证明货物的装卸、运输中的实际情况，明确责任归属的依据。

3. 检验证书的期限

商检机构对检验合格的商品签发检验证书，出具出入境货物通关单并在其上加盖放行章。检验证书的有效期一般货物为 60 天，新鲜果蔬类为 2～3 个星期。货物务必在有效期内进出境，如超过期限，应重新报检。

12.2.3 进出口税费

报关是指进出口货物收发货人、进出境运输工具负责人、进出境物品的所有人或者他们的代理人向海关办理货物、物品或运输工具进出境手续及相关海关事务的过程。

在我国，货物的出口报关应当经过海关审单、查验、征税、放行四个作业环节。出口货物收发货人或其代理人应当按程序办理相对应的出口申报、配合查验、缴纳税费、提取或装运货物等手续，货物才能出境。

1. 进口关税

在国际贸易中，进口关税一直被各国公认为一种重要的经济保护手段。进口关税采用的计征方法有从价税、从量税、复合税、滑准税等，如表 12-2 所示。

表 12-2 进口关税的计征方法

计征方法	具 体 运 用
从价税	以货物、物品的价格作为计税标准，以应征税额占货物的百分比为税率，价格和税额成正比例关系的关税。我国对进口货物征收进口关税主要采用从价税计税标准
从量税	以货物和物品的计量单位，如重量、数量、容量等作为计税标准，以每一计量单位的应征税额征收的关税。我国目前对冻鸡、原油、啤酒、胶卷等类进口商品征收从量税
复合税	一个税目中的商品同时使用从价、从量两种标准计税，按两者之和征收关税。我国目前对录像机、放像机、摄像机、非家用型摄录一体机、部分数字照相机等进口商品征收复合关税
滑准税	当商品价格上涨时采用较低税率，当商品价格下跌时采用较高税率，其目的是使该种商品的国内市场价格保持稳定。如我国对关税配额外进口的一定数量的棉花实行 6%～40% 的滑准税

2. 出口关税

为鼓励出口，世界各国一般不征收出口税或仅对少数商品征收出口税。征收出口关税的主要目的是限制、调控某些商品的过度、无序出口，特别是防止本国一些重要自然资源和原材料的无序出口。

一般出口关税以征收从价税为主，计算公式为：

$$出口关税应征税额＝出口货物完税价格×出口关税税率$$
$$出口货物完税价格＝FOB 价格 ÷（1＋出口关税税率）$$

例 12-1：国内某企业从广州出口一批合金生铁到新加坡，申报出口量 86 吨，每吨价格为 FOB 广州 98 美元。已知外汇折算率 1 美元等于人民币 6.98 元，要求计算出口关税。

解：A)查得合金生铁出口税率为 20%。

B)审定离岸价格为 8 428 美元；折算成人民币为 58 827.44 元。

C)出口关税税额＝FOB 价格÷(1＋出口关税税率)×出口关税税率

$$＝58 827.44÷(1＋20\%)×20\%＝9 804.57(元)$$

3. 海关代征税与其他费用

进口货物和物品在办理海关手续放行后，进入国内流通领域时，由海关代征的进口环节国内税主要有增值税、消费税和船舶吨税 3 种。报关环节还可能产生滞纳金和滞报金等其他费用。

12.2.4　出口报关单

货物出境时，发货人或其代理人应在海关规定的期限内向海关申报。报关时须递交海关规定的包括报关单在内的一系列单据。一般情况下，这些单据应由出口企业填制或提供。

完整、准确、有效地填制出口货物报关单直接关系到报关效率、企业的经济利益、海关征税、减免税及查验、放行等工作。

12.3　任务实施与心得

 任务实施

(1)报检

2010 年 9 月 10 日常信公司的孙大伟填写报检单，并随附合同、信用证、常州兴隆服装有限公司的厂检合格单、包装性能合格单、发票、装箱单等资料，向常州出入境检验检疫局报检。

中华人民共和国出入境检验检疫

出境货物报检单

报检单位(加盖公章)：常州常信外贸有限公司　　　　　　＊编号＿＿＿＿＿＿

报检单位登记号：＊＊＊＊08212　　联系人：孙大伟　　电话：0519-86338171

报检日期：2010 年 9 月 10 日

发货人	(中文)	常州常信外贸有限公司				
	(外文)	CHANGZHOU CHANGXIN IMPORT & EXPORT CORP.				
收货人	(中文)	金山贸易有限公司(法国)				
	(外文)	GOLDEN MOUNTAIN TRADING CO.，LTD				
货物名称 (中/外文)	H.S. 编码		原产国 (地区)	数量/重量	货物总值	包装种类及数量
女式风衣 LADIES COAT	6202.1290		中国	1 248 件	35 817.60 美元	156 个纸箱
运输工具 名称号码	TRIUMPH V991A		贸易方式	一般贸易	货物存放地点	江苏常州

续表

合同号	CZCX080180	信用证号	LCH066/08	用途	
发货日期	2010.09.25	输往国家（地区）	法国	许可证/审批号	
起运地	SHANGHAI PORT CHINA	到达口岸	MARSEILLES PORT	生产单位注册号	JS-CZS1122
集装箱规格、数量及号码	＊＊＊＊＊＊				

合同、信用证订立的检验检疫条款或特殊要求	标记及号码	随附单据（划"√"或补填）	
	FTC CZCX080180 MARSEILLES NO. 1-156	☑合同　☑信用证　☑发票　☑装箱单	☐换证凭单　☑厂检单　☑包装性能结果单　☐许可/审批文件

需要证单名称（划"√"或补填）

				＊检验检疫费
☑品质证书　2 正__副	☐动物卫生证书　__正__副			总金额（人民币元）
☐重量证书　__正__副	☐植物检疫证书　__正__副			
☐数量证书　__正__副	☐熏蒸/消毒证书　__正__副			收费人
☐兽医卫生证书　__正__副	☐出境货物换证凭单			
☐健康证书　__正__副	☑出境货物通关单			计费人
☐卫生证书				

报检人郑重声明：1. 本人被授权报检。2. 上列填写内容正确属实，货物无伪造或冒用他人的厂名、标志、认证标志，并承担货物质量责任。签名：　孙大伟

领取证单	
日期	
签名	

注：有"＊"号栏由出入境检验检疫机关填写

（2）领取通关单和检验证书

常州出入境检验检疫局对报检的 1 248 件女式风衣进行检验，确认是合格的商品。孙大伟向常州出入境检验检疫局领取出境货物通关单和品质检验证书，并对品质检验证书认真审核。

中华人民共和国出入境检验检疫
出境货物通关单

编号：442301104065547

1. 发货人 常州常信外贸有限公司＊＊＊＊＊＊	5. 标记及号码 FTC CZCX080180 MARSEILLES NO. 1-156
2. 收货人 GOLDEN MOUNTAIN TRADING CO.，LTD＊＊＊＊＊＊	
3. 合同/信用证号 CZCX080180 / LCH066/08 ＊＊＊＊＊＊	4. 输往国家或地区 法国

续表

6. 运输工具名称及号码 船舶 TRIUMPH V991A	7. 发货日期 2010.09.25	8. 集装箱规格及数量 ＊＊＊＊＊＊
9. 货物名称及规格 女式风衣 100% COTTON LADIES COAT woven, with bronze-colored buttons, 2 pockets at side	10. H. S. 编码 6202.1290 ＊＊＊＊＊＊ （以下空白）

10. H. S. 编码 6202.1290 ＊＊＊＊＊＊ （以下空白）	11. 申报总值 ＊35 817.60 美元 ＊＊＊＊＊＊ （以下空白）	12. 数/重量、包装数量及种类 ＊1 248 件 ＊3 900 千克 ＊156 纸箱 ＊＊＊＊＊＊ （以下空白）
13. 证明		

13. 证明

上述货物业经检验检疫，请海关予以放行
　　　本通关单有效期至　　　2010 年 10 月 30 日
　　　签字：×××　　　　日期：2010 年 9 月 10 日

14. 备注

中华人民共和国出入境检验检疫
ENTRY-EXIT INSPECTION AND QUARANTINE
OF THE PEOPLE'S REPUBLIC OF CHINA

编号 No.

品质检验证书
QUALITY CERTIFICATE

发货人：
Consignor： 常州常信外贸有限公司 CHANGZHOU CHANGXIN IMPORT & EXPORT CORP.

收货人：
Consignee： GOLDEN MOUNTAIN TRADING CO.，LTD

品名：
Description of Goods： 女式风衣　LADIES COAT

报验数量/重量：
Quantity/Weight Declared： 1 248 件(PC)

包装种类及数量：
Number and Type of Packages： 156 个纸箱(CARTONS)

运输工具：
Means of Conveyance： TRIUMPH V991A

检验结果：
Results of Inspection： 经检验，上述货物符合 CZCX080180 号合同之规定

印章
Official stamp

标记及号码
Mark & No.： FTC S/C
CZCX080180
MARSEILLES
NO. 1-156

签证地点　　　　　　　签证时间
place of issue 江苏 JIANGSU　date of issue SEPT. 14, 2010

续表

授权签字人	签名	
authorized officer	signature	王伟

我们已尽所知和最大能力实施上述检验，不能因我们签发本证书而免除卖方或其他方面根据合同和法律所承担的产品质量责任和其他责任。All inspections are carried out conscientiously to the best of our knowledge and ability. This certificate does not in any respect absolve the seller and other related parties from his contractual and legal obligations especially when product quality is concerned.

（3）出口申报

出口货物的申报期限为货物运抵海关监管区后、装货的 24 小时以前。

常信公司于 2010 年 9 月 24 日向上海浦东海关进行申报。申报单证有报关单以及发票、装箱单、出入境检验检疫局签发的出境货物通关单等。

中华人民共和国海关出口货物报关单

预录入编号：　　　　　　　　　　　　　　　　　　　海关编号：

出口口岸 浦东海关 2250	备案号	出口日期 2010.09.25	申报日期 2010.09.24
经营单位 常州常信外贸有限公司 3204915070	运输方式 江海运输	运输工具名称 TRIUMPH/991A	提运单号 COS3426
发货单位 常州兴隆服装有限公司	贸易方式 一般贸易	征免性质 一般征税	结汇方式 L/C
许可证号	运抵国（地区） 法国	指运港 马赛港	境内资源地 江苏常州其他
批准文号 32A573324	成交方式 CIF	运费 502/1200/3	保费 502/433.40/3	杂费
合同协议号 CZCX080180	件数 156	包装种类 纸箱	毛重（千克） 4 680	净重（千克） 3 900
集装箱号 0	随附单据		生产厂家 常州兴隆服装有限公司	

标记唛码及备注
FTC
CZCX080180
MARSEILLES
NO. 1-156

项号	商品编号	商品名称、规格型号	数量及单位	最终目的国（地区）	单价	总价	币制	征免
01	6202.1290	女式风衣 LADIES COAT	1 248 件	法国	28.70	35 817.60	美元	照章

续表

100% COTTON woven，with bronze-colored buttons，		

税费征收情况

录入员　　　　录入单位	兹声明以上申报无讹并承担法律责任	海关审单批注及放行日期(签章)	
报关员	申报单位(签章)	审单	审价
单位地址		征税	统计
邮编　　　　电话	填制日期	查验	放行

（4）配合海关查验货物

海关查验货物时，常信公司应当到场，配合海关查验，并做好以下工作：负责按照海关要求搬移货物，开拆包装，以及重新封装货物；如实回答查验人员的询问以及提供必要的资料；协助海关提取需要做进一步检验、化验或鉴定的货样，收取海关出具的取样清单；查验结束后，认真阅读查验人员填写的"海关进出境货物查验记录单"，审核主要记录是否符合实际。

（5）缴纳税费，海关放行，装运货物

海关对报关单进行审核，核对税费，开具税款缴款书和收费票据。海关在货运单据上签印放行。出口货物装货起运出境。常信公司在规定期限内缴纳税款。

🛡️任务实施心得

（1）申请报检时，应填制出境报检申请单，向检验检疫机构申请报检。一般每份报检单限填一批货物。

报检日期按检验检疫机构受理报检的日期填写。报检日期和检验证书的签发日期不得晚于出运日期。

填制完毕的报检单必须加盖报检单位公章或已经向检验检疫机构备案的报检专用章，报检人应在签名栏手签，必须是本人手签，不得代签。

（2）报关员在填制报关单时，必须做到真实、准确、齐全、清楚，对申报内容的真实性、准确性、完整性、规范性承担相应的法律责任。

报关单必须真实，做到两个相符：一是单证相符，即报关单与合同、发票、装箱单、提单、批文等相符；二是单货相符，即报关单中所列各项内容与实际出口货物情况相符，不允许有伪报、瞒报或虚报等情况存在。

网站链接：HS 法定检验检疫查询 http：//www.shciq.gov.cn/jsp/ciq＿hsfd-jyjyQy.jsp

12.4　知识拓展

1. 电子报关

我国《海关法》规定："办理进出口货物的海关申报手续，应当采用纸质报关单和电子数据报关单的形式"。这一规定确定了电子报关的法律地位，使纸质报关单和电子数据报关单具有同等的法律效力。纸质报关单形式和电子数据报关单形式是法定申报的两种基本方式。

2. 电子口岸

电子报关是指进出口货物收发货人或其代理人通过计算机系统，按照《中华人民共和国海关进出口货物报关单填制规范》的有关要求，向海关传送报关单电子数据，并备齐随附单证的申报方式。

中国电子口岸系统是指与进出境贸易管理关联的国务院 12 个有关部委利用现代信息技术和电子计算机技术，与本部委管理的进出口业务信息为基础建立的一个公共数据库，以期达到为相关政府部门提供跨部门、跨行业管理核查，为进出口企业提供网上办理各种进出口业务的国家信息系统。

12.5　业务技能训练

12.5.1　课堂训练

1. 商品检验证书有哪些作用？试举例说明。

2. 商品检验报检时，需要提供哪些材料？

3. 简述填制商品检验报检单需要注意哪些问题。

4. 简述出口商品报关的流程。出口商品报关时需要提供哪些单据？

5. 某出口货物成交价格为 FOB 上海 10 000 美元，另外从上海至出口目的国韩国的运费为总价 500 美元，从上海至韩国的保险费率为 3‰。假定其适用的基准汇率为 1 美元＝6.40 元人民币，出口关税税率为 10%。计算出口关税税额。

6. 案例分析题

(1)我国对外出口一批货物，货物在装运前经商品检验检疫局检验合格，并出具品质和数量检验证书，货到目的港后发现货物有短缺，进口商要求我方赔偿，我方应如何处理？

(2)某企业报检一批出口玩具，于 10 月 8 日领取了出境货物通关单，于 12 月 20 日持该出境货物通关单办理报关手续，企业是否需要重新报检？

12.5.2　实训操作

1. 根据常州天信外贸有限公司与加拿大客户 JAMES BROWN&SONS 出口的男衬衫的资料缮制"出境货物报检单"。

报检单位登记号：08214，产品用途为自用，贸易方式为 A，货物暂存于常州。

2. 根据江苏天地木业有限公司与现代公司签订的地板出口合同及单据，填写报检单。

报检单位登记号：08218，产品用途为自用，贸易方式为 A，货物暂存于常州。

3. 常州天信外贸有限公司的男衬衫计划于 10 月 10 日装船。请你填制"出口货物报关单"，向海关报关。

4. 根据江苏天地木业有限公司与现代公司签订的地板出口合同及发票、装箱单等随附单据，填写出口货物报关单。

5. 根据前面自己公司和外商所签订的合同办理相应的报检、报关手续（说明过程，填写相应的单据）。

任务 13

出口货物的运输

知识要点

1. 集装箱班轮运费的组成
2. 提单的种类

技能要点

- 掌握海运班轮运输的流程和集装箱运输的流程
- 能够办理出口货物的运输操作
- 能够制作托运单，审核提单内容的正确性

13.1 任务描述与分析

1. 任务描述

2010 年 9 月 10 日常州兴隆服装有限公司通知常信公司，女式风衣能够按时完成生产。孙大伟在确定采用集装箱班轮运输后，正着手安排货物的运输。

孙大伟首先计算出运货物的毛重和体积，向货代办理海运的托运手续，订舱并说明集装箱装货的地点，支付海运费，拿到提单后，认真审核确保提单正确，以符合信用证的规定。

2. 任务分析

出口货物的运输，是整个出口业务中的重要环节，由谁负责办理运输手续并支付运费，是由买卖双方商定的贸易术语决定的。在 CIF 贸易术语下，出口方要按时安排运输工具，把货物装上装运港船只，及时向进口方发出装运通知，支付运费，并准备移交海运提单。

海运提单是承运人收到承运货物后签发给出口商的证明文件。它是交接货物、处理索赔与理赔以及向银行结算货款或进行议付的重要单据。在象征性交货术语下，提单的作用更为重要，必须做到单据正确，并控制好所有权。

13.2 相关知识

13.2.1 出口货物海运流程

以 CIF、CFR 条件成交的出口货物，由出口方安排运输出口货物，其主要环节和程序如下。

1. 订舱

出口商在备好出口货物、信用证齐备后根据贸易合同和信用证的有关条款，在货物托运前一定的时间，填制订舱单，随附商业发票、装箱单等其他必要单据，向船公司或其代理人申请订舱。

2. 签发装货单

船公司根据具体情况，如果接受出口商的订舱，就确认托运人的订舱，同时把配舱回单、装货单(S/O)等与托运人有关的单据退还给托运人，并告知出口商实际承运的船名和航次。

3. 安排运输

船公司在接受托运申请后，签发装货单，分送集装箱堆场或集装箱货运站，据以安排空箱及办理货运交接。

4. 货物集港

港口在载货船只靠港前，向出口商发送货物集港通知，通知出口商在规定的时间内将货物运至指定码头或集装箱货运站待装。如果是集装箱整箱货，出口商也可以在工厂或仓库自行装箱并加海关封志后按时运到集装箱码头堆场。

5. 货物装船，获取提单

出口商向海关办理报关手续。海关放行后，货物装船。装货后，承运人签发提单给托运人，托运人准备去结汇。

13.2.2 班轮运费的计算

班轮运费包括基本运费和附加费两部分，即班轮运费＝基本运费＋附加费。

1. 基本运费

基本运费是指从装运港到目的港之间收取的运费，也是全程运费的主要部分。

基本运费按班轮运价表（Liner's Freight Tariff）规定的计收标准计收。在班轮运价表中，根据不同的商品，班轮运费的计算标准通常采用下列几种形式。实务中以按重量（W）、体积（M）、重量体积从高计收（W/M）三种方式居多，具体如表 13-1 所示。

表 13-1 班轮基本运费的计算标准

计算标准	计算单位	运价表内的表示方式	说明
重量法	按货物的毛重计收，即重量吨（Weight Ton）	W	1 重量吨一般为 1 公吨 运费＝实际重量吨×单位运费
体积法	按货物的体积计收，即尺码吨（Measurement Ton)	M	1 尺码吨一般为 1 立方米 运费＝实际体积吨×单位运费
从价法	一般以商品的 FOB 价按一定的百分率计收运费	AV 或 Ad Val	适用于体积、重量不大的贵金属、精密仪器、工艺品等货物 运费＝实际 FOB 价×单位费率
选择法	按货物的毛重或体积从高计收	W/M	重量吨和尺码吨统称运费吨（Freight Ton） 运费＝Max（实际运费吨）×单位运费
选择法	按货物重量、体积或价值三者中较高者计收	W/M or AV	
	选择货物的重量、体积从高计收，然后再收取一定比例的从价运费	W/M Plus AV	
按件法	按货物的个数（辆、头……）计收运费	Per ...	适用于车辆、活牲畜等
议定法	船、货双方临时议定运价	Open Rate	适用于大宗低值货物，如粮食、豆类、煤炭等。议价运费通常比较低廉

2. 附加费

附加费一般是在基本运费的基础上加收一定百分比（附加运费率）的费用或根据运费吨收取固定数值的费用。常见附加费大致有以下几种：超重附加费、超长附加费、超大附加费、直航附加费、绕航附加费、转船附加费、港口附加费、港口拥挤附加费、选择港附加费、变更卸货港附加费、燃油附加费、货币贬值附加费等。

3. 班轮运费的计算

班轮运费是按照班轮运价表的规定计算的。不同的班轮公司或班轮公会有不同的班轮运价表。班轮运价表的结构一般为：说明及有关规定、港口规定及条款、货物的分类和分级表、航线费率表、附加费率表、冷藏货及活牲畜费率表等。班轮运费的计算分四步：

第一步，查货物等级表。根据商品的英文名称查出该商品所属等级及其计费标准。

货物分级表是班轮运价表的组成部分，它有"货名"、"等级"和"计算标准"三个项目，如表 13-2 所示。

表 13-2　货物等级表

货名	COMMODITIES	CLASS	BASIS
……	……	……	……
棉布及棉纱	COTTON GOODS & PIECE GOODS	10	M
文具及办公用品	SATATIONERY & OFFICE APPLIANCE	10	W/M
茶叶	TEA	8	M
童车	TRICYCLES, CHILDREN VEHICLES	9	M
瓷砖	TILES，PORCELAIN	7	W
……	……	……	……

第二步，查航线等级费率表。根据商品的等级和计费标准，查该商品某具体航线的基本费率。表 13-3 是中国—澳大利亚航线等级费率表。

表 13-3　中国—澳大利亚航线等级费率表(人民币元)

等级(Class)	费率(Rates)
1	240.00
2	250.00
3	260.00
4	280.00
5	290.00
6	310.00
7	340.00
8	360.00
9	404.00
10	443.00
Ad Val	290.00

注：基本港口为 BRISBANE，MELBOURNE，SYDNEY，FREMANTLE。

第三步，查附加费率。根据该商品本身所经航线和港口，查出有关附加费率。

最后，计算出总的运费。

13.2.3　海运提单

1. 提单的性质和作用

海运提单是承运人或其代理人在收到货物后签发给托运人，证明货物已经收到或已装船，并保证将货物运到指定的目的港的证明性文件。它体现了承运人与托运人之间的相互关系。

提单的性质和作用，主要表现在以下几个方面：

（1）物权凭证

提单代表着货物。货物抵达目的港后，提单的合法持有者凭提单要求承运人交货，而承运人也有义务向提单的持有者交货。提单可以通过背书转让给第三者。此时，货物的所有权也随之转移给了第三者，第三者可凭提单向承运人提货；提单的持有者还可以凭提单向银行办理抵押贷款或押汇。

（2）运输契约证明

海运提单是承运人和托运人之间订立的运输契约的证明。提单上载明了承运人、托运人或提单的持有者等各方之间的权利和义务关系。一旦发生海洋运输方面的争议，它是处理的依据。

（3）货物收据

海运提单是承运人装运货物的收据。提单是承运人应托运人的要求所签发的货物收据，表明货物已经由承运人接收或装船。

承运人填写海运提单要做到准确无误，托运人收到承运人的提单要认真核对。提单的更正要尽可能在载货船舶开航之前进行，以减少因此而产生的费用。开船后要求更改提单的，对于不太重要的项目，可直接修改并加盖签单单位的更正章；对于重要的项目如品名、收货人、目的港等，须经过船公司批准后才可以重新签单，由此产生的责任及费用由要求更改方承担。一般货到目的港后，提单不能更改。

2. 提单的分类

海运提单可以从不同角度进行分类，图 13-1 是提单的分类。下面对部分提单作简单介绍。

提单
- 根据货物是否已装船
  - 已装船提单（On Board B/L；Shipped B/L）
  - 收妥待运提单（Received for Shipment B/L）
- 根据提单上对货物外表是否有不良批注
  - 清洁提单（Clean B/L）
  - 不清洁提单（Unclean B/L）
- 根据提单收货人不同
  - 记名提单（Straight B/L）
  - 不记名提单（Bearer B/L）
  - 指示提单（Order B/L）

图 13-1　提单的分类

（1）清洁提单与不清洁提单

不清洁提单指承运人对货物的表面状况等另加不良批注的提单。例如："一箱破损"、"三件玷污"等。

UCP600 第 27 条规定：银行只接受清洁运输单据。清洁运输单据指未载有明确宣称货物或包装有缺陷的条款或批注的运输单据。带有不良批注的不清洁提单，银行将不予接受。为了安全收汇，在货物装船时，如发现问题，应及时采取措施进行修复或更换，力求取得清洁提单。清洁已装船提单是提单转让的先决条件。

(2)记名提单、不记名提单与指示提单

记名提单是托运人在收货人一栏内指定具体收货人名称的提单。记名提单的收货人已经确定，只能由该特定的收货人提货。托运人不能通过背书的方式将记名提单转让给第三者。因此，只在某些特定的情况下使用。如来证要求"Full set of B/L consigned to A. B. C. Co."，提单收货人栏应填"A. B. C. Co."。

不记名提单是指在提单的收货人一栏内只写明"货交提单持有人"，而不填写具体收货人的名称，承运人应把货交给提单的持有人。不记名提单不需要背书即可转让，只要把提单交给受让人即可。因此，这种提单对买卖双方均有较大的风险，在国际贸易中，使用很少。

指示提单是指在提单的收货人一栏内填写"凭指示"或"凭×××指示"的提单。表示承运人凭指示交货，这种提单可以通过指示人的背书而进行转让。

在信用证方式下，一般常使用指示式提单。记名提单、不记名提单、指示提单的区别如表 13-4 所示。

表 13-4　记名提单、不记名提单、指示提单的区别

	收货人(示例)	可否转让	转让方式	
记名提单	TO ABC CO.，LTD	否	否	
不记名提单	TO BEARER	可	任意转让，无须背书	
指示提单	TO ORDER	可	背书转让	托运人背书
	TO ORDER OF ××			××背书
	TO ××OR ORDER			××背书

提单还可以根据其他标准进行不同的分类，如船公司提单、船公司代理提单、无船承运人提单；预借提单、倒签提单和过期提单等。使用预借提单和倒签提单属于违法的欺骗行为，要负法律责任。

3. 提单的内容

不同的国家、不同的船公司使用的海运提单的格式不尽相同，但其内容基本一致。一般而言，海运提单的正面通常包括的内容有：托运人、收货人、被通知人、收货地点或装货港、目的港或卸货港、船名航次、唛头及件号、货物名称、毛重和体积、运费预付或到付等。表 13-5 以中国远洋运输集团公司出具的海运提单为例，对海运提单加以说明。

表 13-5　海运提单的正面内容

项目	内容	要点提示
1. 提单的号码 B/L No.	由提单签发人填写	

续表

项目	内容	要点提示
2. 托运人 Shipper/ Consignor	发货人的全称和地址	信用证方式下的受益人，托收方式下的卖方
3. 收货人 Consignee	提单的抬头	按照 L/C 的规定在记名收货人、凭指示和记名指示中选一个。托收方式下填写"to order"或"to order of shipper"
4. 被通知人 Notify Party，Addressed to	承运人在货物到港后通知的对象，一般是进口商或其代理人，其全称和详细地址	如信用证未规定，将 L/C 中的申请人名称、地址填入副本 B/L 中，正本先保持空白 如果来证要求两个或两个以上的公司为被通知人，出口公司应把这两个或两个以上的公司名称和地址填入
5. 前程运输 Pre-carriage by	第一程船的船名	如果货物不需转运，保持空白
6. 收货地点 Place of Receipt	收货的港口名称或地点	如果货物不需转运，保持空白
7. 船名、航次 Ocean Vessel Voy. No.	实际货运船名、航次	如货物需要转运，填写第二程船的船名
8. 装运港 Port of Loading	货物实际装船的港口名称	如果货物需要转运，填写中转港口名称
9. 卸货港 Port of Discharge	一般是目的港	
10. 交货地点 Place of Delivery	最终目的地	如果货物目的地是卸货港，保持空白
11. 唛头、集装箱号和封号 Marks & Nos. Container/Seal No.		符合信用证或合同的规定，与发票等单据保持一致。若无，填"N/M"
12. 集装箱数或包装件数 No. of containers or packags		与 16 栏大写一致
13. 包装种类和件数，货物名称 Kind of packags，Description of Goods	商品名称；最大包装件数	商品名称按信用证要求填写，允许使用货物的统称。要按实际包装具体情况填写，如塑料桶（Plastic Drums）、铁桶（Iron Drums）、纸箱（Carton）等，而不可仅笼统地填为件（Packages）。若是散装货物，该栏只需填"In Bulk"

续表

项目	内容	要点提示
14. 毛重 Gross Weight	货物的毛重总数	毛重以千克表示 如果是裸装货,应该在净重前加注 N. W.
15. 尺码 Measurement	货物的体积总数	货物体积以立方米表示,小数点后保留三位
16. 合计 Total Number of Containers or Packages(In Words)	大写表示集装箱或其他形式最大外包装的件数	与前面小写一致
17. 运费支付情况 Freight & Charges		除非信用证另有规定,此栏一般不填运费的具体数额,只填写运费支付情况,具体有以下几种:在 CFR 或 CIF 价格条件下出口,填运费预付(Freight Prepaid)或(Freight Paid);在 FOB 价格条件下出口,填运费到付(Freight Collect)或(Freight Payable at Destination)
18. 运费支付地点 Freight Payable at		
19. 提单签发地点及日期 Place and Date of Issue	承运人实际装运货物的港口与时间	签发地点应为装运港 签发日期,一般为实际装运货物的时间或接受船方监管的时间,它不能晚于信用证规定的最迟装运期
20. 正本提单份数 No. of Original B/Ls		用英文大写数字表示,如:ONE,THREE。每份正本提单的效力相同,当其中一份提货后,其他各份均失效
21. 承运人签字 Signed for the Carrier	船长或承运人或其代理的签字盖章	凡承运人/船长的签署必须可识别其身份,如 COSCO 提单由 COSCO 自行签发时,在签署的橡章上须表示其为 CARRIER。凡由承运人/船长的代理签署时,须有代理的具名,并须表明被代理人的名称和身份。例如 E 公司代理 COSCO 签发提单时,除 E 公司具名和签字的橡章外,还得标明:AS AGENT FOR THE CARRIER—COSCO
22. 装船批注	装船批注、日期和签署	提单上预先印就,如果没有,则需要加注 如要求提供已装船提单,必须由船长签字并注明开船时间 Date:... 和"LADEN ON BOARD"字样

知识链接

关于海运提单的国际公约

提单背面的运输条款是确定承运人和托运人以及提单持有人之间的权利和义务的主要依据。有关提单的国际公约主要有《海牙规则》、《海牙—维斯比规则》、《汉堡规则》等。目前以《海牙规则》为依据的居多，该公约对承运人有利。

13.2.4　其他运输单据

1. 海运单

海运单又称不可转让海运单，其具有运输单据的一般功能。它是承运人收到承运货物的收据，是承运人与托运人之间运输契约的证明，但它不是凭以提货的物权凭证。因此，它是一种不可转让的运输单据。这是不可转让海运单与海运提单的根本区别。

2. 铁路运单

铁路运单是铁路承运人收到货物后所签发的铁路运输单据。国际铁路联运运单使用正副本方式。运单正本随同货物从始发站到终点站交给收货人，作为铁路向收货人交付货物的凭证。运单副本在发货站加盖承运期戳记，作为货物已被承运的证明，发货人凭之向银行要求结汇。国际铁路运单不是物权凭证，不能转让。

3. 航空运单

航空运单是航空公司收到货物后出具的货物收据和运输凭证。航空运单与海运提单性质不同，它只能表示承运人已收到货物，起到货物收据的作用，但不具有物权凭证的性质。货到目的地后，收货人不是凭航空货运单提货而是凭航空公司发出的"到货通知单"提取货物。因此，航空运单不能背书转让，在航空运单的收货人栏内必须填写收货人的全称和详细地址，不能做成指示式抬头。

航空运单根据签发人的不同可分为主运单和分运单。主运单由航空公司签发，分运单由航空货运代理公司签发。

4. 多式联运单据

多式联运单据是指多式联运经营人在收到货物后签发给托运人的单据。按照国际商会《联合运输单证统一规则》的规定，多式联运经营人负责货物的全程运输。多式联运单据是货物所有权凭证，可以凭单据提取货物，也可以进行转让、流通或抵押。

5. 邮政收据

邮政收据是邮政部门收到其负责邮递的信函、样品或包裹等邮件后向寄件人出示的注有寄发日期的货物收据，也是邮件发生灭失或损坏事故后寄件人或收件人向邮政部门索赔的凭证。但是邮政收据不代表货物所有权，既不能转让，也不能凭收据提货。

13.3　任务实施与心得

 任务实施

(1)填写出口托运单，订舱

在出口货物、信用证齐备后，孙大伟根据出口合同和信用证的有关条款，在 9 月 15 日填制出口托运单，随附商业发票、装箱单等单据，委托货运代理人订舱，订一个 20 英尺的集装箱，DOOR TO DOOR。

托运单的内容如下：

出口货物托运单

公司编号：　　　　　　　　　　　　　　　　　　日期：SEPT. 15，2010

1)托运人 CHANGZHOU CHANGXIN IMPORT & EXPORT CORP. NO. 25 MINGXIN RD, CHANGZHOU JIANGSU, CHINA TEL：0519-86338171	4)信用证号码 LCH066/08	
	5)开证银行 BANQUE NATIONAL DE PARIS PARIS FRANCE	
	6)合同号码 CZCX080180	7)成交金额 USD35 817.60
	8)装运口岸 SHANGHAI, CHINA	9)目的港 MARSEILLES, FRANCE
2)收货人 TO ORDER	10)可否转船 ALLOWED	11)可否分批装运 NOT ALLOWED
3)通知人 GOLDEN MOUNTAIN TRADING CO., LTD ROOM 1618 BUILDING G NO.36 THE FIRST LYON STREET, PARIS, FRANCE TEL：019-33-44-55	12)信用证有效期 OCT. 31，2010	13)装船期限 LATEST SEPT. 30，2010
	14)运费 USD 1 200.00	15)成交条件 CIF MARSEILLES
	16)公司联系人 孙大伟	17)电话/传真 0519-86338171/86338176
	18)公司开户行	19)银行账号
20)特别要求		

21) 标记唛码	22) 货号规格	23) 包装件数	24) 毛重	25) 净重	26) 数量	27) 单价	28) 总价
FTC CZCX080180 MARSEILLES NO.1-156	LADIES COAT	156CTNS	4 680KG	3 900KG	1 248PCS	USD 28.70	USD 35 817.60

	29) 总件数	30) 总毛重	31) 总净重	32) 总尺码	33) 总金额
	1 248PCS	4 680KG	3 900KG	24.96M³	USD 35 817.60

(2)报关、装货上船

货运代理订舱后，把配舱回单、装货单等托运单据退还给孙大伟，并告知实际承运的船名和航次为 TRIUMPH V991A，开船日期为 2010 年 9 月 25 日。船公司的集装箱计划于 9 月 23 日到工厂装货。

孙大伟立即和工厂联系，安排工厂于 23 日装箱并按时运到集装箱堆场。9 月 24 日上午向海关顺利完成报关手续后，货物装上了船。

(3)向客户发出装运通知

按照国际惯例，货物装上船后，孙大伟于 2010 年 9 月 24 日向客户发出"装运通知"。

　　装运通知主要内容包括合同号、信用证号、货物名称、数量、总值、唛头、装运口岸、装运日期、船名及预计开航日期等。

　　(4)支付运费,审核船公司的提单

　　货物上船,并于 2010 年 9 月 25 日离开了上海港,常信公司向船公司支付了海运费 1 200 美元和内陆运费 2 100 元人民币,船公司把海运提单传真给孙大伟,让孙大伟认真审核,如果有差错,及时提出,以便船公司更正。

　　下面是孙大伟审核无误的提单。

海运提单 BILL OF LADING

1)Shipper CHANGZHOU CHANGXIN IMPORT & EXPORT CORP. NO. 25 MINGXIN RD, CHANGZHOU JIANGSU, CHINA TEL: 0519-86338171	B/L NO. COS3426 C O S C O 中国远洋运输(集团)总公司
2)Consignee TO ORDER	CHINA OCEAN SHIPPING (GROUP) CO. *ORIGINAL* Combined Transport BILL OF LADING
3)Notify Party GOLDEN MOUNTAIN TRADING CO. , LTD ROOM 1618 BUILDING G NO. 36 THE FIRST LYON STREET, PARIS, FRANCE TEL: 019-33-44-55	

4) Pre-Carriage by	5) Place of Receipt	
6)Ocean Vessel Voy. No. TRIUMPH V991A	7)Port of Loading SHANGHAI, CHINA	
8)Port of Discharge MARSEILLES, FRANCE	9)Place of Delivery	

10)Marks & Nos.　11)NO. of Containers or PKG. Description of Goods　12)G. W. (kg) 13)Meas. (m³)
Container/ Seal No.

FTC CZCX080180 MARSEILLES NO. 1-156	156 CTNS OF LADIES COAT	4 680KG	24. 960M³

FREIGHT PREPAID FREIGHT CHARGES: USD1 200. 00

14)Total Number of Containers
and/or Packages(in words)　SAY ONE HUNDRED AND FIFTY-SIX CARTONS ONLY

FREIGHT & CHARGES USD 1 200. 00	REVENUE TONS	RATE	PER	PREPAID	COLLECT
PREPAID AT	PAYABLE AT			16)PLACE AND DATE OF ISSUE SHANGHAI, SEPT. 25, 2010	
TOTAL PREPAID	15)NUMBER OF ORIGINAL B(S)L THREE			17) × × ×	

LOADING ON BOARD THE VESSEL
DATE SEPT. 25, 2010 BY × × ×

> **注意**
> 根据信用证规定，该提单送银行结汇必须空白背书，即在提单背面加盖托运人印章。

任务实施心得

(1)正确填写和保存出口托运单

托运单填写正确与否，不仅关系到货物能否及时报关出运，还关系到提单的正确性以及结汇的安全性。

在填写托运单时应注意以下事项：

1)填写要严格依照信用证或买卖合同的有关规定。

2)有些栏目不需要出口公司填写，如：提单号、船号、运费等栏目。

3)"可否分批"、"可否转船"栏中只允许填写"允许"或"不允许"，如果合同或信用证对其有其他说明，应在特殊条款栏中作出补充。例如：信用证中规定货物分三批装运，则在托运单"可否分批"栏中填"允许"，特殊条款栏中填"货物分三批装运"。

4)托运单号码一般要与发票号码一致。一是为了使发票填写的内容与实际装货的情况完全一致；二是为了便于查询、核对。

(2)正确处理好提单的交寄

近些年来，来证中有如下语句出现："Beneficiary's certificate certifying that they have sent by speed post one of the three（1/3 original）B/L direct to the applicant immediately after shipment and accompanied by relative post receipt"，是指开证申请人要求卖方在货物装船后给其寄一份正本提单。这种做法于买方提货和转口贸易以及较急需或易腐烂的商品贸易有利，但对卖方却有货物已交出却收不到货款的风险。因而，此处应慎重处理。

13.4　知识拓展

电放

电放是船方不凭正本提单而凭电子单据(包括提单的电传件、传真件、复印件和E-mail 等)放货。一般情况下，发货人是通过银行或直接将提单寄给收货人，收货人拿到正本提单后方可提货。但在近洋运输(如从上海到日本或韩国)时，船期很短，常常货已到港而提单未到。为不影响收货，收货人会要求发货人办理电放手续，货物到港后收货人凭电放提单即可提货。

船公司常要求发货人交 100～200 元的电放费并出具保函(船公司或货代均有其固定的格式)，保证电放造成的一切问题与其无关。

电放后发货人将不再掌握货权，因此办理电放前一定要确认能够安全收款，否则极易造成钱货两空的局面。

下面是无锡一家公司的电放保函式样：

电 放 保 函

我司出运一批货

提单号：LGTVS024268

船名航次：MAY FLOWER V.0810

品名为：FLEXIBLE PIPE，125 CARTONS

从：SHANGHAI

至：DURBAN SOUTH AFRICA

由××要求，特出此保函，请贵司允许将提单电放，

由此产生的责任及费用由我司承担。

电放给 CONSIGNEE：

无锡市×××××有限公司

2010 年 10 月 15 日

13.5　业务技能训练

13.5.1　课堂训练

1. 海运提单具有哪些性质和作用？

2. 记名提单、不记名提单、指示提单有何区别？

3. 我国海运货物出口的流程如何？

4. 学生讨论如何填写提单的收货人，如何进行背书，其依据是什么？

5. 计算题

（1）大连某纺织品进出口公司出口到日本一批纺织品，共 9.6 立方米，运费计算标准为 M，按《中远表》5 号版本 10 级货类计算。从大连至日本横滨 10 级货基本运费为 36 元人民币，燃油附加费每运费吨 18 元人民币，港口拥挤费 25％。试计算其运费为多少？

（2）某公司向西欧推销箱装货，原报价每箱 50 美元 FOB 上海，现客户要求改报 CFRC3 Hamburg。问在不减少收汇的条件下，应报多少？（该商品每箱毛重 40 千克，体积 0.05 立方米。在运费表中的计费标准为 W/M，每吨运费基本运费率为 200 美元，另加收燃油附加费 10％）

（3）某企业出口一批柴油机（该货物为 10 级，计算标准为 W/M），共 15 箱，总毛重为 5.65 公吨，总体积为 10.676 立方米。由青岛装船，经中国香港转船至苏丹港。已知 10 级货从青岛运至中国香港费率为 22 美元，中转费 13 美元；从中国香港到苏丹港费率为 95 美元，苏丹港要收港口拥挤附加费，费率为基本运费的 10％。试计算该企业应付船公司运费多少？

13.5.2　实训操作

1. 常州天信外贸有限公司出口给加拿大客户 JAMES BROWN&SONS 的衬衫，每件纸箱毛重 25KG，净重 24KG，2010 年 10 月 2 日向长荣公司托运。船名为 HAPPY V.86，

开船日期为 2010 年 10 月 5 日；从张家港起运，目的地是加拿大的温哥华，B/L NO. ：LMN 01996，请你缮制提单，并发出装运通知。

2. 江苏天地木业有限公司的地板 2010 年 12 月 20 日由 COSCO 的船 WESTERN V. 92 从宁波港起运。CTN SIZE：1220×200×68mm，GW：15kg NW：14.5kg，B/L NO. ：GN 0867，请你缮制提单。

3. 常州天宁对外贸易有限公司有一批货物从上海运到美国的洛杉矶。请根据以下资料，缮制托运单和提单，并发出装运通知。

DOC. CREDIT NUMBER：20 CM20100943

EXPIRY：31D DATE 081004 PLACE CHINA

ISSUING BANK：51A CENTER BANK （FORMERLY CALIFORNIA CENTER BANK)

　　　　　　LOS ANGELES, CA

APPLICANT：50 SALTEX, INC.

　　　　1117 E. PICO BLVD. LOS ANGELES, CA 90021

BENEFICIARY：59 CHANGZHOU TIANNING FOREIGN TRADE CO. , LTD

　　　　7TH FLOOR XINRUN BUILDING NO. 223 JUQIAN

　　　　STREET CHANGZHOU JIANGSU, P. R. OF CHINA

PARTIAL SHIPMENTS：43P ALLOWED

TRANSHIPMENT：43T NOT ALLOWED

PORT OF LOADING：44E ANY CHINA PORT AND/ OR ANY HONG KONG PORT

PORT OF DISCHARGE：44F LOS ANGELES/ LONG BEACH PORT, CA U. S. A.

LATEST DATE OF SHIPMENT：44C 080930

DESCRIPTION OF GOODS：45A

98/2PCT COTTON/SPANDEX （WOVEN FABRIC）, 14 WAIL CORDUROY

IN PFD COLOR, WIDTH 58″ SALVAGE TO SALVAGE,

SHRINKAGE LESS THAN 4PCT×4PCT, TORQUE 2PCT

CONSTRUCTION 84×143－16×16＋70D

PIECE LENGTH 35PCT-50PCT 80YDS, 65PCT 80YDS AND OVER

FABRIC WEIGHT 9OZ/Y2

Q'TY(YDS)	U/PRICE	AMOUNT(USD)
30 000	USD2. 15	64 500. 00

＋ CIF LOS ANGELES PORT, CA U. S. A.

DOCUMENTS REQUIRED：46A

…

FULL SET AND 3 NON-NEGOTIABLE COPIES OF CLEAN ON BORAD VESSEL MARINE/ OCEAN BILLS OF LADING MADE OUT TO THE ORDER OF CENTER BANK, 2222 WEST OLYMPIC BLVD, LOS ANGELES, CA 90006, USA, MARKED 'FREIGHT PREPAID' AND NOTIFY ACOUNTEE.

…

ADDITIONAL CONDITIONS：47A

...

+ALL DOCUMENTS MUST BEAR THIS CREDIT NUMBER.

+ALL DOCUMENTS MUST BE IN ENGLISH LANGUAGE.

...

其他信息：

唛头	合同/号	208TN4281	发票号	208TN4281
PO： FABRIC DESCRIPTION： CONTENT： CONSTRUCTION： ROLL♯ SHADE♯ YARD： LOT♯ GW： NW： MADE IN CHINA	单价	USD 2.15/YD	数量	30 000YDS/305ROLLS
	总金额	USD 64 500	总毛重	15 149KG
	总净重	14 844KG	总体积	40.90M³
	目的港	洛杉矶	装运港	上海
	B/L NO.	COSU6019576990	船名航次	RIALTO BRIDGE 33E
	开航日期	Sept. 29，2010	运费	USD 2 200
	联系人	谢飞	联系电话	0519-××××××××

4. 每位学生就出口产品和进口商磋商，完成合同货物的出运，缮制订舱委托书和提单，发出装运通知。

任务 14

出口货物的运输保险

ℹ️ 知识要点

    1. 出口货物运输保险单的内容

    2. 出口货物运输保险费的计算

✊ 技能要点

    • 准确办理具体的出口货物运输保险手续

    • 正确填制投保单，审核保险单的内容是否正确

14.1　任务描述与分析

1. 任务描述

常信公司的 156 箱女式风衣已经在 2010 年 9 月 15 日完成托运，并确定已经于 9 月 24 日装上船只，25 日离开港口，现在孙大伟去保险公司办理相应的保险手续。

2. 任务分析

CIF 贸易术语下，出口人在货物出运前，根据合同向保险公司投保合同约定的货物运输保险。保险公司接受保险，在投保人支付保险费后，向出口人出具保险单。保险单作为出口人结汇的单据之一。

现在孙大伟需要按照合同填写投保单，支付保险费，在收到保险公司的保险单后，需要认真审核保险单是否正确。

14.2　相关知识

14.2.1　保险单据

1. 保险单据的种类

保险单据是保险公司和投保人之间订立的保险合同，也是保险公司出具的承保证明，是被保险人凭以向保险公司索赔和保险公司进行理赔的依据。保险单据背面印有规定保险人与被保险人、受让人之间权利与义务关系的保险条款。常用保险单据有：

（1）保险单

保险单是一种正规的保险合同，除载明投保单上所述各项内容外，还列有保险公司的责任范围以及保险公司与被保险人双方各自的权利、义务等方面的详细条款。

（2）保险凭证

保险凭证是一种简化的保险合同，除其背面没有列入详细保险条款外，其余内容与保险单相同。保险凭证也具有与保险单同样的法律效力。

（3）预约保单

为了简化投保手续，防止出现漏保或来不及办理投保等情况，我国进口货物一般采取预约保险的做法。合同中规定承保货物的范围、险别、费率、责任、赔款处理等条款，凡属合同约定的运输货物，在合同有效期内自动承保。

2. 保险单据的填制

保险单据正面记载证明双方当事人建立保险关系的文字，主要有：被保险货物的情况，包括货物项目、标记、包装及数量、保险金额及载货船名、起运地和目的地、开航日期等；承保险别；理赔地点以及保险人关于所保货物如遇风险可凭本保险单及有关证件给付赔偿的声明等。具体内容如表 14-1 所示。

表 14-1　保险单据的正面内容

项　目	内　容	要点提示
1. 保单的号码 POLICY NO.		保险公司编制的保单号
2. 发票号码 IN-VOICE NO.		此处填写发票号码
3. 被保险人 IN-SURED	即投保人，或称抬头	这一栏一般填写出口公司的名称。买卖双方对货物的权利可凭单据的转移而转移，因此交单结汇时，卖方将保险单背书转让给买方 如信用证规定被保险人为受益人以外的第三方，或做成"TO ORDER OF…"应视情况确定接受与否
4. 标记 MARKS AND NOS.	唛头	填写具体的唛头，也可只填"AS PER INVOICE NO. ×××"。如无唛头，可填 N/M
5. 包装及数量 QUANTITY	有包装的填写最大包装件数	煤炭、石油等散装货注明 IN BULK，再填写净重；有包装但以重量计价的，应将包装数量与计价重量注明
6. 保险货物项目 DESCRIPTION OF GOODS		参照发票、提单填写，也可用统称，但应该与提单、产地证的填写一致
7. 保险金额 AMOUNT INSURED	小写金额	一般为发票总金额的 110%，小数点后尾数一律进为整数。例如 USD30 006.06，则填写 USD30 007
8. 总保险金额 TOTAL AMOUNT INSURED	保险金额的大写形式	上面计价货币也应该填写全称，注意大、小写金额保持一致。例如，U. S. DOLLARS THIRTY THOUSAND AND SEVEN ONLY
9. 保费 PREMIUM 和费率 RATE	通常不注明具体数字，由保险公司印就"AS AR-RANGED"(如约定)	有时保费栏也可按信用证要求缮打"PAID"、"PRE-PAID"，或具体金额数目
10. 装载工具 PER CONVEY-ANCE	与提单的运输工具一致。实际货运船名、航次	海运方式下填写船名、航次。例如，FENGNING V. 9406；如整个运输由两程运输完成时，应分别填写一程船名和二程船名，中间用"/"隔开。例如：提单中一程船名为"MAYER"，二程船名为"SINYAI"，可填写"MAYER/ SINYAI"
11. 开航日期 DATE OF COM-MENCEMENT		填写提单的签发日期，或填"AS PER B/L DATE"
12. 起运地和目的地 FROM … TO…	应按提单填写起运地和目的地名称	如发生转船，可填写：FROM (装运港)TO(目的港)W/T 或 VIA(转运港)。例如：FROM SHANG-HAI TO NEW YORK VIA HONG KONG

续表

项　目	内　容	要点提示
13. 承保险别 CON-DITIONS		险别内容必须与信用证规定的保险条款严格一致
14. 保险查勘代理人 Insurance Survey Agent	此栏无论信用证是否有规定，都应注明查勘代理人	由保险公司决定查勘代理人，并应有详细地址，以便收货人在出险后通知其代理人联系有关查勘和索赔事宜 如果信用证规定在目的港以外的地方赔付，例如，目的港在伦敦而赔付地在巴黎，则应注明伦敦的查勘代理人和巴黎的查勘代理人 如果来证规定有两个赔付地，则两个地点的代理人都要注明
15. 赔付地点 CLAIM PAYABLE AT	一般信用证规定在赔付地点后要注明偿付的货币名称，赔款的货币一般与 L/C 的货币一致。例如：AT NEW YORK IN USD	如信用证中并未规定，则应填写目的港。如信用证规定不止一个目的港或赔付地，则应全部照打
16. 保险单的签发日期和地点 DATE AND PLACE OF ISSUE		保险单的签发日期不得迟于提单签发的日期，以证明是在货物发运前办理的投保；签发地点一般为出口商所在地
17. 保险公司签章 AUTHORIZED SIGNATURE		保险单只有经保险公司或其代理人签章后才生效

　　如信用证没有规定具体险别，或只规定"MARINE RISK"、"USUAL RISK"或"TRANSPORT RISK"等，则可投保一切险、水渍险、平安险三种基本险中的任何一种，另外还可以加保一种或几种附加险。如果来证要求投保的险别超出了合同规定，或成交价格为 FOB 或 CFR，但来证却由卖方保险，遇到这种情况，如果买方同意支付额外保险费，可按信用证办理。

　　投保的险别除注明险别名称外，还应注明险别适用的文本及日期。如保险单据表明所出具正本为一份以上，则必须提交全部正本保险单。

14.2.2　保险索赔

　　进出口货物在运输途中遭受损失，被保险人（投保人或保险单受让人）可向保险公司提出索赔。保险公司按保险条款所承担的责任进行理赔。索赔主要程序包括以下三个方面。

1. 损失通知

　　被保险人获悉货损后，应立即通知保险公司或保险单上指明的代理人。后者接到损失通知后应即采取相应的措施，如检验损失，提出施救意见，确定保险责任和签发检验报告等。

2. 采取合理的施救措施

被保险货物受损后，被保险人应迅速对受损货物采取必要合理的施救、整理措施，防止损失的扩大。被保险人收到保险公司发出的有关采取防止或者减少损失的合理措施的特别通知的，应按照保险公司的通知要求进行处理。

3. 备妥索赔单证

提出索赔要求时，除正式的索赔函以外，还应包括保险单证、运输单据、发票，以及检验报告、货损货差证明、列明索赔金额及计算依据，以及有关费用的项目和用途的索赔清单等。

14.3　任务实施与心得

任务实施

（1）办理投保

投保单是投保人要求投保的书面要约，是保险公司签发保险单的依据，进行核保及核定给付、赔付的重要原始资料。各保险公司的投保单，格式有所不同，但内容大体相同，一般均列有：被保险人名称、货物名称、包装及数量、标志、保险金额、装运工具或船名、开航日期、航程、投保险别、赔款地点等栏目。

常信公司一般都是向中国人民保险公司常州分公司办理出口货物运输保险手续，2010年9月24日孙大伟根据买卖合同和信用证规定，在备妥货物并确定装运日期和运输工具后，按规定格式逐笔填制投保单。下面是孙大伟填制的投保单。

中国人民保险公司常州分公司
The People's Insurance Company of China, Changzhou Branch

APPLICATION FORM FOR CARGO TRANSPORTATION INSURANCE

被保险人
INSURED：CHANGZHOU CHANGXIN IMPORT & EXPORT CORP.

发票号（INVOICE NO.）CLK008

合同号（CONTRACT NO.）CZCX080180

信用证号（L/C NO.）LCH066/08

发票金额（INVOICE AMOUNT）　　　　投保加成（PLUS）　10　%

兹有下列货物向　　投保。(INSURANCE IS REQUIRED ON THE FOLLOWING COMMODITIES:)

标 记 MARKS & NOS.	数量及包装 QUANTITY	保险货物项目 DESCRIPTION OF GOODS	保险金额 AMOUNT INSURED
FTC CZCX080180 MARSEILLES NO. 1-156	156CTNS	LADIES COAT	USD39 400.00

续表

起运日期 DATE OF COMMENCEMENT SEPT. 25, 2010	装载运输工具： PER CONVEYANCE：TRIUMPH V991A

自　　　经　　　至
FROM SHANGHAI VIA TO MARSEILLES
赔款偿付地点
CLAIM PAYABLE AT DESTINATION

　　投保险别：(PLEASE INDICATE THE CONDITIONS &/OR SPECIAL COVERAGES：)
　　请如实告知下列情况：(如"是"在[　]中打"√"，"不是"打"×") IF ANY, PLEASE MARK "√"
OR "×".
　　1. 货物种类：袋装[　]　散装[　]　冷藏[　]　液体[　]　活动物[　]　机器/汽车[　]　危险品等级[　]
　　　GOODS：BAG/JUMBO　BULK　REEFER　LIQUID　LIVE ANIMAL　MACHINE/AUTO
DANGEROUS CLASS
　　2. 集装箱种类：普通[　]　开顶[　]　框架[　]　平板[　]　冷藏[　]
　　CONTAINER：ORDINARY　OPEN　FRAME　FLAT　REFRIGERATOR
　　3. 转运工具：海轮[　]　飞机[　]　驳船[　]　火车[　]　汽车[　]
　　BY TRANSIT：SHIP　PLANE　BARGE　TRAIN　TRUCK
　　4. 船舶资料：船籍[　]　船龄[　]
　　PARTICULAR OF SHIP：REGISTRY　AGE
备注：被保险人确认本保险合同条款和内容已经完全了解。
THE ASSURED CONFIRMS HEREWITH THE　　　投保人(签名盖章)
TERMS AND CONDITIONS OF THESE INSURANCE　　APPLICANT'S SIGNATURE
CONTRACT FULLY UNDERSTOOD　　　孙大伟
　　　　　　电话：(TEL)0519-86338171
投保日期：DATE SEPT. 24, 2010　　　地址：(ADD)

（2）交付保险费

投保人交付保险费，是保险合同生效的前提条件。在被保险人支付保险费以前，保险人可以拒绝签发保险单据。

常信公司向保险公司交付保险费 433.40 美元。计算如下，一切险的保险费率为 1%，战争险的保险费率为 0.1%。

$$保险费＝保险金额×保险费率$$
$$＝CIF 价×(1＋投保加成率)×保险费率$$
$$＝USD35\ 817.60×(1＋10\%)×(1\%＋0.1\%)$$
$$＝USD39\ 400.00×1.1\%＝USD433.40$$

（3）领取和审核保险单据

保险公司收到保险费后，传真保险单给常信公司，孙大伟仔细审核保险单的各项内容，如果发现错误或者与信用证内容不符，及时要求保险公司更正，确保内容正确，以保持与信用证要求的一致。

下面是孙大伟审核无误的保险单。

中国人民保险公司
The People's Insurance Company of China

总公司设于北京   一九四九年创立
Head Office Beijing   Established in 1949

保险单
INSURANCE POLICY

发票号(INVOICE NO.)   CLK008   保单号次
                                             POLICY NO. CZPI0998

合同号(CONTRACT NO.)   CZCX080180

信用证号(L/C NO.)   LCH066/08

被保险人:

INSURED: *CHANGZHOU CHANGXIN IMPORT & EXPORT CORP.*

中国人民保险公司(以下简称本公司)根据被保险人的要求,由被保险人向本公司缴付约定的保险费,按照本保险单承保险别和背面所载条款与下列特款承保下述货物运输保险,特立本保险单。

THIS POLICY OF INSURANCE WITNESSES THAT THE PEOPLE'S INSURANCE COMPANY OF CHINA (HEREINAFTER CALLED "THE COMPANY") AT THE REQUEST OF THE INSURED AND IN CONSIDERATION OF THE AGREED PREMIUM PAID TO THE COMPANY BY THE INSURED, UNDERTAKES TO INSURE THE UNDERMENTIONED GOODS IN TRANSPORTATION SUBJECT TO THE CONDITIONS OF THIS OF THIS POLICY AS PER THE CLAUSES PRINTED OVERLEAF AND OTHER SPECIAL CLAUSES ATTACHED HEREON.

标 记 MARKS&NOS.	包装及数量 QUANTITY	保险货物项目 DESCRIPTION OF GOODS	保险金额 AMOUNT INSURED
FTC CZCX080180 MARSEILLES NO. 1-156	156CTNS	100% COTTON LADIES COAT	USD39 400. 00

总保险金额
TOTAL AMOUNT INSURED: SAY U. S. DOLLARS THIRTY-NINE THOUSAND AND FOUR HUNDRED ONLY

保费: 起运日期:
PERMIUM: AS ARRANGED   DATE OF COMMENCEMENT: SEPT. 25, 2010

装载运输工具:
PER CONVEYANCE: TRIUMPH V991A

自   经   至
FROM: SHANGHAI CHINA   VIA TO   MARSEILLES PORT

承保险别:

CONDITIONS:

All Risks, War Risks as per and subject to the relevant Ocean Marine Cargo Clause of the People's Insurance Company of China, dated 1/1/1981.

所保货物,如发生保险单项下可能引起索赔的损失或损坏,应立即通知本公司下述代理人查勘。如有索赔，应向本公司提交保单正本(本保险单共有×份正本)及有关文件。如一份正本已用于索赔，其余正本自动失效。

IN THE EVENT OF LOSS OR DAMAGE WITCH MAY RESULT IN A CLAIM UNDER THIS POLICY, IMMEDIATE NOTICE MUST BE GIVEN TO THE COMPANY'S AGENT AS MENTIONED HEREUNDER. CLAIMS, IF ANY, ONE OF THE ORIGINAL POLICY WHICH HAS BEEN ISSUED IN TOGETHER WITH THE RELEVANT DOCUMENTS SHALL BE SURRENDERED TO THE COMPANY. IF ONE OF THE ORIGINAL POLICY HAS BEEN ACCOMPLISHED. THE OTHERS ORIGINAL(S) TO BE VOID.

中国人民保险公司

The People's Insurance Company of China

赔款偿付地点
CLAIM PAYABLE AT　　MARSEILLES IN USD　　　　　　　×××××××
　　　　　　　　　　　　　　　　　　　　　　　　　Authorized Signature
出单日期
ISSUING DATE　　SEPT. 24，2010

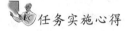
任务实施心得

　　投保人填制投保单时应注意：

　　1)投保单内容须真实，并与出口合同或信用证规定相符。

　　2)对特殊要求的处理。在 CIF 条件下，买方可能临时要求提高保险金额、加保某种特殊附加险以及扩展保险责任等。卖方应认真研究，并与保险公司取得联系，然后决定是否接受这些特殊要求。

　　3)按照一般惯例，我国外贸公司向中国人民保险公司投保条款即认为可以适用中国的有关法律。国外客商如要求按照伦敦协会有关条款投保，中国人民保险公司一般可予接受。

　　审核保险单需要注意以下事项：

　　1)保险单的出具时间不得晚于提单的时间，否则进口商或付款银行有权拒绝付款。

　　2)出口商办理保险，保险单交给银行前应该背书转让。

　　3)当采用 FOB 、CFR 术语出口时，应该考虑到货物从工厂到装运港越过船舷这阶段的风险，并采取相应的保险。

14.4　知识拓展

保险的免赔率

　　对易碎和易短量货物的索赔，应了解是否有免赔的规定。如果不计免赔率，只要标的损失属于承保范围，保险人一律按保险货物的实际损失给予赔偿。如果规定了免赔率，当发生的损失没有超过保险公司规定的免赔率比例时，保险公司不予赔偿。

　　免赔率有相对免赔率和绝对免赔率之分。

　　相对免费率：当保险标的的损失超过了保险单规定的免赔百分比以后，保险人就按实际损失给予赔偿，不扣除免赔率。

　　绝对免赔率：当保险标的的损失超过了保险单规定的免赔百分比以后，保险人只对保险标的的实际损失超过保险单中规定的免赔率的部分给予赔偿。

14.5　业务技能训练

14.5.1　课堂训练

1. 计算题

(1)天津港保税区某公司出口一批货物 CIF 价为 7 800 美元，现国外客户来电要求按 CIF 价加 20% 投保海上一切险，我方照办，如保险费率为 1%，我方应向客户补收多少保险费?

(2)我国某外贸公司以每公吨 1 000 英镑 CIF 伦敦(按加一成投保一切险，保险费率为 1%)，向英商报盘出售一批轻工业产品，该外商拟自行投保，要求改报 CFR 价，问：CFR 价格为多少，出口人应从 CIF 价中扣除多少保险费?

2. 学生讨论如果保险单日期晚于提单日期，会出现什么后果?

3. 案例分析题

(1)北京某外贸公司按 CFR 马尼拉价格出口一批仪器，买方投保的险别为一切险"仓至仓条款"。我方将货物用卡车由北京运到天津港发货，但在运输中，一辆货车翻车，致使车上所载部分仪表损坏。问：对该损失应由哪方负责，保险公司是否应给予赔偿?

(2)上海浦东开发区某厂从英国进口一批货物，英商应我方的要求，将货物交给指定运送人——荷兰某船运公司运到上海。但在卸货时发生短缺，据船公司回答，所有短卸货物已卸在香港，将安排运回上海，约过了 25 天，又发现所短货物未全部运来，而且又无法查清货物究竟在何处，致使该厂的生产计划拖延，生产受到损失。问：①船公司应负何责任? ②该厂是否可就由于生产计划拖延而造成的估计损失要求赔偿? ③在多次转船运输中，买方为避免此损失发生应该投保何种险别较好?

14.5.2　实训操作

1. 常州天信外贸有限公司向加拿大客户 JAMES BROWN&SONS 出口的男衬衫已经装运，装运时间见前一个任务实训。请你办理保险手续。

2. 江苏天地木业有限公司与现代公司的合同是 CFR 术语，不需要出口方办理保险。现在假设合同是采用的 CIF 术语，其他条款内容不变，请你填写保险单。险别为：一切险，其保险费率为 0.85%。

3. 根据任务 13 常州天宁对外贸易有限公司出口货物的资料，以及以下资料，缮制投保单和保险单。险别为：一切险加战争险，其保险费率分别为 1% 和 0.5%。

4. 每位学生就自己公司和外商洽谈签订的合同，确定该由谁进行货物运输的保险工作，由该同学进行保险单的填写。

任务 15

货款的结算

知识要点

1. 结汇单据的主要内容
2. 结汇方式

技能要点
- 正确制作货款结算所需要的单据
- 办理交单结汇手续并处理结算业务中的相关事项

15.1　任务描述与分析

1. 任务描述

常信公司的货物已于 2010 年 9 月 25 日从上海港按期发运，信用证的交单期为 10 天（PRESENTATION PERIOD 48 ：DOCUMENTS TO BE PRESENTED WITHIN 10 DAYS AFTER THE ISSUANCE OF THE SHIPPING DOCUMENTS BUT WITHIN THE VALIDITY OF THE CREDIT.），现业务员孙大伟正抓紧制作单据，早日到银行办理货款结算事宜。

2. 任务分析

现代国际贸易绝大部分采用凭单交货、凭单付款的方式。在信用证业务中，由于银行只凭信用证和单据结算，不管买卖合同和货物，因此对单据的要求非常严格。单证正确与否直接关系到企业的经济利益。顺利结汇的关键在于单证的正确、完整、及时、清晰。

出口商完成了货物的交付后，就要着手结算货款。制作好汇票、发票、装箱单等，并及时从相关机构获取提单、保险单、产地证书、商检证书等单据，审核正确，然后在规定的交单到期日或之前，将各种单据和必要的凭证送交指定的银行办理付款、承兑或议付手续。

15.2　相关知识

15.2.1　常用结汇单据

现简单介绍几种常见的结汇单据及制单时应注意的问题。

1. 发票

发票是商业发票的简称，是出口商向进口商开列的出口货物价目清单，也是进出口报关不可缺少的重要文件之一。商业发票是一笔业务的全面反映，内容包括商品的名称、规格、价格、数量、金额等。商业发票处于全套出口单据的核心地位，发票的缮制如表 15-1 所示。

表 15-1　发票的内容和缮制要点

项　目	内　容	要点提示
1. 出票人和出票地址	即出口人的名称与地址	
2. 发票的名称和种类	如：Invoice	不同发票的名称表示不同用途，要严格根据信用证的规定制作发票名称
3. 出票日期 Invoice Date、发票编号 Invoice No.		在全套单据中，发票是签发日最早的单据。它只要不早于合同的签订日期，不迟于提单的签发日期即可
4. 运输方式和路线 Means of transportation and the route	起运地及目的地，如 From Dalian To Goteborg. Sweden W/T Hong Kong	按合同或信用证规定

续表

项　目	内　容	要点提示
5. 抬头人 To	买方名称	与信用证规定一致。如信用证中无规定，即将信用证的申请人或收货人的名称、地址，填入此栏。如信用证中无申请人名字则用汇票付款人
6. 唛头及编号 Marks and No.	如：收货人简称、目的地、参考号、件号	应严格按照信用证与合同的规定进行刷唛和制单。如未规定，可按买卖双方和厂商订的方案或由受益人自定。无唛头时，应注"N/M"或"No Mark"。如为裸装货，则注明"NAKED"或散装"In Bulk"
7. 品名及货物描述 Description of Goods	货物的名称、规格型号等	严格根据信用证及合同的规定填写
8. 单价 Unit Price，总额 Amount	除非信用证上另有规定，否则货物总值不能超过信用证金额	如涉及佣金和折扣，要注意其处理。来证要求在发票中扣除佣金，则必须扣除；有时证内无扣除佣金规定，但金额正好是减佣后的净额，发票应显示减佣，否则发票金额超证；有时合同规定佣金，但来证金额内未扣除，而且证内也未提及佣金事宜，则发票不宜显示，待货款收回后另行汇给买方
9. 特殊条款 Special terms	如：要求证实货物原产地	按信用证或合同要求注明，起到证明、声明的作用
10. 签署 Signature	出口商公司名称及授权签字人	一般要签署，特别是有证实语句时

2. 装箱单

装箱单是对商业发票的一种补充单据，有装箱单、重量单和尺码单等不同的名称、格式，具体应该按照信用证要求的名称缮制。装箱单是对出口商品的包装、规格、重量、尺码等详细情况说明的一种单据，是买方收货时核对货物的品种、花色、尺寸、规格和海关验收的主要依据。装箱单主要有以下内容：

1) 装箱单名称(Packing List)：应按照信用证规定使用。

2) 编号(No.)：与发票号码一致。

3) 合同号(Contract No.)：注此批货物的合同号。

4) 箱号(Case No.)：如：Carton No. 1-5：…Carton No. 6-10：…有的来证要求此处注明"CASE NO. 1-UP"，UP 是指总箱数，在制单时应把具体箱数写明。

5) 品名和规格(Name of Commodity & Specification)：要求与发票一致。

6) 外包装单位(Unit)和数量(Quantity)。

7) 毛重(Gr. Wt.)：常用计量单位是千克。

8) 箱外尺寸(Measurement)：注明每个包装件的外尺寸，常用计量单位是立方米。

9）唛头（Shipping Mark）：与发票一致。

10）出单人签章：应与发票相同，如信用证规定包装单为"in plain"或"in white paper"等，则在包装单内不应出现买卖双方的名称，不能签章。

3. 汇票

汇票必须记载下列事项："汇票"字样；无条件支付委托；确定的金额；付款人名称；出票日期；出票人签章等。汇票上未记载规定事项之一的，汇票无效。在实际业务中，汇票通常尚需列明付款日期、付款地点和出票地点等内容。

（1）汇票名称

汇票上标明"汇票"（Bill of Exchange)字样。

（2）金额

金额由货币和数额两部分组成，大小写两种表述方式，且大小写必须一致。一般情况下汇票金额应与发票金额一致，但也有例外。

1）信用证上明确规定汇票金额是发票金额的一定百分比。

2）来证要求出具佣金单时：

汇票金额＝发票金额－佣金单金额

如信用证要求佣金在支付时扣除，则汇票金额等于发票金额，但寄单索汇时应少收佣金部分。

3）来证要求运费、保险费或其他费用可在证下或超证支取：

汇票金额＝发票金额＋费用总和

来证要求运费、保险费或其他费用不许超证或证外支付，则须另制费用金额汇票。

4）在部分信用证、部分托收的结算中，需分制不同支付方式下的汇票。

5）当实际装运数量少于规定的数量，或信用证允许分批装运时，发票金额为实际应收金额。

（3）付款期限

汇票期限分为即期和远期。即期用"at sight"或"on demand"表示；远期有多种表示方法，应严格按信用证规定缮制。

（4）受款人

受款人也称"抬头人"或"抬头"。在实际业务中汇票通常作成指示性抬头，即"Pay to the order of…"。

（5）出票条款

出票条款指在 Drawn under 之后缮打开立的信用证号或合同号。与信用证具体规定严格一致。如信用证未要求，则应打开证行名称、地址、信用证号和开证日期。另在出票条款中，按信用证要求也可加注利息条款和费用条款。

（6）付款人

付款人也称受票人，包括付款人名称和地址。汇票付款人的填写要按照信用证的要求填写。

（7）出票地点及日期

出票地点及日期通常一起出现在汇票的右上角。一般在地址之后或之下注明日期。出票日期应晚于提单日，早于议付日或于议付日当天，一般是提交议付行议付的日期，该日期往往由议付行填写。该日期不能迟于信用证的有效期。托收方式的出票日期以托收行寄单日期填列。

（8）汇票编号

汇票编号一般采用发票号码。

（9）出票人

出票人即受益人、合同的卖方或托收方式下托收的委托人。

4. 原产地证书

（1）原产地证书的种类

根据签发者不同，原产地证书一般可分为以下三类：中华人民共和国检验检疫局出具的普惠制产地证格式 A 和一般原产地证书等；中国国际贸易促进委员会出具的贸促会产地证书；制造商或出口商出具的产地证书。

（2）原产地证书的填制

一般原产地证书简称原产地证，是出口商应进口商要求而提供的、由公证机构或政府机构或出口商出具的证明货物原产地的一种证明文件。原产地证是进口商进口报关、享受配额待遇的有效凭证。原产地证的填制规范如表 15-2 所示。

表 15-2　原产地证的填制规范

栏　目	填　制　规　范
1. 编号	应在证书右上角填上证书编号。此栏不得留空，否则此证书无效
2. 出口方	填出口方名称、详细地址及国家（地区）。若经其他国家或地区需填写转口名称时，可在出口商后面加填英文 VIA，然后再填写转口商名称、地址和国家（地区）
3. 最终收货方的名称、详址及国家（地区）	通常是合同的买方或信用证规定的提单通知人。如果来证要求所有单证收货人留空，此栏应加注"To Whom It May Concern"或"To order"。但不得留空。若需填写转口商名称，可在收货人后面加填英文 VIA，然后加填转口商名称、地址、国家（地区）
4. 运输方式及路线	海运、陆运填写装货港（地）、到货港（地）及运输路线，如经转运，还应注明转运地
5. 目的地国家（地区）	国家名或单独关税地区名
6. 签证机构专用栏	此栏为签证机构在签发后发证书、补发证书或加注其他声明时使用。一般情况下，此栏为空白
7. 运输标志	按发票填制
8. 商品名称、包装数量及种类	包装数量要有大小写，本栏的末行要打上表示结束的符号："——"或"＊＊＊＊＊＊＊＊＊＊"
9. 商品编码	此栏要求填写 H.S. 编码
10. 数量/重量	填写出口货物的量值并与商品计量单位联用

续表

栏　目	填　制　规　范
11. 发票号码及日期	其中月份用英文表达，例如：OCT. 10, 2010
12. 出口商声明	该栏由申领单位已在签证机构注册的人员签字并加盖有中英文的印章，并填写申领地点和日期。此日期不得早于发票日期
13. 签证机构证明	由签证机构签字(手签)、盖章。注意签字、盖章不得重合，并填写签订日期、地点。此日期不得早于发票日期和申请日期(一般与发票日期相同)

15.2.2　结汇方式

我国出口信用证结算业务中，通常有下列几种出口结汇办法。

(1)收妥结汇

收妥结汇是指出口地银行收到受益人提交的单据，经审核确认与信用证条款的规定相符后，将单据寄给国外付款行索偿，待付款行将外汇划给出口地银行后，该行再按外汇牌价结算成人民币交付给受益人。

(2)买单结汇

买单结汇又称出口押汇或议付，是指议付行在核实单据后确认受益人所交单据符合信用证条款规定的情况下，按信用证的条款买入受益人的汇票及单据，按照票面金额扣除从议付日到估计收到票款之日的利息，将净数按议付日人民币市场汇价折算成人民币，付给信用证的受益人。

15.2.3　信用证事故的处理

在实际业务中，由于主、客观原因，发生单证不符的情形往往难以完全避免，只能不符点交单，或者开证行判断存在不符点的，都有可能导致单据被拒付。

如果遭到对方拒付，首先要区分责任，判断开证行拒付是否有合理依据、是否符合程序。所谓合理依据，就是开证行提出的不符点应有站得住脚的理由，否则可通过国内银行回复解释申辩。所谓符合程序，开证行必须在5个工作日内审核单证并一次性提出不符点，否则即使有不符点也无权再提。

(1)"单证不一致"的防范与处理

在信用证交易中，业务员应该树立"信用证至高无上"的观念，即使信用证中出现错别字或明显的语法错法，只要不导致产生歧义，在无法修改的情况下，也要将错就错地照样搬到所有单证中去。

不能做到的应事先讲明，因意外而导致失误的(例如提单传递迟误，导致未能按照客户要求及时寄出提单复印件等)，必要的时候，说明一下请客户谅解即可，但单证要完全按照信用证要求出具。

对于不是自己出具，而是由第三方如货运公司出具的提单一类，事先务必与他们仔细核对正确，然后领取正本，领取后再检查一次，看是否正确。对于日期时效方面的不符，可以请货运公司协作，虚打日期以使信用证日期相符。

对于国家机构比如商检局出具的单据，不易灵活处理，因此要慎重一些。如果信用证条款中对这类单证有特别的要求，应先与商检机构沟通咨询，看是否能满足客户要求。无法完全满足的，坚决要求修改信用证条款。因外贸市场灵活多变，品质要求也参差不齐，对于商检局提出异议的产品，可以通过"客户确认"的保函形式协商解决。

(2)"单单不一致"的预防与处理

单单不一致，指同一套单证里不同单据相同栏目的内容不一致。这个问题通常是由于部门在分工协作制单中的疏漏造成的。预防的方法，就是养成事先编制交易档案，按照栏目分别归类，像一个数据库一样，根据交易编码，各部门或者各单证直接调用。

此外，审单证的时候，不但要逐张审核，还可以"横"审，即比对不同单证同一栏目的内容。实务中，也允许有些地方在合理范围内某些栏目单单不一致的情况。比如品名描述栏，在发票中也许细致详实，按照同类产品不同款式逐一分列，而在提单和原产地证中就将其简单合并了。

(3)不符点的处理

单据与信用证存在差异的情况一概称为不符点。轻微的不符点比如某个字母或标点符号的错误，不造成歧义，对交易性质无实质影响的，一般开证行也会接受，但会对每一个不符点扣罚几十美元。如果是较大的错误，特别是数量、金额、交货期方面的错误，开证行会通知受益人不符点的情况，并暂时中止执行信用证支付，待受益人与开证申请人协商，开证申请人愿意接受不符点并同意付款，才会支付，同时不符点费用照扣。可见，不符点将直接导致信用证失效。

一般地，在把单证交付国外开证行之前，国内出口商的信用证议付行会审核一遍，发现确有不符点的，如若来得及换单，会将修改正确的单证补交上去。只要修改后的单据在信用证规定的有效期内提交到指定银行，则视为单据不存在不符点，开证行必须付款。

倘若限于时间，无法在信用证有效期内做到单证相符，或者很多情况既成事实，不符点无法更改，有以下几种处理方式。

1)不符点不严重，可在征得开证申请人同意的前提下，由受益人出具保证书请求议付行"凭保议付"。多数情况下，客户也会同意。

2)不符情况较为复杂，可请议付行电告开证行单据中的不符点，请开证行与开证申请人联系，让开证申请人向开证行确认接受不符点，开证行再向国内银行确认，然后对外寄单。这种操作方式称为"电提不符点"。

3)上述两种方式如开证行均不接受，只能改为"跟证托收"。这种方式风险极大，不能轻易采用。

15.3 任务实施与心得

 任务实施

(1)制作单据

孙大伟在出口货物装运后，根据信用证的要求及时制作汇票、发票、装箱单等单据，以便结汇。(单据见英文部分)

（2）交单

孙大伟从货代公司处取得提单，从保险公司取得保险单，从检验检疫局取得品质证书、产地证等，经仔细审核，连同制作的单证，在 9 月 28 日向银行提交信用证项下的单据，要求银行议付。

（3）结汇

中国银行常州分行在核实单据后，确认常信公司所交单据符合信用证条款规定的要求，按信用证的条款买入受益人的汇票和单据，按照票面金额扣除从议付日到估计收到票款之日的利息，将净数按议付日人民币市场汇价折算成人民币，于 2010 年 10 月 6 日划入常信公司的账户。中国银行于 2010 年 10 月 15 日收到法国付款行的货款。

任务实施心得

在凭单交货、凭单付款方式下，办理货款结算时，单据的制作是关键，一定要树立"单证就是钱"的理念，要仔细审核向银行办理结汇的单据，并在规定的时间内交单，与银行良好协作，顺利结算货款。

业务员在制作结汇单据时，要按照以下几点要求做：

1）正确。单据内容必须正确，要能真实反映货物的实际情况，单据之间的内容不能矛盾，信用证方式下还要符合信用证的要求。

2）完整。单据的份数应符合信用证或合同的规定，不能短少；单据本身的内容应当完备，不能出现项目短缺的情况，信用证或合同的特别要求也应体现。

3）及时。制单应及时，各单据出单时间应合理、有序；交单应及时，信用证业务中应在信用证有效期内、交单期内交单。

4）简明。单据内容应按信用证或合同的要求和国际惯例填写，力求简单明了，切勿加列不必要的内容。

5）整洁。单据的布局要美观、大方，打印的字迹要清晰，不宜轻易更改，尤其对金额、件数、重量等内容不宜改动。

15.4 知识拓展

1. 单据份数的表达

在国际贸易实务中，单据份数的表达方式一般有三种：第一种是"Copy"表达法，in 1 copy，in 5 copies；第二种是"Fold"表达法，in 1 fold，in 5 fold；第三种是固定的表达方式：in duplicate（一式两份），in triplicate（一式三份），in quadruplicate（一式四份），in quintuplicate（一式五份），in sextuplicate（一式六份），in septuplicate（一式七份），in octuplicate（一式八份），in nonuplicate（一式九份），in decuplicate（一式十份）。

2. 单据签发时间之间的关系

每份单据都会标明签发日期，各种单据的签发日期应符合逻辑和国际惯例，以提单上的 ON BOARD DATE 为基准，发票、提单、保险单、产地证、商检证等单据日期之间存在以下先后关系：

发票日期应在各单据日期之首，装箱单日期一般与发票日期相同；提单日不能晚于

L/C 规定的装运期也不得早于 L/C 的最早装运期；保单的签发日应早于或等于提单日期（一般早于提单两天），不能早于发票；产地证的日期不早于发票日期，不迟于提单日；商检证日期不晚于提单日期，但也不能过分早于提单日，尤其是鲜货，容易变质的商品；受益人证明的日期等于或晚于提单日；船公司证明等于或早于提单日；汇票的日期不得早于提单日，一般应晚于发票等其他单据的日期，但不能晚于 L/C 的有效期。

15.5　业务技能训练

15.5.1　课堂训练

1. 简述跟单信用证下各单据签发时间之间的关系。
2. 学生讨论如果信用证结算方式下，出现单证不符的情况，怎样去解决？
3. 案例分析题

(1)某外贸公司出口一批货物，数量为 1 000 公吨，每公吨 USD78CIF Rotterdam。国外买方通过开证行按时开来信用证，证内注明按 UCP600 办理，该证规定：总金额不得超过 USD78 000，有效期为 11 月 30 日。外贸公司于 11 月 4 日将货物装船完毕取得提单，提单签发日期为 11 月 4 日。请问：①外贸公司最迟应在何日将单据交银行议付？为什么？②本批货物最多、最少能交多少公吨？为什么？

(2)我某出口企业收到国外开来不可撤销信用证一份，由设在我国境内的某外资银行通知并加以保兑。我出口企业在货物装运后，正拟将有关单据交银行议付时，忽接该外资银行通知，由于开证银行已宣布破产，该行不承担对该信用证的议付或付款责任，但可接受我出口公司委托向买方直接收取货款的业务。对此，你认为我方应如何处理为好？

15.5.2　实训操作

1. 常州天信外贸有限公司的衬衫出口后，缮制发票、装箱单、汇票、产地证。
2. 江苏天地木业有限公司的地板出口后，缮制发票、装箱单、汇票、产地证。
3. 每位学生就自己公司产品出口后，缮制发票、装箱单、汇票等单据，去银行结汇。
4. 根据所给的内容和信用证条款缮制发票、装箱单、汇票、产地证。

ADVISING BANK：BANK OF COMMUNICATIONS SHANGHAI（HEAD OFFICE）

OPENING BANK：BANGKOK BANK PUBLIC COMPANY LIMITED, BANGKOK

FORM DOC CREDIT	*40A	IRREVOCABLE
DOC CREDIT NUM	*20	0611LC123756
DATE OF ISSUE	31C	061103
DATE/PLACE EXPIRY	31D	070114, BENEFICIARIES' COUNTRY
APPLICANT	*50	MOUN CO. , LTD.
		NO. 443, 249 ROAD
		BANGKOK THAILAND
BENEFICIARY	*59	SHANGHAI FOREIGN TRADE CORP.
		SHANGHAI, CHINA

CURR CODE，AMT	*32B	Code USD Amount 18 000，
AVAILABLE WITH/BY	*41D	ANY BANK IN CHINA BY NEGOTIATION
DRAFTS AT	43D	ISSUING BANK
PARTIAL SHIPMENTS	43P	NOT ALLOWED
TRANSSHIPMENT	43T	ALLOWED
LOADING ON BRD	44A	CHINA MAIN PORT，CHINA
FOR TRANSPORT TO	44B	BANGKOK，THAILAND
LATEST SHIPMENT	44C	061220
GOODS DESCRIPT.	45A	2，000KG. ISONIAZID BP98
		AT USD9. 00 PER KG CFR BANGKOK
DOCS REQUIRED	46A	

+COMMECIAL INVOICE IN ONE ORIGINAL PLUS 5 COPIES INDICATING FOB VALUE, FREIGHT CHARGES SEPARATELY AND THIS L/C NUMBER, ALL OF WHICH MUST BE MANUALLY SIGNED

+FULL SET OF 3/3 CLEAN ON BOARD OCEAN BILLS OF LADING AND TWO NON-NEGOTIABLE COPIES MADE OUT TO ORDER OF BANGKOK BANK PUBLIC COMPANY LIMITED, BANGKOK MARKED FREIGHT PREPAID AND NOTIFY AP-PLICANT AND INDICATING THIS L/C NUMBER

+PACKING LIST IN ONE ORIGINAL PLUS 5 COPIES, ALL OF WHICH MUST BE MANUALLY SIGNED

+CERTIFICATE OF ORIGIN

ADD. CONDITIONS	47A	A DISCREPANCY FEE OF USD50. 00 WILL BE IMPOSED ON EACH SET OF DOCU-MENTS PRESENT ED FOR NEGOTIATION UNDER THIS L/C WITH DISCREPANCY. THE FEE WILL BE DEDUCTED FROM THE BILL AMOUNT.
CHARGES	71B	ALL BANKCHARGES OUTSIDE THAI-LAND INCLUDING REIMBURSING BANK COMMISSION ANDDISCREPANCY FEE (IF ANY) ARE FOR BENEFICIARIES' AC-COUNT.

相关资料：

合同号码：SFT986	发票号码：SHE 02/1845
发票日期：2006 年 11 月 26 日	提单号码：SCOISG7564
提单日期：2006 年 11 月 29 日	船名：JENNY V. 03
装运港：上海港	货物装箱情况：50KG/DRUM
总毛重：2 200KG	总尺码：56CBM
集装箱：1×40'FCL CY/CY UXXU4240250 0169255	运费：USD0. 08/KG

综合训练三

1. 业务背景
接综合训练二，新加坡客户很快会签寄回常州永盛进出口公司缮制的销售确认书。

SALES CONFIRMATION

NO. SC009762

DATE：SEPT. 21，2010

Seller：CHANGZHOU YONGSHENG IMPORT & EXPORT CORP.

88，YANLING ROAD, CHANGZHOU,

JIANGSU, CHINA

Buyer：RAFFLES TRADING CO. LTD. ，

69 INTERNATIONAL TRADE PLAZA，ORCHARD ROAD ，SINGAPORE

The undersigned Sellers and Buyers have agreed to close the following transaction according to the terms and conditions stipulated below：

NAME OF COMMODITY	QUANTITY	UNIT PRICE	AMOUNT
BLACK PENOY BRAND JEANS - 30S×36S 72×69 150CM×42 YARDS	4 200 YARDS	CIF　SINGAPORE USD2. 50/YARD	USD 10 500. 00

TOTAL VALUE：US DOLLARS TEN THOUSAND AND FIVE HUNDRED ONLY

SHIPMENT：BEFORE DEC. 08. ，2010 FROM CHINA PORT TO SINGAPORE WITH PARTIAL SHIPMENT ALLOWED，TRANSSHIPMENT NOT ALLOWED

PAYMENT：BY IRREVOCABLE CREDIT AT 30 DAYS AFTER SIGHT (THE L/C MUST REACH THE SELLER 30 DAYS BEFORE THE TIME OF SHIPMENT)

PACKING：PACKED IN BALES OF 20 PCS EACH

MARKS & NOS. ：AT SELLER'S OPTION

INSURANCE：TO BE COVERED BY THE SELLERS AGAINST ALL RISKS AND WAR RISK，STRIKE RISK AS PER CIC

THE BUYER　　　　　　　　　　　THE SELLER

RAFFLES TRADING CO. , LTD.　　　CHANGZHOU YONGSHENG TEXTILES IMPORT & EXPORT CORP

常州永盛进出口公司 10 月 23 日接到对方开来的信用证。

BANK OF CHINA SINGAPORE　　　Singapore，Oct. 20，2010

IRREVOCABLE LETTER OF CREDIT　NO. 08475 For US $ 10 500. 00

To：CHANGZHOU YONGSHENG TEXTILES IMPORT & EXPORT CORP.

88，YANLING ROAD, CHANGZHOU,

JIANGSU，CHINA

We inform you that we have established our Irrevocable Letter of Credit in your favour，for account of RAFFLES TRADING CO.，LTD. 69 INTERNATIONAL TRADE PLAZA，ORCHARD ROAD ，SINGAPORE for a sum or sums not exceeding a total of US DOLLARS TEN THOUSAND AND FIVE HUNDRED and available by your drafts on us at 30 days after sight for 100% of the Invoice value，accompanied by the following documents.

(1) Signed Invoices in 3 fold indaicating S/C No.

(2) Packing List in 5 fold.

(3) Full set clean shipped on board Bills of Lading marked Freight Prepaid made out to order of shipper and endorsed in blank，notifying applicant.

(4) Insurance Policy in duplicate covering All Risks and War Risk，Strike Risk for 110% of invoice values as per CIC with claims payable in Singapore.

(5) Certificate of Origin issued by CCPIT.

Evidencing shipment of：

4 200 yards of Jeans to be packed in bales as per SC009 762 CIF SINGAPORE.

From China Port to Singapore not later than. Dec. 8，2010.

Partial shipments are allowed.

Transshipment is not allowed.

This Credit is valid for negotiation in China until Dec. 23，2010.

OTHER INSTRUCTIONS：

5% more or less in value and quantity acceptable.

Shipper must cable advise buyer shipment particulars within 24 hours after shipment，one copy of signed invoices and non-negotiable B/L to be airmailed to buyer after shipment.

All Drafts drawn under this credit must contain the clause "DRAWN UNDER BANK OF CHINA，SINGAPORE Credit No. 08475 dated Oct. 20，2010. " This credit is issued subject to Uniform Customs & Practice for Commercial Documentary Credits publication No. 600 (2007 Revision).

We hereby undertake to honor all drafts drawn in accordance with the terms of this credit. One complete set of documents is to be sent by airmail to us in one lot.

2. 训练任务

(1)完成出口合同下的备货任务(签订购货合同、缮制出口货物出境报检单及原产地证明书)；

1)购货合同资料：

合同号码：08CS96

合同供方：常州黑牡丹纺织有限公司

签约时间：2010 年 9 月 29 日

购销价格：每码 15 元

交货期：2010 年 11 月底以前

2）商检、产地证资料：

申请日期：2010 年 11 月 5 日；报验号：3508888878

商品名称编码：5209.4200

申请单位注册号：3508888637；证书号：35080076660

发票号：CS08-556；发票日期：2010 年 11 月 6 日；发票（FOB）总值：USD10 050.00

拟出运日期：2010 年 11 月 25 日；申请日期：2010 年 11 月 6 日

（2）完成信用证的审证、改证等必要工作；

（3）完成货物装运出口任务（填写提单、保险单、出口货物报关单、发装运通知等）；

1）运输、投保资料

货物 2010 年 11 月中旬备妥并办完商检、产地证手续；

11 月中下旬开往新加坡港的可选船舶为 COSCO 公司"HAPPY LIFE V.0688"；

船方确认货物开船日期为 2010 年 11 月 25 日。

2）报关资料

货物 2010 年 11 月 20 日办妥运输手续；报关单预录入及海关编号分别为编号
666456880、350100856；境内货源地为常州市区；出口收汇核销单为 20100666988。

3）装船资料

货物 11 月 25 日全部如数装船出口。

（4）制作出口结汇单据（汇票、发票、装箱单），办理出口结汇手续。

情境 4　进口合同的履行

任务 16
进口合同的履行

知识要点

1. 进口合同的结构和内容
2. 进口贸易合同的履行程序

技能要点

- 能够解决在进口合同履行中可能遇到的问题
- 能够熟练制作进口合同中所用到的各种单证

16.1　任务描述与分析

1. 任务描述

由于一笔出口服装业务的需要，常信公司需从日本老客户三永会社进口一批面料。孙大伟负责该批面料进口的全部工作。

2. 任务分析

根据 WTO 最新统计数据，2009 年中国已成为世界第二大进口国，成为日本、澳大利亚、巴西、南非的第一大出口市场。我国的进口平均关税总水平降至 9.8％，远低于发展中国家 46.6％的平均关税水平；与此同时，我国政府不断出台措施，简化进口程序。据相关机构的预测，我国的进口贸易还将快速发展，进口贸易在我国国际贸易中的地位不断加强，同时也给国家的持续发展带来了强劲的动力。

在进口贸易的整个流程中，涉及多个单位的协作。如进出口国家的银行、货运代理公司、保险公司、检验检疫机构、海关等。还要涉及如信用证申请、租船订舱委托书、投保单、检验检疫申请单、报关单等多种单证。作为进口贸易业务的实际操作人员，必须了解和掌握整个国际贸易进口的流程，把握进口的关键环节，正确填制各种进口相关单证，处理好进口贸易中可能发生的问题。

16.2　相关知识

16.2.1　进口合同的履行程序

按 FOB 条件和信用证付款方式成交的进口合同，其履行合同的一般程序包括开立信用证、租船订舱、接运货物、办理货运保险、审单付款、报关提货、验收和拨交货物、办理索赔等环节，如图 16-1 所示。

1. 开证

作为进口商，应在合同规定的开证时间办理信用证的开证。如合同规定在卖方确定交货期后开证，进口商应在接到卖方上述通知后开证；如合同规定在卖方领到出口许可证或支付履约保证金后开证，进口商应在收到对方已领到出口许可证的通知，或银行转知保证金已收后开证。

一般而言，进口商都在业务往来银行申请开立信用证，具体分为以下几个步骤。

（1）填写开证申请书

需要填写银行统一印制的开证申请书，这一步骤是整个开立信用证过程中最重要的环节，开证申请书是开证银行对外开立信用证的基础和依据。因此，在填写申请时，应与合同条款一致。例如，品质、规格、数量、价格、交货期、装货期、装运条件及装运单据等，应以合同为依据，并在信用证中一一做出规定。

（2）递交有关合同的副本及附件

进口商在向银行申请开立信用证时，应向银行递交有关的进口合同副本及附件，如进口许可证、进口配额证（需要进口许可证及配额时）、某些政府部门的批文等。

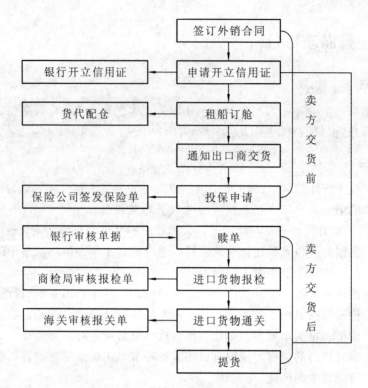

图 16-1   进口贸易业务操作流程(FOB＋L/C)

（3）交纳押金和开证手续费

按照国际惯例，进口商向银行申请开立信用证，应向银行交付一定比例的押金或其他担保金。押金一般为信用证金额的百分之几到百分之几十，根据进口商的资信情况而定。此外，银行为进口商开证时，开证申请人还需按规定支付一定比例的开证手续费。

（4）银行开立信用证

开证行在收到进口商的开证申请后，立即对开证申请书的内容及其与合同的关系、开证申请人的资信状况进行审核，在确信可以接受开证人的申请并收到开证申请人提交的押金及开证手续费后，即向信用证受益人开出信用证，并将信用证正本通过给受益人所在地的通知行将信用证传达给受益人。

2. 租船订舱

履行 FOB 交货条件下的进口合同，应由进口商负责派船到对方口岸接运货物。合同应规定出口商在交货前一定时间内，将预计装运日期通知进口商。进口商在接到上述通知后，应及时向运输公司办妥租船订舱手续，在规定的期限内将船名、船期及时通知出口商，以便出口商备货装船。同时，为了防止船货脱节和出现"船等货"的情况，注意催促对方按时装运。对数量大或重要物资的进口，如有必要，也可以请驻外机构就地了解、督促对方履约，或派人员前往出口地点检验监督。

3. 投保货运险

在 FOB 或 CFR 交货条件下的进口合同，保险由进口商办理。进口商在向保险公司办理进口运输货物保险时，有两种做法，一种是逐笔投保方式；另一种是预约保险方式。

逐笔投保是进口商在接到国外出口商发来的装船通知后，直接向保险公司提出投保申请，填写"起运通知书"，并送交保险公司。保险公司承保后，即在"起运通知书"上签章，进口商缴付保险费后，保险公司出具保险单，保险单随即生效。

预约保险方式是进口商与保险公司签订一个总的预约保险合同，按照预约保险合同的规定，所有预约保险合同项下的按 FOB 或 CFR 条件进口货物的保险，都由该保险公司承保。即每批进口货物，在收到国外装船通知后，即将船名、提单号、开船日期、商品名称等项内容通知保险公司，保险公司则对该批货物负自动承担保险责任。

例 16-1：我国某外贸公司进口成交一批价值为 CFR12 000 美元的货物。现按 CIF 价格加成 10％投保一切险和战争险，业务员应该怎么去办理保险手续？

解：查保费率表得到该货物的一切险和战争险费率分别为 0.5％和 0.04％，则总费率为：

$0.5\% + 0.04\% = 0.54\%$

将 CFR 价值转化为 CIF 价值，即

$CIF = 12\,000 \div (1 - 0.54\% \times 1.1) = 12\,072$（美元）

得出保险费为

$12\,072 \times 1.1 \times 0.54\% = 71.71$（美元）

4. 审单和付汇

出口商在货物装运后，将汇票与全套货运单据经国外银行寄交进口国的开证行。开证行收到国外寄来的汇票和单据后，根据"单证一致"和"单单一致"的原则，对照信用证的条款，核对单据的种类、份数和内容。

如果发现"单证不符"和"单单不符"的情况时，可以有以下处理方法：第一，由开证银行向国外银行提出异议，根据不同情况采取必要的处理办法；第二，由国外银行通知卖方更正单据；第三，由国外银行书面担保后付款；第四，拒付。

如果完全相符，即由开证行向国外付款，并通知进口商按当日外汇牌价付款赎单。进口公司付款后，获得运输单据，凭此提货。

5. 报检和报关

（1）进口货物报检

入境货物检验检疫的报检方式分为进境一般报检和进境流向报检两种。

进境一般报检指法定检验检疫入境货物的货主或其代理人，持有关证单向卸货口岸检验检疫机构申请取得《入境货物通关单》，并对货物进行检验检疫的报检。对进境一般报检业务而言，签发《入境货物通关单》和对货物的检验检疫都由口岸检验检疫机构完成。货主或其代理人在办理完通关手续后，应主动与检验检疫机构联系落实施检工作。

进境流向报检，也称口岸清关转异地进行检验检疫的报检，是指法定入境检验检疫货物的收货人或其代理人，持有关证单在卸货口岸向口岸检验检疫机构报检，获取《入境货物通关单》并通关后，由进境口岸检验检疫机构进行必要的检疫处理，货物调往目的地后再由目的地检验检疫机构进行检验检疫监管。申请进境流向报检货物的通关地与目的地属于不同辖区。

异地施检报检是指已在口岸完成进境流向报检，货物到达目的地后，该批货物的货主或其代理人，在规定的时间内向目的地检验检疫机构申请进行检验检疫的报检。异地施检报检时，应提供口岸检验检疫机构签发的《入境货物调离通知单》。

(2)进口货物报关

进口货物到货后,进口货物的收货人应当自运输工具申报进境之日起 14 日内向海关申报。由进口公司或委托货运代理公司或报关行根据进口单据填具"进口货物报关单"向海关申报,并随附发票、提单、装箱单、进口许可证及审批文件、进口合同、产地证和所需的其他证件。如属法定检验的进口商品,还需随附商品检验证书。

进口货物在办完向海关申报,接受查验、缴纳税款等手续以后,由海关在货运单据上签印放行。收货人或其代理人必须凭海关签印放行的货运单据才能提取进口货物。

6. 货物验收和拨交

进口货物运达港口卸货时,要进行卸货核对。如发现短缺,应及时填制"短卸报告"交由船方签认,并根据短缺情况向船方提出保留索赔权的书面声明。卸货时如发现残损,货物应存放于海关指定仓库,待保险公司会同商检局检验后再做出处理。

对于法定检验的进口货物,必须向卸货地或到达地的商检机构报检,未经检验的货物不准投产、销售和使用。如进口货物经商检局检验,发现有残损短缺,应凭商检局出具的证书对外索赔。

在办完上述手续后,进口公司把进口货物转交给最终用货单位。

7. 争议与索赔

在履行进口合同过程中,往往货到后发现品质、数量和包装等方面有问题,致使买方遭受损失,而需向有关方面提出索赔。进口索赔虽不是每笔交易一定发生,但一旦出现卖方违约或发生货运事故,应切实做好进口索赔工作。根据造成损失原因的不同,进口索赔也可分为向出口商索赔、向运输公司索赔、向保险公司索赔三种情况。

在进口业务中,办理对外索赔时,一般应注意以下事项:

第一,保留索赔证据。对外提出索赔需要提供的证件,首先,应制备索赔清单,随附商检局签发的检验证书、发票、装箱单、提单副本。其次,对不同的索赔对象还要另附有关证件。向运输公司索赔时,需另附由船长及港务局理货员签发的理货报告及船长签发的短卸或残损证明;向保险公司索赔时,需另附保险公司与买方的联合检验报告等。

第二,计算索赔金额。索赔金额,除受损商品的价格外,有关的费用也可以提出。如商品检验费、装卸费、银行手续费、仓租、利息等,都可以包括在索赔金额内。

第三,注意索赔期限。对外索赔必须在合同规定的索赔有效期限内提出,过期无效。如果商检工作可能需要更长的时间,可向对方要求延长索赔期限。

16.2.2　填写信用证申请书

进口商根据银行规定的统一开证申请格式填写信用证申请书,一式三份,其中一份交银行,另两份留公司的业务部门和财务部门。开证申请书是银行开立信用证的依据,必须按合同的具体规定,写明对信用证的各项要求,内容要明确、完整、无词义不清的记载。开证申请书主要包括两部分内容:

1)背面内容。背面内容是开证申请人对开证行的承诺,用以明确双方的责任。

2)正面内容。主要有下列一些内容:①开证行名称;②开证通知方式,要明确指示信用证采用全电、简电或信开方式;③申请日期;④信用证的有效期及地点;⑤通知行名址;⑥申请人名址;⑦受益人名址;⑧金额(大小写)和币别;⑨信用证类型,即明确信用证是即期付款、承兑、议付或延期付款；⑩受益人必须提供的单据种类、正副本份数、内容及要求等；⑪有关货物的简要描述；⑫必要的附加指示，如国外银行费用由谁负担、提交单据的期限、以第三者为发货人的运输单据可否接受等；⑬价格条件及原产国；⑭装运条款；⑮开证申请人签章。

16.3　任务实施与心得

 任务实施

2009 年 8 月 3 日，常信公司同日本老客户三永会社签署一份进口面料的合同，具体内容如下。

PURCHASE CONTRACT

The Sellers：SANYONG TRADE COMPANY　　　　　　　　Contract No.：SYC763/09N

Address：6-14，Fukahori-machi 3-chome，Nagasaki

TEL：0081-08054677434 FAX：0081-08054677435　　　　　　Date：Aug. 3，2009

The Buyers：CHANGZHOU CHANGXIN IMPORT & EXPORT CORP.

Address：NO. 25 MINGXIN ROAD，CHANGZHOU，JIANGSU，CHINA

TEL：0086-0519-86338171 FAX：0086-0519-86338176

This contract is made by and between the Buyers and the Sellers，whereby the Buyers agree to buy and the sellers agree to sell the under-mentioned commodity according to the terms and conditions stipulated below：

Ⅰ **COMMODITY AND SPECIFICATIONS**：

name of the commodities	Specifications	quantity	Unit price	Amount
Blended shell fabric	BRDXK09A38 Composition：80% poly + 20% rayon Weight：206g/m^2 Width：58/59” Density：40s/2 ＊150D / 104 ＊98	2 000M	FOB Osaka USD 2.5/M	USD5 000.00

Total Amout：Say U. S. Dollars Five Thousand Only.

Ⅱ **COUNTRY OF ORIGIN**：Japan

Ⅲ **PACKING**：100meters in one roll，with plastic bag

Ⅳ **TIME OF SHIPMENT**：No later than Sept. 30，2009，transshipment allowed，partial shipment not allowed

Ⅴ **PORT OF SHIPMENT**：Osaka

Ⅵ **PORT OF DESTINATION**：Shanghai，China

Ⅶ **INSURANCE**：To be covered by the buyer for 110% of invoice value covering all risks and war risks as per P. I. C. C.

Ⅷ PAYMENT：To be effected by irrevocable letter of credit available by draft(s) at sight for 100% of invoice value drawn by the Sellers

Ⅸ INSPECTION：Inspection result of CIQ at destination should be final

The Seller：	The Buyer：
SANYONG TRADE COMPANY	CHANGZHOU CHANGXIN IMPORT & EXPORT Co., Ltd.
中村恒介	孙大伟

（1）开立信用证

进口合同签订之后，业务员孙大伟就去常信公司的往来银行中国银行常州分行进行开立信用证的申请，并递交了与合同相关的副本和附件。目前，常信公司的账户上有充足的资金，银行业务员在审核了合同的相关副本之后，交给孙大伟一份《开证申请书》。

孙大伟根据合同中的品质、规格、数量、价格、交货期、装货期、装运条件及装运单据等条款，在信用证申请书中一一填写。

信用证申请书

Application for Issuing L/C

TO：①BANK OF CHINA，CHANGZHOU BRANCH   ③date：090810

⑦Beneficiary (full name and address) SANYONG TRADE COMPANY 6-14，FUKAHORI-MACHI 3-CHOME，NAGASAKI 　　　（also as notifying bank⑤）	L/C NO.：XYZSCC1223 Contract No.：SYC763/09N
	④Date and place of expiry of the credit OCTOBER 15TH AT THE BENEFICIARY'S COUNTRY

⑭ Partial shipments （　）allowed （×）not allowed	⑭ Transshipment （×）allowed （　）not allowed	②（　）Issue by airmail （　）With brief advice by teletransmission （　）Issue by express delivery （×）Issue by teletransmission（which shall be the operative instrument）

⑭ Loading on board / dispatch / taking in charge at / from Osaka	⑧Amount（both in figures and words） USD 5 000 SAY US DOLLARS FIVE THOUSAND ONLY

⑪Description of goods： Blended shell fabric BRDXK09A38 Composition：80%poly＋20%rayon Weight：206g/m² Width：58/59" Density：40s/2 ＊150D / 104 ＊98	⑨Credit available with （　）by sight payment（　）by acceptance（　）by negotiation（　）by deferred payment at （×）against the documents detailed herein and beneficiary's draft for 100 % of the invoice value at sight on BANK OF CHINA，CHANGZHOU BRANCH ⑬（×）FOB　（　）CFR　（　）CIF　（　）or other terms

⑩Documents required：(marked with ×)

• （×）Signed Commercial Invoice in 5 copies indicating invoice NO.，contract NO.

• （×）Full set of clean on board ocean Bills of Lading made out to order and blank endorsed，marked "freight（×）to collect /（　）prepaid（　）showing freight amount" notifying ACCOUNTEE.

续表

- （　）Air Waybills showing "freight （　）to collect / （　）prepaid （　）indicating freight amount" and consigned to _____ .
- （　）Memorandum issued by _____ consigned to _____ .
- （　）Insurance Policy / Certificate in copies for 110 % of the invoice value showing claims payable in China in currency of the draft, blank endorsed, covering （　）Ocean Marine Transportation / （　）Air Transportation / （　）Over Land Transportation）All Risks, War Risks.
- （×）Packing List / Weight Memo in 4 copies indicating quantity / gross and net weights of each package and packing conditions as called for by the L/C.
- （×）Certificate of Quantity / Weight in 2 copies issued an independent surveyor at the loading port, indicating the actual surveyed quantity / weight of shipped goods as well as the packing condition.
- （×）Certificate of Quality in 3 copies issued by （　）manufacturer / （×）public recognized surveyor / （　）
- （×）Beneficiary's certified copy of FAX dispatched to the accountees within 2 days after shipment advising （×）name of vessel / （×）date, quantity, weight and value of shipment.
- （　）Beneficiary's Certificate certifying that extra copies of the documents have been dispatched according to the contract terms.
- （　）Shipping Co's Certificate attesting that the carrying vessel is chartered or booked by accountee or their shipping agents:
- （×）Other documents, if any:
a) Certificate of Origin in 3 copies issued by authorized institution.
b) Certificate of Health in 3 copies issued by authorized institution.

⑫Additional instructions:

1. （×）All banking charges outside the opening bank are for beneficiary's account.
2. （×）Documents must be presented with 15 days after the date of issuance of the transport documents but within the validity of this credit.
3. （　）Third party as shipper is not acceptable. Short Form / Blank Back B/L is not acceptable.
4. （×）Both quantity and amount 10 % more or less are allowed.
5. （　）Prepaid freight drawn in excess of L/C amount is acceptable against presentation of original charges voucher issued by Shipping Co. / Air line / or it's agent.
6. （　）All documents to be forwarded in one cover, unless otherwise stated above.
7. （×）Other terms, if any:
a) Charter party B/L and third party documents are acceptable.
b) Shipment prior to L/C issuing date is acceptable.
Advising bank: Mitsubishi UFJ Trust and Banking 2-7-1, Marunouchi, Chiyoda-ku, Tokyo, Japan

⑮ Applicant: CHANGZHOU CHANGXIN IMPORT & EXPORT CORP.
NO. 25 MINGXIN RD,
CHANGZHOU JIANGSU, CHINA ⑥
TEL: 0519-86338171

中国银行在常信公司缴纳了相关担保金与开证手续费之后，即向三永会社开出信用证，并将信用证正本电传给三菱日联银行，然后由该行将信用证传达给受益人。

Letter of Credit

		BKCHCNJSA08E SESSION: 000 ISN: 000000
		BANK OF CHINA
		CHANGZHOU BRANCH
Issuing bank		NO. 5 DRAGON FLY BRIDGE
		WUJIN DISTRICT
		CHANGZHOU
		CHINA
Destination Bank		MITSUBISHI UFJ TRUST AND BANKING
		2-7-1, MARUNOUCHI, CHIYODA-KU,
		TOKYO, JAPAN
Type of Documentary Credit	40A	IRREVOCABLE
Letter of Credit Number	20	XYZSCC1223
Date of Issue	31G	081309
Date and Place of Expiry	31D	101509 JAPAN
Applicant Bank	51D	BANK OF CHINA CHANGZHOU BRANCH
Applicant	50	CHANGZHOU CHANGXIN IMPORT & EXPORT CORP.
Beneficiary		SANYONG TRADE COMPANY
		6-14, FUKAHORI-MACHI 3-CHOME, NAGASAKI
Currency Code, Amount	32B	USD 5 000
Available with…by…	41D	ANY BANK BY NEGOTIATION
Drafts at	42C	AT SIGHT
Drawee	42D	BANK OF CHINA CHANGZHOU BRANCH
Partial Shipments	43P	NOT ALLOWED
Transshipment	43T	ALLOWED
Shipping on Board/Dispatch/		
Packing in Charge at/ from	44A	OSAKA
Transportation to	44B	SHANGHAI PORT, P. R. CHINA
Latest Date of Shipment	44C	093109
Description of Goods or Services:	45A	Blended Shell fabric
		BRDXK09A38; Composition: 80% poly + 20% rayon; Weight: 206g/m^2; Width: 58/59"; Density: 40s/2 * 150D / 104 * 98
Documents Required	46A	

1. SIGNED COMMERCIAL INVOICE IN 5 COPIES.

2. FULL SET OF CLEAN ON BOARD OCEAN BILLS OF LADING MADE OUT TO ORDER AND BLANK ENDORSED, MARKED "FREIGHT TO COLLECT" NOTIFYING CHANGZHOU CHANGX-IN IMPORT & EXPORT CORP. TEL: 0519-86338171

3. PACKING LIST/WEIGHT MEMO IN 4 COPIES INDICATING QUANTITY/GROSS AND NET WEIGHTS OF EACH PACKAGE AND PACKING CONDITIONS AS CALLED FOR BY THE L/C.

4. CERTIFICATE OF QUALITY IN 3 COPIES ISSUED BY PUBLIC RECOGNIZED SURVEYOR.

5. BENEFICIARY'S CERTIFIED COPY OF FAX DISPATCHED TO THE ACCOUNTEE WITHIN 2 DAYS AFTER SHIPMENT ADVISING NAME OF VESSEL, DATE, QUANTITY, WEIGHT, VAL-UE OF SHIPMENT, L/C NUMBER AND CONTRACT NUMBER.

续表

6. CERTIFICATE OF ORIGIN IN 3 COPIES ISSUED BY AUTHORIZED INSTITUTION.

ADDITIONAL INSTRUCTIONS　　47A

1. CHARTER PARTY B/L AND THIRD PARTY DOCUMENTS ARE ACCEPTABLE.

2. SHIPMENT PRIOR TO L/C ISSUING DATE IS ACCEPTABLE.

Charges　　71B

ALL BANKING CHARGES OUTSIDE THE OPENNING BANK ARE FOR BENEFICIARY'S AC-COUNT.

Period for Presentation　　48

DOCUMENTS MUST BE PRESENTED WITHIN 15 DAYS AFTER THE DATE OF ISSUANCE OF THE TRANSPORT DOCUMENTS BUT WITHIN THE VALIDITY OF THE CREDIT.

Confirmation Instructions　　49　　WITHOUT

Instructions to the Paying/Accepting/Negotiating Bank　　78

1. ALL DOCUMENTS TO BE FORWARDED IN ONE COVER, UNLESS OTHERWISE STATED A-BOVE.

2. DISCREPANT DOCUMENT FEE OF USD 50.00 OR EQUAL CURRENCY WILL BE DEDUCTED FROM DRAWING IF DOCUMENTS WITH DISCREPANCIES ARE ACCEPTED.

（2）派船接运货物

在办妥银行开证申请手续后，孙大伟随即联系上海凯捷货运代理有限公司，并填写了订舱委托书，委托该公司办理进口货物的运输。

进出口货物订舱委托书

公司编号：DL09071226		日期：2009 年 8 月 19 日	
发货人：日本三永会社 SANYONG TRADE COMPANY 6-14, FUKAHORI-MACHI 3-CHOME, NAGA-SAKI	信用证号码：XYZSCC1223		
	开证银行：中国银行常州分行武进区飞龙路支行		
	合同号码：SYC763/09N	成交金额：USD5 000	
	装运口岸：大阪	目的港：上海	
收货人：常州常信外贸有限公司 鸣新路 25 号 电话：0519-86338171	转船运输： 可以	分批装运： 否	
	信用证有效期： 2009 年 10 月 15 日	装船期限： 9 月	
	运费：	成交条件：FOB	
	公司联系人：李华	电话/传真：86632734	
通知人： 常州常信外贸有限公司，鸣新路 25 号	公司开户行： 中国银行常州分行	银行账号： 02000010090 186675678	
	特别要求：		

续表

标 记	货号规格	包装件数	毛重	数量	单价	总价
	BRDXK09A38	20ROLLS	412KG 2 000m	USD 2.5/M	USD5 000	

上海凯捷货运代理有限公司在收到托运单后，审核托运单，确定装运船船舶后，安排运输。我公司随后通知日本三永会社预期装船的港口、船名和时间：即 9 月 3 日大阪港口，VICTORIA.0608 号货轮。9 月 1 日，日本三永会社向我方发来了货物已备妥通知。双方再次核准了装船时间、港口和地点等。

（3）投保货运险

9 月 15 日，孙大伟收到了日本三永会社的已装船通知单（传真）。告知该批货物已经于当日装载至 VICTORIA.0608，预计开航日期为 2009 年 9 月 16 日。其装船通知如下：

Shipping Advice

OSAKA，SEPT. 15th，2009

Messr，

Dear Sirs，

L/C No. XYZSCC1223

Under the captioned Credit and Cover Note(or Open Policy)，Please insure the goods as detailed in our Invoice No. IN/SANY/09108 Enclosed，other particulars being given below：

Carry Vessel's Name：VICTORIA.0608

Shipment Date：on or about Sep. 16th，2009

Covering Risks（as arranged）

Kindly forward directly to the insured your Insurance Acknowledgment.

SANYONG TRADE COMPANY

据此通知，孙大伟立即向中国人民保险公司发出了一份《国际运输预约保险起运通知书》。

国际运输预约保险起运通知书

被保险人：常州常信外贸有限公司   编号：SK030412

唛头	包装及数量	保险货物项目	价格条件	货价（原币）
N/M	20rolls Plastic bag	Blended shell fabric	FOB OSAKA	USD 5 000

合同号：SYC763/09N	发票号：CXC090811		提单号：KKLUAA0166832	
运输方式：海洋运输	运输工具名称：VICTORIA.0608		运费：to collect	
开航日期：2009 年 9 月 16 日	运输路线：自 大阪 至 上海			
投保险别：一切险	费率：0.35%	保险金额：USD5 500		保险费：USD19.25
中国人民保险公司 2009 年 9 月 15 日	常州常信外贸有限公司 被保险人签章 2009 年 9 月 15 日		备注	

本通知书填写一式五份送保险公司。保险公司签章后退回被保险人一份。

（4）审单和付汇

汇票及全套单据于 2009 年 9 月 19 日顺利传递至中国银行常州分行。根据银行的通知，孙大伟当日便去审核单据。审核的单据包括：商业发票、海运提单、品质证书、装箱单、原产地证书。经审核完全无误，我方予以付款。

（5）报检和报关

9 月 20 日货物顺利到达上海港口。接到通知后，孙大伟立即向上海出入境检验检疫局提出检验申请，填写了报检单，随后向上海海关提交了报关单。海关工作人员依法查验后，对货物征收了进口关税。具体税款的计算如下：

已知海运费用为人民币 2 040 元，保险费用为人民币 131 元。转化为 CIF 价为 RMB（5 000×6.8＋2 040＋131），即海关完税价格为人民币 36 171 元。经查询混纺布料的 H.S. 编码为 6114900011，进口关税为 15%。则常信公司应该缴纳的进口关税＝（5 000×6.8＋2 040＋131）×15%＝5 425.65（元）。

各种手续办好之后，上海海关即在货运单据上签印放行。

中华人民共和国出入境检验检疫
入境货物报检单

报检单位（加盖公章）：常州常信外贸有限公司　　　　　　　　编号 CX061008
报检单位登记号：3100600018　　联系人：张三　电话：0519-86338170　报检日期：2009 年 9 月 20 日

发货人	（中文）日本三永会社　（外文）SANYONG TRADE COMPANY　6-14, FUKAHORI-MACHI 3-CHOME, NAGASAKI				
收货人	（中文）常州常信外贸有限公司　（外文）CHANGZHOU CHANGXIN IMPORT & EXPORT CORP.　NO. 25 MINGXIN RD, CHANGZHOU JIANGSU, CHINA				
货物名称（中/外文）	H. S. 编码	产地	数/重量	货物总值	包装种类及数量
混纺布料 Blended shell fabric	6114900011	日本	2 000m	USD5 000	20 rolls
运输工具名称号码	VICTORIA . 0608	贸易方式	一般贸易	货物存放地点	上海
合同号	SYC763/09N	信用证号	XYZSCC1223	用途	
到货日期	2009 年 9 月 20 日				
起运地	大阪				
集装箱规格、数量及号码					

续表

合同、信用证订立的检验检疫条款或特殊要求	标记及号码	随附单据(划"√"或补填)
	N/M	合同、发票、海运提单、品质证书、装箱单

需要证单名称(划"√"或补填)		检验检疫费	
品质证书 √	植物检疫证书	总金额(人民币/元)	
重量证书 √	卫生证书	计费人 王强	
兽医卫生证书	健康证书	收费人	
动物卫生证书			

报检人郑重声明: 1. 本人被授权报检。 2. 上列填写内容正确属实,货物无伪造或冒用他人的厂名、标志、认证标志,并承担货物质量责任。 签名:孙大伟	领取证单	
	日期	
	签名	

中华人民共和国进口货物报关单

预录入编号:459785468-8   海关编号:459785468-8

进口口岸 吴淞海关(22/02)		备案号	进口日期 2009/09/20	申报日期 2009/09/20
经营单位 常州常信外贸有限公司 320495 *****		运输方式 江海运输	运输工具名称 维多利亚 0608	提运单号 KKLUAA0166832
收货单位 金山服装厂		贸易方式 一般贸易(0110)	征免性质 一般征税	征税比例
许可证号		起运国(地区) 日本	装货港 大阪	境内目的地 常州其他
批准文号	成交方式 FOB	运费 142/2 040/3	保费 142/131/3	杂费
合同协议号 SYC763/09N	件数 20	包装种类 卷	毛重(千克) 412	净重(千克) 399
集装箱号	随附单据	发票、装箱单	用途:	
标记唛码及备注				

项号	商品编号	商品名称、规格型号	数量及单位	最终目的国(地区)	单价	总价	币制	征免
1	BRDXK09A3	Blended shell fabric	20 rolls	日本	2.5/M	5 000	USD	照章

续表

税费征收情况		
录入员 录入单位	兹证明以上申报无讹 并承担法律责任	海关审单批注及放行日期(签章)
报关员		审单　　　　审价
单位地址	申报单位(签章)	征税　　　　统计
	常州常信外贸有限公司	
邮编　　　电话	填制日期 2009/09/20	查验　　　　放行

(6)货物验收和拨交

海关放行后,孙大伟会同相关人员一起查验货物,发现一切正常,于是将货物发至金山服装厂。

任务实施心得

在做完这一份进口合同之后,孙大伟对国际贸易的操作又有了不少新的体会和认识。这一份 FOB 贸易合同的履行程序一般包括:开证、租船订舱、装运、办理保险、审单付款、接货报关、检验、拨交和索赔。在实际操作中要特别注意以下环节:

1)开证。开证内容必须与合同内容一致,做到完备、明确、具体。

2)做好催交、租船订舱、派船工作。进口商可采用预约保险或逐笔保险方式办理保险。

3)进口商应在规定时间内对银行转来的单据认真审核。

4)进口商或其代理人在货到目的港后须按海关规定的办法报关纳税,并由进口商向中国商检局申请商品检验。

5)发现质量、重量和包装等方面有问题,进口商应在分清责任的基础上,及时向有关方提出索赔。

此外,在履行凭信用证付款的 FOB 进口合同时,上述各项基本环节是不可缺少的,但是在履行凭其他付款方式和其他贸易术语成交的进口合同时,则其工作环节有别。例如,在采用汇付或托收的情况下,就不存在买方开证的工作环节;在履行 CFR 进口合同时,买方则不负责租船订舱,此项工作由卖方办理;在履行 CIF 进口合同时,买方不仅不承担货物从装运港到目的港的运输任务,而且不负责办理货运投保手续。此项工作由卖方按约定条件代为办理。这就表明,履行进口合同的环节和工作内容,与出口合同履行一样,也主要取决于合同的类别及其所采取的支付条件。

16.4 知识拓展

进口采用 FOB 贸易术语比较有利

在 CIF 术语下,运输由出口方来安排。运输公司给进口方提供的服务可能较差,但收费可能较高。出口方也可以通过运输公司了解到最终买家的身份,从而绕过进口方直接与最终买家合作。

在 FOB 术语下,运输公司由进口方指定,拥有了直接磋商的机会,从而降低了货物的运输成本。进口方可以通过运输公司来核实出口商提供的信息，并及时了解货物的动态，拥有了完全的掌控权，可以避免出口方的欺骗行为。在国际运输中，经常出现的倒签提单就是 CIF 条款的产物。如果是 FOB，那么进口方自己指定的运输商不大可能去配合卖方倒签提单来欺骗进口方。

16.5　业务技能训练

16.5.1　课堂训练

1. 采用 FOB 贸易术语进口时，对于买卖双方来说存在着船货衔接的问题。请问可以通过什么样的途径加以解决？

2. 如果南京一外贸公司准备进口一批美国大豆，请陈述进口的流程。

3. 案例分析题

甲方按 FOB 条件向乙方购买一批大宗商品，双方约定的装运期限为 2010 年 5 月，后因买方租船困难，接运货物的船舶不能按时到港接运货物，出现较长时期的货等船情况。卖方便以此为由撤销合同，并要求赔偿损失。你认为卖方的做法是否合理？为什么？

16.5.2　实训操作

1. 请根据信用证预审单的相关信息，为上海新联纺织品股份有限公司拟写一封信函，对其中标出的 3 个问题进行修改。

开证行	BANK OF NAGOYA LTD.	开证日期			Oct. 6th, 2003					
申请人	THE GENRRU TRADING CO. LTD.	受益人			SHANGHAI NEW UNION TEXTILES IMP&.EXP. CORP. PUDONG COMPANY 3409 NEW DENG ROAD SHANGHAI CHINA					
信用证金额	①USD172 006 （应为 USD172 066）	信用证号			NLC031059					
汇票付款人	开证行	汇票期限			②见票后 60 天（应为即期）					
可否转船	可以	可否分批装运			可以					
装运期限	Dec. 15th, 2003	有效期	Dec. 30th, 2003		到期地点		③KOBE			
唛头	未指定	交单日			提单日后 3 天					

单据名称	提单	发票	装箱单	重量单	保险单	产地证	FORM A	寄单证明	寄单邮据	寄样证明	寄单邮据	寄样证明
银行	3/3	3	3		2	2		3				3

提单或承运单据	抬头	To order		一切险加战争险			
	通知	applicant	保险	加成 10%	赔款地点	目的港	
	注意事项	注明运费已付					
备注							

2. 请根据常州天信外贸有限公司和 JAMES BROWN&SONS 的贸易函电，拟定一份

进口合同。

June. 20，2010

Dear Sirs，

Thanks for your acceptance of Jan. 18th. And hereby we are pleased to send you our sales confirmation No. 04DRA207 for your signing.

Portable Mixer Pm-23	US＄23 FOB Toronto /Set	100Sets	US＄2 300. 00
Vacuum Cleaner Vc-18	US＄47 FOB Toronto /Set	100Sets	US＄4 700. 00

Terms：As usual

We hope that the goods will be shipped by Aug. 30th. And we ensure L/C will reach you not later than July 1.

Yours Faithfully，
(Signature)

Buyer：

CHANGZHOU TIANXIN IMPORT & EXPORT CORP.

Room 2601，Changzhou International Trade Center

801 Yan Ling Road(w)，Changzhou，Jiangsu 213001

Seller：

JAMES BROWN&SONS.

♯304-310 JaJa Street，Toronto，Canada

综合训练四

1. 业务背景

2010 年 10 月，常州永盛进出口公司与澳大利亚一家公司磋商，准备进口牛肉罐头。双方进行了多次谈判，并于 11 月 8 日签订了进口合同，合同如下。请以公司业务员身份，完成该合同下的各项履约任务。

PURCHASE CONFIRMATION

NO. ：08CY56

DATE：NOV. 08，2010

THE BUYER：CHANGZHOU YONGSHENG IMPORT & EXPORT CORP.

88，YANLING ROAD，CHANGZHOU，

JIANGSU，CHINA

THE SELLER：BMV TRADING CORP.

75 ROUTE 96570 ADELAIDE，AUSTRALIA

FAX ：0061-418-62345668 TEL：0061-418-62345688

BUYER'S ORDER NO. ：FE021G

THIS PURCHASE CONFIRMATION IS HEREBY MUTUALLY CONFIRMED，

TERMS AND CONDITIONS ARE AS FOLLOWS：

NAME OF GOODS AND SPECIFICATIONS	QTY	UNIT PRICE	AMOUNT
Canned Beef			CFR SHANGHAI
ITEM NO. SL100	1 000CTNS	USD20. 00/ CTN	USD20 000. 00
ITEM NO. SG120	2 000CTNS	USD15. 00/ CTN	USD30 000. 00
ITEM NO. SF200	3 000CTNS	USD30. 00/ CTN	USD90 000. 00
TOTAL	6 000CTNS		USD140 000. 00
SAY DOLLARS ONE HUNDRED AND FORTY THOUSAND ONLY			

PACKING：ONE DOZEN CANNED IN ONE CARTON

SHIPMENT：FROM ADELAIDE TO SHANGHAI NOT LATER TNAN DEC. 20, 2010.

PARTIAL SHIPMENTS AND TRANSHIPMENT TO BE ALLOWED.

PAYMENT：L/C AVAILABLE BY DRAFTS AT SIGHT FOR 100% OF INVOICE VALUE.

INSURANCE：TO BE EFFECTED BY THE BUYER.

SELLER ： BUYER：

SHEMSY NEGOCE ID CORP. CHANGZHOU YONGSHENG IMPORT & EXPORT CORP.

2. 训练任务

(1)根据买卖合同要求，到中国银行常州分行填写信用证开证申请书，申请开立信用证。

(2)12 月 16 日接到客户装船通知，请向中国人民保险公司办理货物进口投保手续(有预约保险协议)；制作保险单(投保一切险，保险费率为 1%)。

DEAR SIRS,

WE ARE PLEASED TO ADVISE YOU OF THE SHIPPING DETAILS AS FOLLOWS：

L/C NO：0809021198

CONTRACT NO. ：08CY56

INVOICE NO. ：HSC990723/1

COMMODITY：Canned Beef

B/L NO. ：SKLU805007

NAME OF VESSEL：FOREVERV. 86W

DATE OF SHIPMENT：DEC. 14，2010

FROM ：FROM ADELAIDE TO SHANGHAI

NET-WEIGHT：22. 50MTS

GROSS-WEIGHT：24. 00MTS

SHIPPING MARK：08CY56

SHANGHAI CHINA

VALUE OF SHIPMENT：USD140 000.00 CFR SHANGHAI

WE HEREBY CERTIFY THAT THE ABOVE CONTENT IS TRUE AND COR-RECT.

BEST WISHES

YOURS FAITHFULLY

×××××××××

（3）填写报检单，向检验检疫局办理货物进口报检手续。

（4）填写报关单，向上海海关办理货物进口通关手续。

情境 5　业务善后

任务 17

业务争议的处理

知识要点

1. 各国关于违约责任的规定及争议解决方式
2. 不可抗力的含义、构成要件及处理
3. 仲裁的特点，仲裁条款的内容

技能要点

- 能根据实际情况，选择合适的争议解决方式
- 能正确处理合同履行中遭受的不可抗力

17.1 任务描述与分析

1. 任务描述

常信公司第一次出口到法国公司(GOLDEN MOUNTAIN TRADING CO.，LTD)的服装，双方合作良好，法国公司很满意，接着下了第二笔订单，数量金额都和第一次的一样，交货期为 2010 年 10 月 30 日。

为及时履行合同，孙大伟通知工厂于 10 月 26 日把货物运送、存放于上海港码头的一个仓库里。10 月 28 日凌晨 2 点，该仓库因雷击起火；起火后，仓库管理员及时组织扑火，但终因火势过大，货物全部被烧毁。由于该批货物是为 GOLDEN MOUNTAIN TRADING CO.，LTD 特别定制，如果重新生产，至少在 11 月下旬才能生产完毕。事发后，孙大伟把常信公司遭遇不可抗力一事及时通知 GOLDEN MOUNTAIN TRADING CO.，LTD 和 Paul，并随后寄去了常州贸促会出具的相关证明。但 Paul 认为常信公司不能够按时交货，就构成违约，要求常信公司按照合同支付违约金；而常信公司坚持认为属于不可抗力，双方协商未果。

GOLDEN MOUNTAIN TRADING CO.，LTD 根据合同中的仲裁条款向中国国际经济贸易仲裁委员会上海分会提出仲裁申请，要求常信公司赔偿损失。

常信公司与 GOLDEN MOUNTAIN TRADING CO.，LTD 合同的违约金、不可抗力和仲裁条款如下：

除本合同列举的不可抗力原因外，卖方不能按时交货，在卖方同意由付款银行在议付货款中扣除违约金或由买方于支付货款时直接扣除违约金的条件下，买方应同意延期交货。违约金率按每 7 天收取延期交货部分总值的 0.5% 收取，不足 7 天者以 7 天计算。但违约金不得超过延期交货部分总金额的 5%。如卖方延期交货超过合同规定期限 10 周时，买方有权撤销合同，但卖方仍应不延迟地按上述规定向买方支付违约金。

因人力不可抗拒事故使卖方不能在本售货合约规定期限内交货或不能交货，卖方不负责任，但是卖方必须立即以电报通知买方。如果买方提出要求，卖方应以挂号函向买方提供由中国国际贸易促进委员会或有关机构出具的证明，证明事故的存在。买方不能领到进口许可证，不能被认为属人力不可抗拒范围。

仲裁：凡因执行本合约或有关本合约所发生的一切争执，双方应以友好的方式协商解决；如果协商不能解决，应提交中国国际经济贸易仲裁委员会，根据该会的仲裁规则进行仲裁。仲裁裁决是终局的，对双方都有约束力。

2. 任务分析

在实际的进出口贸易中，发生争议、索赔的事例是很多的。我们必须严肃对待和认真处理。要处理好这项工作必须熟悉国际惯例和国际法律，注意调查研究，弄清事实，合理解决，做到有理、有利、有节。在解决国际贸易纠纷时，最好能在尽可能短的时间内、以尽可能少的费用解决纠纷，且尽量不要伤害彼此的感情。仲裁是国际贸易使用最多的一种争议解决方式。

在市场情况发生变化，进出口商人觉得履约对他们不利时，往往寻找各种借口拒不履约或拖延履约，甚至弄虚作假或提出无理要求，不可抗力就是其中一个常见的借口。判断是否构成不可抗力，主要是看事件是否符合不可抗力的 3 个构成条件。

17.2 相关知识

17.2.1 争议与索赔

1. 争议

争议是指交易的一方认为另一方未能部分或全部履行合同规定的义务而引起的业务纠纷。在国际贸易中，这种纠纷屡见不鲜，究其原因，主要有以下几个方面：

1)卖方不交货，或未按合同规定的时间、品质、数量、包装条款交货，或单证不符等，或者是买方违约造成的。

2)合同条款的规定欠明确，买卖双方所属国家的法律或其对国际贸易惯例的解释不一致，甚至对合同是否成立有不同的看法。

3)在履行合同过程中遇到了买卖双方不能预见或无法控制的情况，如某种不可抗力，双方对其有不一致的解释等。

2. 违约责任

买卖合同是对缔约双方均具有约束力的法律文件。任何一方违反了合同规定，都应承担违约的法律后果，受损方有权提出损害赔偿要求。但是，各国法律及国际公约对于违约方的违约行为、由此产生的法律后果及处理有不同的规定和解释。

(1)《联合国国际货物销售合同公约》的法律规定

与英国、美国法律不同，《联合国国际货物销售合同公约》根据违约的后果及其严重性进行判断，将违约分为根本性违约和非根本性违约。

根本性违约是指由违约方的故意行为造成的违约，比如卖方完全不交货，买方无理拒收货物或拒付货款，其结果给受损方造成实质损害。如果一方当事人根本违约，另一方当事人可以宣告合同无效，并可要求损害赔偿。

非根本性违约是指违约的状况尚未达到根本违反合同的程度，受损方只能要求损害赔偿，而不能宣告合同无效。

(2)我国的法律规定

我国《合同法》规定，一方当事人违反合同规定，以致另一方订立合同时所期待的经济利益受到影响，另一方当事人有权要求解除合同。同时也规定，合同的变更、解除或终止并不影响当事人要求赔偿损失的权利。可见，我国《合同法》的规定与《联合国国际货物销售合同公约》基本一致。

3. 索赔

索赔是指在合同的履行过程中，受损方向违约方提出赔偿的要求。理赔是违约方对受损方所提出的赔偿要求予以受理并进行处理的行为。涉及国际货物买卖的索赔一般有三种情况。

(1)买卖索赔

它是以买卖合同为基础的，当一方当事人违反买卖合同规定时，受损方可依据买卖合同规定和违约事实提出索赔。属于卖方违约的，主要表现为交货的时间、品质、数量、包装等不符合合同的规定；属于买方违约的，主要表现为不按时接货、付款、办理租船订舱等。

（2）运输索赔

它是以运输合同为基础的。如收货人持有清洁提单而收到的货物却发生了残损短缺，这与发货人无关，收货人只能凭运输合同向承运人索赔。

（3）保险索赔

它是以保险合同为基础的，当发生保险合同承保范围内的风险并由此造成损失时，被保险人可向保险公司索赔。例如，按 CIP 条件成交的货物，在运输途中遭遇暴雨致水浸损坏，由于投保了水渍险，买方可凭保险合同向保险公司索赔。

索赔时，依照索赔情形、对象不同索赔的依据也有所不同。向贸易对方索赔，销售合同为主要依据；向承运人索赔须提供运输合同或提单；向保险公司索赔，保险单据为主要凭证，而检验证书则是任何索赔均必须出具的。

索赔条款示例

订立索赔条款通常有两种方式：

（1）索赔条款

该条款针对卖方交货品质、数量或包装不符合合同规定而订立。

例：买方对于装运货物的任何异议，必须于装运货物的船只到达提单所指定的目的港的 30 天内提出，并须提供经卖方同意的公证机构出具的检验报告。如果货物已经过加工，买方即丧失索赔的权利。

（2）违约金条款

违约金是指合同当事人一方未履行合同义务而向对方支付约定的金额。只要一方违反合同，不管其违约行为有没有给对方造成损失，都必须向对方支付违约金。违约金条款一般适用于卖方延期交货，或者买方延迟开立信用证和延期接运货物等情况。

通常因为卖方没有按照合同发货而由买方向卖方提出索要违约金。

例：除本合同第_____条所列举的不可抗力原因外，卖方不能按时交货，在卖方同意由付款银行在议付货款中扣除罚金或由买方于支付货款时直接扣除罚金的条件下，买方应同意延期交货。罚金率按每 7 天收取延期交货部分总值的 0.5%，不足 7 天者以 7 天计算。但罚金不得超过延期交货部分总金额的 5%。如卖方延期交货超过合同规定期限 10 周时，买方有权撤销合同，但卖方仍应不延迟地按上述规定向买方支付罚金。

注意：英美法系国家的法律，只承认损害赔偿，不承认带有惩罚性的违约金。所以在与英、美、澳、新等国贸易时，应注意约定的违约金额的合法性。违约金条款常用于大宗商品或成套设备的合同中。

17. 2. 2　不可抗力

不可抗力又称人力不可抗拒，是指合同签订后，不是由于当事人一方的过失或故意，发生了当事人在订立合同时所不能预见，对其发生和后果不能避免并且不能克服的事件，以致不能履行合同或不能如期履行合同。遭受不可抗力事件的一方，可以据此免除履行合同的责任或推迟履行合同，对方无权要求赔偿。因此，不可抗力是一项免责条款。

1. 不可抗力的特点

不可抗力是一项免责条款，所以区分商业风险和不可抗力事故显得非常重要。根据国际贸易惯例的解释：货价的变动、运价的变动、汇率的变动等不属于不可抗力，是正常的商业风险。构成不可抗力一般应当具备以下条件：

1)事件必须发生在合同签订以后。

2)事件不是因为合同当事人自身的过失或故意导致。

3)事件是合同当事人不能控制、不能预见、无法避免的。

2. 不可抗力的范围

不可抗力通常包括两种情况：一种是自然原因引起的，如水灾、旱灾、暴风雪、地震等；另一种是社会原因引起的，如战争、罢工、政府禁令等。但不可抗力事件目前在国际上并无统一的明确的解释，可由买卖双方在合同的不可抗力条款中约定。

3. 不可抗力事件的处理方式

发生不可抗力事件后，应按约定的处理原则和办法及时进行处理。不可抗力的后果有两种：一是解除合同；二是延期履行合同或部分履行合同。

究竟如何处理，应视事件的原因、性质、规模及其对履行合同所产生的实际影响程度，由买卖双方磋商而定。

4. 不可抗力的通知

不可抗力事件发生后，如影响合同履行，发生事件的一方当事人应按约定的通知期限和通知方式，将不可抗力事件情况如实通知对方，一般先用电报通知对方，并在 15 天内以航空信提供事故的详尽情况和影响合同履行的程度的证明文件。对方在接到通知后，应及时答复，如有异议也应及时提出。

值得注意的是，有关不可抗力的通知，必须确保对方能够收到；否则，遭受不可抗力的一方，必须对另一方"未收到通知而造成的损害"而非"因遭受不可抗力而造成的损害"负赔偿责任。

5. 不可抗力事件的证明

在国际贸易中，当一方援引不可抗力条款要求免责时，必须向对方提交有关机构出具的证明文件，作为发生不可抗力的证明。在国外，一般由当地的商会或合法的公证机构出具。在我国，由中国国际贸易促进委员会(CCPIT)或其设在口岸的贸促分会出具。

不可抗力条款示例

我国进出口合同中的不可抗力条款，通常有下列 3 种规定办法。

(1)概括式规定

概括式规定指在合同中不具体规定不可抗力事件的范围，只作概括的规定。这类规定方法由于对不可抗力范围定得过于笼统，一旦发生问题，容易引起贸易纠纷，难以作为解决问题的依据，一般很少采用。

例：如果由于不可抗力的原因导致卖方不能履行合同规定的义务时，卖方不负责任。但卖方应立即通知买方，并须向买方提交证明发生此类事件的有效证明书。

(2)列举式规定

列举式规定指在合同中明确规定不可抗力事件的范围，凡在合同中没有明确规定的，均不能作为不可抗力事件加以援引。

　　例：如果由于战争、洪水、火灾、地震、雪灾、暴风等原因致使卖方不能按时履行义务时，卖方可以推迟这些义务的履行时间，或者撤销部分或全部合同。

　　(3)综合式规定

　　综合式规定指采用概括和列举综合并用的方式。这种方法既明确，又有一定的灵活性，在我国进出口贸易业务中，多采用此种表示方法。

　　例：如因战争、洪水、火灾或其他人力不可控制的原因，买卖双方不能在规定的时间内履行合同，如此种行为或原因在合同有效期后继续 3 个月，则本合同的未交货部分即视为取消，买卖双方的任何一方，不负任何责任。

17.2.3　仲裁

　　在国际贸易实践中，对于争议和索赔的处理，通常采用友好协商、调解、仲裁或诉讼的方式来解决。与友好协商和诉讼相比，仲裁是最被广泛采用的解决国际经济争议的一种方式。

　　仲裁是指买卖双方在争议发生之前或发生之后，签订书面协议，自愿将争议提交双方所同意的第三者予以裁决，而这个裁决是终局性的，对双方都有约束力，双方都必须遵照执行。

　　1. 仲裁的特点

　　1)仲裁是双方自愿的。仲裁气氛缓和，当事人双方感情上有回旋余地。

　　2)仲裁的立案时间快，费用较低。

　　3)仲裁时当事人双方可以选择仲裁员。

　　4)仲裁裁决一般是终局裁决，对双方都有约束力。

　　2. 仲裁协议

　　一般来说，仲裁协议主要有以下两种形式：

　　1)仲裁条款是双方当事人在争议发生之前订立的，通常作为合同中的一项条款出现，表示自愿把将来可能发生的争议交付仲裁机构解决的书面文件。

　　2)提交的仲裁协议是双方当事人在争议发生以后订立的，表示自愿把已经发生的争议提交仲裁解决的协议。

　　这两种形式的仲裁协议虽然在形式上有所区别，但其法律效力却是相同的。按照大多数国家的法律规定，仲裁协议的作用主要有以下三个方面：

　　1)约束双方当事人只能以仲裁方式解决其争议，且不得向法院起诉。

　　2)排除法院对有关案件的管辖权。

　　3)仲裁机构取得争议案件管辖权的依据。

　　3. 仲裁条款的内容

　　仲裁条款的规定，应当明确合理，不能过于简单，其具体内容一般应包括仲裁地点、仲裁机构、仲裁规则、仲裁裁决的效力、仲裁费的负担等。

　　仲裁条款示例

　　凡因执行本合约或有关本合约所发生的一切争执，双方应以友好方式协商解决；如果协商不能解决，应提交中国国际经济贸易仲裁委员会，根据该会的仲裁规则进行仲裁。仲裁裁决是终局性的，对双方都有约束力。

17.3　任务实施与心得

 任务实施

(1)提出仲裁申请

GOLDEN MOUNTAIN TRADING CO.，LTD 认为此次不能够及时交货的原因是雷击起火，不属于不可抗力，于是将所发生的争议根据合同的仲裁条款向中国国际经济贸易仲裁委员会上海分会提出仲裁申请。

(2)组织仲裁庭

根据我国仲裁规则的规定，常信公司和 GOLDEN MOUNTAIN TRADING CO.，LTD 各自在仲裁委员会仲裁员名册中指定一名仲裁员，并由仲裁委员会主席指定一名仲裁员为首仲裁员，共同组成仲裁庭审理该争议案件。

(3)作出裁决

仲裁庭作出裁决如下：

火灾发生在合同订立后，满足"不能预见"、"不能避免"、"不能克服"三项条件，且当事人均无过错，因此，火灾构成不可抗力。

火灾发生后，常信公司及时通知对方，并提供当地贸易促进委员会的证明，且因货物全部烧毁，故常信公司有权延期履行合同或终止履行合同。常信公司不需要向 GOLDEN MOUNTAIN TRADING CO.，LTD 进行赔偿。

任务实施心得

(1)合同要明确规定双方应承担的义务、违约的责任

许多合同只规定双方交易的主要条款，却忽略了双方各自应尽的责任和义务，特别是违约应承担的责任。合同文字如果含糊不清，模棱两可，在执行过程中，往往争议纷纷，扯皮不断，甚至遗祸无穷。

(2)援引不可抗力条款和处理不可抗力事件应注意的事项

当不可抗力事件发生后，合同当事人在援引不可抗力条款和处理不可抗力事件时，应注意如下事项：

1)发生事故的一方当事人应按约定期限和方式将事件情况通知对方，对方也应及时答复。

2)双方当事人都要认真分析事件的性质，看其是否属于不可抗力事件的范围。

3)发生事件的一方当事人应出具有效的证明文件，以作为发生事件的证据。

4)双方当事人应就不可抗力的后果，按约定的处理原则和办法进行协商处理。处理时，应弄清情况，体现实事求是的精神。

17.4　知识拓展

索赔期限

索赔方向违约方逾期索赔，违约方可不予受理。索赔期限的规定要根据商品性质以及

检验所需时间等因素确定。

　　实际业务中的习惯做法是：一般货物的索赔期限为货到目的港后 30～45 天；食品、农产品等易腐烂变质商品的索赔期限可以再短些；机器设备的索赔期限分数量和品质作不同的规定，数量方面的索赔期限一般为货到目的港后 60 天，品质方面的索赔期限一般为 1 年或 1 年以上，并通常规定其为质量保证期。

　　《联合国国际货物销售合同公约》第 39 条规定："无论如何，如果买方不在实际收到货物之日起两年内将货物不符合同情形通知卖方，他就丧失声称货物不符合同的权利，除非这一时限与合同规定的保证期限不符。"

17.5　业务技能训练

17.5.1　课堂训练

1. 合同中的哪些变更构成实质性变更？
2. 不可抗力的构成要件是什么？不可抗力可能有哪些后果？
3. 简述仲裁条款的作用和仲裁裁决的效力。

17.5.2　实训操作

　　1. 常州天信外贸有限公司男衬衫出口后，收到加拿大客户 JAMES BROWN&SONS 的来信，声称有 200 件男衬衫的衣袖存在色差，要求天信外贸公司赔偿 1 万美元。请你用 E-mail 回复，妥善处理此事。

　　2. 江苏天地木业有限公司收到现代公司的传真，称有两个型号的地板质量有问题，要求降价 20%。请你回复传真，提出处理意见。

　　3. 每位学生就自己公司和客户洽谈的商品出口产品，订立合同的索赔条款、不可抗力条款和仲裁条款。

综合训练五

　　1. 业务背景

　　常州永盛进出口公司于 2010 年 12 月 8 日收到出口货款，2011 年 1 月，公司收到客户 RAFFLES TRADING CO.，LTD. 寄来 SGS 新加坡公司的检验报告，证明我方所交货物数量短少 300YARDS。

　　2. 训练任务

　　(1)出口退税计算

　　常州永盛进出口公司收到货款后办理核销，请你描述出口收汇核销手续的流程以及所需要递交的单据。然后去国税局退税(退税率 14%)，问：可得多少退税？

　　(2)写理赔函

　　公司接到对方索赔电函后，经查此次短少系我方工作疏忽所致。现在请写一封回函，提出两种解决办法：以空邮方式将短少数量补齐，或者把短少的金额电汇给客户，向客户保证今后将不再发生此事。

Workshop 1
Preparation for International Trade

Task 1

Getting Familiar with International Trade Policies and Measures

 Knowledge objectives: students are expected to know

- ◆ what is international trade
- ◆ types of policies on international trade
- ◆ tariff barriers and non-tariff barriers
- ◆ characteristics and developing trend of international trade

Skill objectives: students are expected to

- ◆ get updated with local policies and measures on foreign trade
- ◆ know the policies and measures of trading countries

1. 1   Task Description and Analysis

1. Task description

In July 2010, David Sun graduated from a higher vocational college in Nanjing and worked in CHANGZHOU CHANGXIN IMPORT & EXPORT CORP. (CCIEC) , which specializes in exporting textiles, garments, laminate flooring and electronic products since its establishment in 1985. He was assigned to work in the export department under the guidance of Chen Ming, a senior merchandiser. What he should do first is to get familiar with policies and measures on foreign trade and international trade environments.

CHANGZHOU CHANGXIN IMPORT & EXPORT CORP.

NO. 25 MINGXIN ROAD, CHANGZHOU, JIANGSU, CHINA

TEL: 0086-519-86338171

FAX: 0086-519-86338176

E-mail: czdavid@126. com

2. Task analysis

CCIEC imports timbers and exports garments, laminating flooring and electronic products, the commodities with competitive advantages.

International trade is conducted among different countries or regions; it involves international trade theories and policies, international trade laws and conventions, international settlements, international finance, international transportation and insurance etc. Thus, when taking up international trade, one should have a good command of relevant theories and skills about international trade.

International trade is greatly influenced by a country's macroeconomic policies. Therefore, it is a great necessity for trade persons to know foreign trade policies, measures of our country and of our trading partners, and to get familiar with related international conventions and regulations.

1. 2   Knowledge Highlight

1. 2. 1   Concepts of International Trade

1. International trade & foreign trade

International trade, also known as world trade, refers to the exchange of goods and services among countries or regions. Composed by each country's or each region's foreign trade, it is the total sum of foreign trade of different countries in the world.

Foreign Trade is the exchange of goods and services with other countries or regions from a certain country's point of view. Some island countries, such as Britain and Japan, also call it overseas trade.

2. Import trade & export trade

International trade is composed of import and export. To the countries of inputting goods or services, it is import; while to the countries of outputting, it is export.

If the transportation of export goods has to pass a third country before arriving in the destination country, this transaction is called transit trade.

A country has usually both import and export. In a certain period of time (suppose one year), if a country's export is more than its import, we call it net export; otherwise we call it net import.

3. Value of foreign trade & value of international trade

Value of foreign trade is the trade volume expressed in currency. In a certain period, the value of the goods imported from other countries is called total amount of imports; the value of the goods exported to the other countries is called total amount of exports. Total amount of imports and exports is the total value of the amount of imports and the amount of exports. This is an important index to reflect a country's scale of international trade. The statistics of each country's value of foreign trade issued by the UN is expressed in US dollars.

The total value of the world imports or the total value of the world exports is calculated by adding all the countries' value of imports or exports in the same currency. Since all the countries calculate their values of exports on the basis of FOB, and imports on CIF, the total value of the world exports is a little smaller than that of the world imports. In view of international trade, a nation's export is another nation's import. So if we take the sum of each nation's value of imports and exports as the total value of international trade, the number is calculated twice. Thus, total value of international trade is the total value of world exports only.

4. Visible trade & invisible trade

Visible trade involves the importing and exporting of tangible goods, whereas invisible trade involves the service exchange between countries.

In Standard International Trade Classification (SITC, REV3), the goods can be classified as follows:

00—Food and edible live animals

01—Beverages and tobacco

02—Crude materials, inedible, except fuels

03—Mineral fuels, lubricants and related materials

04—Animal and vegetable oils, fats and waxes

05—Allowed chemicals and related products

06—Manufactured goods classified chiefly by material

07—Machinery and transport equipment

08—Miscellaneous manufactured articles

09—Commodities and transactions not classified elsewhere in the SITC

The value of visible trade can be reflected in a country's customs statistics, while the invisible can not, but it can be shown in a country's Balance of Payments.

5. Trade surplus & trade deficit

Balance of Trade refers to the balance between the total value of export and import in a certain period of time such as one year, half a year, a season, a month, etc.

If the total value of exports equals to that of imports, it is called the balance of trade. When the total value of exports exceeds that of imports, it is called favorable balance of trade and expressed by positive numbers; on the contrary, it is called unfavorable balance of trade and expressed by negative numbers.

6. Direct trade, indirect trade & entrepot trade

Direct Trade refers to the trade directly conducted between the country in which the commodity is produced and the country in which it is consumed.

Indirect Trade refers to the trade indirectly conducted between the above mentioned two countries via a third country. To the commodity producing country, it is indirect export; to the commodity consuming country, it is indirect import; to the third country, it is entrepot trade.

7. Composition of international trade and direction of international trade

Composition of International Trade is the mixture of different categories of commodities or a certain commodity in a country's whole international trade in a certain time. It reflects the economic development, levels of industrial structure and scientific and technological development of a country or of the world.

Direction of International Trade, also called International Trade by Regions, reflects the position of different continents, different countries or regions in international trade. By observing and studying the direction of international trade of various periods, we can grasp the development and change of the world market, be aware of the close exchange relations among different countries and develop new markets. In 2009, the leading trade partners of China are EU, US and Japan.

8. Ratio of dependence on foreign trade

Foreign trade dependency ratio is the ratio of total foreign trade valve to GDP. It is an index to measure the degree of dependence on foreign trade of a nation's economy. The ratio of dependence on foreign trade is different from one country to another because each country has its own economic development level, foreign trade policy and domestic market scale.

1. 2. 2   Foreign Trade Policy

The purpose of foreign trade policy is to protect local market, to promote export, to improve industry structure, to accumulate capital and to maintain the home country's political and economic relations with other countries.

Foreign trade policies of different countries or of a country in different periods keep changing. With the development of world economy and international trade, free trade policy as well as protectionism is widely adopted.

1. Free trade policy

Free trade policy is adopted by many developed countries. Countries adopting this policy abandon barriers and restrictions as well as priorities and preferences on import and export of commodities, service trade and investments related to trade. It helps companies to compete freely in both domestic and foreign markets.

In recent years, with rapid development of global and regional economic integration, there are many new forms of regional trade agreements (RTA). Major countries and regional groups in the world rapidly develop free trade zones and there is a striving interest in free trade. To go with the stream, we focus on the construction of free trade zones and have achieved a great success.

2. Trade protectionism

Protectionist policy comes from the country who sets different barriers, applies different trade restrictions on import to protect the homemarket in order to avoid competitions from foreign commodities, services, technologies and investments, and provides preferences and subsidies for export.

1. 2. 3   Foreign Trade Measures

As we discussed in the previous section, trade protectionism is the use of government regulations to limit the import of goods and services. Advocates of trade protectionism believe it allows domestic producers to survive and grow, and creats more jobs. Most trade barriers, i. e. the trade protection hurdles, are designed to restrict imports. Two of the most important barriers are tariff and non-tariff ones.

1. Tariff

Tariff, also called duty, is imposed on imports or exports to increase the government revenues, to weaken the competitiveness of the imported goods.

Import duties are classified as most-favored nation's (MFN) duties and general duties. The rate of MFN duty is much lower than that of general duties.

Categorized by special and differential treatment, besides the usual import duties, there are import surtaxes, preferential duties, penalty duties, retaliatory duties and so on.

(1) Import surtaxes

Import surtax, is an extra tax on imports, in addition to ordinary customs duties as a temporary means of discouraging imports, usually applied by the government of a country that is in difficulties with its balance of payments. It has three forms: Countervailing Duty, Anti-dumping Duty, Variable Levy.

(2) Preferential duty

It is an import duty at a specially low rate on goods from a country that is being favored, usually because it is a member of a certain group of countries, but it doesn't apply to the importation from countries or regions without agreements.

Generalized System of Preference (GSP) is a tax preference offered by developed nations to the developing nations. Under this program, developed nations are to offer generalized, non-reciprocal, and non-discriminatory tariff preference for importing finished and semi-finished products from the developing nations.

2. Non-tariff barriers

In addition to tariffs, other methods are also adopted to restrict imports. They are called Non-tariff Barriers(NTBs). After the 2nd World War, many countries became members of GATT; the tariff levels of many countries have been lowered. Therefore, NTBs are more and more widely used. The major non-tariff barriers include:

(1)Import quota system

Import quota system is the most common form of non-tariff barriers. An import quota limits the cumulative quantity or amount of the import commodity during a given period of time. The quotas may be on a country basis or global without reference to countries. The goods with import quotas can be imported and the ones without quotas can't be imported, or be imported after paying extra tariffs, surtaxes or fines.

(2) Voluntary export quotas

The export quotas may be imposed unilaterally and can also be negotiated on a so-called voluntary basis. Obviously, exporting countries do not readily agree to limit their sales. Thus, the "voluntary label" general means that the importing country has threatened to impose even worse restriction if voluntary cooperation is not forthcoming.

(3) Import license system

This is a way to limit the quantity of the imports. The importing countries rule the certain kinds of goods being imported under import license. Without the required license, they cannot be accepted by the customs. The importing countries can directly control the kinds of commodities, quantity, origin, price and time of importing.

(4) Newtrade barriers

The new trade barriers are centered on the technical barriers, including all the newly appeared barriers which hamper the free trade such as the environmental barriers, green trade barriers and social barriers.

There are still some other non-tariff barriers such as foreign exchange control, customs valuation, state monopoly of import and export, discriminative government procurement policy, minimum price, embargoes, import deposit scheme, etc.

3. Export encouraging policies

Many countries adopt tariff and non-tariff measures to restrict the importation, and they also adopt measures to encourage exportation.

(1) Export credit

Export credit refers to loan, finance, or guarantee provided by a government or a financial institution enabling companies to export goods and services in situations where payment for them may be delayed or subject to risk, such as full set of equipment or vessels which are expensive and with a long transacting time period. It can be divided into Seller's Credit and Buyer's Credit.

(2) Export subsidy

Export subsidies are either cash allowances (direct subsidies) or financial preference (indirect subsidies), such as tax exemption, freight reduction, etc. granted by government to decrease the price of export goods, which makes the goods more competitive in foreign markets.

(3) Dumping

Dumping is defined as the act of a manufacturer in one country exporting a product to another country at a price which is either below the price it charges in its home market or is below its costs of production in order to penetrate foreign market.

Since these practices are naturally considered to be unfair competition by manufacturers in the country in which the goods are being dumped, the government of the foreign country will be asked to impose "anti-dumping" duties.

(4)Exchange dumping

Exchange dumping is a special measure for export enterprises to penetrate foreign markets when its domestic currency is depreciated. With the depreciation, the price of exports in foreign currency decreases, which makes the goods more competitive. On the other hand, the price of imports increases, which limits the importation.

(5) Other measures

Some countries establish administration bodies to help the import and export. Specific research organization is shaped to study and work out export strategy and commercial information website is established to strengthen information service. Trade centers are built; exhibitions are held and exporter appraisal activities are organized.

In the countries where foreign exchange control is imposed, measures such as foreign exchange retained (bonus) and export incentive system are adopted to promote exportation.

4. Export control

Export control is a multi-faceted body of laws and regulations governing the export of sensitive items, including equipment and technology used in research, which can affect a research institution in many different and unexpected ways.

1.3 Task Performance and Reflections

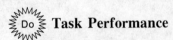 **Task Performance**

Knowing foreign trade policies and measures via websites

Being open-minded to and well-informed of what is going on in the economic world,

David Sun has formed a good habit of browsing government websites, caring policies and measures of different countries and searching latest related trade policies and measures.

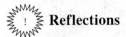 **Reflections**

Practice of International Trade is a course focusing on the exchange of goods and services among various countries; it is of vital importance to the people who intend to participate in foreign trade. The learners should learn the course through practice. Please pay attention to the followings:

1. To apply theory to practice, and to pay more attention to the international business conventions

Learning should be guided by the principal theories of international trade and our country's rules and policies in foreign trade; what has been learned should be put into practice to improve competency of analyzing and solving the practical problems.

It is necessary, with consideration of the realities in our country, to study the international business conventions and practice, such as the *INCOTERMS 2000*, *URC522* and *UCP600*.

2. To focus on case study and skill training

Practice of International Trade is an applied course with strong practicality. After learning each chapter, pay more attention to the case study and skill training after class and take every possible opportunity to conduct field observation to promote the learners' practical competency.

3. To learn a foreign language and to strengthen the application of the learned knowledge

To learn a foreign language well is of great importance to trade persons, since it is a tool for business communications, negotiations, writing and replying foreign trade correspondence and making foreign trade documents. If one's foreign language is not very good, it is very difficult for him to do his work well. Thus, it is necessary to learn a foreign language well.

1. 4   Knowledge Extension

1. Exchange earnings for export verification

It is a kind of supervision after the deal tracking from the export goods to the final payment by State Administration of Foreign Exchange (SAFE). The purpose of the system is to supervise the exporting companies to receive the payment of export in time.

In·practice, the exchange earnings for export verification should follow the next procedures.

a. Receipt Requisition

The exporter should obtain export receipt of SAFE verification form (the "Verification Form") before conducting export. On the spot, the enterprises fill in the verification form.

Export verification form filling should be done before declaration.

b. Declaration

The exporter should make the declaration of the customs within the specified time with the official seal of verification forms and related documents.

c. Customs returning the verification form

The customs returns the verification forms affixed with a security label, stamped customs, "Examined" of the export declaration.

d. Verification Exporters handle export receipt in SAFE with verification and "special joint export exchange verification" issued by bank. SAFE will audit related documents, and verification will be completed.

2. Export rebates

Export rebates refer to the measure of the refunding to exporters some or all of the domestic tax which has been collected. Export tax rebate is an international practice returning domestic exports tax to balance the tax burden of domestic products, to make their products enter the international market without tax, to compete with foreign products on equal terms, thereby to enhance their competitiveness and expand export.

In 1985, China introduced the export tax rebate policy; since then the policy has been adjusted for several times.

Under present tax regulations, tax refund in China is a kind of turnover tax either from value-added tax or consumption tax.

Tax refunding application should be accompanied by the following documents: declarations form, sales invoices, purchase invoices, receipt notice, product revenue show that export exchange has written off as well as other documents related to the export tax rebate.

Task 2

Knowing Procedures of International Trade

 Knowledge objectives: students are expected to know

- ◆ the basic international trade procedures
- ◆ the steps of business negotiation
- ◆ the constitution of offer and acceptance

Skill objectives: students are expected to know

- ◆ international trade procedures as well as the products and clients
- ◆ the writing of commercial correspondence

2. 1 Task Description and Analysis

1. Task description

A week later, David Sun got familiar with the foreign trade policies and measures in our country, particularly familiar with the alternation of tax refund rate of related products. And during this period of time, Mr. Chen taught David the business procedures of the last month's order of 8 000 pairs of trousers exported to Los Angeles, USA. At the same time, he also showed all the copied documents to David.

On July 10, Mr. Chen forwarded to David an E-mail from a French company on buying garments, requiring his independent fulfillment of the transaction, including getting in touch with the company, making an offer, etc. The following is the contacting information of the French company.

GOLDEN MOUNTAIN TRADING CO. , LTD

ROOM 1618 BUILDING G

NO. 36 THE FIRST LYON STREET,

PARIS, FRANCE

TEL: 0019-33-44-55   FAX: 0019-33-44-56

E-MAIL: paul@hotmail. com

2. Task analysis

For the people who want to engage in international trade, it is necessary to have a good knowledge of international trade procedure to guarantee the smooth conduction of international trade. Compared with domestic trade, international trade has its own features which are quite different from those of domestic trade in terms of procedure, trade terms, business practice and the laws concerned. Both exporters and importers should comply with the correct international trade procedure to get the expected profits. Any mistake in the procedure may lead to great losses.

International trade is in principle not different from domestic trade as the motivation and the behavior of parties involved in a trade do not change fundamentally regardless of whether trade is across a border or not. The main difference is that international trade is typically more costly than domestic trade.

2. 2 Knowledge Highlight

In the actual international trade, different deals, different terms of trade require different procedures. On the whole, whether it is an import or export trade, the principal procedures include the preparation before business negotiation, the business negotiation and the conclusion of a contract, and the performance of the contract. The following is the flowchart of international trade.

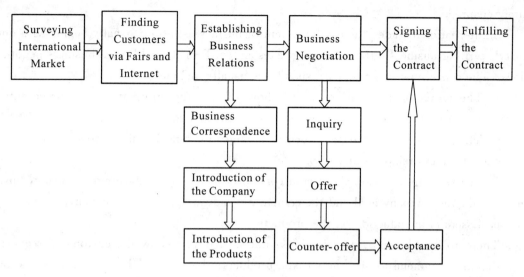

Figure 2-1   The Flowchart of International Trade

2. 2. 1   Preparations before Transactions

Making preparations before business transactions is the first step in the procedure of international trade; it is also the basis of the whole transactions. The preparations of business transactions includes the international market research, customer-hunting and establishment of business relations.

1. International market research

International market research aims to obtain various relevant information, to find out the features of international market by analyzing the above information, to judge the possibility of the transaction and finally to make suitable trade plans. The core part of international market research is the customer research.

Customer research refers to knowing the basic information about the foreign customers with whom you want to do business. The information usually includes the history of the company, his business scope, his capability of business operation, his credit status as well as the past and present situation of doing business with his worldwide (include China) customers. In practice, there are many cases of great losses occurred because the two parties do not know each other well. Therefore, it is necessary to know the financial standing and credit information of your foreign customers well before we do business with them.

2. Hunting for customers

Market positioning and hunting for prospective customers are what foreign trade enterprises do after the market research, which they obviously will do its utmost to do. There are many channels to hunt for possible customers, such as through a third person (party), via mass media and by participating in traditional trade fairs, etc.

3. Establishing business relations

Business relationship can be established only when the customers' credit status is definitely ensured.

In international trade, the establishment of business relations usually begins with one party's writing business letters, sending faxes and/or E-mails and formal business negotiations. The concerning business correspondence usually includes:

a. The source of information, that is how you get the information of your potential customers: from the internet or by recommendations and so on.

b. The purpose of your letter, such as hoping to extend business scope, to establish long-term business relations and so on.

c. Necessary information about your company, including the nature of company, business scope, the company goal and the comparative advantages of the company.

d. Essential introduction on the products

There are two kinds of introductions: one is that you know the customers' request, you should recommend to him the specific products; the other is that if you do not know the customers' detailed requirements, you can give a general introduction of your products (you'd better enclose a catalogue, a price list or samples for reference).

e. The ending of your letter, which should show your eagerness for your customers' quick response.

2.2.2　Business Negotiation

Oral negotiation and written negotiation are most commonly used in international trade. In the former case, traders talk about the terms and conditions of a transaction with each other in person or by telephone. As to the latter one, communications through letters, faxes, or E-mails are the usual means. In practice, letter-writing plays a major role and that is why a prosperous trader always has a great deal of correspondence to deal with.

Enquiry, offer, counter offer and acceptance are generally the four steps to reach an agreement in the international business negotiation, among which only offer and acceptance are the two required steps, and they are essential to make a contract.

1. Enquiry

An enquiry is usually made by a buyer, enquiring a seller about the terms of a sale. It can also be made by a seller, who may initiate the negotiation by making an enquiry to a foreign buyer, stating his intention of selling a certain kind of goods to the buyer.

The following is an example of a buyer's enquiry:

Want to buy middle-size T-shirt 1 500 dozen please offer the lowest price and the earliest delivery.

The following is an example of a seller's enquiry:

Can supply T-shirt 2 000 dozen.

Attention:

> Whoever makes an enquiry is not obliged to buy or sell, and the other party, at the same time, can make no reply at all. But, as is the general practice in international trade, the receiver of an enquiry will respond without delay with an offer, quotation, or bid, book, and order.

2. Offer

An offer, which is made from one individual or one firm to another, can be also called bid. It is a declaration that he or it is willing to sell or buy a certain amount of specified goods, at specified price, under specified terms. An offer becomes legally binding upon the parties involved upon its acceptance. The United Nations Convention on Contracts for the International *Sale of Goods* (CISG) stipulates "A proposal for concluding a contract addressed to one or more specific persons constitutes an offer if it is sufficiently definite and indicates the intention of the offeror to be bound in case of acceptance. "

The offerors can be both buyers and sellers. The offer made by a seller is called the selling offer, while the offer made by a buyer is called the buying offer.

(1) The requirements for an offer

CISG stipulates an offer must satisfy four requirements to make it legally effective:

a. The offeree must be specified.

b. Its contents must be definitely certain.

c. The offeror must show his intention to conclude a contract and abide by the contract.

d. The offer must reach the offeree.

(2) The validity of an offer

Any offer has a validity, which the offeror should abide by strictly. Usually the validity is clearly given in an offer. But sometimes, when an offer, whose price is fixed and its supply is sufficient, intends to sell goods the offeror might not state the validity in the offer. Under such cases, an offer expires within a reasonable period of time. There are three kinds of ways to stipulate the validity.

a. State clearly the deadline. For example:

Subject to march 20

Valid in 7 days

b. The validity is not exactly stated in the offer. However, this offer is not permanently effective, according to the provision 18th of CISG. The offeree should respond within a "reasonable time", otherwise the acceptance will be regarded as invalid. However, the explanation of "reasonable time" varies with nations. That's why this way is seldom used.

c. According to CISG, rerbal offers are only valid when the offeree accepts at their meeting nuless it has been otherwise agreed between the offeror and the offeree.

(3) The withdrawal and revocation of an offer

The offeror can withdraw his offer if the withdrawal has reached the offeree before or at the same time with the offer.

The continental laws stipulate that offers can not be revoked during the period of validity. In case it does not have a definite period of validity, it should not be revoked during a reasonable period of time.

British and American laws stipulate that in general an offeror can revoke his offer before it is accepted even though the offer would be good for a stated period and that period had not yet expired.

(4) The termination of an offer

An offer terminates under the following circumstances:

a. When counter-offered or rejected by the offeree; b. When revoked before acceptance; c. By non-acceptance within the time limit, by non-acceptance within a reasonable time if no time limit is specified; d. Some particular situations stipulated by laws. For example: The offeror become bankrupt or lost ability to fulfill the order; The offeror is deprived of managerial authority; The goods concerned is prohibited from exporting or importing or disappear, etc.

3. Counter-offer

A counter-offer is an offer made on the basis of the original one by the offeree to the offeror, showing offeree's willingness to accept some terms and change some terms. In fact, a counter-offer is a partial rejection of the original offer. It is a new offer, at the same time, the original offer lapses. Examples are as follows:

Your offer of Oct. 8 acceptable if payment by D/P.

We think your offer is too high, which is difficult for us to accept.

4. Acceptance

An acceptance is an assent to terms of an offer or a counter-offer. An acceptance means the formation of the contracted relationship of the two parties, who then can begin their business now even if they have not signed a written contract or a sales confirmation. For example:

We accepted "red star" gloves 2 000 dozen HK $ 3. 50 per dozen CIF LONDON shipment during July payment in sight irrevocable L/C.

(1) The requirements of an acceptance

An acceptance must meet four requirements:

a. It must be made by the person or firm to whom the offer has been delivered, that is, the acceptance must be made by the offeree.

b. An acceptance must be shown either by words or actions or in a written form.

c. An acceptance should be an unconditional assent to all the terms designated in the offer.

d. Acceptance must reach the offeror within the validity of the offer.

(2) The alternation of an acceptance

An acceptance means that all the terms and conditions of the offer are accepted. If it contains additional or different terms, that is, if it alternates the offer, this kind of acceptance is a kind of counter offer, not an acceptance in strict meaning.

(3) The withdrawal of an acceptance

An acceptance becomes effective when it has reached the offeror and a contract comes into effect. So an acceptance can be withdrawn only if the withdrawal reaches the offeror before or at the same time of the arrival of the acceptance.

(4) Late acceptance

A late acceptance is one which arrives at an offeror after the expiry of the validity. Generally a late acceptance is not valid. But Article 21 of CISG stipulates the following exceptions:

a. A late acceptance is nevertheless effective as an acceptance if, without delay, the offeror orally informs the offeree or dispatches a notice to that effect.

b. If a letter or other writing containing a late acceptance would have reached the offeror in due time, the late acceptance is effective as an acceptance unless, without delay, the offeror orally informs the offeree that he considers his offer as having elapsed or dispatches a notice to that effect.

Attention:

Whether the late acceptance is effective or not will be determined by the offeror. Thus, when the offeror receives a late acceptance, whether he accepts or refuses the acceptance, it is necessary to reply to the other party in time and in this way future disputes can be avoided.

2. 2. 3   The Formation and Performance of a Contract

After business negotiation, if both parties agree with each other on the terms of the contract, they both will draft and sign a written contract. A written contract endorsed by both parties of the deal constitutes the evidence of the formation of a contract, and a written contract forms the foundation upon which the parties concerned perform their contract. After signing the contract, both parties should perform the contract.

1. The performance of export contract

Having finished business negotiation and signed a contract, both the exporter and importer should take further steps to perform the contract. The performance of the contract refers to the process through which the exporter should be obliged to deliver the goods punctually and get back the payment in time. Nowadays a lot of export transactions are concluded under CIF and sight L/C terms. Six steps are usually involved in the performance of the contract, that is, preparing goods for shipment; examination and modification of the L/C; chartering or booking shipping space; customs formalities, insuring goods, and bank negotiation, etc.

2. The performance of import contract

The performance of import contract is the process during which the importer should pay for the goods and discharge the goods legally according to the contract. FOB terms as well as L/C are usually adopted in importing. Major steps include opening letter of credit, chartering the vessels, covering insurance, settling the payment, customs clearance, receiving the goods, etc.

2.3　Task Performance and Reflections

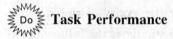 **Task Performance**

David Sun wrote a letter of establishing business relations with his potential customer and made a specific enquiry on his products.

Dear Sirs,

We learned from the Internet that you are one of the major exporters of TEXTILES AND GARMENTS in your country. We are writing to enter into business relations with you on the basis of mutual benefits and common interests.

Our corporation is a state-owned foreign trade organization, dealing in the import and export of TEXTILES AND GARMENTS. Our products are of fashionable design, comfortable feeling and high quality, which enjoy high reputation both in America and Asia.

As requested, enclosed is our latest catalogue. If you have special requirements, please inform us.

Looking forward to your prompt reply.

Yours faithfully,

David Sun

(signature)

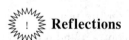 **Reflections**

Customers are of great importance to a person who engages in international trade, and to find customers always takes a lot of time. However, finding your prospective customers and establishing business relations with them are just the first step in international trade, business negotiation, including enquiry, offer, counter-offer and so on, is even tougher than that.

Offer, counter-offer and acceptance are based on cost accounting and the analysis of market trend. To an exporter, the procedures of performing business transactions are preparation of goods, shipment and customs formalities, delivery of the goods, and so on, among which the production cost and expenses constitute the major factors influencing the prices of the exporting goods. In actual offers, full consideration should be made on pricing due to its complication.

2. 4   Knowledge Extension

Modes of International Trade

1. Exclusive sales

Exclusive Sales is also called Exclusive Distribution, it is a situation in which only certain dealers are authorized to sell a specific product within a particular territory. The legality of an exclusive distribution agreement can vary depending on the specifics of the case.

The relationship between the exporter and the distributor is the same as the relationship between the buyer and the seller. The distributors buy goods from the principals on their own account and resell them to their customers in their territory. The remuneration is mainly from the margin between the prices at which he buys and the prices at which he sells.

2. Agency

Agency refers to a relationship between two parties, that is, the exporter and the agent. An agent is a middleman who acts on behalf of a principal in specific matters. At present there are different types of agents actively engaged in different international business domains, for example, forwarding agents in transportation, brokers in customs delaration, etc.

According to the rights that the principal has entitled to an agent, the agency can be divided into three kinds: general agency, exclusive agency and commission agency.

3. Consignment

Under consignment, the consignor sends the goods to a foreign consignee who will sell the goods for the consignor according to the agreed terms and conditions. The core of consignment is that goods exported on the consignment remain the property of the exporter. Therefore, consignment exports are not really exports because the exporter reserved the right of the goods until the importer sells the goods to final customers or third parties.

The consignee, who usually works for a commission, does not own the goods, although usually having the possession of them. Consignment is favorable to the consignee, and used only when the goods are difficult to sell.

4. Tender-inviting and tender-submitting

Tendering is widely used in international trade, especially in government construction projects and the purchase of goods in large quantities.

Tender-inviting means that the tenderee publicizes the announcement of invitation for tener through proper means to all prospective tenderers to bid at the designated time and place, and according to the prescribed procedures. In tender-inviting, trading terms about quality, quantity and delivery time and so on are listed specifically.

Tender-submitting refers to the tenderer, in accordance with the request of the tenderee, the bidding in the stated time and conditions.

5. Auction

Auction is a method of sales in which goods are sold in public to the highest bidder. Auctions are used for certain commodities, such as tea, bristles, wool, furs, antique furniture, works of art, etc., which must be sold as individual lot, rather than on the basis of a standard sample or grading procedure.

In most auctions the goods to be sold are available for viewing before the sale and the seller or the auction gallery would not be responsible for the quality of the auction goods. Of course, the higher the quality, the more expensive the auction would be. And usually it is the seller who sets an upset price on the article offered. Therefore, this mode of trade is highly appreciated by the seller.

6. Fairs and sales & processing trade

Fairs and Sales is a mode of international trade which means that the exporter displays and sells his goods by joining or holding exhibitions, fairs and expos, etc.

Processing Trade is a kind of processing the supplied materials and then re-export business. It integrates the processing and export expansion with the processing fees earning. At present, this trade covers three types: processing with supply materials, processing with imported materials and assembling with imported components.

Workshop 2
Contract Negotiation and Conclusion

Task 3

Conclusion of the Clauses on Subject Matter

 Knowledge objectives: students are expected to know

◆ how to qualify commodities

◆ the components of shipping marks

◆ the content of more or less clause

◆ how to calculate the weight of commodities

Skill objectives: students are expected to be able to

◆ use proper ways to express the quality of commodities

◆ calculate the quantity of the goods in one container

◆ make sure the proper quantity in more or less clause and use proper shipping marks

◆ conclude the clauses on the quality, quantity and packing of commodities

3. 1   Task Description and Analysis

1. Task description

CCIEC has established the business relations with Golden Mountain Trading Co. LTD, a French company, which is intended to purchase Chinese consumer goods, such as garments, toys, etc. , and would like to start the business by placing an initial order of garments.

CCIEC usually uses cartons for garment export. The method of packing is of two types: solid color and size and assorted color and size. It usually offers the price on the basis of the minimum order of the quantity fit for a 40ft container. Since it is the first time to do business with CCIEC, the French company has placed a trial order of the quantity fit for a 20ft container. If the sales go well, it will further increase orders.

David has entered into the negotiation with Pual, the French representative, and they have agreed to start a transaction of ladies coats. At present, the detailed discussion has been undergoing with regard to the name, quality and packing of the garments, the clauses of which are also in the process of preparation.

2. Task analysis

In international business transactions, the name, quality and quantity of commodities are the first conditions and physical foundations for both sellers and buyers. Without specific and concrete names, quality and quantity, the two parties have then no reference to negotiate and the transactions cannot be conducted.

As CISG prescribes, the delivered goods should be in accordance with the name, quality and quantity stipulated in the contracts. If the goods delivered by the seller are not in conformity with the agreed name and quality of the commodity, the buyer reserves the right to lodge a claim for repair, substitution, or compensation, to reject the goods or even to cancel the contract. The seller must deliver the goods which are of the quantity required by the contract. If the seller delivers a quantity of goods greater than that provided for in the contract, the buyer may take delivery or refuse to take delivery of the excess quantity. If the quantity delivered is found to be less than that called for in the contract, the seller should delivered the missed quantity on condition that the buyer should not bear the relevant inconvenience and/or unreasonable expense. Furthermore, the buyer has the right to reject the goods. If the goods delivered by the sellers do not conform to the agreed packing terms or are not in accordance with the usual practice, the buyers are entitled to reject the goods.

In contracts for the international sales of goods, the contents of the clause on quality varies from the different goods to the methods expressing quality of goods, and includes the names, specifications, grades, brands, standards, etc. The basic contents of the quantity clause consist of two parts—the quantity to be delivered and the measurement to be used. If the goods are measured by weight, the way of calculation should also be indicated.

If the goods are measured by the number, a clause of more or less should be added. The packing clause mainly includes packing materials, packing methods, packing specifications, packing marks, packing charges and the quantity or weight of the goods in each package.

3.2　Knowledge Highlight

3.2.1　Names of Commodities

Names of commodities should be specified clearly and concretely when the seller and the buyer negotiate and conclude the contract. The common names should be used to avoid future trouble.

1. Names of commodities & Harmonized System (HS)

The classifying principle, structure and names of commodities adopted in our country are in complete conformity with those in HS, which divides the commodities into 22 categories, 98 chapters. Therefore, it is very important for us to nominate our products by using the names which are in conformity with HS.

2. The contents of the name of commodity clause

The requirements and formats of the name of commodity clause are usually negotiated by sellers and buyers. The name of commodity is on most occasions listed below the title: Commodity Name, which is sometimes omitted, and replaced by a sentence indicating the seller and the buyer agreed to transact ×××commodity.

When the clause of the name of commodity is set, the following should be considered:

a. Be clear, specific and realistic. The name of commodity in the contract should be clear, specific and free from ambiguous expressions so as to avoid trouble in the execution of the contract. Exaggerated or unnecessary descriptions should not be used. The name of commodity stipulated in the contract must be in conformity with the goods that the seller is able to produce or supply and that the buyer requires.

b. Try to adopt a name of commodity which is widely accepted internationally. The name used should be categorized precisely in HS.

c. Select appropriate names of commodities to facilitate importing and reduce customs duties and freight charges.

In international trade, tariff rates and freight rates may be different for the same commodity with different names. Therefore, choosing an appropriate name as the name of commodity in the contract can be beneficial to both the exporter and the importer.

3.2.2　The Quality of Commodities

The quality of commodities is of great significance and it has the influence not only on positioning the price but also on promoting the goods and its reputation. Some countries even stipulate that the commodities, the quality of which is not in conformity with the prescriptions in their laws, are not allowed to import. To improve the quality of commodities so as to reach the requirements of the laws in different countries is one of the effective ways to expand export and break the trade barriers in foreign trade.

In international trade, the categories of commodities are diversified and the ways to stipulate the quality of commodities are also very varied. Generally speaking, there are two types.

1. Sale by sample

A sample is a small quantity of products, often taken out from a whole lot or specially designed and processed. It is usually given to encourage prospective customers to buy the product or set aside as the quality standard of the whole consignment. If the goods are sold by sample, the goods to be delivered must be in full conformity with the sample.

In international trade, sale by sample can be classified into three types from the perspective of the sample supplier: Sale by seller's sample, sale by buyer's sample and sale by counter sample.

Table 3-1   Sample Classification

	Seller's sample	Buyer's sample	Counter sample
Definition	Sample provided by the seller	Sample provided by the buyer	The seller duplicated the buyer's sample and then send the duplicate to the buyer for confirmation.
Sale by sample	Sale by seller's sample. Goods delivered are of the same quality as shown.	Sale by buyer's sample	In practical business transactions, the cautious seller is usually not willing to accept a sale by the buyer's sample, just to avoid the risks of compensation and reject of goods due to the inconformity between the delivered goods and the sample.
Stipulations in contract clause	In the contract for sale, it should be clearly stated: " Quality as per seller's sample".	In the contract for sale, it should be clearly stated: "Quality as per buyer's sample".	The seller's sample is used, instead of the buyer's sample, so as for the seller to have the initiative.
Requirements for delivered goods	The quality of the delivered goods should correspond with the provided sample.	The quality of the delivered goods by the seller should correspond with the buyer's sample.	The quality of the delivered goods should correspond with the counter sample.

In the case of sale by seller's sample, the seller should keep a duplicate sample or keep sample of the original sample or type sample so that they can be used as reference when the production is arranged, when the commodities are delivered or when the quality disputes arise. If necessary, the same coding numbers can be added in the original sample and the duplicate sample to indicate the concrete delivered date. The duplicate sample can serve as proof of quality if a dispute about the quality of goods occurs.

In the case of sale by buyer's sample, the seller should fully consider the practicability of raw materials supply, application of the processing technology and equipment, and production schedule to assure the implementation of the contract in future. In the meantime, attention should be paid to not infringing the third party's industry property right. Therefore, it should be made clear in the contract that if the infringement of the third party's property right arise, caused by the buyer's sample, the buyer bear the liability.

Attention:

Some samples are marked as being "sample for your reference only". They are then reference samples and are not binding upon the seller. They are for sales promotion and better understanding of each other. Under such circumstances, if there are no words indicating "goods delivered as per given sample" and no other means are used to express quality, it is not the sale by sample.

Samples usually represent the integrated quality of commodities, but some samples are only used to reflect a few respects of commodities, e. g. color sample, patter sample. As far as the other respects of commodities are concerned, they are usually expressed in words.

In case of sale by sample, the delivered goods should be in full conformity with the sample. Otherwise, the buyer has right to claim for compensation or even reject the goods. Therefore, sale by sample should not be the first consideration when more scientific methods can be used to show the quality. If the quality of commodities cannot be definitely described, flexible prescriptions should be made in contracts. For example, *Quality is nearly the same as the sample* can be used.

When the scientific ways are not suitable to describe the quality, or there are special requirements for color, fragrance, taste, or form, *sale by sample* is the first choice. This method is usually applicable to arts, garments, light industry products and native products.

2. Sale by description

In most cases, sale by description is the method to indicate the quality of the commodity. Sale by description may take the form of sale by specification, sale by grade, sale by standard, sale by trade mark or brand, sale by name of origin and sale by illustration.

Table 3-2　Classification of Goods Quality by Description

	Attended tips	Examples	Suitable commodities
Sale by specification	The main indices such as composition, content, purity, strenghth, size, etc. should be included in the contract. As for the same commodity, different usages may require different specifications.	Chinese Groundmut 2007 Crop, F. A. Q. Moisture (max.) 13% Admixture(max.) 5% Oil content (min.) 44%	Most commodities
Sale by grade	Some products can be divided into different grades based on different specifications, such as large, medium, small or Grade A, Grade B, Grade C….	Chinese Green Tea, Special Chunmee, Special Grade, Art No. 41022	Commodities that have clear classification, such as mineral products, etc.

Continued

	Attended tips	Examples	Suitable commodities
Sale by stand-ard	It is recommended that the international standards be used to enlarge the export. When the standard is used, it is important to mark the publication year of the standard to avoid the disputes.	GB 172323-1988 (compulsory national standard) GB/T 17392-1988 (recommended national standard) Rifampicin B. P. 1933	Commodities that have uniform standards
Sale by trade mark or brand name	It is necessary to stipulate the type or specification of the goods with the same brand or trade mark.	SONY Brand Color TV Set Model: KV-2553 TC	Commodities with renowned brands in international market
Sale by name of origin	The name of origin should represent the quality of the goods and enjoys good reputation.	Sichuan Preserved Vegetable	Commodities that possess the distinguished styles, features or local flavors, etc.
Sale by illustration	To protect the buyer's interest, in the contract, the clause of quality contains not only the name of commodity, the brand but also the instructions to illustrate the sturcture and functions of the product.	Qulaity and technical data to be strictly in conformity with the description submitted by the seller.	Machinery, instruments, apparatuses, equipments, transportation tools, Technology-intensive commodities

Under the circumstance of sale by grade, it is suggested that both the grades and the specification in each grade be clarified. For example, the exported tungsten ore by our country is classified into 3 grades in accordance with the contents of tin and tungsten trioxide.

Table 3-3   Standards for the Grades of the Exported Tungsten Ore

Grade	WO_3 (min.)(%)	Sn (max.) (%)	As(max.) (%)	S (max.) (%)
Special Grade	70	0. 2	0. 2	0. 8
Grade 1	65	0. 2	0. 2	0. 8
Grade 2	65	1. 5	0. 2	0. 8

In international trade, the quality of some special commodities cannot be described by words, and cannot also be represented by sample, such as jewels, calligraphies, paintings, artworks, etc. The buyer and the seller can only make the sale by inspection. In many cases, the buyer may be advised to arrange for inspection of the goods before or at the time they are handed over by the seller for carriage (pre-shipment inspection or PSI). The buyer or his/her agent inspects the goods one by one. If both sides have no dissatisfaction, the deal is then concluded. This practice is usually employed in consignments, auctions, exhibition sales, etc.

3. 2. 3   Unit of Measurement and System of Measurement and Weight

The unit of measurement and weight is compulsory to indicate the quantity of commodity. To know the measurement system and to be familiar with the special meanings of the units of measurement, and the ways of calculating the quantity are the fundamental skills for international traders.

1. Unit of measurement

The following table shows some common units of measurement used in international trade:

Table 3-4 Units of Measurement

Measurement	Common measurement units	Used for the goods	Examples
Weight	metric ton, long ton, short ton, kilogram, pound, ounce, carat, etc.	agricultural products, mineral products and some industrial finished products, etc.	grain, cotton, wool, mineral products, medicines, etc.
Number	piece, package, dozen, pair, set, unit, head, case, bale, barrel, drum, bag, et.	consumer goods, light industrial products, native produce & animal by-products, etc.	stationery, toys, garments, vehicles, live stocks, etc.
Length	meter, foot, yard, centimeter, etc.	textiles, rope, metal cord, cable, etc.	
Area	square meter, square foot, square yard, square centimeter, etc.	textiles, building materials, animal by-products, plastic products, etc.	plastic floor board, leather, etc.
Volume	cubic meter, cubic foot, cubic yard, cubic inch, etc.	timber, natural gas, chemical gases, etc.	
Capacity	liter, gallon, bushel, etc.	liquid products, agricultural produce, etc.	wheat, corn, petroleum, alcohol, bear, etc.

2. System of measurement and weight

In international trade, besides the differences in the units and the methods of measurement and weight, the systems adopted in different countries are also different. The following four systems are used in international trade.

a. Metric System: popular in the countries in East Europe, Latin America, South East Asia, and Africa.

b. British System: popular in Great Britain, New Zealand, and Australia.

c. U. S. System: popular in North America.

d. International System of Unit/SI: being adopted by more and more countries.

Under different systems, the same number with different unit implies the different quantity of commodity, as shown in Table 3-5. Therefore, it is quite necessary to know the different systems of measurement and weight because it relates with the usual practice of using units and regulations, etc. in the imported countries.

Table 3-5　Metric Ton, Long Ton, Short Ton

	Kilogram	Pound
SI —Metric Ton	1 000	2 204. 60
BS—Long Ton	1 016	2 240
U. S. S—Short Ton	907. 20	2 000

3. 2. 4　Calculation of Weight

In international trade, goods are most often measured in weight. The methods to measure the weight of goods are stated as follows.

1. Gross weight

Gross weight means the over-all weight of the commodity, including the tare, i. e. the package weight. It is suitable for the goods of low-value.

2. Net weight

Net weight of the goods refers to the weight of the commodity alone, the tare is not counted in.

As for some agricultural products or other products with low value, *gross for net* is used to calculate the weight. e. g. when rice, bean, etc. are weighed, the weight of the gunny bags are not excluded, that is, the gross weight is used as the basis to calculate the price and delivered weight.

Because this way of calculating the weight directly influences the price, the words *Gross for Net* should be added to both the quantity clause and the price clause. For example, Walnut, 100 Metric Ton, USD 300 per Metric Ton, gunny bag with single layer, gross for net.

3. Other methods of calculations

a. Conditioned weight

Conditioned weight means the weight derived from the process with which the moisture content of the commodity is removed and standardized moisture content added by scientific means. Conditioned weight is usually applicable to such goods as raw silk and wool, which are of high economic value and with unsteady moisture content.

The formula of calculating conditioned weight is given as follows:

$$\text{Conditioned weight} = \frac{\text{actual weight} \times (1 + \text{standard regaining rate of water})}{1 + \text{actual regaining rate of water}}$$

b. Theoretical weight

Commodities such as galvanized iron and steel plate have regular specifications and regular size. They are often subject to the use of theoretical weight. Their unit weight is the same and the theoretical weight is got by multiplying the unit weight with the total number of the goods.

c. Legal weight

Legal weight is the weight of the goods and the immediate packages of the goods.

Such kinds of goods include cans, small paper boxes, small bottles, etc. The weight excluding the package weight is the net weight. Both of these two methods are the basis of special duty imposed by Customs.

In international trade, it is the usual practice to measure the goods in net weight, when no specific method is stipulated to weigh and to price the goods.

3.2.5　Types of Packing

The types of packing of goods are various in international trade. In terms of the functions of packing in the process of circulation, packing can be divided into transport packing and sales packing.

1. Transport packing

Transport packing is also referred to as outer packing and is mainly used for protecting the goods and facilitating loading/unloading, stowage, transport and sorting & counting of the goods.

According to the method of packing, transport packing can be divided into unit outer packing and assemblage outer packing.

（1）Unit outer packing

Unit outer packing means single piece packing in the course of transportation as shown in Table 3-6.

Table 3-6　Unit Outer Packing

Types	Suitable goods	Packing method
case	cargoes that cannot be pressed, such as glassware, fruits, etc.	wooden case, crate, carton, corrugated carton, skeleton, etc.
drum, cask	liquid, powder, chemicals, paint, etc.	wooden cask, iron drums, barrel, hogshead, plastic cask, etc.
bag	cement, fertilizer, flour, oil cakes, animal feeding products, chemicals, etc.	paper bag, gunny sack, plastic bag, etc.
bundle, bale	cargoes that can be pressed, such as cotton, wool, sheepskins, carpet, packaging paper, etc.	cotton bale, jute bale, etc.

Moreover, demijohn, cylinder, basket, jar, tin, bottle, etc. are also used in unit packing.

（2）Assemblage outer packing

Assemblage outer packing means that unit goods are assembled or consolidated into large containers. Packing goods in such a way facilitates loading and unloading by mechanical handling. It also reduces the intensity of laboring, saves cost, lowers the risks of damage to the goods and promotes the modernization of transportation.

The commonly used assemblage packing is of three types: large metal containers, flexible containers and pallets.

2. Sales packing

The sales packing is used to promote the sales and goes directly into the retail market with the commodities. It is also called inner packing.

(1) The decorations and descriptions of sales packing

The decoration of the sales packing should highlight its feature of being commodity. Meanwhile, the import countries' customs, the hobbies and taboos of colors, pictures and numbers should also be attended.

The verbal descriptions, the sticking or hanging trade marks or bands should fit for the regulations of the import countries. e. g. Japanese government stipulates that besides the ingredients and usages of the imported medicines, their functions should also be described. Moreover, some countries stipulate that the verbal descriptions of the imported products should be in the native language or in several languages. Take Canada for example, the medicine imported should carry English and French explanations. The properness should be specially attended when foreign languages are used.

(2) Product code

A product code (bar code) is an encoded set of lines and spaces that can be scanned and interpreted into numbers to identify a product.

There are two main bar codes internationally. One is UPC (Universal Product Code— USA), the other is EAN (European Article Number).

3. 2. 6   Marking of Goods

Marks are the pictures, numbers and words printed or stenciled on transporting packing. The correct and complete marking of goods helps to prevent incorrect handling, incorrect delivery, losses of weight and volume and customs fines. Generally marks are classified into three categories: shipping marks, indicative marks and warning marks. Moreover, there are marks of weight, marks of origin, etc.

1. Shipping mark

Shipping marks are usually composed of numbers, alphabets, and simple words.

Shipping marks can also prevent the goods from being wrongly delivered or shipped. The ISO has recommended a type of standards shipping mark to all countries, which cover four parts as follows:

a. Abbreviations of consignee or buyer, e. g. ABCCO.

b. Reference number. It can be the number of sales confirmation, order, or letter of credit, e. g. SC9750.

c. Port of destination. The name of the final destination should not be abbreviated. If the several ports have the same name, the country name should be added. If transshipment is needed, the word "TRANSSHIPMENT" or the name of transferred place should be added. For example, London via Hong Kong.

d. Package number. The shipper should list in the shipping mark the total number of the whole lot of consignment and the number of the individual packages consecutively. For example: Nos. : 1/100, which means that the total number of the goods is 100 pkgs, the goods itself is the first package. If the total number is not decided, the expression can be "C/ Nos. : 1/Up". This can always be seen in the customers' orders or the correspondence.

The following is an example of a shipping mark:

ABC   CO.   ⟶ Name of consignee or buyer

SC9750   ⟶ Contract number

LONDON via HONG KONG   ⟶ Port of destination and transshipment

No. 1-100   ⟶ Package number

Sometimes, pictures such as triangles, diamonds and squares, inside which some numbers or alphabets are printed, are also used as shipping marks.

2. Indicative mark

Indicative marks are to remind the porters and the container-openers that improper handling might cause damage to the goods. They consist of simple and eye-catching figures and written languages. For exported commodities, English is used. The indicative marks are usually found on the exterior package during the transit.

3. Warning mark

Warning marks are also called dangerous cargo marks. They are used to remind the cargo handlers to take necessary safety measures. They are stenciled clearly on outer packages with warning phrases. They are usually composed of figures and written language. The following marks are usually found on the exterior packages of the goods.

Figure 3-1   Warning Marks

In our country, two sets of warning marks should be marked on the outer packages of dangerous cargoes, one set issued by our government and another issued by International Maritime Organization lest that unnecessary losses arise for the ship is not allowed to call at the destination port.

When dangerous cargoes are transported, warning marks should be printed or stenciled on the eye-catching part of the packages. Meanwhile, colors should be bright, firmly set, anti-falling, and anti-decoloring.

4. Weight, volume & origin marks

Weight such as gross weight, net weight and volume is usually marked on the transport packing to facilitate the arrangement of storing, loading and unloading as well as liner space.

The origin of the goods is the basis of Customs' statistics and duties and is indicated in the certificate of origin. We generally mark the origin on both the inner packing and the outer packing.

e. g.

GROSS WEIGHT   108kg
NET WEIGHT   103kg
MEASUREMENT   50cm×45cm×30cm
MADE IN CHINA

3. 3   Task Performance and Reflections

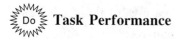 **Task Performance**

(1) David and Paul have had better understanding of each other after communication. The French company plans to import a certain number of ladies coats. David sent the sample (Ref. Num. - LJ 566) to Paul on August 15, 2010. On receipt of the sample, the French company inspected the quality and accepted the quality of the sample. Then both sides agreed to stipulate in the clause on quality:

LADIES COATS, woven, with bronze-colored buttons, 2 pockets at side, like orignial sample No. LJ566 sent on AUG. , 15, 2010.

(2) The volume of a 20ft container is 25m³ or so; the size of each carton is 50cm×40cm×80cm, the volume is about 0. 16 m³. By calculating, 25 m³/0. 16 m³ = 156 cartons; each carton can contain 8 pieces of garment; therefore, the total number of the garment for one container is 1 248pcs. To avoid mistakes, it is acceptable to draw a 5% more or less clause.

David reached the agreement with Paul on the quantity of the garment, and stipulated the quantity clause as follows:

QUANTITY: 1 248pcs, 5% more or less at seller's option.

(3) After discussion, both sides also agreed to adopt the packing: assorted color and size, 8 pieces per carton, 1 container of 20 feet for the initial delivery. The agreed packing clause is as follows:

8 pcs per carton, assorted color and size, per piece in polybag.

W×H×L: 50cm×40 cm×80 cm

SHIPPING MARK: FTC
                CZCX080180
                MARSEILLES
                NO. 1-UP

 **Reflections**

(1)Proper selection of the ways to express the quality of goods

Generally speaking, sale by specification, sale by grade, and sale by standard are proper to be employed for the goods whose quality can be represented by scientific indices; sale by brand or trade mark is for the goods with stable quality and features; sale by illustration is for the machinery with complicated structures and performance; and sale by sample is suitable for the goods that are hard to be specified or standardized.

Under the circumstance of sale by sample, the serial number of the sample and the date of post should be clearly stated. Sometimes, *The quality of the delivered goods is about equal to that of the sample.* should be added.

The methods to express the quality of goods rests on the features of the goods. Two or more than two methods should be avoided if one method is enough to express the quality just in order to simplify the production and delivery of the goods.

(2) Packing materials and packing methods

The packing materials and packing methods should be clearly stated in the clause. If the packing materials are supplied by the buyers, the time of provision should be made clear, and the buyer should bear the responsibility for the delayed delivery due to the late provision of the packing materials. Meanwhile, the fillings, paddings and strengthening materials should be also clearly stated.

Usually, there is no need to stipulate packing marks in the contract, as they are usually decided by the seller. But on condition that the buyer nominates it, it is necessary to stipulate the details of the shipping mark; and the final date that the buyer should inform the seller the shipping marks should be stipulated, or else the seller can make decision.

Packing charges are usually included in price. But if the buyer asks for special packing, we should make it clear as to who shall bear the additional charges. The time and methods of payment should also be stated. In exporting goods, the goods requiring technology-intensive packing in particular, the words *Packing Charges Included* should be added after the price clause so as to avoid the disputes.

(3) To clarify the systems of measurement and weight to avoid misunderstanding

In quantity clause, it is necessary to clarify what system of measurement and weight is adopted. If *Ton* is used, then *Long Ton* or *Short Ton* should be made clear. As for the screw threads of some mechanical products, it is compulsory to make clear whether British system or metric system is employed to avoid misunderstanding.

It is quite necessary to make certain the delivered quantity according to the loading capacity of transporting vehicles so as to save the cost. If containers are used, the delivered quantity should be similarly equal to the one fit for full container load to make full use of the load capacity. The LCL will add much to the cost.

In practice, it is sometimes hard to control strictly the quantity of some bulk cargoes like agricultural products, mineral products. Besides, owing to changes to supplies and limitation to processing conditions, the actual quantity may be somewhat more or less than the contracted quantity. Under such circumstances, more or less clause is usually stipulated in the contract so that the seller can fulfill the contract more smoothly. The more or less clause is a clause which stipulates that the quantity delivered can be more or less within certain extent (range). The most commonly used way is allowing some percentage more or less. Generally, it is from 3% to 5%. The proportion of the percentage usually lies in the party who is responsible for the chartering and booking the cargo space.

(4) Stipulations on approximate quantity in UCP600

Sometimes an approximate quantity clause is also used to indicate the tolerance of the actual quantity to be delivered. In such a clause, the words like "about", "circa" and "approximately" are used to define the quantity of goods. UCP 600, Article 30 provides that the words "about" or "approximately" used in connection with the amount, the quantity or the unit price to which they refer. A tolerance not to exceed 5% more or 5% less than the quantity of the goods is allowed, provided the credit does not state the quantity in terms of a stipulated number of packing units or individual items and the total amount of the drawings does not exceed the amount of the credit. However, it should be noted that different countries may interpret these words differently, i. e. these words represent a different amount of quantity allowance in different countries. Therefore, it is advisable not to use this method in international trade practice.

Examples for the Quality Clause of Other Commodities

1) Tea Cups Quality Same as Sample No. CT78 Airmailed on May 16

2) Multi-shuttle Box Loom Model 1515A, Detailed Specifications as per attached Descriptions and illustrations.

3) 9971 China Green Tea Special Chummed Grade 1 Art. No. 9307

4) Tetracycline HCL Tablets(sugar coated)250mg inconformity with B. P. 1980

5) White Rice, Long-Shaped

Broken Grains(max)25%

Admixture(max)0. 25%

Moisture(max)15%

Examples for the Quantity Clause of Other Commodities

1) Northeast Small Red Beans, 100 metric tons packed in single new gunny bags of about 100kg. each, gross for net.

2) 500m/t, with 5% more or less at seller's option.

3) Quantity: 1000M/T, the Sellers have the option to load 5% more or less than the quantity contracted if it is necessary, such excess or deficiency to be settled of contracted price.

4) Place a trial order for 1 000 dozen of fireworks and 500 cartons of mosquito coil incense.

Examples for the Packing Clause of Other Commodities

1)In wooden cases of 50 kilos net each.

2)Packing: In cartons containing 60 tins of 1000 tab. each.

3)Each piece in a polybag, half dozen in a box and 10 dozen in a wooden case.

4)In cartons, each containing 4 boxes about 9 pounds, each fruit waxed and wrapped with paper.

5)Each set packed in one export carton, each 810 cartons transported in one 40ft container.

3. 4　Knowledge Extension

1. Two methods to express the flexibility in quality clause

(1) Quality Latitude

Quality latitude means that the seller and buyer agree that the quality of the delivered goods can vary within an agreed range. Three ways commonly used are *Allowed Deviation*, *Maximum* & *Minimum*, *Flexible Range*. Quality latitude is mainly suitable for primary products and is used as the quality index of some industry products.

(2)Quality Tolerance

Quality tolerance is the internationally accepted deviation from a given standard of size, content, performance, purity, or some other measurable characteristics in the specifications of a product, that is, the tolerance within which the quality of the delivered goods from the seller can be higer or lower.

e. g. :

China Sesame seed　　Moisture (max.) 8%; Admixture(max.) 2%;

　　　　　　　　　　Oil Content (wet basis ethylether extract) 52% basis;

2. Neutral packing and packing with designated brand

(1)Neutral packing

Neutral packing is the one that makes no mention at all of the name of the country producing the goods and name of the manufacturer on the comodity and on the outer and inner packages. The purpose of using neutral packing is to break down high customs duties or get round quota and other barriers of the importing countries, thereby making it possible for the exporters to market their goods profitably.

(2)Packing with designated brand

Packing with designated brand means the brand and / or trade mark designated by the buyer are marked out on the product and / or package.

The usual practice in our country is as follows:

a. Only the brand and / or trade mark designated by the foreign merchants are put on the commodities, the country of origin and the name of exporting manufacturers are not indicated.

b. Both the foreign and native brands and / or trade marks are indicated on commodities.

c. While the brand and / or trade mark designated by the foreign buyers are put on the commodities, the words MADE IN CHINA are printed below.

Task 4

Conclusion of Price Clause

 Knowledge objectives: students are expected to know
- ◆ the definition, importance of trade terms
- ◆ the rights and liabilities of buyers and sellers under main trade terms

Skill objectives: students are expected to be able to
- ◆ choose the appropriate trade terms and understand the rights and liabilities of buyers and sellers
- ◆ convert prices between trade terms
- ◆ draw the price clause of export contracts

4.1　Task Description and Analysis

1. Task description

David Sun have obtained quotations from a few suppliers with whom he cooperated many a time. The purchasing cost of the ladies coats is RMB 160 per piece, including 17% value added tax; the export tax refund rate is 11%; the company's operate cost rate is 5%; and the expected profit rate is 10%.

Now David is going to negotiate the price with Paul and draw the price clause. At the moment the price of fabric is on the rise and the exchange rate of US dollar to RMB keeps going low.

2. Task analysis

The cargo price in international trade covers *Total Amount* and *Unit price*. The unit price is, with commission and discount included sometimes, usually composed of employed currencies, trade terms, measurement unit, and unit price figure.

As a core in international trade, the price is usually the focus of negotiation between buyers and sellers because it is directly related to both parties' profits.

In export, when negotiating and stipulating the price clause, companies should follow the prevailing price in international market and set the price for the goods with the combined consideration of its business intention and the various policies in different countries and regions. The currencies and trade terms should also be attended, and the methods of price setting should be illustrated. If necessary, price adjustment clause should be added. The commission and discount clause should be decided on specific conditions.

4.2　Knowledge Highlight

4.2.1　Introduction of Trade Terms

1. The role of trade terms

Trade terms, also known as price terms or delivery terms, are an important composition of cargo price. It refers to a simple expression or three English letters abbreviated from three English words to describe the place and manner for the transference of the goods from the seller to the buyer. These trade terms may also define a variety of other matters, including the price, the time when the risk of loss shifts from the seller to the buyer, and the costs of freight and insurance.

The use of trade terms in quotations helps clarify the composition of the price, the respective liabilities, costs and risks to be undertaken by each party, thus greatly simplifying the process of negotiation of contract, saving time and cost for businessmen.

2. Introduction to INCOTERMS 2000

By the late 1920s, commercial traders had developed a set of trade terms to describe their rights and liabilities with regard to the sales and transport of goods. These trade terms consisted of short abbreviations for lengthy contract provisions. Unfortunately, there was no uniform interpretation of them in all countries, and therefore misunderstandings often arose in cross-border transactions.

International Rules for the Interpretation of Trade Terms, short for INCOTERMS, is now the most widely used in international trade. Most contracts made after 1st January, 2000 referred to the latest edition of INCOTERMS, which came into force on that date.

(1) The scope of INCOTERMS 2000

It should be stressed that the scope of INCOTERMS is limited to matters relating to the rights and obligations of the parties to the contract of sale with respect to the delivery of goods sold (in the sense of "tangible", not including "intangibles", such as computer software). INCOTERMS do not deal with the consequences of breach of contracts and any exemptions from liability owing to various impediments. These questions must be resolved by other stipulations in the contract of sales and the applicable laws.

(2) The structure of INCOTERMS 2000

For ease of understanding, the terms were grouped in four basically different categories: namely starting with the term whereby the seller only makes the goods available to the buyer at the seller's own premises (the "E"-term Ex works); followed by the second group whereby the seller is called upon to deliver the goods to a carrier named by the buyer (the "F"-terms FCA, FAS and FOB); continuing with the "C"-terms where the seller has to contract for carriage, but without assuming the risk of loss of or damage to the goods or additional costs due to events incurring after shipment and dispatch (CFR, CIF, CPT, and CIF); the "D"-terms whereby the seller has to bear all costs and risks needed to bring the goods to the place of destination (DAF, DES, DEQ, DDU and DDP). The following chart sets out this classification of the trade terms.

Table 4-1   INCOTERMS 2000

Group E—departure	EXW	Ex Works (… named place)
Group F—main carriage Unpaid	FCA	Free Carrier (… named place)
	FAS	Free alongside Ship (… named port of shipment)
	FOB	Free on Board (… named port of shipment)
Group C—main carriage Paid	CFR	Cost and Freight (… named port of destination)
	CIF	Cost, Insurance and Freight (… named port of destination)
	CPT	Carriage Paid to (… named place of destination)
	CIP	Carriage and Insurance Paid to (… named place of destination)
Group D—arrival	DAF	Delivered at Frontier (… named place)
	DES	Delivered Ex. Ship (… named port of destination)
	DEQ	Delivered Ex Quay (… named port of destination)
	DDU	Delivered Duty Unpaid (… named place of destination)
	DDP	Delivered Duty Paid (… named place of destination)

(3)Tips for attention when INCOTERMS 2000 used

INCOTERMS 2000 is itself not the law and has no compulsory quality. The international trade practice of trade terms is based on "autonomy of will". What trade terms the involved parties choose to use and under what practice the chosen terms are governed are completely relied on the principle of being voluntary. If the involved parties hope to employ INCOTERMS 2000, when signing the sales contract, it should be clearly stipulated in the contract that the contract is governed by INCOTERMS 2000 so as to avoid unnecessary disputes, e. g. CIF New York INCOTERMS 2000.

4. 2. 2　The Most Frequently Used Trade Terms

1. FOB

Free on Board (... named port of shipment) means the seller fulfills his obligation to deliver when the goods have passed over the ship's rail at the named port of shipment and bears all costs and risks of loss of or damage to the goods before that moment.

This term can only be used for sea or inland waterway transport. In FOB, the buyer and the seller should bear respective responsibilities, costs and risks, which are illustrated in Table 4-2.

Table 4-2　Responsibilities, Costs and Risks Borne by the Buyer and the Seller under FOB

Parties Obligations	The seller	The buyer
Responsibilities, costs, risks	①Obtaining export license or other official documents and carrying out all customs formalities for the export of the goods; Paying all costs relating to the goods until such time as they have passed the ship's rail at the named port of shipment; and the costs of customs formalities necessary for export as well as all duties, taxes and other charges payable upon export. ② Delivering the goods on board the vessel designated by the buyer at the port of shipment within the period stipulated in the contract; giving the buyer sufficient notice that the goods have been delivered. ③Providing the commercial documents or its equivalent electronic message to the buyer.	① Obtaining all kinds of documents required for import clearing and carrying out import formalities; paying all costs relating to the goods from the time they have passed the ship's rail at the named port of shipment; and any additional costs incurred, either because the vessel nominated by him fails to arrive on time, or is unable to take the goods etc. ; all duties, taxes and other charges as well as the costs of carrying out customs formalities payable upon import of the goods and for their transit through any country. ② Chartering ships or booking liner spaces, paying the freight, informing the seller of the name and the date of arrival of the ship; contracting at his own expense for the carriage of the goods from the named port of shipment. ③Taking delivery of the goods, making payment to the seller.

After the contract has been concluded under FOB term, both the buyer and the seller, besides undertaking the respective obligations, should note the following tips.

(1)The passing point of risk

Under FOB term, according to INCOTERMS 2000, the seller fulfills his obligations to deliver when the goods have passed over the ship's rail at the named port of shipment, but it is often the practice that the seller sees the goods to be delivered on board. Under such cases, the ship's rail can be taken as the point where the seller and the buyer divide their risks. Since it is not a law, INCOTERMS is not mandatory. Businessmen may therefore otherwise stipulate their responsibilities or risks in their contract. For example, the seller is required to provide "shipped on board Bill of Lading". That means the buyer and the seller have made an arrangement which requires the seller to be responsible for all the risks and charges until the goods have been shipped on board the vessel. The date of B/L is the date from which the buyer is held responsibilities for all risks.

(2)Linkage between ships and goods under FOB

Under FOB, it is the buyer who arranges the ship for the shipment of the goods. So the parties must try to ensure that the goods and the ship arrive at the same loading port at the same time. The loss caused by the untimely arrival or delay of the ship should be compensated by the buyer while the loss arising from the untimely arrival or delay of the goods will be covered by the seller. Under FOB, the seller sometimes also makes the charter party. But it is on the buyer's behalf and the cost as well as the risk should be covered and borne by the buyer.

(3)FOB in the *Revised American Foreign Trade Definitions* 1941

There are six kinds of FOB in the *Revised American Foreign Trade Definitions* 1941. And only the fifth FOB, i. e. FOB vessel is close to the FOB in INCOTERMS. But under this FOB, the buyer is responsible for export clearing, as opposed to countries like the United States, Canada, we should not only put the word Vessel after FOB, but also make it clear that the other side, i. e. "the seller must obtain at his own risk and expense any export license or other official authorization and carry out customs formalities necessary for the export of the goods", or the contract might refer to FOB (INCOTERMS 2000).

2. CIF

"Cost, Insurance and Freight(…named port of destination)" means that the seller is responsible for chartering and booking space, shipping the goods on board ship within the contracted time limit; the seller should cover the transport insurance, pay the freight and insurance premium, and undertake all the risks and charges before the goods are loaded on board. Here, the freight only refers to the normal one when the ship sails along the usual route, excluding all extra fees occurred in the transport journey.

CIF term is only applicable to marine ocean transport and inland water transport. According to INCOTERMS 2000, under CIF term, the liabilities, charges and risks undertaken by the buyer and the seller are illustrated in Table 4-3.

Table 4-3 Liabilities, Costs and Risks Undertaken by Concerned Parties under CIF

Party Obligations	The seller	The buyer
Liabilities, cost and risks	Goods—Provides the goods, commercial invoice or electronic message, and other documentation as required by the sales contract. Licenses and Customs Formalities—Obtains at own risk and cost any export licenses and authorizations and carries out all export formalities and procedures. Carriage and Insurance—Contracts for and pays costs of carriage by sea or inland waterways and insurance for 110 percent of the value of the contract to the named port of destination. The insurance policy should allow the buyer to make a claim directly from the insurer. Deliver the insurance to the buyer. Delivery—Delivers the goods on board the named vessel at the named port and on the date or within *the time period* stipulated in the sales contract. Risk Transfer—Assumes all risks of loss of or damage to the goods until they have passed the ship's rail at the port of shipment. Costs—Pays all costs of carriage and insurance until the goods have been delivered to the named port of shipment and have passed the ship's rail, plus costs of loading, carriage to the port of destination and normal unloading. Also pays all costs related to the export including duties, taxes and customs formalities. Notice to the Buyer—Provides sufficient notice to the buyer that the goods have been delivered on board the named vessel. Proof of Delivery, Transport Documents—Provides the buyer with a transport document that allows the buyer to claim the goods at the destination and (unless otherwise agreed) allows the buyer to sell the goods while in transit through a transfer of the transport document or by notification to the sea carrier. Checking, Packing, Marking—Pays all costs associated with checking that the quality and quantity of the goods is in conformity with the sales contract. Provides appropriated packing (unless the goods are traditionally delivered unpackaged) as required for the transport of the goods, to the extent that the buyer has made transport circumstances known to the seller prior to the execution of the sales contract. Provides marking appropriate to the packaging. Other—Provides the buyer at the buyer request, risk and cost any and all assistance in securing documentation originating in the country of export or origin required for import and for transshipment.	Payment—Pays for the goods as provided in the sales contract. Licenses and Customs Formalities—Obtains and pays costs of all import licenses and authorizations and carry out all import formalities. Carriage and Insurance—Is under no obligation of the seller to pay for carriage or insurance. Taking Delivery—Takes delivery of the goods at the port of destination as provided in the sales contract. Risk Transfer—Assumes all risk of loss of or damage from the time the goods have passed the ship's rail at the port of shipment. Costs—Pays all supplemental costs for the goods once they have passed the ship's rail at the port of shipment, including unloading, lighterage and wharfage at the port of destination. Pays all costs relating to import formalities including duties, taxes and other charges including transshipment. Notice to the Seller—If, according to the sales contract, the buyer is able to specify a time for shipping and / or to specify a port of destination, gives the seller sufficient notice. Proof of Delivery, Transport Document—Accepts the seller's transport document so long as it is in conformity with the sales contract. Inspection(s)—Pays for the costs for pre-shipment inspection except inspections as required by the country of export. Other—Pays costs of securing documentation from the country of origin or export as required for import. Reimburses seller such costs. Provides information as necessary to obtain insurance.

When transaction is conducted under CIF term, the following tips should be attended.

(1) Contracts under CIF term are "Shipping Contracts"

It should be clarified that under CIF term and the terms of its variations such as CFR, CPT, CIP, being similar to F group terms such as FCA, FAS, FOB, the seller fulfills his obligation of delivery of goods at the place of shipment. Contracts under these trade terms are of the quality of "shipping contracts". The seller undertakes no liabilities for the might-occurred risks of cargoes after he completes the shipment of goods at the shipping place in accordance with the contract.

(2) Insurance cover

Under CIF, it is the seller who effects and pays the insurance. The covered risks and the insured amount should be previously negotiated and stated in the contract to avoid unnecessary disputes.

If no certain risks are specified, according to INCOTERMS 2000 the seller can insure the lowest coverage; when required by the buyer, the seller should effect, at the buyer's expense, war, strikes, riots, and civil commotion risk insurances if procurable. The minimum amount of insurance shall be the 110% of invoice value and shall be provided in the currency of the contract.

(3) Chartering and booking space

Under CIF, one of the obligations of the seller is to charter and book cargo space, and to handle the relevant affairs of the transport from the port of shipment to the port of destination. If no special agreements on transportation are made, the seller is only responsible for chartering and /or booking space, and transporting the goods to the port of destination by adopting the usual sailing route. Without special agreements, the seller can refuse any special requirements by the buyer on the nationality, type, age, classification of the vessel, and on using the vessel of the appointed liner company.

(4) Symbolic delivery

Under CIF, the seller is obliged to effect insurance coverage, but he does not bear the risk of loss of or damage to the goods during transit. Once he has delivered the goods and acquired the necessary documents, he is entitled to the payments of the goods even if the cargoes are lost. This is called symbolic delivery or documentary transaction. And if the goods are lost during transit, the buyer, instead of the seller, is to ask the insurance company to cover the losses, and usually the seller will render the necessary support.

The transaction under CIF is actually a documentary one, so the shipping documents are of great significance.

3. CFR

"Cost and Freight (… named port of destination)" means that the seller must pay the costs and freight necessary to bring the goods to the named port of destination but the risk of loss of or damage to the goods, as well as any additional costs due to events occurring after the goods have been delivered on board the vessel, is transferred from the seller to the buyer when the goods pass the ship's rail at the port of shipment.

Under CFR term, compared with FOB, the seller, besides the obligations under FOB, should also undertake the liabilities of arranging the transport, paying the freight to the appointed port of destination; compared with CIF, the seller is not responsible for effecting insurance and paying insurance charges and does not provide insurance policy. Moreover, both CFR and CIF share almost the same division of obligations for the buyer and the seller.

The seller under CFR must give the buyer sufficient notice that the goods have been delivered on board the vessel as well as any other notice required in order to allow the buyer to effect cargo insurance in time. The risks and losses occurred in transport, resulting from the delayed shipping advice, should be borne by the seller.

Under CFR, the import business in our country usually adopts the practice that the seller arranges the shipment and the importer is liable to effect insurance. Therefore, the importer should select customers with good credit and put forward proper requirements for vessels lest the seller collude with the shipping company, present false bill of lading, book non-seaworthy vessels, or forge certificates of quality and origin. If so, the importer will sustain unexpected losses.

FOB, CFR and CIF are identical in the ways of delivering goods, the places of delivery, and the passing point of risks. The differences among them mainly rest on who should be responsible for the transport, insurance and relevant costs, which is illustrated in Table 4-4.

Table 4-4　Similarities and Differences between FOB, CFR, CIF

Similarities	Transport: waterway transport
	Passing point of risks: the rail of vessels at the port of shipment
	Place of delivery: port of shipment
	Mode of delivery: symbolic delivery, documentary sales
	Person to handle import & export formalities: the seller handles the formalities of export; the buyer handles the formalities of import.
Differences	The liabilities and charges undertaken by the seller: CIF>CFR>FOB The rail of vessels at the port of shipment is treated as the passing point of risks, but under FOB, clear B/L should be obtained, under CFR, the seller pays the general freight, under CIF, the seller pays the freight and insurance premium.

4. Variations of trade terms

The loading and unloading charges are usually included in liner freight and the liner does not undertake the charges. In order to avoid possible disputes, the seller and the buyer should reach agreement on who is to pay the cost of loading and unloading when voyage charter is adopted. The variations of FOB are thus generated.

(1) Loading charge bearers and FOB variations

Under FOB, to specify the payer of the loading charge, the seller and the buyer will negotiate to add other conditions, such as FOB Liner Terms, FOB Under Tackle, FOB Stowed, FOB Trimmed FOB Stowed and Trimmed, etc.

(2) Unloading charge bearers and CIF variations

Under CIF and CFR, the loading charge is usually borne by the seller; which party should bear the unloading charge is specified via the variations of CIF and CFR, such as CIF Liner Terms, CIF Landed, CIF Ex Tackle, CIF Ex Ship's Hold, etc.

4.2.3   Three Trade Terms Implying Goods to be Delivered to Carrier

FCA, CPT and CIP are applicable to any modes of transport, including multimodal transport. They belong to symbolic delivery, and "the carrier to whom the goods are delivered" is treated as the passing point of risks.

In INCOTERMS 2000, carrier means any person who, in a contract of carriage, undertakes to perform or to procure the performance of carriage by rail, road, sea, air, inland waterway or by a combination of such modes.

1.   FCA

"Free Carrier (… named place)" means that the seller delivers the goods, cleared for export, to the carrier nominated by the buyer at the named place. It should be noted that the chosen place of delivery has an impact on the obligations of loading and unloading the goods at that place. If delivery occurs at the seller's premises, the seller is responsible for loading. If delivery occurs at any other place, the seller is not responsible for unloading. *This term may be used for all modes of transport.* If the buyer nominates a person other than a carrier to receive the goods, the seller is deemed to have fulfilled his obligation to deliver the goods when they are delivered to that person.

In accordance with INCOTERMS 2000, under FCA, the liabilities, charges and risks borne by the seller and the buyer are illustrated as Table 4-5.

Table 4-5   Liabilities, Charges and Risks Borne by the Seller and the Buyer under FCA

Party Obligations	The seller	The buyer
Liabilities, charges, risks	Licenses and Customs Formalities—Obtains at own risk and cost any export licenses and authorizations and carries out all export formalities and procedures; also pays all costs related to the export including duties, taxes and customs formalities. Delivery—Delivers the goods as per the agreed mode or local practice to the carrier at the named port and on the date or within the time period stipulated in the sales contract. Notice to the Buyer—Provides sufficient notice to buyer that the goods have been delivered the named carrier.	Licenses and Customs Formalities—Obtains and pays costs of all import licenses and authorizations and carry out all import formalities; Pays all costs relating to import formalities including duties, taxes and other charges including transshipment. Carriers—appoints the carrier. Transport contract—concludes the transport contract stipulating the carriage from the named place to the place of destination. Notice to the Seller—If, according to the sales contract, the buyer is able to specify a time for shipping and / or to specify a port of destination, gives the seller sufficient notice.

Continued

Party / Obligations	The seller	The buyer
	Proof of Delivery, Transport Documents—Provides the buyer with a transport document that allows the buyer to claim the goods at the destination or the electronic documents with the same legal validity. Risk Transfer—Assumes all risks of loss of or damage to the goods until they have been passed to the carrier.	Insurance—Is under the obligation of the seller to pay for insurance. Proof of Delivery, Transport Document—Accepts the seller's transport document so long as it is in conformity with the sales contract. Taking Delivery—Takes the delivery of the goods at the port of destination as provided in the sales contract. Payment—Pays for the goods as provided in the sales contract. Risk Transfer—Assumes all risk of loss of or damage to the goods from the time they have been passed to the carrier.

2. CIP

"Carriage and Insurance paid to (… named place of destination)" means that the seller delivers the goods to the carrier nominated by himself and pay the cost of carriage necessary to bring the goods to the named destination. This means that the buyer bears all risks and any additional costs occurring after the goods have been so delivered. However, in CIP the seller also has to procure insurance against the buyer's risk of loss of or damage to the goods during the carriage. Consequently, the seller contracts for insurance and pays the insurance premium.

In accordance with INCOTERMS 2000, under CIP, the liabilities, charges and risks borne by the seller and the buyer are illustrated as Table 4-6.

CIP and CIF are almost the same and they both cover the freight and the agreed insurance charges. The contracts under these two terms are "shipping contracts", that is, the seller delivers the goods via documents and the buyer pay the goods against the documents.

Table 4-6   Liabilities, Charges and Risks of the Seller and the Buyer under CIP

Party / Obligations	The seller	The buyer
Liabilities, charges, risks	Licenses and Customs Formalities—Obtains at own risk and cost any export licenses and authorizations and carries out all export formalities and procedures; also pays all costs related to the export including duties, taxes and customs formalities. Carriage and Insurance—Contracts for and pays costs of carriage by sea or inland waterways and insurance for 110 percent of the value of the contract to the named port of destination. The insurance policy should	Payment—Pays for the goods as provided in the sales contract. Licenses and Customs Formalities—Obtains and pays costs of all import licenses and authorizations and carry out all import formalities. Taking Delivery—Takes delivery of the goods at the port of destination as provided in the sales contract. Risk Transfer—Assumes all risk of loss of or damage to the goods from the time they have been passed to the first carrier.

Continued

Party Obligations	The seller	The buyer
	allow the buyer to make a claim directly from the insurer. Deliver the insurance to the buyer. Delivery—Delivers the goods on board the named vessel at the named port and on the date or within the time period stipulated in the sales contract. Risk Transfer—Assumes all risks of loss of or damage to the goods until they have been passed to the carrier. Costs—Pays all costs of carriage and insurance until the goods have been delivered to the first carrier. Also pays all costs related to the export including duties, taxes and customs formalities. Notice to the Buyer—Provides sufficient notice to buyer that the goods have been delivered on board the named vessel. Proof of Delivery, Transport Documents—Provides the buyer with a transport document or electronic one with the same legal validity that allows the buyer to claim the goods at the destination and (unless otherwise agreed) allows the buyer to sell the goods while in transit through a transfer of the transport document or by notification to the sea carrier.	Costs—Pays all supplemental costs for the goods once they have been passed to the first carrier. Pays all costs relating to import formalities including duties, taxes and other charges including transshipment. Notice to the Seller—If, according to the sales contract, the buyer is able to specify a time for shipping and / or to specify a port of destination, gives the seller sufficient notice. Proof of Delivery, Transport Document—Accepts the seller's transport document so long as it is in conformity with the sales contract.

3. CPT

"Carriage paid to(⋯ named place of destination)" means that the seller delivers the goods to the carrier nominated by him, but the seller must in addition pay the cost of carriage necessary to bring the goods to the named destination. This means that the buyer bears all risks and any other costs occurring after the goods have been so delivered.

The buyer takes the delivery of the goods at the named destination and pays for the goods and the import duties and all the relevant charges incurring in the carriage. Meanwhile, the buyer should bear all risks after the goods have been passed to the first carrier.

Under CPT, the division of the liabilities and charges between the seller and the buyer lies between FCA and CIP.

As above-mentioned, FCA, CPT and CIP are all applicable to any mode of transport. The delivery place and the passing point of risks are also the same. Furthermore, the contracts under these three terms are all "shipping contracts". The differences between them rest mainly on transport handling, liabilities of insurance, freight payment and the insurance amount.

4. The comparison between FCA, CPT, CIP and FOB, CFR, CIF

The terms of FCA, CPT and CIP derive from the terms of FOB, CFR, CIF. These two categories of terms share the following similarities:

a. All of them are symbolic delivery of goods and the corresponding sales contracts are shipping contracts.

b. The exporter handles the export formalities and the importer handles the import formalities.

c. The liabilities of transport and insurance undertaken by the seller and the buyer are corresponding with each other. That is, under FCA and FOB, the buyer performs the transport; under CPT and CFR, the seller handles the transport; under CPT and CFR, the seller bears the responsibilities of transport and insurance.

The differences between these two categories of terms are:

a. Being applicable to different modes of transport. FCA, CPT, CIP are applicable to all modes of transport, including the multimodal one, the carrier of which can be shipping company, the railway administration, airliner, and the operator of a multimodal transport company while FOB, CFR, CIF are only applicable to ocean and inland waterway transport, the carrier of which is usually the shipping company or its agent.

b. Possessing different passing point of risks. Under FCA, CPT, CIP, the passing point of risks is "the carrier to whom the goods are passed", while in traditional terms, the point is "passing over the rail of the ship". Therefore, the delivery time of the former terms is the shipping time while the latter, the delivery time cannot be treated as the shipping time.

c. Loading and unloading charges borne by different parties. Under FCA, CPT, CIP, it is the carrier who pay the loading & unloading charges, thus no relevant variations are used; under FOB, CFR, CIF, when voyage charter is adopted, the loading & unloading charges should be stipulated under their variations.

d. Having different transport documents. Under FOB, CFR, CIF, the seller should present a clean bill of lading while under FCA, CPT, CIP, the transport documents presented by the seller vary according to the modes of transport. If the ocean and inland waterway transport is employed, the seller should present transferable B/L, sometimes non-transferable B/L can also be provided. If the modes of transport by rail, road, air or the multimodal transport are employed, the railway airway bill or multimodal transport documents should be provided respectively.

Therefore, except the different passing point of risks, the modes of transport under

FCA，CPT，CIP can be treated as the extension under FOB，CFR，CIF from the ocean transport to all modes of transport.

4. 2. 4　The Other Trade Terms

1. EXW

"Ex Works(…named place)"means that the seller delivers when he places the goods at the disposal of the buyer at the seller's premises or another named place (i. e. workshops, factory, warehouse, etc.) not cleared for export and not loaded on any collecting vehicle. This term thus represents the minimum obligation for the seller，and the buyer has to bear all costs and risks involved in taking the goods from the seller's premises. However，if the parties wish the seller to be responsible for the loading of the goods on departure and to bear the risks and all the costs of such loading，this should be made clear by adding explicit wording to this effect in the contract of sale. The term is applicable to all modes of transport.

2. FAS

"Free Alongside Ship(…named port of shipment)" means that the seller delivers the goods when the goods are placed alongside the vessel at the named port of shipment. This means that the buyer has to bear all costs and risks of loss of or damage to the goods from that moment. The "alongside ship" is treated as the passing point for the buyer and the seller to bear the respective charges and risks. This term is only applicable to ocean and inland waterway transport.

3. Trade terms of delivering goods at destinations

In INCOTERMS 2000，there are five terms indicating goods are delivered at destinations, such as: DAF (Delivered At Frontier), DES (Delivered Ex Ship), DEQ (Delivered Ex Quay), DDU, DDP (Delivered Duty Paid).

Contracts concluded under D terms are called "arrival contracts"，which evidences the biggest difference from the other trade terms. Under D terms，the seller has to bear muchmore risks.

4. 2. 5　Incoterms® 2010

In order to meet the fast development of world trade and its changing practice，ICC has made revisions to Incoterms 2000. Thus Incoterms® 2010 comes into effect from the January 1st，2011.

The Incoterms® 2010 rules take account of the continued spread of customs－free zones，the increased use of electronic communications in business transactions，heightened concern about security in the movement of goods and changes in transport practices.

Incoterms® 2010 includes 11 rules，deleting DAF、DES、DEQ and DDU. They are presented in two distinct classes:

The first class includes the seven Incoterms® 2010 rules that can be used irrespective of the mode of transport selected and irrespective of whether one or more than one mode of transport is employed. EXW, FCA, CPT, CIP, DAT, DAP and DDP belong to this class.

In the second class of Incoterms® 2010 rules, the point of delivery and the place to which the goods are carried to the buyer are both ports, hence the label "sea and inland waterway" rules. FAS, FOB, CFR and CIF belong to this class. Under the last three Incoterms rules, all mention of the ship's rail as the point of delivery has been omitted in preference for the goods being delivered when they are "on board" the vessel. This more closely reflects modern commercial reality and avoids the rather dated image of the risk swinging to and fro across an imaginary perpendicular line.

Moreover, Incoterms® 2010 are applicable to both internaitonal and domestic sales contracts.

4.2.6 Price Accounting

1. Price accounting

When we quote the price and make price clause, we should attend the budgeting of the cost of the goods so as to increase the economic benefit. The main indices of cost budget include currency exchange cost, balance rate, and foreign exchange rate.

The price of commodities is composed of three parts: cost, expense and profit.

The cost of commodities is the one excluding the export refund from the purchasing cost, that is, actual purchasing cost. The expense can be divided into two categories: domestic expense including packing charge, storage and disposal charge, domestic freight, cost of inspection and proof certificate, loading charge, export taxed, post and cable fees, banking charges, predicted loss, pre-paid interest, business charges, etc; overseas expense, under different trade terms, including ocean transport charge, land transport charge, air transport charge and transport insurance fee, and commission paid to brokers. The profit is the predicted profit of an exporting company.

FOB price= purchasing cost+domestic expense+net profit

CFR price= purchasing cost+domestic expense+ocean freight+net profit

CIF price= purchasing cost+domestic expense+ocean freight+ocean premium+net profit

FOB price to other prices:

CFR price=FOB price +ocean freight

CIF price=(FOB price +ocean freight)/(1-(1+10%)× premium rate)

CFR price to other prices:

FOB price=CFR price -ocean freight

CIF price=CFR price /(1-(1+10%)× premium rate)

CIF price to other prices:

FOB price=CIF price×(1-(1+10%)× premium rate)-overseas freight

CFR price=CIF price×(1-(1+10%)× premium rate)

The price composition of FCA, CPT, CIP are similar to those of FOB, CFR, CIF.

2. Commission and discount

(1) Commission

In international trade, some transactions are negotiated by agents or brokers. What is paid to agents or brokers for their efforts in negotiating the sales is called commission. Price is of two types: price including commission and net price.

When the price of commodities includes commission, words should be used to express, e. g. USD 200 per M/T CIF San Francisco including 2% commission. Another way to express the price with commission included is to add the first letter of the word *commission* and the relevant percentage to the trade term, e. g. USD 200 per M/T CIFC 2% San Francisco. The commission included in the price can also be expressed in concrete and absolute numbers, e. g. To pay USD 25 as commission per metric ton.

The stipulation of commission should be rational; the percentage is usually between 1% and 5% of the price.

The usual formula is as follows:

Commission = Price (commission included) × commission rate

Net price = Price (commission included) × (1− commission rate)

Price (commission included) = net price ÷ (1− commission rate)

(2) Discount

Discount is a favor granted to the buyer by the seller for various purposes. In international trade, there are quite a few types of discount, such as quantity discount to enlarge sales, special discount for special purposes, and turnover bonus, etc.

In international trade the discount is also expressed in verbal form in the price clause of sales contracts. For example: *USD 200 per metric ton CIF London including 3% discount* or *USD 200 per metric ton CIF London less 3% discount*. Moreover, discount can also be expressed in concrete and absolute numbers: USD 6 discount per metric ton.

4.3　Task Performance and Reflections

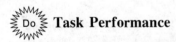 **Task Performance**

(1) To select proper trade terms

Though the freight is changing due to the price fluctuation of crude oil, David has decided to adopt CIF MARSEILLES, because under CIF, he has more control over the shipment and transport of the cargoes.

(2) To calculate and to quote the price

David is now calculating the price of the goods: the purchasing cost is CNY 160 per pc, including 17% value added tax; the export refund rate is 11%; the company's operation cost rate is 5%; the freight of 20' FCL from Shanghai to Marseilles is CNY 9380; the company will insure 110% of total value of the cargoes against All Risks and War Risk at the buyer's request; the premium rate is 0.8% and 0.02%; the predicted profit is 10%.

Under CIF, the RMB quotation is:

CIF = actual purchasing cost + operation cost + freight +premium + profit

$$= 160 - 160 \div (1 + 17\%) \times 11\% + 160 \times 5\% + 9\,380 \div 1\,248 +$$
$$\text{CIF} \times 110\% \times 0.82\% + \text{CIF} \times 10\%$$

CIF = CNY 180.11/pc, exchange rate between USD & CNY is 6.47

CIF = USD 27.84/pc

In negotiation, the importer requires 3% of commission. David re-calculates the price including commission on the basis of the net price USD 27.80 per piece, CIF Marseilles.

Price (commission included) = net price / (1−commission rate) = 27.84/(1−3%) = USD 28.70/pc

(3)To conclude price clause

After calculating the price and considering the fast delivery, David has not set price adjust clause and the clause of value maintenance of foreign currency, though US dollar is depreciating and the price of raw materials is on the rise. He has raised the price a bit and negotiated with Paul, thus concluding the following price clause:

Unit price: USD 28.70 per piece CIF Marseilles including 3% commission.

Total Value: USD 35817.60(Say U.S. Dollars thirty-five thousand eight hundred and seventeen and cents sixty only)

Other price clauses for reference:

Unit Price: USD 120 per M/T CIF Bangkok

Total Value: USD 13000 (Say U.S. Dollars thirteen thousand only)

Price including commission

Unit Price: GBP 15 per box FOB Guangzhou including 2% Commission

Total Value: GBP14350 (Say Pounds Sterling fourteen thousand three hundred and fifty only)

Price with deduction

Unit Price: USD 100 per yard FOB Shanghai including 2% discount

Fixed price clause

Price: USD 235 Per M/T CIFC 2% New York. No price adjustment shall be allowed after conclusion of this contract.

Reflections

When concluding the price clause, we should first calculate the price, taking all the factors influencing the price into account. To make the price clause more reasonable, the following tips should be attended:

(1) To select the proper trade terms according to the business intention and actual sit-

uation

In international trade, nowadays, the trade terms of symbolic delivery are more employed, that is, the transactions are conducted by means of delivering the goods at the shipping port or shipping place. CIF and CIP terms are favorable to exporter while FOB and FCA are more favorable to importer.

When the methods of paying upon the delivery of the goods or collection are used, FOB or CFR terms should not be used.

(2) To correctly write unit of measurement, loading and unloading places in the unit price

The contents of the price clause should be in conformity with those in other clauses, such as unit of measurement, loading and unloading places, etc.

In different trade terms, the referred places should be in accordance with the trade terms; for example: in the terms of F Group, the referred place is the shipping place; in C Group, the referred place is the unloading place; the referred place in FOB, CFR, CIF is the port; and the place in FCA, CPT, CIP can be the port and airport and so on.

(3) To take into account all factors influencing the price to work out reasonable prices

If there is a tolerance about the quality and quantity of the delivered goods, the price of the "more or less" part should also be stipulated. For example, when packing materials and packing charge are calculated separately; its pricing methods should be stated clearly; as for port congestion surcharge, optional fees, etc. , they should also be specified in the price clause if the buyer bears the charge.

4.4　Knowledge Extension

1. *Warsaw-Oxford Rules* 1932 and *Revised American Foreign Trade Definition* 1941

Besides INCOTERMS 2000, there are two other influencing practices of trade terms:

Warsaw-Oxford Rules 1932, specially made by International Law Association to interpret CIF contracts.

Nine American Trade Bodies made *Revised American Foreign Trade Definition* 1941. It includes six types of trade terms: EX (Point of Origin), FOB(Free on Board), FAS (Free Along Side), C&F(Cost and Freight), CIF(Cost Insurance and Freight), EX Dock (Named Port of Importation).

2. To choose the proper currency for foreign exchange exposure

In import and export trade, the widely used currencies are: USD, GBP, EUR, CAD, HKD, JPY CHF, etc.

In export trade, hard currencies are always used because they are comparatively stable and tend to appreciate while in import trade, soft currencies are recommended to be used because their exchange rate has the tendency of decreasing. In addition, other methods can also be adopted to avoid the risks, such as to lower the importing price and to raise the export price; to combine the uses of hard currencies and soft currencies; to adopt forward transaction, optional transaction, swap transaction, etc.

Task 5

Conclusion of Transportation Clause

 Knowledge objectives: students are expected to know
- ◆ what is loading port, destination port
- ◆ what is partial shipment and transshipment

 Skill objectives: students are expected to be able to
- ◆ choose the proper mode of transportation in accordance with specific conditions
- ◆ conclude the clause of transportation for export

5.1 Task Description and Analysis

1. Task description

CCIEC and the French Company have agreed to conclude a contract of a 20ft container of garments. David Sun, representing the Chinese company, is discussing with Paul from the French company how to stipulate the transportation clause and what mode of transportation to be adopted.

2. Task analysis

Different from inland transportation, international transportation has to go through many intermediate procedures, unpredictable changes and high risks. Thus, the cooperation and reasonable arrangement are essential for the concerned parties.

In international trade, both the seller and the buyer should negotiate and stipulate the terms and conditions of the shipment clause, including shipment date, port of shipment and destination, partial shipment, transshipment, shipping notice, shipping documents, etc. Without specific stipulations of the shipment clause in the sales contract, disputes would arise when the sales contract is performed, which causes serious troubles.

5.2 Knowledge Highlight

5.2.1 Modes of International Transport

There are many modes of transport in international cargo transport, such as marine transport, rail transport, air transport, parcel transport, international multi-modal transport, containerization, etc. Marine transportation and container transportation will be mainly discussed in the following.

1. Marine transportation

Marine/Ocean transport is the most widely used form of transportation in international trade. 80% of the world total volume is now transported by sea. It is generally considered as a cheap mode of transport for delivering large quantities of goods over long distances. According to ways of operations, ocean transport can be divided into liner transport and charter transport.

(1)Liner transport

A liner is a passenger vessel or a cargo vessel that operates over a regular route according to an advertised timetable, calls at certain fixed ports. The freight is charged at pre-published rate. At present liner transport has become one of the most welcomed modes of international marine transportation. It has the following characteristics:

1) Fixed sailing date (an advertised schedule), fixed route (operating on a regular route), fixed calls at scheduled ports and relatively fixed freight rate.

2) Liner freight covers loading and unloading charges, so the carrier is responsible for

the loading and unloading. Therefore, liner transport does not cover loading and unloading time, demurrage and dispatch; the charge of loading and unloading is included in the freight and is actually undertaken by the freight payer.

(2)Charter transport

Charter transport here refers to the practice of paying money to a shipping company to use their ships. Charter rate is much cheaper than that of the liner. Shippers may choose direct route. Therefore it is widely used in transport of bulk cargo. There are two types of charter transport, i. e. voyage charter transport and time charter transport.

According to a voyage charter contract, the freight is usually charged at the quantity of cargoes, regardless of the time the voyage will take. Lenders bear the time risk. In order to urge renters to finish the loading and unloading, to complete the contracted voyage and to obtain more freight, lenders usually stipulate Dispatch Money and Demurrage in contracts. The lenders reward the renters if the cargoes are loaded or unloaded ahead of time; while the renters will have to pay fine if they cannot finish loading or unloading within the contracted time. The dispatch money is usually a half of the demurrage.

2. Container transport

Container transport is a mode of distributing merchandise in a unitized form, suitable for ocean, rail, and multimodal transport. At present, containerized ocean transport has already become a dominating mode in international liner routes.

The widely used containers in international trade are of the sizes of 20ft (Twenty-foot Equivalent Unit/ TEU) and 40ft (Forty-foot Equivalent Unit/FEU).

There are full container load/FCL and less than container load/LCL. The loading of FCL is usually at the factory or the warehouse by the consignor, and then it is sent to the container yard /CY for consolidation by the carrier. When the cargoes arrive at the destination, the consignee can carry away the containers. Less than container loads require the carrier pack the cargoes from different consignors into one container at the container freight station/CFS. When the cargoes arrive at the destination, it is up to the carrier to unload the container and dispatch the goods to different consignees. The usual interchanging ways of containers are illustrated in Table 5-1.

Table 5-1   The Usual Interchanging Ways of Containers

Ways	Loading	Unloading	Interchanging Place/ Expressions
FCL/FCL	Consigner	Consignee	Door to Door, CY to CY, Door to CY, CY to Door
LCL/LCL	Carrier	Carrier	CFS/CFS
FCL/LCL	Consigner	Carrier	Door to CFS, CY to CFS
LCL/FCL	Carrier	Consignee	CFS to Door, CFS to CY

Notes: Door refers to the factory or warehouse of consignor or consignee; CY refers to Container Yard; CFS refers to Container Freight Station.

3. Other modes of transport

(1)Rail transport

Rail transport is a major means of transport regarding to loading capacity, second only to ocean transport. It is very popular in multi-modal transport and transshipment especially in land bridge. It is capable of achieving relatively high speed, and is particularly economical if it provides the complete trainload for a shipper on a regular basis. Besides, it is less influenced by poor weather conditions. The most import document for rail transport is consignment note. Once the forwarding railway station has accepted the goods for carriage together with the consignment note, the contract of carriage comes into effect.

(2)Air transport

Air transport is one of the modern forms of transport, with the merits of quick delivery, saving the cost of package and storage, and no limitation to ground conditions. Because of its high freight, it is usually desirable for consumer cargoes such as badly needed goods, precision instruments, fresh goods, seasonal goods, and the goods of high value but low volume.

Air transport services are divided into four categories: scheduled airlines, chartered carriers, consolidated consignments and air express service. The air express service is the fastest transport, especially suitable for transportation of badly needed goods and files.

Air express service is cooperation between express service companies and airliners. It provides the services: the goods are got from the consigner's place by express service company, and then delivered by the fastest airline to the destination, where a specially assigned person will pick up the goods and go through all the imported formalities, and finally send the goods to the consignees. This way of transport is thus called "Desk to Desk Service".

(3) Parcel post transport

Parcel post transport is simple and convenient. This is used only for the delivery of very small quantity of goods, with the weight not exceeding 20kgs, and with the length not exceeding 1 meter. It is desirable for goods such as samples, medicine, machinery parts, and valuable goods. International parcel post can be divided into two categories: letter post and parcel post.

(4) International multi-modal transport or international combined transport

Following the containerization of international transport, a brand new mode of transport, "international multi-modal transport" has been introduced in the transport industry. International multi-modal transport means the carriage of cargo by at least two modes of transport on the basis of a multi-modal transport contract from a place of one country where the cargoes are collected to a place designated for delivery in another country. Although different modes of transport (sea, air, rail, etc.) are combined, only one multi-modal transport operator is responsible for taking the cargo from the consignor and delivering them to the consignee.

The definition of International Multi-modal Transport as per *United Nations Conven-*

tion on International Multimodal Transport of Goods comprises the following characteristics:

a. Multi-modes: At least two different modes of transport are employed in transiting the goods among different countries.

b. One contract: A combined transport contract is used to stipulate the obligations, responsibilities and exemption of the respective parties.

c. One copy of documents: One copy of combined transport documents is required during the whole journey.

d. One freight rate: All through the journey, only one freight rate is used, which covers the sum of charges at separate voyages, management fees and reasonable profit.

e. One operator: There is only one representative on behalf of the multi-modal transport runner to be responsible for the whole process of cargoes delivery.

International multi-modal transport simplifies the procedures, reduces the intermediate links, fastens the delivering speed, lowers the transport cost, and promotes the transport efficiency. It is an effective approach to realize "door to door" transport.

5.2.2   Time of Delivery

On the basis of FOB, CIF, CFR, the seller usually completes its delivery at the shipping port. Therefore, the time of delivery conforms to the time of shipment.

Shipping time is a vital term in international sales contracts. The buyer is entitled to cancel the contract for the delayed delivery and lodge a claim for compensation; the buyer can accept or reject the early delivery, but cannot cancel the contract for this reason.

The usual practice for shipping time is:

a. To specify the time of shipment. It can be stipulated within a specific month or specific months to finish the shipment; it can also be stipulated that the shipment should be completed not later than a certain time. E. g. :

Shipment during March;

Shipment before June 30;

Shipment no later than June 30;

Shipment on or before June 30;

Shipment during February /March

b. To specify to finish the shipment with ×× days upon receiving L/C. To protect his own interest, the seller should stipulate clearly the date on which the L/C should arrive so as to avoid the buyer's delaying of opening L/C or rejecting of opening L/C.

E. g. : *Shipment within 30 days after receipt of L/C subject to buyer's L/C reaching the seller before March 1.*

c. To specify to finish the shipment within ×× days upon receiving the payment. It means that the buyer should pre-pay the goods. It is most favorable to the seller.

5.2.3　Port of Shipment and Port of Destination

Port of shipment refers to the port where the goods are loaded on board while port of destination refers to the port where the goods arrive and are unloaded. It is usually the seller who assigns the port of shipment with the approval from the buyer. The port of destination is usually assigned by the buyer with the seller's approval.

The choice of port of shipment and port of destination should consider the rational goods flow and implement the principle of proximity. Meanwhile, facilities, loading and unloading conditions at the ports should also be considered.

The usual practice for the stipulation of port of shipment and port of destination is:

a. It is generally accepted to assign one port of shipment and one port of destination. E. g. : *Port of Shipment : Qingdao; Port of Destination : London.*

b. Two or more than two ports of shipment and ports of destination are also accepted under actual circumstances. E. g. : *Port of Shipment : Qingdao, Dalian and Shanghai; Port of Destination : London and Liverpool.*

c. If it is hard to determine the port of shipment and the port of destination during negotiation, optional ports can be chosen. E. g. : *Port of Shipment : Qingdao/Dalian/Shanghai; Port of Destination : London/ Liverpool.*

5.2.4　Partial Shipments and Transshipment

Partial shipments and transshipment are directly relevant with both buyers' and sellers' benefit. Sellers usually welcome partial shipments and transshipment, but buyers generally do not want the goods partially-shipped or transshipped unless the market requires him to do so. The non-stipulation of the partial-shipment in the sales contract, as per some countries' Contract Law, does not mean that partial shipments are allowed. However, in UCP, it states that partial shipments or transshipment is allowed unless the credit has particular stipulations. To prevent misunderstandings, in our country's usual export practice, clear stipulations on partial shipments and transshipment should be made.

1. Partial shipments

In case of an export business covering a large quantity of goods, it is necessary to make shipment in several lots by several carriers sailing on different dates. This is done because of the limitation of shipping space available, poor unloading facilities at the port of destination, a dull market season, or possible delay in the process of manufacturing of goods, etc. This is allowable only if the clause "Partial shipments to be allowed" is agreed upon in the sales contract. If partial shipments are not permitted, the clause "no partial shipments" or its like should be inserted in the contract.

In the sales contract there are three ways to stipulate the clause of partial shipments.

a. Only "Partial shipments allowed" is made, the specific time, lots and quantity are not stipulated. This is more convenient for the seller because the seller can flexibly arrange the goods according to the transporting conditions and the source of the goods.

b. The number of the lots of the goods is stipulated but the quantity of each lot is not.

c. The specific time, the number of the lots and the quantity of each lot are clearly stated. This way is completely at the buyer's demands and has more strict confinement on the seller. E. g. , Shipment during March / June in four equal monthly lots.

2. Transshipment

Transshipment in ocean transport is the movement of goods in transit from one carrier to another at ports of transshipment before the goods reach the port of destination. The transshipment may not only waste time, add cost, and cause loss of goods so that buyers usually do not accept transshipment. However, when direct sailing to the port of destination is not available, the port of destination does not lie along the sailing route of the liner, or the amount of cargo for a certain port of destination is so small that no ships would like to call at that port, the seller should insist on concluding the clause of transshipment to be allowed in the contract.

5. 3　Task Performance and Reflections

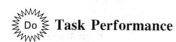 **Task Performance**

(1) To select modes of transport

Considering the situations, the containerized liner is usually chosen. Sometimes, in full season, air transport is selected if the prompt delivery by other modes is not available.

(2) To decide shipping time and ports of shipment

Via Jincheng Logistics Network, there is no direct liner to Marseille. Shanghai Port, Ningbo Port, Dalian Port can be chosen as the Port of Shipment, and transshipment is quite possible during the voyage. Therefore, when the transport clause is being concluded, Chinese ports should be assigned as ports of shipment and transshipment should be allowed. Considering the voyage from Shanghai to Marseille is one month or so, the shipping time is stipulated in September.

(3) To draw shipping clause

Shipment: from Shanghai, China to Marseille, France by sea between 20 Sept. , 2010 and 30 Sept. , 2010; otherwise to transport from Shanghai China to Marseille, France between 1 Oct. , 2010 and 15 Oct. , 2010 on seller's account by air. Transshipment is allowed. Partial shipment is not allowed.

More examples of shipping clause

The shipping clause usually includes the stipulations on shipping time, ports of shipment and ports of destination, partial shipment and transshipment. Sometimes, the documents by the seller and a shipping notice are also stipulated. More examples are illustrated as follows:

1)Shipment: on or before May 31st from Shanghai to Wellington. Partial shipments and transshipment are allowed. The seller should fax the shipping details to the buyer within two days after shipment.

2)Shipment during May from London to Shanghai. Partial shipments are allowed and transshipment is not allowed. The seller should advise the buyer the goods will be ready for shipment 45 days before the month of shipment.

3)During March/ April in two equal monthly shipments, to be transshipped at Hong Kong, 1/3 original B/L and one set of not-negotiable document to be sent to the buyer within 3 days after shipment by DHL.

4)Shipment advice shall be cabled by the seller with indication of quantity shipped, invoice value carrying vessel, ETD (expected time of departure), port of loading, etc. , to enable the buyer to cover proper insurance accordingly.

5)Destination port: One port at buyer's option. The buyer must declare the definite port of destination to the carrier five days before the vessel's expected time of arrival (ETA) at the first port of discharge and bear the optional fees thus incurred.

! Reflections

When David finished drawing the clause of transport, he got the following tips:

(1)The shipping time should be specific

With the consideration of the goods supply and vessels, the time of shipment should be specific; and expressions such as Prompt Shipment, Immediate Shipment, Shipment as soon as possible etc. should be avoided. Meanwhile, suitable shipping periods and concrete date of credit issuing should also be attended.

In export, as for some seasonal goods, the foreign customers demand that shipping time and delivery time should be stipulated in the contract. It is not the usual case in international trade.

(2)The port of shipment and port of destination should be specific

The stipulations on the port of shipment and port of destination should be clear and concrete; base ports are usually chosen. In our country, European Main Ports and U. S. Main Ports are not used for the port of destination in export and the port of shipment in import. However, a Chinese port is used for the port of shipment in export and the port of destination in import for the purpose of Chinese companies enjoying more options when chartering ships or booking cargo space.

Inland cities cannot be assigned as ports of shipment and ports of destination. In winter season, seasonal ports should not be used for vessels being not able to call at by frozen ice. If there is no direct liner, the clause that transshipment is allowed should be added in the contract. Ports in places where wars and political commotions occur should not be used as ports of shipment and ports of destination.

(3) The same names of foreign ports should be attended

In order to avoid mistakes, the country and specific locations should be stated clearly for those ports with the same name. The names such as Victoria, Tripoli, Portland, Boston, etc. are used to refer to different ports. Therefore, the regional names or country names should be added after these names.

5. 4   Knowledge Extension

Relevant stipulations on partial shipment in UCP 600:

a. The consequence of the non-shipment of one installment on the stipulated date. The Article 32 in UCP 600 states: If a drawing of shipment by installments within given periods is stipulated in the credit and any installment is not drawn or shipped within the period allowed for that installment, the credit ceases to be available for that and any subsequent installment. Therefore, in export, caution is needed in negotiating this clause. However, from perspective of the buyer, partial shipment can help him reasonably arrange its sales and financing.

b. Some cases cannot be treated as partial shipment, such as: using the same vehicle, presenting transport documents at one time, the same voyage and the same destination. The article 31, Clause b states: A presentation consisting of more than one set of transport documents evidencing shipment commencing on the same means of conveyance and for the same journey, provided they indicate the same destination, will not be regarded as covering a partial shipment, even if they indicate different dates of shipment or different ports of loading, places of taking in charge or dispatch. If the presentation consists of more than one set of transport documents, the latest date of shipment as evidenced on any of the sets of transport documents will be regarded as the date of shipment. A presentation consisting of one or more sets of transport documents evidencing shipment on more than one means of conveyance within the same mode of transport will be regarded as covering a partial shipment, even if the means of conveyance leave on the same day for the same destination.

Task 6

Conclusion of Insurance Clause

 Knowledge objectives: students are expected to know

◆ the categories and characteristics of international cargo insurance

◆ actual total loss, constructive total loss, general average, particular average

Skill objectives: students are expected to be able to

◆ choose the proper categories of marine cargo insurance according to specific conditions

◆ master the contents of marine cargo insurance and conclude the clause of insurance

6. 1   Task Description and Analysis

1. Task description

Under most circumstances, CCIEC handles export under CIF basis and import under FOB basis. David Sun has reached the agreement with the French company on transport clause. Because CIF term is used, it is up to the seller to cover insurance. Now David is discussing with Paul the cargo insurance and drawing the insurance clause.

2. Task analysis

In international trade, it is usually a long distance for the goods to be shipped from the seller to the buyer. Many perils will be encountered resulting in losses of or damage to the goods. Importers and exporters usually change the uncertain risks into fixed charges by effecting insurance. They would be compensated if any unfortunate incidents within the range of the insurance occurred in the carriage of the goods. The perils and losses sustained are various. For identifying responsibilities, insurance clauses of the insurance companies stipulate different articles by which different perils and losses are covered.

Because marine transport dominates international trade transport, the marine cargo insurance thus becomes the dominant one. Here, the covering range for different risks should be clarified. Insurance companies usually undergo the compensations according to the stipulations on different risks, losses, and fees in insurance clauses.

6. 2   Knowledge Highlight

6. 2. 1   Risks Coverage for Ocean Transportation

On ocean voyage, the ship and goods may suffer a variety of natural calamities such as bad weather, thunder and lightening, flood, floating, drift ice, earthquake, tsunami and other irresistible disasters; various fortuitous accidents such as ship stranding, striking upon rocks, sinking, colliding with icebergs or other objects, fire, explosion and ship missing; some general extraneous risks such as theft, breakage, leakage, contamination, sweat and heating, taint of odor, hook damage, shortage, rain, etc. ; and also special extraneous risks caused by military affairs, political and administrative rules such as war, strikes, refusal to delivery of cargo, etc.

The damage to or the loss of the insured cargoes in marine transport is called Average. According to the extent of the damage or loss, the average falls into two categories: total loss and partial loss.

1. Total loss

Total loss means all the goods insured suffered loss. It can be subdivided into actual total loss and constructive total loss.

(1)Actual Total Loss

Where the subject matter insured is destroyed, or so damaged as to cease to be a thing of the kind insured, or where the insured is irretrievably deprived thereof, there is an actual total loss. Furthermore, actual total loss, within the meaning of the definition, may be construed in three distinct ways, namely: when the subject matter is totally destroyed; when the subject matter is so damaged as to cease to be a thing of the kind insured, and when the insured is irretrievably deprived thereof.

(2)Constructive Total Loss

The concept of constructive total loss, whereby the subject matter insured is effectively lost to the assured, but is not actually destroyed, is unique to marine insurance. There is a constructive total loss where the subject matter insured is reasonably abandoned on account of its actual total loss appearing to be unavoidable, or because it could not be preserved from actual loss without an expenditure which would exceed its value when the expenditure had been incurred.

2. Partial loss

Partial loss is any loss other than a total loss. A partial loss may include a particular average loss, a general average loss and particular charges. Thus there are two distinct types of partial loss:

(1)General Average(GA)

General average applies to a loss (sacrifices of property and expenditure involved) intentionally incurred in the general interest of the ship owner and the owners of the various cargoes. For example, a ship goes around on her voyage and both ship and cargo are in a perilous position. With a view to save her from breaking up, the captain's all efforts to refloat her have failed, he may decide to jettison part of the cargo on board to lighten the ship. The loss, the sacrifice of that part of cargo, is borne by all concerned in proportion. The same applies to additional expenditures incurred in the common interest, such as the towage, port of refuge expenses, and other salvages.

General Average is a kind of loss encountered in ocean transport, but not all the losses caused by accidents or disasters occurred at sea can be categorized as general average. General average is usually of the following elements:

a. The perils are encountered. The perils resulting in general average really exist and are unavoidable, but not subjectively assumptive.

b. Measures are taken to protect the ship and cargoes. The losses caused only by protecting the ship or the cargoes cannot be classified as general average.

c. The expenditure is extra and the loss is extraordinary.

d. Reasonable measures are taken automatically and intentionally.

(2)Particular Average

Particular average means a partial loss which is suffered by the one whose goods are partly lost or damaged. When there is a particular average loss, other interests in the voyage (such as the carrier and other cargo owners whose goods were not damaged) do not contribute to the partial recovery of the one suffering the loss. An example of a particular average occurs when a storm or fire damages part of the shipper's cargo and no one else's cargo has to be sacrificed to save the voyage. The cargo owner whose goods were damaged turns to his insurance company for payment, provided, of course, his policy covers the specific type of loss suffered.

3. Expenses

Losses of the insured cargoes not only come from the risk of the loss of the goods or the damage done to the goods, but also from the expenses the insured spends in rescuing the goods in damage. Therefore, losses, damages, and expenses are all covered by the transportation insurance. The main expenses are as follows.

Sue and labor expense are the expenses arising from measures properly taken by the insured, the employee and the assignee, etc. , to minimize or avoid losses caused by the risks covered in the insurance policy. The insurer is liable to compensate for such expenses.

Salvage charges are expenses resulting from measures properly taken by a third party other than the insured, the employee and the assignee, etc.

6. 2. 2　Ocean Marine Insurance under C. I. C.

Insurance is actually a scope of responsibilities that the insurer should undertake for the risks and the losses. It is also a foundation on which the insurer and the insured perform their rights and obligations, according to which the extent of the liabilities the insurer should bear and the insurance premium the insured should pay can be decided.

In our country, China Insurance Clauses /C. I. C. are the most used insurance clauses in ocean transportation of import and export, which is made and issued by People's Insurance Company of China. As per different modes of transport, there are ocean marine insurance, overland transport insurance, air transport insurance and parcel post insurance.

The China Insurance Clauses provides both basic risks coverage and additional risks coverage for marine cargo transport. Basic risks coverage can be filed solely while additional risks coverage can only be added to certain basic risks coverage.

1. Basic risks coverage for ocean transportation

Under China Insurance Clauses, basic risks coverage falls into three types: free from particular average, with average, and all risks. The insured may choose any one suitable for the carriage of his goods.

(1)Free from Particular Average (F. P. A.)

Free from particular average, basically, is a limited form of cargo insurance cover in as much as that no partial loss or damage is recoverable from the insurers unless that actual vessel or craft is grounded, sunk or burnt. Under the latter circumstances, the F. P. A. cargo policy holder can recover any losses of the insured merchandise which was on the vessel at the time as would obtain under the more extensive W. P. A. policy. The F. P. A. policy provides coverage for total losses and general average emerging from actual "marine perils".

(2) With Average/ With Particular Average (W. A. / W. P. A.)

This insurance covers wider than F. P. A. Apart from the risks covered under F. P. A. conditions as mentioned above, this insurance also covers partial losses of the insured goods caused by heavy weather, lightening, tsunami, earthquake and/or flood.

(3) All Risks (A. R.)

All Risks is the most comprehensive of the three in coverage. Aside from the risks covered under F. P. A. and W. P. A. , this insurance also covers all risks of loss or damage to insured goods whether partial or total. Arising from external causes in transit, it should be noted that "All Risks" does not, as its name suggests, really cover all risks. The "All Risks" clause excludes coverage against damage caused by war, strikes, riots, etc. These perils can be covered by a separate clause. And it covers only physical loss or damage from external causes.

Besides the above basic risks coverage, there are conditions of exclusions. Exclusions refer to losses and expenses for which the insurance company declares clearly not to be responsible. The usually include: loss or damage caused by the intentional act or fault of the insured; loss or damage falling within the liability of the consignor; loss or damage arising from the inferior quality or shortage of the insured goods prior to the attachment of this insurance; loss or damage arising from normal loss, inherent vice or nature of the insured goods, loss of market and / or delay in transit and any expenses arising therefrom; risks and liabilities covered and excluded by the war risks clause and strikes, riot and civil commotion clauses under C. I. C.

2. Additional risks coverage for ocean transportation

Additional risks coverage is the supplement and extension of the basic risks coverage. In ocean transportation, the insured can select one or several additional risks coverage in accordance with the nature of goods and actual need. Additional risks under C. I. C. fall into general additional risks and special risks.

(1) General Additional Risks

General additional risks cover the losses caused by extraneous risks. If the goods are covered against All Risks, it is not necessary to ask for general additional risks. General additional risks under C. I. C. fall into 11 types: theft, pilferage, and non-delivery (T. P. N. D.); fresh water and / or rain damage(F. W. R. D); shortage; intermixture and contamination; leakage; clash and breakage; taint of odor; sweat and heating; hook damage; breakage of packing; rust.

(2) Special Additional Risks

Special additional risks cover losses caused by special extraneous risks. Normally, they fall into 8 types: war risk; strike risk; on deck risk; import duty risk; rejection risk;

Aflatoxin risk; failure to deliver risk; fire risk extension clause for storage of cargo at destination Hong Kong including Kowloon or Macao.

More details are given on war risk and strike risk as follows:

1) War risks

This covers losses attributable to war, piracy, armed conflict, warlike or antagonistic acts, detention, seizure, and confinement because of acts therefrom. It also covers the general average, salvage charges, and sue and labor expenses arising from the above-listed acts. Losses caused by torpedoes and bombs of various kinds (except atomic bombs) are also answerable by war risk.

2) Strike risks

This covers the losses caused by strikes, civil commotion and riot. There will not be additional charges for strikes if the insured has effected war risks.

3. Commencement and termination of insurance coverage

The commencement and termination of all the risks coverage under Ocean Marine Transportation Insurance of China, except war risks, follow the international practice of using Warehouse to Warehouse (W/W), that is, the liabilities of the insurer begins from the warehouse at the shipping port stipulated in the insurance policy, where the goods insured are shipped to the warehouse at the port of destination stipulated in the insurance policy. The liability terminates when the goods are delivered to the consignee's warehouse. However, the insurance terminates immediately after 60 days when the goods are unloaded at the port of destination, regardless if they are moved into the consignee's warehouse or not.

Warehouse to warehouse clause is not applicable to war risks under ocean marine cargo transport insurance. The liability of this risk starts when the goods insured are loaded on board the ship at the port of shipment and ends when the goods are unloaded from the ship or the lighter at the port of destination. If the goods insured have not been unloaded from the ship or the lighter, the insurance coverage naturally expires 15 days later counting from the midnight when the goods reached the port of destination. If transshipment is allowed, the insurance coverage remains effective for 15 days, counting from the midnight when the ship reaches the transit port or unloading place, regardless if the goods are unloaded or not. The insurer resumes his liability when the ship restarts its voyage.

The time effect of claiming for compensation under the three types of basic risks in Ocean Marine Cargo Transport Insurance remains effective for not more than two years counting from the time when the goods insured are unloaded from the ship.

6.2.3　Other Cargo Transport Insurances

The cargo shipped by sea must be insured and the cargo transported by land, air and parcel post should also be insured, for risks also lie in these means of transportation. However, the insurance company may have different clauses and terms to meet the needs of different modes of transport.

Overland cargo transportation insurance falls into two types: overland transportation risks and overland transportation all risks. Air transport insurance includes air transport risks and air transport all risks. Parcel post transport insurance has also two types: parcel post risks and parcel post all risks.

Moreover, there are overland transport insurance "Frozen Product", and additional risks such as overland transport cargo war risks (trains), air transport war risks, and parcel post transport war risks, etc.

6.3 Task Performance and Reflections

Do Task Performance

In CIF or CIP contract, the clause should make it clear as to who is responsible for effecting insurance, the risks covered, the methods of ascertaining the insurance amount, and the insurance clauses adopted. Ambiguous clauses as "usual risks" or "customary risks" should be avoided.

After negotiation, David and Paul have concluded the following insurance clause:

Insurance: To be covered by the seller for 110% of total invoice value against all risks, war risks as per and subject to the relevant ocean marine cargo clause of the People's Insurance Company of China, dated January 1st, 1981.

! Reflections

Insurance clause is one of the important parts of international sales or purchase contract. The contents are different when different trade terms are chosen.

In FOB, FCA, CFR and CPT contract, the insurance clause may simply be stipulated as: "*Insurance: To be covered by the Buyer.*" If the buyer entrusts the seller to effect insurance, items like amount insured, risks covered, clauses applied and so on should be clearly stipulated in the contract.

In CIF contract, the following tips should be attended:

a. To choose the right insurance clause. The China Insurance Clauses by the People's Insurance Company of China dated January 1st, 1981 is conventionally employed. It is also acceptable to adopt Institute Cargo Clause (ICC) under the demand of the foreign customers, but the concrete insurance coverage should be chosen in accordance with the nature of the goods and actual conditions.

b. To choose the proper insurance coverage. The nature of the goods and actual conditions should be accounted when the two parties choose to insure the goods against F. P. A. or W. P. A., or A. R. It is also necessary to note clearly in the contract that what additional risks should be added.

c. To decide the markup percentage. The markup percentage is usually 10% of the total invoice value. If the buyer demands a higher percentage and the insurance company a-grees to underwrite the insurance, the seller can accept the requirement. But the buyer should, in principle, bear the increased insurance premium. If there are no concrete stipu-lations on the markup percentage, the seller is subject to insure 110% of the total invoice value under CIF or CIP terms with conformity to the stipulations in *INCOTERMS* 2000 and *UCP* 600.

d. To clarify the insurance policy. The name of the insurance documents (the insur-ance policy or insurance certificate) presented by the insured should be noted in the con-tract.

> More examples:
> Insurance: To be effected by the sellers on behalf of the buyers for 110% of total in-voice value against W. A. including Taint of Odors, premium to be for buyer's account as per and subject to the relevant Ocean Marine Clauses of the People's Insurance Company of China, dated January 1st, 1981.
> Insurance: To be covered by the seller for 120% of total invoice value against ICC (A), as per Institute Cargo Clause dated January 1st, 1982.

6.4 Knowledge Extension

1. Insurance Interest

The subject matter the insurer underwrites is the object to be secured. What the in-sured has effected is not the subject matter itself, but the ownership of the interest of the subject matter. If the insured does not have the interest, the insurance contract is of no force.

The same is true of the international cargo transportation insurance. The insured's possession of the interest of the insured subject matter is embodied by the ownership of the insured subject matter and the reliabilities undertaken.

Under FOB or CFR terms, the buyer undertakes the risks when the goods pass the ship's rail. The losses of the goods directly results in the losses of the buyer, so the buyer possesses the insurance interest. Therefore, it is the buyer, as the insured, who effects the insurance and the insurance contract does not come into effect until the goods pass the rail of the ship. Before the goods pass the rail, the buyer does not have the insurance interest, so the insurer do not need to undertake the liability if losses occur.

Under CIF terms, it is the obligation of the seller to effect insurance and the seller has the ownership of the goods, thus possessing the insurance interest. The insurance contract comes into force when the goods leave the place of departure.

2. Institute Cargo Clauses (ICC)

The Institute Cargo Clauses, shortened as I. C. C. were set forth by the Institute of

London Underwriters. They have exerted great influences in the development of international insurance. Chinese firms usually adopt CIC. But if the foreign clients request to adopt ICC, it may also be acceptable.

The ICC was initially published in 1912 and has been amended many times. The latest version was completed on January 1st, 1982 and came into force from April 1st, 1983, in which six insurance clauses are provided, namely:

(1)Institute Cargo Clause A, or ICC (A);

(2)Institute Cargo Clause B, or ICC (B);

(3)Institute Cargo Clause B, or ICC (C);

(4)Institute War Clause—Cargo;

(5)Institute Strikes Clause—Cargo;

(6)Malicious Damage Clause.

Among the above six clauses, ICC(A) is equivalent to All Risks under CIC, with wider coverage, that is, it covers all risks of loss of or damage to the subject matter insured. ICC (B) is equivalent to W. A. , and ICC(C) is equivalent to F. P. A. but with smaller coverage.

The first three kinds of coverage are main insurance and can be effected separately, while the latter three are additional risks and generally cannot be effected separately. At special request, Institute War Clause and Institute Strikes Clause can be effected separately.

Task 7

Conclusion of Commodity Inspection Clause

 Knowledge objectives: students are expected to know

◆ the inspection and quarantine organization of exported goods

◆ the inspecting time and place of exported goods

Skill objectives: students are expected to

◆ master the main contents and the specified methods in inspection clause

◆ be able to conclude the clause of inspection

7.1 Task Description and Analysis

1. Task description

The quantity and quality of the delivered goods are always the focus of the disputes between the buyer and the seller. Therefore, the inspection of the goods is very important to both the buyer and the seller and each of them will try to make the method of inspection convenient to him respectively in the sales contract.

CCIEC and Golden Mountain Trading Co., LTD have already agreed on the other clauses except the inspection clause. Now David Sun is going to negotiate with the French company about the inspection and to conclude the clause of inspection and quarantine.

2. Task analysis

It is closely related with the inspection of goods whether the goods are able to be delivered smoothly, or whether the claim for the loss is able to be made when problems arise. This should be made clear in the clause of inspection in the sales contract.

The inspection clause of export contracts generally includes time and places of inspection, inspection organization, inspection certificates, reinspection, etc. The contents of inspection clause are very important to the benefit of the buyer and the seller.

When the inspection clause is made, the contents of the clause should be in conformity with the other clauses, such as the quality clause, the quantity clause, etc. so that conflicts are avoided.

7.2 Knowledge Highlight

Commodity inspection and quarantine refers to the check of the quality, quantity, weight, packing, security, health, shipping conditions of the delivered goods and the check of infectious diseases, pests, epidemics of men, animals, and plants by commodity inspection and quarantine bodies.

7.2.1 Inspection Bodies

In international trade, the inspection and quarantine of imported and exported goods are of great significance. The selection of inspection bodies will directly decide who is up to inspect the goods and issue the certificate, which will greatly influence the benefit of the concerned parities in the contract. Therefore, it should be clearly stipulated that which inspection organization is chosen.

In international trade, specialized inspection bodies are entitled to carry out the inspection. Outside China, according to the nature of the possession of inspection bodies, there are governmental organizations, trade associations or institutes, or private managed agencies; there are also semi-governmental organizations. The names of the inspection bodies are also diversified, such as *inspection companies, fair trade houses, identification companies, laboratories or claimed measuring men*, etc.

According to the Law of the People's Republic of China on Import and Export Commodity Inspection and the Regulations for the Implementation of the Law of the People's Republic of China on Import and Export Inspection, the State Commodity Inspection Authorities are responsible for the inspection of import and export commodities throughout the country.

The Import and Export Inspection Corporation of China and its branches designated by the China Exit and Entry Inspection and Quarantine Bureau at different places also carry out the inspection and identification business in the name of the third party.

7.2.2   Time and Places of Inspection

To decide the time and places of inspection of the goods is actually to determine who, the buyer or the seller, has the right to perform the inspection.

According to the international usual practice, there are three ways to stipulate the time and places of inspection.

1. Inspection at the export country

The inspection at the export country can be sub-divided into two types: inspection at the place of production and inspection at the port of shipment.

(1) Inspection at the place of production

It means that the seller or the inspection bodies entitled by the seller performs the inspection before the goods leave the producing places, such as factories, farms or mines. The seller is responsible for the goods before the goods leave the producing places. After the inspection, the buyer should bear the liabilities if the problems of the quality, quantities, etc. arise in the transport. The important goods or the huge equipment imported to our country are usually inspected, installed and tested before they leave the manufacturing factories.

(2) Inspection at the port of shipment

It is also named Shipping Quality and Shipping Weight. Before the goods are shipped, the inspection organization agreed by both parties inspects the goods and issues the certificate which functions as the final evidence of the quality and weight of the goods. When the goods arrive at the port of destination, the buyer may re-inspect the goods. Even if the problems arise, the buyer cannot reject the goods or claim for compensation.

2. Inspection at the port of destination

This means inspection carried out at the port of destination by the agreed inspection organization is to be final. It is also called Landed Quality and Landed Weight. As far as technology-intensive goods or the goods which are not suitable to be unpacked after unloaded are concerned, they can also be inspected at the buyer's place or the end user's place.

This arrangement is favorable to the buyer. It is not usually adopted.

3. Inspection at the port of shipment and reinspection at the port of destination

It means after inspection at the port of shipment, the buyer retains the right to re-inspect and claim for compensation if the goods delivered don't comply with the contract. This method is favorable to both parties and therefore is widely used in international trade.

7.3　Task Performance and Reflections

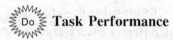 **Task Performance**

CCIEC and the French company have concluded the clause of inspection as follows:

It is mutually agreed that the certificate of quality issued by the China Exit and Entry Inspection and Quarantine Bureau at the port/place of shipment shall be part of the documents to be presented for negotiation under the relevant L/C. The buyers shall have the right to reinspect the quality of the cargo. The reinspection fee shall be borne by the buyers. Should the quality be found not in conformity with that of the contract, the buyers are entitled to lodge with the sellers a claim which should be supported by survey reports issued by a recognized surveyor approved by the sellers. The claim, if any, shall be lodged within 180 days after arrival of the goods at the port of destination.

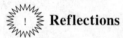 **Reflections**

In inspection clause the nature of the goods should be taken into consideration when the expiry date of claim and the re-inspecting time are to be decided. The period from 30 days to 180 days upon the arrival of the goods is usually accepted.

The other tips with attention are as follows:

a. The clause of quality and packing should be clear and concrete. Otherwise the inspection cannot be performed.

b. The inspection organization should be agreed by both parties and its legality should be ascertained. The name and copies of the issued certificate should be made certain and be presented to different bodies.

c. The inspection standards, the sampling ways and the inspection methods can be specified in accordance with the concrete business. Our country's relevant standards and sampling ways are generally adopted.

d. The hygiene inspection of the exported goods and animal product should be complied with the relevant regulations and laws of our country. If foreign buyers raise special requirements or demand the inspection be conducted by observing the other countries' standards, they should present relevant materials, and the approval from China Exit and Entry Inspection and Quarantine Bureau of our country should be obtained. Otherwise, their requirements cannot be accepted.

7. 4   Knowledge Extension

The world-famous inspection bodies

The international inspection of commodity is mainly undertaken by non-governmental-bodies which have the same legal status as notary bodies. The notable bodies are Societe Generale De Surveillance S. A. (SGS) in Geneva, Swiss, Underwriter Laboratory (UL) in the USA, Lloyd Surveyor, B. V. in Britain and Japan Marine Surveyor & Swron Measurer's Association (NKKK), etc.

Headquartered in Switzerland, SGS is the world's leading inspection, verification, testing and certification company. Founded in 1878, SGS is recognized as the global benchmark in quality and integrity. SGS-CSTC Standards Technical Services Co. , Ltd was founded in 1991 as a joint venture between SGS Group and China Standard Technology Development Corp. (http: //www. cn. sgs. com/zh/)

Task 8

Conclusion of International Payment Clause

 Knowledge objectives: students are expected to know

◆ bill of exchange/draft, promisory note, and check

◆ the categories, process and characteristics of remittance and collection

◆ the process and characteristics of letter of credit

Skill objectives: students are expected to

◆ properly choose the payment methods and instruments

◆ master the contents of payment clause and to be able to conclude the payment clause

8.1　Task Description and Analysis

1. Task description

It is the first time for CCIEC and Golden Mountain Trading Co. , LTD, to do business transaction. Both sides are not sure of the counterpart's credibility. Therefore, David and Paul have paid a lot of attention to the choice of payment methods and instruments when concluding the payment clause.

2. Task analysis

In international trade practice, the buyer is obliged to pay the seller the agreed amount, in the agreed currency, within the agreed period of time and by the agreed method of payment. Therefore, it is of essential importance to stipulate in the contract the various terms of payments.

The payment methods are the main contents in the payment clause, including: letter of credit, remittance and collection. Among the factors influencing the effective payment, the safe payment should be put in the first place, the time of funds flow is another important factor, and the procedure handling and bank fee should also be attended.

8.2　Knowledge Highlight

8.2.1　Payment Instruments

Bills are the acceptable instruments of payment, among which the draft is used as the most common payment instrument, and promissory note and check are also sometimes used.

1. Definition and chief contents of a draft

A draft or bill of exchange is defined as an unconditional order in writing, addressed by one person to another and signed by the first person, requiring the second person to whom it is addressed to pay on demand, or at a fixed or determinable future time, a certain some of money to the order of a specified person, or to the order of him.

2. Types of drafts

Drafts or bills of exchange can be sorted according to different criteria. They can be classified into the following types, as illustrated in Table 8-1.

Table 8-1　Categories of Drafts

Classification Criteria	Types	Description
According to whether the shipping documents are attached or not	Clean bill	It is a bill without shipping documents attached thereto.
	Documentary bill	It is a bill with shipping documents attached thereto.

Continued

Classification Criteria	Types	Description
According to the tenure	Sight bill or demand bill	It is a bill payable on demand or at sight or on presentation.
	Time bill or usance bill	It is a bill payable at a fixed or determinable future time.
According to the drawer	Banker's bill/bank's bill	It is a draft drawn by a bank on another bank.
	Trade bill / commercial bill	It is a bill issued by a trader on another trader or on a bank.
According to the acceptor	Commercial acceptance bill	It is a time bill drawn on a trader and accepted by him.
	Banker's acceptance bill	It is a time bill drawn on a bank and accepted by this bank. This kind of bill is more preferable and negotiable than the trader's acceptance bill and is more acceptable in the discount market.

Time draft or usance draft is a bill payable at a fixed or determinable future time. The time may be expressed in the following four ways: a. at … days after sight; b. at … days after date; c. at … days after date of B/L; d. at a fixed date in future.

In international trade, the documentary bill is usually adopted; after the delivery of the goods, the consignor collects the payment by presenting the documents. Clean bill is rarely used, and it is only used to collect payment balance, commission or disbursement. Banker's draft is usually used in bank remittance while commercial bill is usually used to collect payment and often adopted in letters of credit and collections.

It should be made clear that one draft can sometimes be of several above-mentioned qualities. For example: a commercial bill can be both time bill and documentary bill; a usance documentary commercial bill can also be a banker's acceptance bill.

3. Parties of a draft

The parties concerned in a commercial bill are payees, payers/drawees, drawers. Besides, there are endorser, acceptor, holder, bona fide holder, etc.

4. Procedures of bills of exchange

The procedure of sight draft is: to issue, to present and to pay, as illustrate in Figure 8-1. The procedure of time/usance draft is: to issue, to present, to accept and to pay, as illustrated in Figure 8-2. If transference is required, the endorsement is necessary. If the draft is dishonored, the protest should be made and the right of recourse should be pursued.

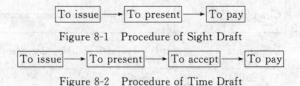

Figure 8-1　Procedure of Sight Draft

Figure 8-2　Procedure of Time Draft

(1) To issue

To issue means that the drawer draws and signs the draft, and delivers it to the payee. The payer, the amount, the time and place of payment, and the payee should be written clearly in the draft.

The title of the draft can be written in the following forms:

a. Restrictive Title: *Pay A Co. only* or *Pay A Co. Not negotiable*. This type of draft cannot be transferred and the payment can only be collected by the addressee.

b. Indicating Title: *Pay A Co. or the order* or *Pay to the order of A Co.*

This type of draft can be endorsed and transferred.

c. To bearer: *Pay bearer*. This draft can be transferred without endorsement.

(2) To present

To present is to produce a draft to a party liable to pay on it for that party's acceptance (i. e. commitment to pay) or payment.

(3) To accept

Acceptance means the drawee writes down the word "Accepted", marks the date and signs his name across on the face of the bill. This action means the payer promise to pay at the date of payment. In doing so, the drawee (acceptor) commits himself to paying the bill upon presentation at maturity. After accepting the bill, the drawee should return it to the holder who will present it for payment at maturity.

(4) Payment

On the expiry date of draft, the payer makes sufficient payment to the legal bearer, the latter then writes off the draft and returns it to the payer as a receipt. The currency for the payment should also be stated.

(5) Endorsement

Endorsement means the holder of a draft transfers the draft by signing his name on the back of the draft or together with the name of the transferee/endorsee. By endorsement, the holder transfers all the rights or part of the rights to the endorsee. A draft can be transferred many times by endorsement before it matures.

The endorsement can be divided into three types: restrictive endorsement, special endorsement and blank endorsement.

(6) Dishonoring and protesting

Dishonoring means the payer refuses or fails to pay or accept the bill when the holder makes presentation to him. When dishonored, the holder shall pursue the right of recourse by giving notice of dishonor to the drawer and each endorser.

Protest is a written statement under seal drawn up and signed by a Notary Public or other authorized person for the purpose of giving evidence that a bill of exchange has been presented by him for acceptance or for payment but dishonored.

After a bill is dishonored by non-acceptance or by non-payment, and a notice of dishonor is sent, the holder may hand the bill to a Notary Public who will present it again for acceptance or for payment as the case may be, so as to obtain a legal proof of the act of dishonor. As it is dishornored again, the Notary Public then draws up a protest, i. e. , an official certificate evidencing the act of dishonor and stating the reason for the protest, demands made on the drawee (or the acceptor) and the response receive.

5. Promissory note

A promissory note is an unconditional promise in writing made by one person to another signed by the maker, engaging to pay, on demand or at a fixed date or determinable future time, a certain sum of money, to, or to the order of , a specified person or to bearer.

Promissory notes can be made by commercial firms or bankers, namely commercial promisory notes or banker's promisory notes. They are all sight notes whose expiry period cannot exceed two months since they are issued according to Clause 79 in Law of Bills of China.

The promisory note used in the international trade are mainly bank notes, which concern two parties and not necessary to be accepted.

6. Check

A check/cheque is defined as an unconditional order in writing addressed by the customer (the drawer) to a bank (the drawee) signed by the customer authorizing the bank to pay on demand a specified sum of money to or to the order of a named person or to bearer (payee).

Checks are all at sight, not necessary to be accepted. In nature, a check is an unconditional paying order, and concerns three parties. The payer of the check must be a bank or other financial bodies.

8. 2. 2　Remittance

Remittance refers to the transfer of funds from one party to another among different countries, that is, a bank (a remitting bank), at the request of its customer (the remitter), transfers a certain sum of money to its overseas branch or corresponding bank (the paying bank) instructing them to pay to a named person or corporation (the payee or beneficiary) domiciled in that country.

1. Parties related to a remittance

In remittance, there are four parties involved:

(1)Remitter

A remitter is the person who requests his bank to remit funds to a beneficiary in a foreign country. He is also called the payer.

(2)Payee or beneficiary

A person who is addressed to receive the remittance is called the payee or beneficiary.

(3)Remitting bank

A remitting bank is the bank transferring funds at the request of a remitter to its correspondent or its branch in another country and instructing the latter to pay a certain amount of money to a beneficiary.

(4)Paying bank

A paying bank is the bank entrusted to by the remitting bank to pay a certain amount of money to a beneficiary named in the remittance advice.

2. Ways of transfer

Generally speaking, there are three types of remittance: Telegraphic Transfer (T/T), Mail Transfer (M/T) and Demand Draft (D/D).

(1)Telegraphic transfer

Among the three types, T/T is the mainstay means. It is a method of transferring funds by telecommunications system such as telex or cable. The advantage is the fast speed. A payment can be made within two or three banking days. The disadvantage is the relatively high cost.

(2)Mail transfer

A mail transfer means that payments instruction given by the remitting bank is transmitted by mail or courier. Payment instruction is in a form of Payment Order. Procedure of M/T is almost the same as the T/T. Owing to the mail time being much longer than that of telecommunication and has more paper work than Demand Draft, the M/T is not broadly used in international trade.

(3)Demand draft

Demand draft is also called remittance by banker's demand draft. The payment instruction is written down directly on the surface of the bank draft. A bank draft is a negotiable instrument drawn by the remitting bank in its overseas correspondence bank, ordering the latter to pay on demand the stated amount to the holder of the draft. It is often used when the client wants to control the funds-transfer. After being issued, the bank draft should be handed over to the remitter, who may dispatch or even bring it to the beneficiary abroad.

3. Application of remittance

Remittance has the merits of easy and convenient procedures, low cost, but is a kind of commercial credit, which is less secure than a banker's credit. It has the disadvantages of high risks, imbalance of fund obligation, etc. before the mutual trust has been achieved between the importer and the exporter.

Attention:

In the current international trade, there are "T/T in advance" and "T/T against B/L". "T/T in advance" means the exporter delivers the goods after the importer pays for the goods, and importer has to face the high risk. "T/T against B/L" means the exporter delivers the goods, then the importer pays for the goods, and the exporter has to face the high risk. When the payment is settled, the combination of "T/T in advance" and "T/T against B/L" usually employed. E. g. , if 30% of the payment is settled by means of "T/T in advance", the balance will be settled by means of "T/T against B/L".

Therefore, in international trade remittance is usually employed to pay the incidental charges, such as freight, insurance, commission, compensation, down payment, interest, payment balance, etc.

In practice, remittance can be adopted in Payment in Advance ("T/T before Shipment" is often used), Cash with Order, Cash on Delivery ("T/T against B/L" is often used) Cash against Documents, Open Account Trade—O/A. Both the importer and the exporter should take measures to reduce risks when handling the complicated conditions in import and export trade.

8.2.3　Collection

Collection means that the exporter issues a draft to the bank and entrust the bank to collect the payment from the importer. It is an adverse exchange and it belongs to commercial credit.

1. Parties involved in collection

(1)Principal

It refers to the exporter, also called the drawer, for the exporter usually draws a draft to collect payment for the goods.

(2)Remitting bank

The remitting bank is the seller's local bank which sends instructions to its branch bank or a correspondent bank in the importing country to collect payment for the goods.

(3)Collecting bank

The collecting bank is the bank in the buyer's country entrusted by the remitting bank with collecting the money for the buyer.

(4)Payer

The payer is the importer, also called the drawee, for the importer is generally the drawee of the draft.

Besides the above-mentioned four parties, occasionally two other parties might be involved, i. e. the presenting bank and the customer's representative in case-of-need.

2. Types of collection

Collection can be divided into two categories: Clean Collection and Documentary Collection.

Clean collection refers to collection of financial documents not accompanied by commercial documents. It is often used to collect remaining funds, advance in cash, sample expenses, etc. in international trade payment. The seller draws merely bills of exchange in buyer, not accompanied by any shipping documents, and entrusts bank to collect funds from the buyer.

Documentary collection can be further divided into two types: Documents against Payment—D/P and Documents against Acceptance—D/A.

(1) Documents against payment, D/P

When entrusting the bank to collect, the principal instructs the bank to deliver the documents when payment has been made. According to the different time of payment, it is divided into D/P at sight and D/P after sight.

a. The draft issued is a demand draft. When the collecting bank makes presentation to the drawee (the importer), the latter should make payment upon presentation. The collecting bank will then deliver the documents to him.

b. Time draft is used in D/P after sight. When the collecting bank makes presentation, the buyer shall first make acceptance after checking the documents, and will make payment on the date of expiry of payment. In order to encourage the importer to fasten the payment, the exporter usually requires adding interest clause in the collection letter.

Under D/P after sight, in order to avoid possible delay and to get the goods as soon as possible, the buyer can present a trust receipt and borrow the shipping documents from the collecting bank and upon the maturity of the draft, effect payment of the goods. Trust receipt is a written document presented by the buyer to the collecting bank, by which he expresses his wish to take delivery of the goods, make customs clearance, effect storing and make sales of the goods on behalf of the collecting bank. He also acknowledges that the title of the goods and the sales proceeds belong to the collecting bank and also he is obliged to make the payment of the goods at the maturity of the draft.

This financing convenience is usually offered to the buyer by the collecting bank and the collecting bank is then to hold itself responsibility to the remitting bank and the principal for the payment of the goods upon the maturity of the draft. Should the principal agree that the drawee gets the shipping documents with trust receipt, the risks will be borne by the principal.

(2) Documents against acceptance, D/A

It means that the exporter presents the documents on condition that the importer accepts the draft. After shipping the goods, the exporter gets the shipping documents, entrusts the bank to collect the payment and in the collection letter instructs the bank to release the shipping documents to the importer after the importer accept the time draft.

D/A is only applicable to time draft. This greatly conveniences the buyer, but it means much more risk for the seller, for once he has delivered the shipping documents, he will have lost his title to the goods. Therefore, the seller should be very cautious in the settlement by D/A.

3. Features and application of collection

Collection uses commercial credit and the banks run business at the principal's instructions without obligations to inspect the documents and undertake the payer's compulsory payment. Generally speaking, collection is more favorable to the importer, and unfavorable to the exporter.

Therefore, when this method is used, the following tips should be attended:

a. The seller needs to have a good understanding of the credit status of the buyer and its operation style, and have a good knowledge of the transacted amount.

b. It is advisable not to use collection if the importing country has strict control over foreign exchanges or foreign trade so as to avoid the losses caused by non-permission of import or non-remittance by the importing country. Meanwhile, it is also advisable to understand the importing country's usual practice of collection.

c. The deal should be done under CIF, the seller covers cargoes insurance or effects the exporting credit insurance; if CIF term cannot be agreed, the insurance should be effected in favor of the seller.

d. Under collection, the system of regular inspection should be set up, the urgent recall and payment clearance should be made on time, and relevant measures should be taken to tackle the problems so as to avoid or reduce the possible losses.

To mediate the contradicts among the parties involved and to facilitate the carrying-out of the commercial and financial activities, the International Chamber of Commerce issued, in 1955, the latest revised edition, *Uniform Rules of Collection*, shortened as UCR522. This *Uniform Rules* is the most important international practice adopted by banks to make collections.

8.2.4 Letter of Credit

1. Definition of letter of credit

As one of the most acceptable methods of payment in international trade, a letter of credit, according to the draft of UPC600 is thus defined:

For the purpose of these articles, the expressions "documentary credits", and "standing letter of credit" (hereafter referred to as "Credits"), mean any arrangement, however named or described, whereby a bank (the "Issuing bank") acting at the request and the instructions of a customer (the "Applicant") or on its own behalf.

(1)is to make a payment to or to the order of a third party (the "beneficiary"), or is to accept and pay bills of exchange (Drafts) drawn by the beneficiary;

(2)authorizes another bank to effect such payment, or to accept and pay such bills of exchange (Draft);

(3) authorizes another bank to negotiate, against stipulated document(s), provided that the terms and conditions of the credit are compiled with.

For the purpose of these articles, branches of a bank in different countries are considered another bank.

2. Features of letter of credit

(1)A banker's credit

Under letter of credit, the issuing bank undertakes the primary liability for payment. As long as the exporter presents the documents conforming to the terms and conditions of the letter of credit, no matter who will be the payer, the importer or the issuing bank, no matter whether the importer can fulfill the obligation of payment, the issuing bank should pay the beneficiary or its appointed bank.

(2) A self-sufficient instrument

Although the credit is issued on the basis of the sales contract, banks are in no way concerned with or bound by such contract, even if any reference whatsoever to such contract is included in the credits. The bank, when issuing the credit has no regard for the sales contract but follows an application handled in by the buyer.

(3) L/C only involves the documents

Under L/C, the exporter can get the payment from the bank only by presenting the documents, the superficial contents of which are in compliance with the stipulations of L/ C. The bank bears no liabilities as for the documents' forms, completeness, correctness, authenticity, forgery, or legal effect, and the written or added general or particular conditions in the documents. However, even if the goods conform with the contract, and if the documents are not in line with the stipulations of L/C, the bank has the rights to refuse to pay. Therefore, only the strict conformity between the documents and L/C, between the document and the document are achieved, the payment can thus be safely and promptly effected by the bank.

3. The parties involved in L/C

There are quite a few parties involved under L/C, such as applicant, opener, issuing bank /opening bank, advising bank /notifying bank, beneficiary, negotiating bank, paying bank /drawee bank.

Besides the above-mentioned parties, sometimes the following parties are also involved: reimbursing banks, confirming banks and transferees.

4. Procedures of letter of credit operations

The basic chain of operations of letters of credit is almost the same with some slight differences owing to different types of L/Cs. Figure 8-3 shows the operation processes of a documentary L/C.

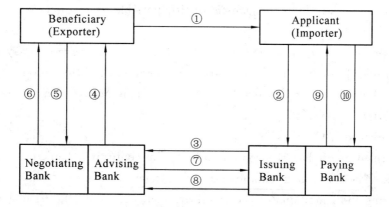

Figure 8-3　The Flow Chart of a Documentary Credit

① Letter of credit is accepted as payment method and stipulated in the sales contract.

②The exporter (beneficiary) applies to their bank for a letter of credit in favor of the applicant (the importer).

③The issuing bank (opening bank) issues an L/C and forwards it to the advising bank in the exporter's country.

④The advising bank passes the documentary credit to the beneficiary after verifying the genuineness of the credit.

⑤On receiving the L/C, the exporter checks the terms and conditions of the credit based on the sales contract. If there is a discrepancy, the beneficiary may have the option to accept it as it stands or to ask the applicant to have it amended so as to be in line with the contract. The exporter then presents the documents to the negotiating bank for the negotiation after shipment.

⑥After receiving the documents, the negotiating bank will check the documents against the terms and conditions of the L/C. If all are in order, the above bank will effect payment to the beneficiary.

⑦The negotiating bank forwards the documents to the paying bank or the bank authorized by the issuing bank to ask for reimbursement.

⑧The paying bank, after receiving the documents from the negotiating bank, will examine them carefully to see whether the documents are in compliance with the L/C. If the documents conform to the L/C, the paying bank will reimburse the negotiating bank.

⑨The issuing bank will notify the importer of the arrival of the documents and ask him to pay the bank for the documents.

⑩The importer will pay money to the bank and get the documents for claiming the merchandise.

5. Classification of letters of credit

(1) Documentary credit

A documentary credit is universally used as a method of payment in international trade. It is a credit under which payment will be made against documents representing title to the goods and thus making the transfer of title possible.

(2) Clean credit

A clean credit is a credit against which the beneficiary of the credit may draw a bill of exchange without presentation of documents. Payment will be effected only against a draft without any shipping documents attached there to or sometimes, against a draft with an invoice alone attached thereto.

(3) Confirmed L/C

A confirmed credit has the commitment of the confirming bank besides that of the issuing bank. The confirming bank guarantees payment if the issuing bank cannot pay provided the terms and conditions of the credit are met. And only the issuing bank may request another bank to add its confirmation.

(4) Unconfirmed L/C

An unconfirmed L/C contains the commitment of the issuing bank only. There is no undertaking on the part of the advising bank or other bank.

(5) Sight L/C

A letter of credit calling for the presentation of sight drafts is a sight credit, under which the beneficiary (the drawer) is entitled to receive payment at once on presentation of his draft to the drawee bank or to the issuing bank if drawn on the issuing bank, once the relevant documents have been checked and found to be in order.

(6) Usuance or time credit

If a letter of credit specifies that drafts are to be drawn at any length of time, such as 30 days, 60 days, 90 days or 120 days, after sight, it is called a usuance or time credit. Under such credit, the drafts may be drawn on and accepted by the opening bank, or the paying bank as indicated therein. In this case, the exporter issues his draft, presents it for acceptance, together with all the shipping documents, to the issuing bank or to the confirming bank or the paying bank, as stipulated in the credit. Once the draft is accepted, this means that the accepting bank promises to pay the full amount of the draft at a specified future date. The accepted usance draft can be discounted in the discount market.

Usance credit may require no drafts at all.

(7) Payment L/C

A payment credit is a credit available by payment, under which a bank specifically nominated therein is authorized to pay against the shipping documents with or without a draft presented in conformity with the terms of the credit.

If the payment cannot be recalled from the issuing bank, the paying bank cannot reimburse from the beneficiary, thus the bank has to undertake the high risk. Therefore, banks usually refuse to use this letter of credit.

(8) Deferred payment L/C

A deferred payment L/C is a kind of usance L/C, but is different from the usance L/C in common use. It does not require a bill of exchange and hence cannot be discounted at the discount house. This kind of L/C is chiefly used in the sale of capital goods. Under such cases, the beneficiary cannot get the payment by discount.

To use deferred L/C means more risks for the beneficiary than acceptance L/C. So if the beneficiary worries about the credit of the issuing bank, he may require the L/C to be confirmed.

(9) Acceptance L/C

If the L/C designates a certain bank to accept a time draft drawn by the seller and does not declare it is a negotiation credit, it will be an acceptance L/C before the validity of the L/C expires.

The bank designated by the L/C is usually the advising bank which is located in the country of the exporter. So having made the delivery of the goods, the seller should come to the bank and present the draft for acceptance before the validity of the L/C expires and get the payment of the goods at the maturity of the draft. Also, the payer of the draft should be the bank which accepts and pays it.

(10) Negotiation L/C

A negotiation L/C is a credit under which a bank specifically nominated therein is authorized to negotiate, or a credit or a time credit, calling drafts to be drawn on the issuing bank or on any other drawee bank.

Besides the above-mentioned categories of L/C, there are quite a few other categories, such as revolving L/C, back-to-back L/C, Reciprocal L/C, etc.

6. Uniform Customs and Practice (UCP)

The full name of Uniform Customs and Practice is Uniform Customs and Practice for Documentary Credit (UCPDC).

This is the internationally recognized codification of rules unifying banking practice regarding documentary credits. The Uniform Customs and Practice 600(UCP 600)is composed of seven parts and put into implementation in 2007.

8. 2. 5　Combined Use of Different Methods of Payment

International trade, usually only one method is used for a deal. But sometimes more than one method is used for the payment of the goods.

1. Combination of remittance and collection

The down payment is usually effected by remittance while the balance of the payment of the goods is made by documentary collection.

E. G. : Shipment to be made subject to an advanced payment amounting USD 10 000 to be remitted in favor of sellers by telegraphic transfer with indication of S/C No. 12 345 and the remaining part on collection bases, documents will be released against payment at sight.

2. Combination of remittance and L/C

Payment made in this way is partly done by L/C and partly by remittance. If the remittance is made before the shipment of the goods, the money is taken as down payment or advanced payment. If it is done after the shipment of the goods, it is often used for the balance of the payment for the consignment which can be varied in amount.

E. G. : 30% of the total contract value as advance payment shall be remitted by the buyer to the seller through telegraphic transfer within one month after signing this contract, while the remaining 70% of the invoice value against the draft on L/C basis.

3. Combination of remittance and banker's letter of guarantee or standby L/C

This payment is usually made in trades of large machines or complete set of equipment. The importer effects the down payment and interest by remittance, and the banker's letter of guarantee or standby L/C are used to guarantee the payment of the exporter.

E. G. : 30% of the total contract value as advance payment shall be remitted by the buyer to the seller through telegraphic within one month after signing this contract, while the remitting 70% of the contract available by D/P at sight with a standby L/C in favor of the seller for the amount of USD 1 000 000 as under taking. The standby L/C should bear the clause: In case the drawee of the Documentary collection under S/C No. 123 fails to honor the payment upon due date, the payment on S/C No. 123 dishonored.

4. Combination of L/C and collection

Payment effected in this way will partly be made by L/C and partly by collection. This will require the buyer to open an L/C for a certain percentage of the whole payment of the goods, the balance is to be collected. Also in the sales contract, it should be declared clearly that the amount of payment under L/C will be available against a clean draft, while the balance of the payment will be available against documentary draft on collection basis. The shipping documents will not be released to the buyer unless he has effected all the payment.

E. G. : Payment by irrevocable letter of credit to reach the sellers 45 days before the month of shipment stipulating that 50% of the invoice value available against clean draft, while the remaining 50% against the draft at sight on collection basis. The full sets of shipping documents shall accompany the collection draft and shall only be released after full payment of the invoice value. If the buyers fail to pay the full invoice value, the shipping documents shall be held by the issuing bank at the seller's disposal.

5. Combination of collection and banker's letter of guarantee or standby L/C

The payment of the goods is made by collection. At the same time, the importer should provide banker's letter guarantee or standby L/C to guarantee the payment of the exporter.

8. 3   Task Performance and Reflections

Do Task Performance

In international trade, the exporter should select the proper instrument and method of the payment, conclude the suitable payment clause.

In the present case, David discussed with his business partner, and agreed to settle the payment of the goods by L/C at sight. The clause of payment is drawn:

The buyer shall open through BANQUE NATIONAL DE PARIS an irrevocable sight letter of credit to reach the seller 45 days before the month of shipment, valid for negotiation in China until the 10th day after the month of shipment, but within the validity of the L/C.

Other payment clauses for reference:

(1)Payment by remittance

a. The buyer shall pay 100% the sales proceeds in advance by T/T to reach the sellers not later than Oct. 15.

b. 30% of the total contract value as advance payment shall be remitted by the buyer to the seller through telegraphic transfer within one month after signing this contract. The remaining 70% of the contract value shall be remitted by the buyer to the seller through telegraphic transfer not later than 2 days after receipt of the fax documents listed in the contract.

(2)Payment by collection

a. Upon first presentation, the buyers shall pay against documentary draft drawn by the sellers at sight. The shipping documents are to be delivered against payment only.

b. The buyers shall duly accept the documentary draft drawn by the sellers at 60 days sight upon first presentation and make payment on its maturity. The shipping documents are to be delivered against payment only.

c. The buyers shall duly accept the documentary draft drawn by the sellers at 60 days sight upon first presentation and make payment on its maturity. The shipping documents are to be delivered against acceptance.

(3)Payment by L/C

a. The buyer shall open through a bank acceptable to the sellers an irrevocable sight letter of credit to reach the seller 45 days before the month of shipment, valid for negotiation in China 15 days after the month of shipment, failing which the seller shall not be responsible for shipment as stipulated and shall have the right to rescind this contract and claim for damages against the buyer.

b. The buyer shall open through a bank acceptable to the sellers an Irrevocable Letter of Credit at 30 day's sight to reach the seller 45 days before the month of shipment, valid for negotiation in China until the 15th day after the month of shipment. The buyer shall stipulate in the L/C: Port congestion surcharges, if any, at the time of shipment is for opener's account and shall be paid to the beneficiary in excess of the credit amount against their invoices and shipping company's original receipt showing actual surcharges paid.

! Reflections

(1)In selecting the proper payment method, attention should be paid:

1) Customers' credit;

2) Intention of management;

3) Trade terms; Under different trade terms, such as CIF, CFR, CIP, CPT, etc. different payment methods should be used;

4) Transportation documents.

(2)Proper instrument of payment should be chosen to reduce the draft risks

The often-used ways to cheat are the forgery of drafts, the modifying of drafts and the coloning of drafts.

8. 4　Knowledge Extension

1. Banker's letter of guarantee

A banker's letter of guarantee (L/G) or bond is a contract by which a bank (the guarantor) agrees to pay another's debt or to perform another's obligation only if that other individual or legal entity fails to pay or perform. A banker's letter of guarantee is usually a separate contract from the principal agreement, and therefore the letter of guarantee is secondarily liable to the third person.

Banker's letter of guarantee cannot only be used in international trade, but also be widely used in the field of international economic co-operations, such as international engineering contract, bid and tender, debt and credit.

2. Standby L/C

Standby L/C is a kind of clean L/C. It is a document by which the opening bank promises to the beneficiary that it will bear some liabilities on behalf of the applicant if the latter has not duly fulfilled his obligations as required by the contract.

Should the applicant have duly fulfilled his obligations, the standby L/C will not be used while if he has not, the beneficiary is to render a written document stating that the applicant has not duly performed the contract and ask the opening bank to make recompense.

Standby L/C is widely used in international trade, debt and credit, engineering bidding, etc. If the applicant duly fulfills the obligations of the contract, the beneficiary needs not to ask the issuing bank to pay the goods or compensate, thus the standby letter of credit automatically lose its validity.

Task 9

Conclusion of an Export Contract

 Knowledge objectives: students are expected to know
- ◆ the form and contents of international sales contracts
- ◆ the contents of CISG

 Skill objectives: students are expected to be able to
- ◆ draw a written contract for export

9.1   Task Description and Analysis

1. Task description

CCIEC usually adopts its own modal contract. When both parties agree on the terms and conditions of the contract and sign it, the contract thus comes into effect.

On July 20, 2010, after harsh negotiation, David and Paul finally reached the agreement on all the terms and conditions of the contract. He prepared the contract, gave it the General Manager to sign, and faxed it to Paul. Paul would send it back after the contract was counter signed.

2. Task analysis

After turns of negotiations, the buyer and the seller reach the agreement on the terms and conditions of the sales contract, the contract thus comes into being. However, according to the usual practice in our country, after the buyer and the seller reach the agreement by means of oral negotiations or correspondence, a formal written international sales contract should be drawn and endorsed to stipulate both parties' liabilities and obligations, thus facilitating the performance of the contract.

In international trade, a sales contract is a legal document made by and entered into between a seller and a buyer on the basis of their offer and acceptance. In the contract the right and obligation of both parties are definitely stipulated to avoid unnecessary disputes and contradictions.

In this case, David and Paul have already reached the agreement on all the clauses of the contract. What should be done is to draw a written contract. With the endorsement of both parties, the contract will thus come into effect.

9.2   Knowledge Highlight

9.2.1   Form and Function of the Contract

In international trade practice, there are three forms of contract: a written form, an oral one, and a behavioral one. The written form includes quite a few categories: contracts, confirmations, agreements and orders. Among them, the most used ones are sales contracts, purchase contracts, sales confirmations, purchase confirmations, orders and intents. In recent years, electronic contracts are accepted more and more widely as a substitute of paper contracts, and they also possess the same legality as the paper contracts.

The functions of contracts are usually classified as follows:

a. Working as evidence. In the present legal system of our country, the stipulations on the oral contract are not clear enough. In practice, when the agreement has been reached orally, a written one will be endorsed to avoid troubles.

b. Working as a basis to perform the contract. After the endorsement of the contract, both parties are bound by the contract and should fulfill the liabilities and obligations respectively.

c. Working as a condition for the contract coming into effect. In the process of offer and acceptance, if both parties claim that the activities should be based on the written contract, the oral agreement is thus invalid.

9.2.2　The Contents of Contracts

In international trade, a written contract refers to a formal written document endorsed by both parties to the transaction. It can be divided into three parts: the heading, the body, and the ending.

The heading of the contract usually includes: the corporate or personal names of the contracting parties and their nationalities and principal places of business or domicile; the date and place of the signing of the contract; the type of contract and the kind and scope of the object of the contract.

The body part usually includes: the technical conditions, quality, standard, specifications and quantity of the object of the contract; the time limit, place and method of payment, and various incidental charges; whether the contract is assignable and, if it is, the conditions for its assignment; liability to pay compensation and other liabilities for breach of contract, methods for settling contract disputes.

The ending part is usually composed of the number of copies of the contract, appendix, the languages in which the contract is to be written and its validity, the time, place of the legality of the contract, and the signatures of the concerned parties.

9.2.3　United Nations Convention on Contracts for the International Sale of Goods

United Nations Convention on Contracts for the International Sale of Goods (shortened as CISG) is a uniformed law of international sales issued in 1980 by United Nations Commission on International Trade Law, which came into effect on January 1, 1988.

CISG is not applicable to the contracts that stipulates most of the liabilities of the supplier are to provide labor service or other forms of service, e.g. Consultation Service Contracts; and also not applicable to the damage to or the death of people caused by the goods, e.g. quality disputes.

9.3　Task Performance and Reflections

 **Task Performance**

Both parties in this case concluded a written sales contract as follows.

SALES CONTRACT

The Buyers: GOLDEN MOUNTAIN TRADING CO. , LTD

Contract NO. : CZCX080180

ROOM 1618   BUILDING G

NO. 36 THE FIRST LYON STREET,   Signed at: CHANGZHOU, CHINA

PARIS, FRANCE

TEL. : 019-33-44-55   Date: JULY 20, 2010

The Sellers: CHANGZHOU CHANGXIN IMPORT & EXPORT CORP.

NO. 25 MINGXIN RD, CHANGZHOU JIANGSU, CHINA

TEL: 0519-86338171

The Buyers agree to buy and the Sellers agree to sell the following goods on terms and conditions as set forth below:

Name of Commodity, Specifications and Packing	Quantity	Unit Price	Total Value
LADIES COAT , woven, with bronze-colored buttons, 2 pockets at side, like original sample NO. LJ566 sent on AUG. , 15, 2010 100% COTTON	1 248pcs	USD 28. 70	CIFC 3% MARSEILLES USD 35 817. 60
Total Amount: SAY U. S. DOLLARS THIRTY FIVE THOUSAND EIGHT HUNDRED AND SEVENTEEN AND SIXTY CENTS ONLY			

(Shipment Quantity 5% more or less allowed)S, 416 pcs, M, 416 pcs, L , 416 pcs

Packing: 8pcs per carton, assorted colors and size, per pc in polybag. W×H×L: 50 ×40×80 cm.

SHIPPING MARK: FTC

CZCX080180

MARSEILLES

NO. 1-UP

Time of Shipment: 20 Sept. , 2010-30 Sept. , 2010 by sea; otherwise 1 Oct. , 2010-15 Oct. , 2010 on seller's account by air

Port of Loading: SHANGHAI CHINA

Port of Destination: MARSEILLES FRANCE

Insurance: To be covered by the <u>seller</u> for 110% of the invoice value against <u>All Risks, War Risks</u> as per and subject to the relevant ocean marine cargo clause of the People's Insurance Company of China, dated 1/1/1981.

Terms of Payment: The buyer shall open through BANQUE NATIONAL DE PARIS an irrevocable sight letter of credit to reach the seller 45 days before the month of shipment, valid for negotiation in China until the 10th day after the month shipment, but within the validity of the L/C.

It is mutually agreed that the certificate of quality issued by the China Exit and Entry

Inspection and Quarantine Bureau at the port/place of shipment shall be part of the documents to be presented for negotiation under the relevant L/C. The buyers shall have the right to reinspect the quality of the cargo. The reinspection fee shall be borne by the buyers. Should the quality be found not in conformity with that of the contract, the buyers are entitled to lodge with the sellers a claim which should be supported by survey reports issued by a recognized surveyor approved by the sellers. The claim, if any, shall be lodged within 180 days after arrival of the goods at the port of destination.

Other terms:

The contents of the covering letter of credit shall be in strict conformity with the stipulations of the Sales Contract. In case of any variation there of necessitating amendment of the L/C, the buyers shall bear the expenses for effecting the amendment. The sellers shall not be held responsible for possible delay of shipment resulting from awaiting the amendment of the L/C and reserve the right to claim from the buyers for the losses resulting therefrom.

Sellers: Buyers:

陈哲   PAUL

 ! Reflections

Because the concerned parties in an international sales contract locate in different countries or regions, both parties should have a good command of the relevant laws of these countries and the usual practice in international trade.

In negotiation, we should try our best to win the chance to draft the contract. If it is not available, we should draft the contract together with the counterparty, and let the counterparty countersign the contract. If the contract is a purchase contract by the buyer, when endorsing it, we should read it carefully lest the buyer add an unfavorable clause or miss a clause that stipulates the liabilities the buyer should undertake so as to avoid the unnecessary troubles and unexpected economic losses.

9.4   Knowledge Extension

Application of e-contract

Newly-occurred e-contracts are being accepted as substitutes of paper ones, for they have the same legal validity. Meanwhile, their predominant advantages, such as facilitating the data filing and searching in computers, has brought great convenience for enterprises. Moreover, e-contracts can be introduced into ERP system, which can also greatly facilitate enterprises' account check, payment settlement and capital management. The year of 2004 witnessed the enforcement of *Law of Electronic Signature*, which admits that electronic documents possess the same legality as paper ones. Therefore, e-documents will enjoy increasingly wide application.

Workshop 3
Fulfillment of an Export Contract

Task 10

Examination and Modification of Letters of Credit

 Knowledge objectives: students are expected to know
- ◆ main contents of a Letter of Credit (L/C)
- ◆ notes on L/C examination and modification procedure
- ◆ contents of UCP600

Skill objectives: students are expected to be able to
- ◆ understand L/C contents and analyze terms of L/C correctly
- ◆ modify L/C according to UCP600 and sales contract

10. 1   Task Description and Analysis

1. Task description

CCIEC signed a contract on Jul. 20th, 2010, but he didn't receive L/C on Aug. 10 as agreed. So David Sun sent an E-mail to Mr Paul, the customer, requesting the opening of L/C. On Aug. 15th, Bank of China Changzhou Branch informed CCIEC that the L/C was received. Now David is examining L/C to make sure every term is correct so that he can fulfill the contract smoothly.

2. Task analysis

L/C is a conditional payment undertaking made by a bank which engages to honor prescribed documents within the prescribed time limit. L/C must abide by the "the doctrine of strict compliance", which means that all documents must literarily conform to the terms of the L/C, and keep consistent among each other as well. Otherwise, the exporter will not be able to receive the funds safely. Therefore the L/C itself should be correct and the exporter is able to meet the L/C requirements.

The exporter, as the beneficiary of the credit, must review every term of the L/C. If the L/C doesn't match with contract or transaction terms, or even though the L/C itself is correct, there might be failures in meeting the requirements of L/C due to exporter's difficulties of fulfilling the contract. The exporter should request the applicant to amend L/C immediately.

10. 2   Knowledge Highlight

10. 2. 1   Contents of L /C

The contents of L/C are constituted by basic provisions, texts and notes, including the following aspects.

1) The relative parties to L/C: beneficiary, applicant, issuing bank, notifying bank, negotiating bank, paying bank, etc.

2) Notes of L/C: including L/C number, issuing date and place, expiry date and place, amount, currency and type of credit, etc.

3) Clause of draft: drawer, payer, terms, amount and issuing date of draft.

4) Clause of documents: type and number of copies of documents that should be submitted by beneficiary.

5) Clause of goods: description of goods, quality, specifications, quantity, packing, price and INCOTERMS, shipping mark, etc.

6) Clause of transportation: port of loading and destination, term of delivery, partial shipments and transshipment, etc.

7) Clause of charges: it indicates clearly who should bear the bank charges occurred in

the L/C.

8) Other clauses: issuing bank's responsibility, instructions to negotiating bank, special clauses, additional texts and statements that the L/C is in compliance with UCP600 etc.

E. g.

FROM: INDUSTRIAL BANK OF JAPAN, TOKYO

TO: BANK OF CHINA, SHANGHAI

SQUENCE OF TOTAL: 27: 1/1

FORM OF DOC. CREDIT: 40A: IRREVOCABLE

DOCU. CREDIT NO. : 20: ILC136107800

DATE OF ISSUE: 31C: 071015

DATE N PLACE OF EXP. : 31D: 071215 IN THE COUNTRY OF BENEFICIARY

APPLICANT: 50: ABC COMPANY, 1-3 MACHI KU STREET, OSAKA, JAPAN

BENEFICIARY: 59: SHANGHAI DA SHENG CO. , LTD. UNIT C 2/F JINGMAO
　　　　　　　　TOWER, SHANGHAI , CHINA.

CURRENCY CODE, AMOUNT: 32B: USD21240. 00

AVAILABLE WITH /. BY … 41D: ANY BANK BY NEGOTIATION

DRAFTS AT: 42C: SIGHT FOR 100PCT INVOICE VALUE

DRAWEE: 42D: THE INDUSTRIAL BANK OF JAPAN, HEAD OFFICE

PARTIAL SHIPMENTS: 43P: ALLOWED

TRANSSHIPMENT: 43T: NOT ALLOWED

LOAD/DISPATCH/FROM : 44A: CHINESE PORTS

TRANSPORTATION TO: 44B: OSAKA/TOKYO

LATEST DATE OF SHIPMENT: 44C: 071130

DESCRIP GOODS/SERVICE: 45A: 4 000 PCS "DIAMOND" BRAND CLOCK ART
　　　　　　　　NO. 791 AT USD5. 31 PER PIECE CIF OSA-
　　　　　　　　KA/TOKYO PACKED IN NEW CARTONS

DOCUMENTS REQUIRED: 46A: IN 3 FOLD UNLESS OTHER WISE STIPU-
LATED:

1. SIGNED COMMERCIAL INVOICE

2. SIGNED PACKING LIST

3. CERTIFICATE OF CHINESE ORIGIN

4. BENEFICIARY'S CERTIFICATE STATING THAT ONE SET OF ORIGINAL SHIPPING DOCUMENTS INCLUDING ORIGINAL FORM A HAS BEEN SENT DIRECTLY TO THE APPLICANT

5. COPY OF TELEX FROM APPLICANT TO SUPPLIERS APPROVING THE SHIPPING SAMPLE.

6. INSURANCE POLICY OR CERTIFICATE ENDORSED IN BLANK FOR 110 PCT OF CIF VALUE, COVERING W. P. A RISK AND WAR RISK

7. 2/3 PLUS ONE COPY OF CLEAN ON BOARD OCEAN BILLS OF LADING MADE OUT TO ORDER AND BLANK ENDORSED MARKED FREIGHT PREPAID AND NOTIFY APPLICANT.

ADDITIONAL CONDITION: 47A: ALL DRAFTS DRAWN HEREUNDER MUST BE MARKED "DRAWN UNDER INDUSTRIAL BANK OF JAPAN, LTD. , HEAD OFFICE, CREDIT NO. ILC136107800 DATED OCT. 15, 1999" AND THE AMOUNT OF SUCH DRAFTS MUST BE ENDORSED ON THE REVERSE OF THIS CREDIT.

DETAILS OF CHARGES 71 B: ALL BANKING CHARGES OUTSIDE JAPAN ARE FOR BENEFICIARY'S ACCOUNT

PRESENTATION PERIOD 48: DOCUMENTS MUST BE PRESENTED WITHIN 10 DAYS AFTER THE DATE OF ISSUANCE OF THE SHIPPING DOCUMENTS BUT WITHIN THE VALIDITY OF THE CREDIT.

CONFIRMATION 49: WITHOUT

SPECIAL INSTRUCTION TO THE ADVISING BANK: ALL DOCUMENTS INCLUDING BENEFICIARY'S DRAFTS MUST BE SENT BY COURIER SERVICE DIRECTLY TO OUR HEAD OFFICE. MARUNOUCHI, CHIYODA-U, TOKYO, JAPAN 100, ATTN. INTER-NATIOANL BUSINESS DEPT. IMPORT SECTION, IN ONE LOT. UPON OUR RECEIPT OF THE DRAFTS AND DOCUMENTS, WE SHALL MAKE PAYMENT AS INSTRUCTED BY YOU.

10. 2. 2　Examination of L /C

L/C is a new agreement independent of a sales contract. When L/C is adopted, exporter should review the contents of the L/C carefully. It is essential for exporter to get payment on time. So the exporter should fully understand the terms of L/C and ensure that they are consistent with the sales contract. Otherwise it is likely for the exporter to fail in fulfillment of sales contract, which may result in delay or reject of payment.

The exporter examines the L/C according to domestic laws and regulations, sales contract, UCP600, and practical situations of operation.

The principle of L/C examination is as the follows:

Amend L/C when the terms of L/C are stricter than that of sales contract (It may be kept unchanged if they don't affect the export to fulfill sales contract and get payment.);

No amendment to L/C when the terms of L/C are less strict than that of sale contract.

1. Key issues in L/C examination

(1) The wording in L/C

According to trade practice, L/C becomes effective when it is received by the beneficiary. But there are unreasonable restrictive provisions in some credits, such as *"This credit is operative only after the buyer obtains the import license"*.

So the exporter should pay attention to such words as the followings:

——L/C is not effective or there are restrictive provisions in the L/C;

——L/C is revocable;

——No statements showing the payment guaranteed;

——No statements confirming UCP600 applicable;

——L/C is not confirmed as per sales contract requirements;

——L/C identification code is wrong.

(2)The validity of L/C

L/C without expiry date is invalid; expiry place is outside of China; expiry date conflicts with shipment date; shipment date, expiry date and documents submission date are different from those in contracts; shipment date or expiry date is contradicory from submission date; submission date is too early.

(3) The relative parts to L/C

The applicant's name or address is different from that in contract; beneficiary's name or address does not match with the contract.

(4)Currency and amount

Unit price and total amount of L/C should be consistent with those in the sales contract; the currency in L/C should be the same with that in the contract. If there is more or less clause in the contract, amount of the L/C should cover the *more part* of the amount.

In reviewing the amount, different cost such as freight and insurance premium should be paid highly attention to. For example, under the terms of FOB conditions, it is unreasonable that L/C requires the seller to make insurance and shipping, and cover the expenses cause by them.

(5)Draft

The drawee is not the issuing bank or its designated negotiating bank; the term of the payment date is different from that of sales contract or not practical.

(6) Transportation

Port of loading and destination, shipment date, partial shipments and transshipment requirements in the L/C are not consistent with those in the contract. If the opening of L/C is delayed and the exporter is not able to deliver goods on time, he should promptly call the buyer to extend the shipment date; If partial shipments are allowed, the exporter should check carefully whether he is able to ship the specific quantity before the specific date of each lot required in L/C. If there are special requirements for the age and nationality of the vessel, port and shipping company etc. , the exporter should check the feasibility.

Attention:

The 3rd clause of UCP600 formulates, "on or about ××" means five days before or after the written date, including the start and the end date; "to / until / till / from / between ××" includes the written date when it is used to specify the shipment date; "before/ after ××" does not include the written date; "from / after ××" doesn't include the written date when specifying a maturity date.

(7)Goods

Name and specifications of goods do not match with the contract; quantity is wrong; package is not appropriate; trade term is incorrect; terms and conditions are contradictory; unit price multiplying quantity doesn't equal to the total amount; contract number and date is not correct; and more or less clause is omitted.

(8) Documents Clauses

The type of documents is not in line with the trade terms. Such as ocean B/L is required when the air freight is adopted; Insurance Policy is required under FOB terms, etc.

The difficulties for beneficiary in preparing and presenting documents. The beneficiary should check whether he is able to submit on time the special documents required in L/C, such as licenses, freight receipts, inspection certificates and other documents certified by special bodies.

(9)Soft clause

The beneficiary may suffer a loss even though he has completely fulfilled the contract if soft clause appears in an irrevocable L/C. Soft clause, in various forms, itself does not betray the principle of UCP600. The risks to beneficiary are potential.

Attention:

Examples of L/C soft clause

Soft clause 1: One of the three original B/L should be sent to the applicant directly. As we know, goods could be drawn upon just one original B/L. Once this clause comes into force, customer can withdraw the goods before bank negotiation, and the beneficiary will face the risk of losing both money and goods.

Soft clause 2: Goods must be inspected and certified by the applicant before delivery, and the inspection certificate is one of the documents for negotiation. The risk here is, if the market changes and customer tends to violate contract, he would deliberately delay the inspection or the issuance of inspection certificate so that the beneficiary can't deliver goods on time and submit inspection report as required in L/C.

The common characteristic of soft clause is to reduce the independence and irrevocability of L/C. Soft clause makes it possible for the customer to take various means and terminate L/C from his side during its implementation. So the foreign trade specialists should learn to identify soft clause. The shortcut is: customers shall not be permitted to take away goods before payment or redeeming of the bills; all documents shall be collected unilaterally by the exporter without relying on the applicant.

Attention:

Appropriate soft terms can be considered acceptable under cautious and careful consideration. Beneficiary can also put some terms of restriction on the applicant to meet the requirements of the applicant and to reduce the risks of the beneficiary.

For example, if the importer is a reputable firm with a long history, and the issuing bank is also well-known and reliable, we can consider to accept the clause of sending original B/L to the applicant, but put the consignee as "TO THE ORDER OF ×××BANK (the issuing bank)". So even the customer gets our original bill of lading, it has to be endorsed by the issuing bank, avoiding the risk of customers taking the goods without notifying the bank. Or it can be modified to "the copy of the bill of lading should be submitted to the applicant", so customers can take goods with the copy in the provocation of some guarantee. At the same time, the guarantee provided also ensures the rights and interests of the beneficiary.

(10) Other terms

All clauses regarding bank charges or route of reimbursement shall be appropriate and convenient.

2. The three key dates in L/C

The three key dates in L/C are validity date, shipment date and documents presentation date. Usually, documents shall be presented to bank within 10 or 15 days after the date of transportation documents, so that there could be enough time to prepare documents for payment.

The 14th rule of UCP600 states: the transportation documents of products must be submitted before the 21st calendar day by the beneficiary or the representative, according to the relative provisions. However, it cannot be later than the credit documents' period of validity in any case.

10.2.3　Modification of L/C

1. Beneficiary requests applicant to modify L/C

Beneficiary usually writes a letter to applicant, asking him to modify L/C via opening bank. Such a letter contains three main parts: firstly, appreciating applicant's help in opening the L/C; secondly, listing all discrepancies and state clearly how to modify them; finally, expressing wishes to receive L/C amendment as soon as possible to ensure on time delivery.

E. g. : *Samples of letter requesting L/C amendment*

We are pleased to have received your L/C No. ×× against S/C No. ×× for tablecloth.

However, we find that the L/C stipulates for the invoice to be certified by your consul, which is unacceptable to us as there is no consul of your country here.

It is our usual practice to have our invoice certified by the China Council for the Promotion of International Trade and this has universally been accepted by our clients abroad. We hope you will agree to it as well.

You are, therefore, requested to contact your bank to delete this clause immediately upon receipt of this letter, or you may replace it by inserting the clause to read "Invoice in triplicate to be certified by the China Council for the Promotion of International Trade".

If your amendment could reach us by the end of this month, we would effect shipment in the first half of next month.

We thank you in advance for your co-operation.

2. The applicant requests the opening bank to amend L/C

L/C is usually amended in the following circumstances:

(1) Request from the exporter (the beneficiary)

The beneficiary asks for the amendment when terms of L/C are different from the contract, or he is not able to meet some requirements in L/C. For example, L/C does not allow transshipment, but in fact there is no direct vessel to the destination. And extension of L/C validity is required when the beneficiary is not able to prepare goods on time or the sailing schedule from shipping company is changed.

(2) Request from the importer (the applicant)

The importer asks to amend L/C when the market changes. For example, to advance or delay the shipment; to increase or decrease the quantity; to modify the variety of the goods; to change the unit price and total amount of the L/C, etc.

The L/C should also be amended when international political and economical environment dramatically changed. For example, special documents are required to import certain goods under the new policies of an import country. The goods should be further insured by war insurance or delivered via different route when war breaks out.

(3) The opening bank's printing or transmitting errors

The printing or transmitting errors resulted from the carelessness of the opening bank should be corrected.

3. The beneficiary receives L/C amendment from the notifying bank via the opening bank

When the beneficiary receives the L/C amendment, he should pay attention to the followings:

a. The beneficiary formally confirms the acceptance or refusal to the L/C amendment. He may also just follow the L/C amendment to show his acceptance.

b. The beneficiary should check L/C amendment immediately to see whether he accepts the amendment or propose a new amendment.

c. Either total acceptance or total refusal should be proposed against modifications, partial acceptance of the modifications will be invalid.

d. Only the amended L/C advised by the original notifying bank is true and valid. Neither the amendment application form nor the copy of the L/C amendment which is directly sent by the applicant is deemed as valid.

e. Generally the amendment fee is born by the party who causes the modification.

10.3　Task Performance and Reflections

Do Task Performance

(1)To urge the opening of an L/C

In order to fulfill the sales contract smoothly, David Sun sent an E-mail to Paul, asking him to open an L/C.

The covering letter of credit is expected to reach here before 15 Aug., since the stipulated date of shipment is 20 Sept.—30 Sept., considering the preparation of the shipment timely, we are looking forward to your immediate covering letter of credit.

(2)To check the L/C

As agreed in sales contract, BANQUE NATIONAL DE PARIS opened L/C against French customer's application on Aug. 12, 2010. Bank of China Changzhou Branch informed Changzhou Changxin Foreign Trade Co. Ltd of the receipt of L/C on Aug. 15.

Now David is examining the L/C, filling out the L/C analysis form, making preparation for the shipment.

! Reflections

To urge, examine and amend L/C is very important. Please pay attention to the followings:

a. Documents clause, validity date and place are the most important and difficult areas to check. So the types, copies, contents and issuers of documents should be carefully examined. If there are abnormal clauses, such as soft clause, the beneficiary should handle seriously.

b. If L/C is adopted, the opening date of L/C should be agreed with that in sales contract. And the exporter should keep pushing the importer to open the L/C. If we prepare the goods before the receipt of L/C and if the importer should fail to open L/C, the goods may become overstock; on the other hand, if we prepare goods and wait for L/C before shipping the goods, we may be short of time to deliver on time.

Generally a letter to urge the opening of L/C contains the followings: the opening date of L/C required in sales contract, time needed to prepare goods; statement that it will be regarded as violating the contract if he does not open a L/C on time.

c. The examination of the L/C is also one of the most important steps.

d. It is the opening bank that amends the L/C against applicant's application form. The exporter should only effect the shipment against receipt of correct L/C amendment.

10. 4   Knowledge Extension

SWIFT letter of credit

SWIFT is short for the Society for Worldwide Interbank Financial Telecommunication. The organization is an international interbank of non-profit and international cooperation organization, specializing in the delivering of non-public international financial telecommunications, including foreign exchange trading, securities trading, opening of letters of credit, bills of exchange under the credit and collection and other business.

Because SWIFT has the features of standard, uniform format, the advantages of safe, high speed, low cost and automatically authentification, the banks use it to open letters of credit.

The letter of credit opened or informed by SWIFT is called SWIFT Credit, with special format designed by SWIFT network system, based on form designing of telecommunications credit made by International Chamber of Commerce.

Task 11

Preparation for Export

 Knowledge objectives: students are expected to know
- ◆ the format and contents of procurement contract
- ◆ the requirements of preparation for export

Skill objectives: students are expected to be able to
- ◆ negotiate with a supplier and sign a purchase order according to the sales contract
- ◆ prepare, pack and mark the goods as per sales contract requirements

11. 1　Task Description and Analysis

1. Task description

On receipt of an enquiry from GOLDEN MOUNTAIN TRADING CO. , LTD in France, David contacted many domestic garment factories immediately and worked out an offer after his sufficient analysis on the cost.

Once the sales contract was signed with GOLDEN MOUNTAIN TRADING CO. , LTD. , David negotiated with two suppliers among which one will be chosen as the final partner.

David examined the L/C from GOLDEN MOUNTAIN TRADING CO. , LTD. And the L/C was correct. So David signed purchase order with Changzhou Xing Long Garment Co. , Ltd. on Aug. 15th, 2010.

2. Task analysis

Both parties of the contract must strictly fulfill the contract. The seller's obligation is to deliver goods and relevant documents in accordance with contract requirements.

Some manufacturers export their own products while most foreign trade companies usually export the goods purchased from domestic suppliers. After the export contract is signed, the business persons should find domestic suppliers, ask for quotations, compare prices, negotiate terms, and finally sign up a purchase order.

As a foreign trade company, CCIEC also purchases garments from domestic factories for export. David has made lots of preparations and now he is preparing goods for export.

11. 2　Knowledge Highlight

11. 2. 1　Signing a Purchase Contract

In order to ensure on time delivery, foreign trade company should sign a purchase contract with a domestic supplier once the export contract is signed. The clauses in the purchase contract should be helpful to the fulfillment of the export contract.

The clauses of quality and packing of the goods in the purchase contract should be in line with those in the export contract. The quantity purchased may be more than the one required in the export contract. The delivery date should be earlier than the shipping date so as to arrange the shipment.

The foreign trade company is responsible for the local transportation from the factory to the port of loading when the delivery is conducted at the factory. The company may pick up the goods or arrange containers to load the goods in the factory. If the place of delivery is the port of loading, it is the factory who arranges the local transportation.

The purchasing price should be well calculated and negotiated to ensure the trade company's profit. The terms of payment should also be in line with the export contract, which reduces the use of company's capitals.

11.2.2　Preparing Goods

The preparation of goods includes, as per sales contract, to push the supplier to manufacture the products or to push the storage section to arrange the goods, to verify the goods process, arrangement, pack and mark, and to tally and accept the goods. The following tips should be attended.

Make sure on time delivery. Goods should be ready before the sailing date which should not be later than the date of shipment in sales contract and L/C.

Check the quality and specifications of goods. The quality and specifications of goods must be consistent with the agreed requirements. If the requirements are not able to be met, actions such as sorting, processing should be taken.

The quantity of goods should be guaranteed. Goods shall be prepared with the agreed quantity and a few more for replacement when necessary. The quantity should be big enough to meet more or less clause requirements.

Correct packing and the number of packages. The goods should be packed as per agreements and the packing is suitable for protection to goods during long-distance transportation.

Check shipping marks and signs. All the shipping marks and signs should be consistent with the agreed contract.

11.3　Task Performance and Reflections

Do　Task Performance

(1)Finding suppliers

Changzhou is one of the famous textile and garment cities in China and there are a large number of garment factories. David chose Changzhou Xinglong Garment Co., Ltd. as his supplier because the two companies have established long-term business relations and the supplier provides a good discount at price.

(2)Signing the purchase contract

Hereby CCIEC (The buyer) and Changzhou Xinglong Garment Co., Ltd (The seller) agree and sign the contract, upon which the seller will complete production of high quality ladies' coats on time.

(3)Checking the quality, quantity and packing of goods

In order to be able to deliver the goods on time, David contacts the supplier everyday to check the production schedule. If any problems occur during the production, he will promptly take reasonable measures to ensure the delivery.

Quality control means the quality of products should be the same as that of samples.

And it is also required to check the shipping marks for accuracy.

Pack the goods with assorted colors and sizes as per contract requirements.

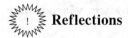 **Reflections**

The quantity, quality and packing of the goods provided by the manufacturers are directly related with the fulfillment of export contract. Therefore, it's vital to choose a supplier with good business relationships, which can help fulfill the export contract successfully and enlarge the business scopes and scales.

The purchase contract should be based on the export contract and relevant clauses should be kept consistent. The quantity in the purchase contract should be bigger and the shipment date is earlier than those in the export contract. The value-added tax invoices from the supplier should be required, for they enable the export company to gain the export tax rebates.

After signing the purchase contract, the exporter should focus on the communication with the supplier to supervise the quality and production schedule. It often happens that the supplier is not able to deliver qualified products on time.

The supplier converts the signed contract into production orders, which are given to specific workshops. The information of foreign customers, the price and the other confidential data should be deleted. The specifications, quantity, packing and shipment date should be stated clearly. The feedback on the receipt of the information from the workshop should be obtained.

11. 4   Knowledge Extension

1. Countermeasures against delayed schedule

Once the supplier drops behind production schedule, we need to analyze the reasons together with the supplier and take practical measures to recover.

If there is sufficient time left, we can add workers and equipments. Otherwise, we can try to extend working hours, recruit temporary workers, and turn single-shift into two shifts, or three shifts.

We may improve the production efficiency by adopting better management methods, timely resolving abnormal affairs to ensure the equipments running.

We can also arrange some appropriate orders to other workshops or outsource some orders. We can also adjust production plan by postponing the production of other orders.

If all the above measures have been taken, the supplier is still behind schedule. The business man should inform the customer of the production delay and ask for the extension of shipment date.

2. The selection and management of supplier

The basic criterion for the selection of supplier is "Q. C. D. S. ", which means that quality, cost, delivery and service are equally important.

Quality: Make sure whether the supplier has Quality Assurance System, and sufficient production equipment and competent technique to produce the requested products.

Cost and Price: Do cost—analysis on related goods, save cost by win-win negotiations. Low prices sometimes bring inferior products.

Delivery: Make sure whether the supplier has sufficient production capacity, adequate human resources, and potentials to expand production.

Service: Check the supplier's records on pre-sale and after-sale service.

Task 12

Commodity Inspection and Customs Declaration

 Knowledge objectives: students are expected to know

- ◆ the procedures of export commodity inspection declaration
- ◆ the procedures of customs declaration
- ◆ the calculation of Duties

Skill objectives: students are expected to be able to

- ◆ fill out export commodity inspection declaration form
- ◆ complete customs declaration for the goods export
- ◆ fill out customs declaration form properly

12. 1　Task Description and Analysis

1. Task description

Changzhou Xing Long Garment Co. , Ltd. completed 80% of the total production task for ladies coats purchased by CCIEC on Sept. 10, 2010. Ladies coats are subject to mandatory inspection. And the L/C also requires the inspection certificate. So David declared inspection to China Entry-Exit Inspection and Quarantine Bureau (CIQ).

Upon the completion of inspection, David booked shipping space. The vessel was scheduled to sail on Sept. 25. He should also prepare a full set of documents, including export customs declaration form, and declare to customs 24 hours before the vessel sailing. Only when the customs officers approve the documents and confirm the release can the goods be loaded on board the vessel. He is now filling out customs declaration form and going through the relevant customs formalities to avoid any delay of shipment.

2. Task analysis

Commodity inspection and customs declaration are crucial procedures in international business.

All commodities included in the List of Commodities, which is established by the State Administration of Commodity Inspection, must undergo inspection procedures. The commodity inspection declaration form should be submitted to local CIQ at least ten days before customs declaration or goods leaving the country.

The relative party should apply for pre-inspection by local CIQ for the partial or consolidated shipments. These shipments can only be sent to ports from inland when they are proved up to standard. CIQ in ports will issue releasing notice for goods to be cleared through customs.

In practice, the buyer usually requires, in the contract and L/C, the inspection certificate as per the relevant state laws, regulations and trade practices. Such certificate is usually issued by the mentioned inspection and quarantine party according to the specific requirements of sales contract and L/C.

Chinese Customs Law states: "In China, the carrying vessels, goods and articles must be imported or exported from the sites where customs are in place. "

12. 2　Knowledge Highlight

12. 2. 1　Filling out Export Commodity Inspection Form

Export commodity inspection procedure includes declaration, inspection, action and release.

As per regulations on registration, a company will be given a registration number when he registers in CIQ. After obtaining the registration number, the company can then start to apply for inspection. The inspection declaration form can only be submitted by qualified inspection declaration specialist, who is granted a professional certificate by CIQ. The company can also entrust an agent to complete inspection declaration, but it should provide the agent with a letter of entrustment.

The exporter should submit inspection declaration form to CIQ, which is filled out as per CIQ requirements.

The relevant information on inspection declaration form should be in line with the physical goods as well as other documents. The form should keep complete, accurate and faithful. No amendments are allowed.

12. 2. 2　Inspection Certificate

1. Types of the inspection certificate

All kinds of certificates and appraisal reports issued by inspection bodies based on the results of inspection or different projects to import and export commodities are called inspection certificates.

Inspection certificates in China are of over ten types: Certificate of Quality, Certificate of Weight and Quantity, Certificate of Fumigation, Certificate of Value, Veterinary Inspection Certificate, Sanitary Inspection Certificate, Certificate of Disinfection, Certificate of Temperature, Certificate of Damage, Certificate on Cargo Weight & Measurement.

2. Functions of the inspection certificate

Generally speaking, the inspection certificate has the following functions:

(1)An evidence to prove the quality, weight, packing and sanitary conditions of the goods in line with the requirements stipulated in sales contract.

(2)An evidence for buyers to raise a claim, reject cargos, apply for compensation, and solve disputes.

(3)One of the essential documents submitted to bank for negotiation by sellers.

(4)One of the effective documents against which the customs release the goods.

(5)A proof to show the status of the goods during loading, unloading and transportation. It helps to judge which party should be responsible for the damage, if any.

3. Time limit of the inspection certificate

The inspection organization issues certificates for the qualified commodities with a stamps. For general commodities the validity of the certificate is 60 days, but for fresh vegetable and fruit, it is only 2 or 3 weeks. The goods should be imported or exported within the validity of the certificate; otherwise a new certificate has to be obtained.

12. 2. 3　Import and Export Tariffs

Declaration is the behavior whereby the consigner, the consignee, the person of the carrying vessels, the owner of articles or their agents indicated in the prescribed form and manner wish to place the goods, articles or transportation tools under a given customs procedure.

In China, the export customs declaration includes four steps: documents examination, physical goods check, tax imposition and goods release. Therefore the exporter or his agent should prepare and submit the documents for export customs declaration, assist customs' physical goods check, pay the duty and related fees and load goods on board the vessel before the goods can be finally exported.

1. Import duty

In international trade, Import duty is a well-known method to protect a country's economy. There are several ways of calculating import duty as follows.

Table 12-1   The Ways of Import Duty Calculation

Ways	Applications
AD valorem duties	The rate is percentage of the price. The higher the price is, the more the duty is. It is the major way for import duty in China.
Specific duties	It is based on the unit of measurement of the goods and articles, such as weight, quantity, volume etc. The rate is based on the unit. Goods: Iced chicken, oil, beer, films etc.
Mixed or compound duties	The HS code maybe subject to both price and volume. Then the duty is the sum of the above two. Samples: video tape recorder, video-player, etc.
Sliding rate based on changing price	When the price of goods rises, the lower rate is adopted and vice versa. The purpose is to stabilize domestic market price. For example, some imported cotton beyond quota is subject from 6% to 40% sliding rate.

2. Export duty

To encourage exportation, usually no country imposes export duty or just a few products are subject to export duty. The purpose of export duty is to control the export and prevent certain products from being over sold to overseas, especially those important natural resources and raw materials.

Normally the export duty is AD valorem duty, which is based on the price.

Formula:

Export duty=CIF price of export goods×rate of export duty

CIF price=FOB price÷(1+rate of export duty)

3. Taxes and other fees

After the import customs procedures are fulfilled and customs authorities release the goods, the consignee has to pay other taxes where necessary before the goods can be finally sold in domestic market. They are mainly VAT, consumption duties and vessel tonnage taxes. Other fees may also occur during the customs declaration, such as fine for delayed payment of tariffs and taxes or delayed declaration.

12.2.4   Export Customs Declaration Form

Consignee or its agent should declare to customs before the goods are exported. A full set of documents has to be submitted to customs, including customs declaration form. Normally these documents are provided by exporters.

The completeness, accuracy and effectiveness of the information in customs declaration form directly affects the export efficiency, enterprise's economic benefits, customs' tax collection, duty exemption, on site check and release etc.

12.3   Task Performance and Reflections

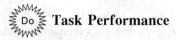 **Task Performance**

(1) Inspection declaration

David from CCIEC filled out the inspection declaration form on Sept. 10, 2010. He submitted it together with the sales contract, the L/C, the quality check report at the factory, the qualified packing report, the invoice and the packing list etc. to Changzhou CIQ.

(2) Obtaining the export cargo inspection certificate

Changzhou CIQ was satisfied with the quality after inspection of 1248 pieces of ladies coats. David obtained the inspection slip and certificate from CIQ and carefully examined them.

(3) Export customs declaration

The customs declaration should be completed after the goods' arrival at the area subject to the customs supervision and 24 hours before the goods to be loaded on board the vessel.

CCIEC filed the declaration to the Customsat Pudong, Shanghai. The applying documents cover the customs declaration form, the invoice, the packing list, the export cargo inspection certificate, etc.

(4) To assist customs officer to complete the physical goods check

During the customs physical goods check, CCIEC should be on site to help customs execute physical examination on the goods, such as to move the goods, to open the package and repack the goods as per customs instructions; to answer the customs' inquiries and to provide the documents where necessary; to prepare the sample goods for customs' further inspection, test, appraisal; and to keep the sample list signed by customs; after the check, to read "the customs check records of import and export goods" to ensure it stating the fact.

(5) Duty payment, goods release and load

Customs officers check the customs clearance form, and examine the physical goods where necessary, and issue the charge note.

Customs officers will seal the shipping documents and release the goods against the completion of customs declaration procedures. The goods can be loaded on board vessel and exported now.

 **Reflections**

(1) The export commodity inspection declaration form should be submitted to CIQ. One form is only for one shipment.

The declaration date is the date on which CIQ receives the application. The declaration date and inspection date should never be later than the shipment date.

The declaration form should be signed by the qualified inspection declaration specialist and stamped with the company's seal.

(2) When the customs declaration specialist is filling out the customs clearance sheet, he must legally be responsible for its truth, accuracy, completeness and compliance.

The customs clearance form must show the fact. It must match with the contract, invoice, packing list, bill of lading and licenses etc. It must also match with the physical goods. Any means of deception is prohibited.

12. 4　Knowledge Extension

Electronic customs declaration

China *Customs Law* states that the customs clearance form in paper and in electronics should be submitted for the customs declaration of import and export goods. This means the customs clearance form in paper and in electronics is equally accepted by the customs.

They are the two basic ways of mandatory customs declaration. Electronic Customs Declaration is one way of declaration where the shipper or consignee of the import and export goods or its agent submits the electronic data to customs via computer system according to the requirements of *Standards of Filling out Import and Export Goods Customs Clearance Form* together with the full set of supplementary documents.

China Electronic Ports System is a public data pool based on the information provided by 12 state ministries related to import and export trade. It helps the audit on the management from different departments and industries, and enables the enterprises to undergo the import and export procedures on line.

Task 13

Export Transportation

 Knowledge objectives: students are expected to know
  ◆ container liner freight
  ◆ types of Bill of Lading

Skill objectives: students are expected to
  ◆ master the procedures of ocean liner transportation and container transportation
  ◆ be able to arrange the export transportation
  ◆ work out space booking note and examine Bill of Lading

13.1   Task Description and Analysis

1. Task description

Changzhou Xing Long Garment Co. , Ltd. informed CCIEC on Sept. 10, 2010 that ladies coats could be ready for shipment on time. David therefore arranged container transportation.

David calculated the gross weight and the volume of the goods, booked shipping space
and informed the forwarder of the shipping place and paid the freight. After he got the Bill
of Lading, he examined it carefully to ensure that the Bill of Lading is in conformity with
the terms of L/C.

2. Task analysis

Export transportation is also a key step in export procedure. The trade term agreed by
both the buyer and the seller shows clearly who will be responsible for the export transportation and pay the freight. Under CIF, it's the exporter who should arrange transportation
on time, including booking shipping space, loading the goods, sending the shipping advice
to the importer, paying the freight as well as handing over the Bill of Lading.

Bill of Lading is one of the most important documents for handing over of the goods,
claiming for compensation, and settling payment. It is even more important under *Symbolic Delivery*, because it may decide who has the possession of the goods. Therefore, it must
be accurate.

13.2   Knowledge Highlight

13.2.1   Ocean Transport Procedures for Export

If CIF or CFR terms are adopted, it is the exporter who arranges the transportation.
The procedures are discussed as the follows.

1. Booking shipping space

When the goods are ready and letter of credit is checked correct, the exporter should
fill out Shipping Space Booking Note as per L/C and contract requirements. The exporter
submits it together with business invoice, packing list and other necessary documents to
the shipping company or its agent.

2. Issuing Shipping Order

If the shipping company accepts the booking, he will send back the confirmation form
and Shipping Order(S/O), from which exporter obtains the information about the vessel
name and voyage number.

3. Arranging transportation

The shipping company sends the S/O to the container yard for preparation of the emp-
ty containers and goods picking-up.

4. Consolidating goods at port

When the vessel is coming, the shipping company notifies all the exporters to deliver goods to a designated dock or a container yard within a specific period.

5. Loading the goods and obtaining Bill of Lading

The goods are loaded on board the vessel after they are released by customs. Then, the carrier issues the bill of lading and sends it to the exporter.

13. 2. 2   Container Freight

Liner freight is the sum of basic freight and additional freight or surcharge.

1. Basic freight

Basic freight is the freight for the transportation from the port of loading to the port of destination. It is the main part of the total freight.

Basic freight is charged as per liner freight tariffs. Shipping companies will normally charge the freight by weight (W), measure (M) or W/M, whichever is the greater, by value (Ad Val), etc.

2. Additional freight / Surcharge

Additional freight is normally a certain percentage amount based on the basic freight. It may also be charged by a fixed rate multiplying actual weight tons.

The followings are the common types of additional freight: Heavy Lift Additional, Long Length Additional, Surcharge of Bulky Cargo ... Direct Additional, Deviation Surcharge, Transshipment Surcharge, Port Surcharge, Port Congestion Surcharge, Optional Fees ... Bunker Adjustment Factor (BAF), Currency Adjustment Factor (CAF) ...

3. The calculation of liner freight

Liner freight is calculated as per liner's freight tariff. It differs from one shipping company to another. The tariff usually includes classification, route rates, additional rates, and the relevant interpretation. It goes through four steps to work out the liner freight.

Firstly, to find out the class and the calculating criteria of the goods as per its English name in the commodity classifications.

Secondly, to find out basic rate for a specific ocean route as per the class of the commodity.

Thirdly, to find out the rate of surcharge according to the ship route that the goods will go along with and the ports the goods will call.

Finally, to calculate the total sum of the freight.

13. 2. 3   Bill of Lading

1. The characteristics and functions of the Bill of Lading

Bill of Lading (B/L) is issued by the carrier or its agent to the exporter after receiving the goods. It shows the goods have been received or on board the vessel, and will be delivered to the designated port of destination. It manifests the relations between the exporter and the carrier.

The characteristics and functions of B/L are as follows:

(1) A document of title to the goods

Owning B/L means owning the title to the goods. When the goods arrive at the port of destination, the legal holder of the B/L requests the carrier to release the goods. It is the obligation of the carrier to give the goods to the holder of the B/L. B/L can be forwarded to the third party by endorsement. The title of the goods is transferred to the third party too. So the third party can request the goods from the carrier. The holder of B/L can also obtain the loan against B/L.

(2) Evidence of a transportation contract

Ocean B/L is the evidence of a contract issued by the shipping company to carry the goods from the shipping port to the port of destination. It states clearly the rights and obligations of the shipping company, the exporter or the holder of the B/L. It is the basis on which the disputes are to be settled in marine transport.

(3) A receipt for the goods

Ocean B/L is the receipt for the consigned goods issued by the carrier. It indicates that the goods are in the custody of the carrier or on board the vessel.

The shipping company should be careful enough in the issuance of the B/L to ensure its accuracy. The exporter should also examine the B/L carefully. To minimize the revision fee, the amendment should be completed before the sailing of the vessel. After sailing, only the minor information can be amended directly with the correction chop; amendments to the name of goods, consignee, port of destination etc., should be approved by the shipping company. All the additional duties and fees are born by the request part of the amendments.

2. Types of Bill of Lading

(1) Clean B/L and Unclean B/L

The carrier adds the unfavorable remarks about the goods' appearance on the B/L, thereby causing the B/L to be "unclean".

E. g. *One Package in Damaged Condition or Three Packages Stained etc.*

As per Article 27 UCP600, banks only accept clean B/L. A clean B/L is one which states that the goods have been "shipped in apparent good order and condition". Therefore, the exporter always tries to get a clean B/L. He will improve or replace the packages which are not in apparent good condition during the goods loading on board the vessel.

(2) Straight B/L, Bearer B/L and Order B/L

A straight B/L is a bill that is made out so that only the named consignee at the destination is entitled to take the delivery of the goods under the bill. The shipper can not transfer the bill to a third party by endorsement. So a straight bill finds very restricted application in export trade. The consignee should be "A. B. C. Co. " if the L/C requires "Full set of B/L consigned to A. B. C. Co. ".

A bearer B/L contains no definite consignee of the goods. There usually appear in the box of consignee words like "To Bearer". The carrier should deliver the goods to the holder of B/L. The transfer of a bearer B/L is completed by mere delivery of the bill to the person whom it is intended, for involving no endorsement at all. Because the risks involved within such bill, are exceedingly high, it is seldom used in international trade.

An order B/L is a bill that is made out "To order" or "To order of ..." a named person. Such bill is transferrable by endorsement. An order bill can be further classified into a special endorsement and a blank endorsement.

A special endorsement defines the order of the bill, usually "To Order of ..." For example, to order of shipper, to order of ... bank or to ... bank's order, to order of A. B. C. Co. The B/L here should be endorsed by shipper, bank or the credit applicant (i. e. to sign and chop on the back of the bill).

A blank endorsement shows "To Order" in the box of consignee, so it is also called blank order. Such bill is only transferable with the endorsement of the shipper.

Generally order B/L is often used under letter of credit.

B/L can also be classified according to other standards, such as Carrier's B/L, Agent's B/L, NVOCC B/L; Advanced B/L, Anti-dated B/L, Stale B/ L. It is illegal to adopt advanced B/L or anti-dated B/L.

3. Contents of Bill of Lading

The format of ocean B/L differs from country to country and company to company. But the basic information on the B/L is almost the same. In general on the front of the bill the following information is covered: shipper, consignee, notify party, place of receiving goods or port of loading, port of destination or port of unloading, name of the vessel and voyage, shipping marks and number of packages, goods name, gross weight and cubic meters, freight prepaid or to collect etc.

International Conventions on Bill of Lading

The transportation clauses printed on the back of Bill of Lading stipulate the rights and obligations of the carrier, the exporter and the bill of lading holder. *Hague Rules*, *Hague-Visby Rules* and *Hamburg Rules* are the major three conventions relating to Bill of Lading, among which *Hague Rules* is most commonly used and most favorable to carriers.

13. 2. 4 Other Transportation Documents

1. Seaway bill

Seaway bill is also called non-negotiable seaway bill. It is the receipt of goods and evidence of the transportation contract, but it is not document of title to goods. So it is not transferable, which makes it different from ocean bill of lading.

2. Railway bill

Railway bill is a transportation document issued by the railway carrier when he receives the goods. International railway transportation document has original and duplicate copies. The original copy is attached to the goods against which the goods are delivered. The duplicate copy with the date of transportation is the evidence of transportation against which the shipper requests payment from the bank. The international railway transportation document is not the document of title to goods, so it is not transferable.

3. Airway bill

Airway bill is a receipt from the airline acknowledging that it has received the consignment from the shipper. And it is a contract between the shipper and the airline for moving the goods. But it is not the document of title to goods. The consignee picks up the goods against "Arrival Notice" sent by airline rather than the airway bill itself. So airway bill is not transferable. The full name and address of the consignee should be shown on the bill.

Airway bill can be classified into MAWB, Master Air Waybill and HAWB, House Air Waybill. The former is issued by an airline and the latter is signed by its agent.

4. Multi-modal transportation document

Multi-modal transportation document is issued by a multi-modal transport operator to the shipper when he receives the goods. As per the stipulations of *Uniform Rules for a Combined Transportation Document*, 1973, the multi-modal transport operator is responsible for the whole conveyance of the cargo. A multi-modal transportation document represents the title of goods, so it is transferable and can be circulated and mortgaged.

5. Parcel post receipt

Parcel post receipt is a receipt issued by the post office to the sender when he receives the letters, samples or parcels. It is the evidence document for raising a claim where the parcel is lost or damaged. But parcel post receipt doesn't present the title of the goods, so it is not transferable and it is not used for picking up goods.

13. 3　Task Performance and Reflections

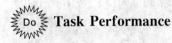 **Task Performance**

(1)Filling out the shipping order and booking the shipping space

Both the L/C and the goods are ready. David filled out the shipping order as per contract and L/C requirements on Sept. 15. He sent the form together with the invoice and packing list to the forwarder to book a 20FT container with the term of DOOR TO DOOR.

(2)Completing customs declaration and loading the goods on board

Forwarder sent back the shipping order (S/O) to David. The name of vessel and voyage is TRIUMPH V991A, sailing date is Sept. 25, 2010. The container will come to the factory on Sept. 23 to pick up the goods.

David informed the factory of the picking-up date. The container with goods arrived at container yard on time that day. The export customs declaration was completed on Sept.

24 morning and the goods were loaded on board the vessel.

(3)Sending the Shipping Notice to the customer

After the goods were loaded on board the vessel, David sent the Shipping Notice to customer on Sept. 24. It contains contract number, L/C number, goods name and descriptions, quantity, total value, shipping marks, port of loading, shipping date, name of vessel, voyage and estimated date of dispatch etc.

SHIPPING ADVICE

Messrs: GOLDEN MOUNTAIN TRADING CO. , LTD

Dear Sirs:

　Re: Invoice No.　CLK008　　　　　L/C No.　　LCH066/08

We hereby inform you that the goods under the above mentioned credit have been shipped. The details of the shipment are as follows:

Commodity: LADIES COAT

Quantity: 1248 PIECES

Bill of Lading No. : COS 3426

Port of Loading: SHANGHAI, CHINA

Date of Shipment: SEPT. 25, 2010

Amount: USD 35 817. 60

Ocean Vessel: TRIUMPH V991A

Port of Destination: MARSEILLES, FRANCE

We hereby certify that the above content is true and correct.

Company name: CHANGZHOU CHANGXIN IMPORT & EXPORT CORP.

Address: NO. 25 MINGXIN RD, CHANGZHOU JIANGSU , CHINA

Signature: ×××

(4)Paying freight and verifying the Bill of Lading

The goods were loaded on board the vessel and the vessel dispatched on Sept. 25. CCIEC paid sea freight USD 1 200 and local transportation fee RMB 2 100. Forwarder faxed the bill of lading to David. David examined it carefully and asked for modifications.

The following is the correct bill of loading examined by David.

BILL OF LADING

1)Shipper CHANGZHOU CHANGXIN IMPORT & EXPORT CORP. NO. 25 MINGXIN RD, CHANGZHOU JIANGSU , CHINA TEL: 0519-86338171	B/L NO. COS3426 COSCO
2)Consignee TO ORDER	CHINA OCEAN SHIPPING(GROUP) CO. *ORIGINAL* Combined Transport BILL OF LADING
3)Notify Party GOLDEN MOUNTAIN TRADING CO. , LTD ROOM 1618　BUILDING G NO. 36 THE FIRST LYON STREET, PARIS, FRANCE TEL. : 019-33-44-55	
4) Pre-Carriage by　　　　5) Place of Receipt	

Continued

6) Ocean Vessel Voy. No. TRIUMPH V991A	7) Port of Loading SHANGHAI, CHINA	
8) Port of Discharge MARSEILLES, FRANCE	9) Place of Delivery	

10) Marks & Nos. Container/ Seal No.	11) NO. of Containers or PKG. Description of Goods	12) G. W. (kg) 156 CTNS OF4680KG	13) Meas. (m³) 24. 960M³

FTC
CZCX080180
MARSEILLES   LADIES COAT
NO. 1-156

FREIGHT PREPAID   FREIGHT CHARGES: USD 1 200. 00

14) Total Number of Containers
and/or Packages(in words)   SAY ONE HUNDRED AND FIFTY-SIX CARTONS ONLY

FREIGHT & CHARGES USD 1 200. 00	REVENUE TONS	RATE	PER	PREPAID	COLLECT
PREPAID AT	PAYABLE AT		16) PLACE AND DATE OF ISSUE SHANGHAI, SEPT. 25, 2010		
TOTAL PREPAID	15) NUMBER OF ORIGINAL B(S) L THREE	17) ×××			

LOADING ON BOARD THE VESSEL
DATE   SEPT. 25, 2010   BY   ×××

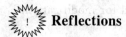 **Reflections**

(1) Filling out the shipping order carefully and keeping it properly

The accuracy of the shipping order not only influences the speed of export customs clearance but also affects the accuracy of the bill of lading, which is issued according to the related information on the form.

So the followings are very important:

a. Filling out the form strictly as per the terms of L/C and contract.

b. Leaving the fields belonging to the shipping company in blank, such as: B/L number, vessel name, freight, etc.

c. Only showing "Yes" or "No" in the fields of "Partial shipments" and "Transshipment" and showing other requirements in the remark field. If L/C requires partial shipments in three, fill out "Yes" in "Partial shipments allowed" field and remark "partial shipments in three" in the remark field.

d. S/O number should be the same as the invoice number. This helps cross reference and consistence.

(2)Being very careful with sending original B/L

Recently it is seen often in L/C: "Beneficiary's certificate certifying that they have sent by speed post one of the three (1/3 original) B/L direct to the applicant immediately after shipment and accompanied by relative post receipt. " The applicant requests the exporter to send him one original B/L after shipment. This helps the buyer to get the goods in time when the goods are perishable or in urgent need. It helps the buyer to arrange carrying trade too. But to the exporter, the risk of not getting paid is very high; special attention should thus be paid to the release of B/L.

13. 4   Knowledge Extension

Telex Release

Telex Release refers that the carrier releases the goods against electronic documents, including B/L by telex, fax and E-mail or copy etc. , which replace the original B/L. In general, the exporter posts the original B/L to consignee directly or via bank, and the consignee pick up the goods by presenting original B/L to the carrier. When the goods are shipped from Shanghai to Japan or Korea, it only takes a few days. It often happens that the goods have already arrived at the port, but the original B/L has not been received by the consignee. In order to avoid any delay in pick-up, the consignee usually requests telex release. It enables the consignee to get the goods immediately after the goods arrival via telex release.

The carrier normally charges RMB 100-200 per telex release. He requires a guarantee letter from the shipper, which states that the carrier and forwarder is not responsible for any problems resulting from telex release.

The exporter no longer holds the title to the goods after telex release. So the exporter must ensure to receive the payment from the consignee before he agrees with telex release. Otherwise, he may easily loose the goods without getting paid.

Task 14

Transportation Insurance of Exported Cargoes

 Knowledge objectives: students are expected to know
- ◆ the contents of insurance policy
- ◆ the ways of calculating premium

Skill objectives: students are expected to be able to
- ◆ perform the formalities of covering transportation insurance
- ◆ fill in the insurance policy and examine its contents

14. 1   Task Description and Analysis

1. Task description

CCIEC booked shipping space for 156 cartons of ladies coats on Sept. 15, and was told that the goods would be loaded on board the vessel on Sept. 24 and the vessel was to sail on Sept. 25. Now David Sun is insuring the goods with an insurance company.

2. Task analysis

Under CIF term, the exporter should insure the goods as per sales contract before shipment. The insurance company issues the insurance policy after he gets the premium from the exporter. The insurance policy is one of the documents required to settle the payment.

Therefore, David Sun should fill out the application form for insurance as per sales contract, pay the premium and carefully examine the obtained insurance policy from the insurance company.

14. 2   Knowledge Highlight

14. 2. 1   The Classification of Insurance Policy

An insurance document is a contract signed by the insurer and the insurant. It serves as an evidence of insurance, against which the insured lodges a claim and the insurer settle the claim. Insurance clauses, stating the rights and obligations of the insurer and insured, are pre-printed on the back of an insurance document.

Insurance documents are mainly classified as insurance policy, insurance certificate, open cover, etc.

1. Insurance policy

An insurance policy is a written legal contract between the insurer and the insured listing all terms and conditions of the agreement, such as the extent of the insurer's responsibility, the rights and obligations of parties concerned, etc. It is also called a formal insurance document.

2. Insurance certificate

An insurance certificate is a simplified contract without terms and conditions on the back of document. It is called informal insurance document. An insurance certificate contains all the information that shows on the face of an insurance policy, so they are of the same legal effect.

3. Open cover

In order to simplify insurance procedure and avoid delay or neglect in insurance arrangement, the practice of open cover is usually adopted in import trade.

An open cover is an insurance document by which the underwriter undertakes to issue a specific policy subsequently in conformity with the terms of open cover, it is also called a general insurance for the recurring shipment. The insurer and the insured sign an insurance contract, pre-defining the insured goods, insurance coverage, premium rate, responsibilities, claims settlement, etc. Any goods covered in the insurance contract are automatically insured within the validity of the contract.

14. 2. 2　The Completion of Insurance Policy

The information on the face of an insurance document proves the contractual relationship between the insurer and the insured. The information on the insured goods covers items, labeling, packing, quantity, insured amount, vessel's name, place of departure and arrival, sailing date, etc. Other information includes insurance coverage, place of claim settlement, and statement of insurer that the compensation will be given against this insurance policy as well as other relevant supporting documents, etc.

If an L/C doesn't indicate a specific insurance coverage, or just states "MARINE RISK", "USUAL RISK" or "TRANSPORT RISK" and so on, the beneficiary may take out one of the three basic insurance risks coverage, all risks, WA and FPA, plus one or several additional risks.

When the insurance coverage required in L/C is beyond the sales contract, or insurance documents is required under FOB and CFR terms, the beneficiary may insure the goods as per L/C requirements should the buyer agrees to pay extra premium.

The applicable version and date of the insurance coverage should be indicated after its name. For example: Covering all risks and war risks as per Ocean Marine Cargo Clause & Ocean Marine War Risks Clauses of the People's Insurance Company of China dated January 1st, 1981.

A set of insurance policy, issued by China People's Insurance Company, includes 5 copies in total: 1 ORIGINAL, 1 DUPLICATE and 3 copies. As per UCP600, all the originals of an insurance policy should be submitted for negotiation when more than one original is issued.

14. 2. 3　Insurance Claim

When there is a loss in the transit of import and export goods, the insured (policy holder or insurance assignee) may lodge a claim to the insurance company. The insurance company should settle the claim according to the stipulated insurance clauses. The below three steps should be followed when a claim is lodged:

1. To inform the loss

Once the insured knows the damage to the cargo, he should immediately notify the insurance company or the designated agent on the policy. The latter should promptly take appropriate measures, such as to inspect the loss, to provide the suggestions, to reduce the losses, to identify liabilities and to issue the inspection report, etc.

2. To take reasonable remedy measures

Whenever the loss occurs, the insured shall promptly take necessary and reasonable measures to prevent more losses.

Sometimes the insurance company sends a special notice to the insured, providing reasonable measures to prevent or minimize the losses. The insured must follow the instructions.

3. To prepare documents for claim

The following documents are required when a claim is lodged:

——Formal letter to lodge a claim

——Insurance policy

——Invoice

——Inspection Report on the Loss

——Damage/Shortage Certificate

——List of details: claim amount, calculation formula, expense items etc.

14. 3   Task Performance and Reflections

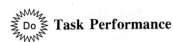 **Task Performance**

(1)Covering insurance

An application form for cargo transportation insurance is a written offer from the insured to the insurer. If the insurer accepts the offer, he will issue an insurance policy accordingly. The application form is the first hand source material which provides reference on the insurance cover and claim settlement. The format of application form from different insurance company may not be the same, but they share the same key information: name of the insured, descriptions of the goods, packing and quantity, shipping marks, the insured amount, conveyance, date of commencement, voyage or route, insurance coverage, place of claim payment, etc.

The export goods from CCIEC are usually insured by PICC, Changzhou Branch. On Sept. 24, 2010, with the confirmed sailing date and the vessel name, David filled out the application form for cargo transportation Insurance in accordance with the stipulations of sales contract and L/C.

(2)Paying premium

The insurance is only effective when the insured pays premium. The insurer may not issue insurance documents if he is not paid.

CCIEC paid US $ 433. 40 to the insurance company. The premium rate for All Risks is 1% and War Risk 0.1%, so

Premium = insured amount × premium rate

= CIF price × (1+ additional percentage) × premium rates

= USD 35 817. 60 × (1+10%) × (1%+0. 1%)

$$= USD\ 39\ 400.\ 00 \times 1.\ 1\% = USD\ 433.\ 40$$

(3)Getting insurance documents and checking them

After getting the premium, the insurance company faxed the insurance policy to CCIEC. David checked the policy against the sales contract and L/C. Should there is any mistake or discrepancy, he should ask the insurance company to amend the policy, so that the policy can strictly conform to the L/C.

! Reflections

When the insured is filling out the application form for cargo transportation insurance, he should pay attention to the followings:

a. The contents should be truthful.

b. The contents should conform with those in the sales contract and L/C.

c. Handling special requirements. Under a CIF contract, the buyer may increase the insured amount, ask for additional risk coverage, etc. The seller should carefully study these requirements and consult the insurance company before he makes up any decisions.

d. The goods of Chinese foreign trade companies are normally insured by PICC, which usually applies China's relevant laws. PICC also accepts Institute Cargo Clauses according to customers' requirements.

When one checks an insurance policy, the followings should be paid attention to:

a. The issuing date of the insurance policy should be not later than B/L date, otherwise the importer or the paying bank may refuse to pay for the goods.

b. When the exporter arranges the insurance, the insurance policy should be endorsed before it is presented to the bank for negotiation.

c. In a FOB or CFR contract, necessary inland insurance coverage should be taken out to avoid the risks occuring from the factory to the ship's rail in the port of shipment.

14. 4   Knowledge Extension

Irrespective of Percentage

When a claim is lodged for fragile and bulk goods, irrespective of percentage (abbreviated as IOP) should always be considered. If IOP is not applicable, the insurer compensates the actual losses as long as these losses are covered by the insurance. If IOP is applicable, the insurance company shall not compensate for the losses when the actual losses are not beyond IOP.

IOP is furthered classified into franchise and deductible.

a. Under franchise, when the losses are beyond IOP, the insurer compensates all the actual losses without deducting IOP.

b. Under deductible, when the losses are beyond IOP, the insurer only compensates the actual losses exceeding the IOP.

Task 15

Settlement of Payment

 Knowledge objectives: students are expected to know
- ◆ the documents of payment settlement and its contents
- ◆ payment settlement methods and its operation

Skills objectives: students are expected to be able to
- ◆ prepare the documents of payment settlement
- ◆ submit the documents and resolve other related issues

15. 1 Task Description and Analysis

1. Task description

CCIEC has exported goods at Shanghai port on Sept. 25, 2010 as required in L/C. Credit says that documents should be presented within 10 days. (Presentation period 48: documents to be presented within 10 days after the issuance of the shipping documents but within the validity of the credit.) Now David Sun is making the documents for the payment.

2. Task analysis

Delivery against documents and payment against documents are the most favorable methods used in current international trade. When the letter of credit is adopted, the bank pays the money in strict accordance with the documents without caring the contract and physical goods. The documents must be accurate, complete, timely and clear to guarantee the benefits of the exporter.

After the delivery of goods, the exporter works for the payment settlement. He makes the draft, invoice, packing list etc., obtains in time the bill of lading, insurance policy, certificate of origin, inspection certificate etc., examines them to ensure accuracy, and then submits all the documents and necessary certificates to the designated bank for payment, acceptance, or negotiation on or before the required date.

15. 2 Knowledge Highlight

15. 2. 1 Documents for Payment Settlement

The contents and preparations of payment settlement documents are briefly introduced as follows:

1. Invoice

Invoice is the shortened form for commercial invoice, which is issued by the exporter to the importer, showing the price of the goods. It is the key document in the customs clearance. Commercial invoice shows the whole picture of a business transaction. It contains the name, specification, price, quantity, amount, etc. It is the basis of the full set of export documents and the key document in the customs clearance.

2. Packing list

Packing list is the supplement document to commercial invoice, composed of a packing list, a weight list or a measurement list. It must be prepared strictly as per the requirements of the letter of credit.

Packing list is the document showing the details of the goods' package, specification, weight, measurement, etc., upon which the buyer and the local customs can check the goods at the destination port.

3. Draft (Bill of Exchange)

The followings must be shown on the draft: the word of "Draft", order of unconditional payment, specific amount, the name of payer, the date of draft, signature of the drawer, etc. Should any of the above is missing, the draft is invalid. In practice, the draft must also show the date and place of payment as well as the issuing place, etc.

4. Certificate of origin

Certificate of origin varies with issuers. It is usually of three types: GSP FORM A issued by CIQ, CERTIFICATE OF ORIGIN drawn by CCPIT, and the one made by the exporter of the manufacturer.

Table 15-1　How to Make the Certificate of Origin

Items	What to fill in boxes
Code Number	To be filled at the upright corner of the certificate, where the filling is compulsory.
Goods Consigned from	Type the name, address and country of the exporter. The name must be the same as the exporter described in the invoice.
Goods Consigned to	Type the name, address and country of the importer. The name must be the same as the importer described in the invoice. For third party trade, the words "To Order" may be typed.
Means of Transport and Route	State in detail the means of transport and route for the products exported. If the L/C terms etc. do not require such details, type "By Air" or "By Sea". If the products are transported through a third country this can be indicated as follows: e. g. *"By Air" "Laos to India via Bangkok"*
Gross Weight or Other Quantity	Type the gross weight or other quantity (such as pieces, kg) of the products covered by the certificate.
For Official Use	Reserved for use by certifying authority.
Marks and Numbers of Packages	Type the marks and numbers of the packages covered by the certificate. This information should be identical to the marks and numbers on the packages.
Tariff Item Number	Type the 4-digit HS heading of the individual items.
Number and Kind of Packages; Description of Goods	Type clearly the description of the products exported. This should be identical to the description of the products contained in the invoice. An accurate description will help the Customs Authority of the country of destination to clear the products quickly.
Number and Date of Invoices	State number and date of the invoice in question. The date of the invoice attached to the Application should not be later than the date of approval on the certificate.
Declaration by the Exporter	The term "Exporter" refers to the shipper who can either be a trader or a manufacturer. Type the name of the producing country and the importing country and the place and date when the declaration is made. This box must be signed by the company's authorized signatory.
Certification	The certifying authority will certify in the appointed box.

15. 2. 2　Methods of Payment under L /C

In the export transactions of our country, the following payment settlement via letter of credits adopted.

1. Settlement against payment

Settlement against payment means the local bank in export country accepts the documents presented by the beneficiary which conforms to the terms of L/C. The local bank forwards the full set of documents to oversea reimbursing bank. The local bank pays the beneficiary after he receives the money from the oversea reimbursing bank.

2. Settlement against documents

Settlement against documents is also called export mortgage or negotiation. The negotiating bank buys the beneficiary's draft and documents which conforms to the terms of L/C. He pays the beneficiary the net amount with the deduction of the interest for the period from negotiating day to the day he may get the payment.

15. 2. 3　Disposal of the Issues in Letter of Credit

In practice, the discrepancy may occur due to various reasons. Any discrepancy, found by the issuing bank may result in the draft being dishonored.

When the payment is refused, the first thing to do is to find out which party should bear the responsibility and whether the rejection is reasonable according to the procedure. If the rejection is not reasonable, our domestic bank may help argue. As per the procedure, the issuing bank must complete the check of documents within 5 working days and raise all the discrepancies at one time. Any discrepancy found later is not acceptable.

1. How to avoid and respond to the "discrepancy between documents and credit"

As a core document, if there are mistakes such as wrong words or grammar errors in L/C, which may not cause misunderstandings and can not be modified, these mistakes should be repeated in conformity with the credit in all the other documents.

The shipper should notify the customer immediately if he failed to post the bill of lading in time as per the customer's request due to the delay of obtaining it. But the documents should still be prepared according to the letter of credit.

The shipper should pay more attention to those documents, which are not issued by himself but the 3rd party, such as the bill of lading from the forwarder. The shipper should check the bill of lading carefully and ask for revision where necessary. The shipper should check the original documents again once he receives them. Ask for the updating immediately if errors still exist. If the date is not in conformity with the letter of credit, ask the forwarder to update the date as required in the letter of credit.

It's difficult to change the documents issued by national bodies, such as Inspection Bureau. Extra effort is thus needed. The exporter should consult the Inspection Bureau for any special documents required in the letter of credit. The credit should be modified if the exporter can't provide them. On the other hand, the international market is changing, and the quality requirement for goods also varies. If Inspection Bureau doesn't satisfy the quality of the product, the exporter may submit the confirmation letter issued by the buyer to Inspection Bureau in exchange for the quality certificate.

2. How to avoid and respond to the "discrepancies among different documents"

This means the discrepancies of same fields on different documents. This is usually caused by difference in the work of different team members. A good solution is to establish a transaction data pool, from which the data can be accurately picked up or cross reference with transaction code.

Crossing check is also very important. The same field in different documents should be filled with the same information. In practice, the contents in the same fields may reasonably be different. E. g. in the name and description field, more detailed information (including different types and specifications under each product name) is shown on the invoice while only the product name is shown on the bill of lading and inspection documents.

3. How to handle the "discrepancy"

Any difference between the documents and the letter of credit is named as discrepancy. The issuing bank may accept the minor errors, such as a wrong letter or mark, which doesn't cause any misunderstanding or affect the business transaction. But certain amount of discrepancy fee, e. g. USD40 per discrepancy, will be deducted from payment. If the mistakes are serious, especially involving quantity, amount and delivery date, etc. , the issuing bank will notify the beneficiary and postpone the payment under credit. Once the applicant of credit accepts all the discrepancies and agrees to effect the payment after the negotiation with the seller, the issuing bank will then pay the money with the discrepancy fee to be deducted. Therefore, the discrepancy may directly invalidate the letter of credit.

In general the domestic negotiating bank examines the documents once again before posting them to the oversea issuing bank. The wrong documents should always be replaced with the revised ones within time limit. As long as the full set of correct documents is submitted to the local negotiating bank before the expiry date of credit, no discrepancy exists and the issuing bank must pay.

If it is impossible to correct the mistakes in time, the following solutions may be helpful:

a. For minor errors: With the approval from the applicant, the beneficiary may ask for negotiation against letter of guarantee. On most occasions customers will agree to do so.

b. For complicated errors: The shipper may ask the negotiating bank to inform the issuing bank of the discrepancies. The issuing bank contacts the applicant and asks for his acceptance. When he receives the acceptance of discrepancy, the domestic negotiating bank then posts the documents to the issuing bank. This is called "inform the discrepancy via electronic means".

c. The credit payment is changed into collection with credit, should all the above solutions fail. Therefore, the risk becomes very high. So never adopt it unless there are no other better alternatives.

15.3   Task Performance and Reflections

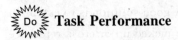 **Task Performance**

(1) Making documents

The export goods were delivered. In order to get payment on time, David is now making the draft, invoice and packing list, etc. as per letter of credit.

Bill of Exchange

Drawn under   BANQUE NATIONAL DE PARIS FRANCE

L/C NO.   LCH066/08   Dated AUG. 12, 2010

NO: CLK008   Exchange for USD35817.60   China   SEP. 27, 2010

At * * * * * * * * sight of this First of Exchange(Second of Exchange Being unpaid)

Pay to the order of BANK OF CHINA CHANGZHOU BRANCH

The sum of SAY U. S. DOLLARS THIRTY-FIVE THOUSAND EIGHT HUNDRED SEVENTEEN AND CENTS SIXTY ONLY

TO BANQUE NATIONAL DE PARIS FRANCE

CHANGZHOU CHANGXIN IMPORT & EXPORT CORP.

陈哲

CHANGZHOU CHANGXIN IMPORT & EXPORT CORP.

NO. 25 MINGXIN RD, CHANGZHOU JIANGSU, CHINA TEL: 0519-86338171

COMMERCIAL INVOICE

TO: GOLDEN MOUNTAIN TRADING CO., LTD   INVOICE NO. CLK008

ROOM 1618   BUILDING G   INVOICE DATE SEPT. 15, 2010

NO. 36 THE FIRST LYON STREET,   CONTRACT NO. CZCX080180

PARIS, FRANCE   L/C NO. LCH066/08

FROM SHANGHAI CHINA TO MARSEILLES PORT FRANCE

MARKS & NOS.	DESCRIPTION OF GOODS	QUANTITY	UNIT PRICE	AMOUNT
FTC CZCX080180 MARSEILLES NO. 1-156	100% COTTON LADIES COAT woven, with bronze-colored buttons, 2 pockets at side,	1248pcs	USD28.70/ PC	CIFC3% MARSEILLES USD35817.60

AMOUNT IN WORDS: SAY U. S. DOLLARS THIRTY-FIVE THOUSAND EIGHT HUNDRED SEVENTEEN AND SIXTY CENTS ONLY

CHANGZHOU CHANGXIN IMPORT & EXPORT CORP.

陈哲

CHANGZHOU CHANGXIN IMPORT & EXPORT CORP.
NO. 25 MINGXIN RD, CHANGZHOU JIANGSU, CHINA TEL: 0519-86338171
PACKING LIST

TO: GOLDEN MOUNTAIN TRADING CO., LTD
ROOM 1618 BUILDING G
NO. 36 THE FIRST LYON STREET,
PARIS, FRANCE

INVOICE NO. CLK008
INVOICE DATE SEPT. 15, 2010
CONTRACT NO. CZCX080180
L/C NO. LCH066/08

MARKS & NOS.	DESCRIPTION OF GOODS	QTY	CTNS	G. W. (KG)	N. W. (KG)	MEAS.
FTC CZCX080180 MAR- SEILLES NO. 1-156	100% COTTON LADIES COAT woven, with bronze-col- ored buttons, 2 pockets at side,	1248PCS	156CTNS	30/4680	25/3900	@ 50X40X80 CM / 24. 96CBM

PACKAGES IN WORDS: SAY ONE HUNDRED AND FIFTY-SIX CARTONS ONLY

CHANGZHOU CHANGXIN IMPORT & EXPORT CORP.
陈哲

Certification of origin

<table>
<tr><td colspan="2">1. Exporter(full name and address)
CHANGZHOU CHANGXIN IMPORT & EXPORT CORP.
NO. 25 MINGXIN RD, CHANGZHOU JIANGSU , CHINA</td><td colspan="3" rowspan="2">Certificate No.
CERTIFICATE OF ORIGION
OF
THE PEOPLE'S REPUBLIC OF CHINA</td></tr>
<tr><td colspan="2">2. Consignee(full name, address, country)
GOLDEN MOUNTAIN TRADING CO., LTD
ROOM 1618 BUILDING G, NO. 36 THE FIRST LYON STREET, PARIS, FRANCE</td></tr>
<tr><td colspan="2">3. Means of transport and route
FROM SHANGHAI TO MARSEILLES PORT BY SEA</td><td colspan="3" rowspan="2">5. For certifying authority use only</td></tr>
<tr><td colspan="2">4. Country/region of destination
FRANCE</td></tr>
<tr><td>6. Marks and numbers
FTC
CZCX080180
MARSEILLES
NO. 1-156</td><td>7. Description of goods. Number and kind of packages
LADIES JACKET
woven, fur at collar, with bronze-colored buttons, 2 pockets at front and 2 pockets without flaps at chest, like original sample sent on July, 15, 2010.
ONE HUNDRED AND FIFTY-SIX (156)CARTONS
* * * * * * * * * * * * * * * * * *</td><td>8. H. S. Code
6202. 1290</td><td>9. Quantity

1248PCS</td><td>10. Number and date of invoice.
CLK008
Sept.
15, 2010</td></tr>
</table>

Continued

11. Declaration by the exporter The undersigned hereby declares that the above details and statements are correct that all the goods were produced in China and that they comply with the Rules of Origin of the people's Republic of China.	12. Certification It is hereby certified that the declaration by the exporter is correct.
CHANGZHOU Sept. 20, 2010 孙大伟 Place and date. Signature and stamp of authorized signatory	CHANGZHOU Sept. 21, 2010 王伟 Place and date. Signature and stamp of Certifying authority.

(2)Documents presentation

In order to improve the quality of the documents and ensure the safe and timely payment settlement, the bank accepts both partial documents without bill of lading or full set of documents.

David obtained the Bill of Lading from the forwarder, Insurance Policy from the insurance company, Quality Certificate and Certificate of Origin from CIQ, and checked all the documents carefully. He submitted all the documents together with the draft prepared just now to local bank for negotiation on Sept. 28.

(3)Payment settlement

The Bank of China Changzhou Branch examined the documents from CCIEC and concluded that the documents met the requirements of the letter of credit. The bank bought the beneficiary's draft and documents, deducting the interest from the negotiation date to the payment receiving date. The negotiating bank converted the net amount in foreign currency into RMB at the exchange rate on the negotiation day. The money was remitted to the account of CCIEC on Oct. 6, 2010. The Bank of China received the payment from the reimbursing bank in France on Oct. 15, 2010.

! Reflections

When the mode of delivery against documents or the payment against documents is adopted, making documents is critical to the success of payment settlement. *The concept that documents are money* should be always kept in mind. The negotiation documents should be examined carefully and submitted to the bank in time.

When documents are made, the following tips should be attended:

a. Accuracy: The contents of the documents should reflect the fact and there should be no conflict information among different documents. All the requirements in the letter of credit must be met.

b. Completeness: The copies of documents should be complete as per the letter of credit or the contract. All the necessary information should be.shown on the documents. All the special requirements in the letter of credit and contract should also be shown on the documents.

c. Promptness: The documents must be prepared on time. The date on different documents must be reasonable and logical; documents must be submitted within the expiry date of the credit, before the presentation date of the required documents and within 21 days after the date of bill of lading.

d. Simplicity. The contents should be simple and clear as per the requirements of letter of credit, contract and international practice. The unnecessary information should be avoided.

e. Cleanness: The layout of the documents should be tidy. The words should be clearly printed and difficult to be changed, especially for the words of the amount, packages, and weight etc.

15. 4   Knowledge Extension

1. Three expressions for number of documents:

"Copy", e. g. in 1 copy, in 5 copies

"Fold", e. g. in 1 fold, in 5 fold

English Words: e. g. in duplicate, in triplicate, in quadruplicate, in quintuplicate, in sextuplicate, in septuplicate, in octuplicate, in nonuplicate, in decuplicate.

2. The logic relationship of the issuing date on each document

Each document marks the issuing date. The date should be logical and accord with the international practice. Take the on board date on the Bill of Lading as the base, the logical order of the dates on the documents of Invoice, Bill of Lading, Insurance Policy, Certificate of Origin and inspection certificate etc. are as follows:

Invoice date is the earliest, and Packing List date is the same as that on the invoice; Bill of Lading date should not be later than the shipment date and not earlier than the earliest shipment date in L/C; Certificate of Origin date is not earlier than the invoice date and not later than the bill of lading date; inspection date is not later and not too much earlier than the bill of lading date, especially for the fresh goods. The date of beneficiary's certificate should be the same with or later than the bill of lading date; the date of carrier's certificate should be earlier or equal to the bill of lading date.

The date of draft should not be earlier than the bill of lading date. And it is usually later than the invoice date and other documents date, but never later than the L/C expiry date.

Workshop 4
Fulfillment of an Import Contract

Task 16

Performance of an Import Contract

 Knowledge objectives: students are expected to know

◆ structures and contents of import contracts

◆ performance procedures of import contracts

Skills objectives: students are expected to be able to

◆ deal with the problems which may arise during the performance of the contract

◆ make all the necessary documents

16. 1　Task Description and Analysis

1. Task description

To fulfill a contracted tansaction, CCIEC plans to import the reqired fabrics from Sanyong Trading Company, a Japanese company and one of its regular customers. David now is in charge of this task.

2. Task analysis

According to the latest statistics from WTO, China has become the world's second largest importer in 2009. Data show that in 2009 China has become the largest export market of Japan, Australia, Brazil, South Africa, etc. China's average import tariff has dropped to 9.8%, which is much lower than other developing nations; at the same time, the government has continuously introduced measures to simplify import procedures. According to the prediction of the relevant agencies that there will be great development in import trade, which would be more and more important in international trade and help improve China's economy development.

The operation of an import transaction involves the cooperation between different bodies, such as banks, freight agencies, insurance companies, inspecting and quarantine organs/agencies, customs, etc. Operators should master the process of making relevant documents such as application of L/C, application for insurance, insurance policies, custom declaration documents, etc. and be able to cooperate well with other business clients.

16. 2　Knowledge Highlight

16. 2. 1　Performance of the Procedures of Import Contracts

Under FOB term and with L/C as the payment tool, the procedure of import can be summarized as follows:

1. Opening a letter of credit

Generally speaking, the importer should apply for issuing a letter of credit within the reasonable time after signing of the contract. The definite time for application of L/C should be decided according to the contract.

The importer usually applies for an L/C in his account bank, through which most of his business and currency transactions are conducted. The general procedures for opening a letter of credit are as follows:

(1)Filling in the L/C application form

The filling-in of the application form is of great importance during the procedures of opening the L/C, because the opening bank will issue the L/C according to the application. Therefore, the importer should be very careful when filling in the application documents. All the items, such as quality, quantity, specification, price, delivery term, shipment period, shipment conditions and shipment documents, etc., should be in exact accordance with the sales contract.

(2)Submitting a copy of the contract and relevant attachments

When making application for the L/C the importer should submit a copy of the contract and relevant attachments, such as the import license, the import quota(if necessary) and the approval certificate issued by the authorized government department.

(3) Paying the handling charge and deposit

According to the international trade practice the applicant should pay a certain amount of money as the handling charge and deposit. The deposit is usually a certain percent of the L/C amount varying with the credit of the importers.

(4) Issuing an L/C

As soon as the opening bank receives the application, they should carefully examine the application, sales contract and applicant's credit conditions. After the applicant's the deposit and service charge, the opening bank should issue the letter of credit for the beneficiary, and send it to the beneficiary's bank.

2. Booking space or chartering vessel

Under FOB, the buyer is responsible for booking space or chartering ships. As the contract stipulates the seller should notify the importer of the expected shipment period. As soon as the importer books the space, they should notify the exporter about the expected arrival time and the shipment port. In order to avoid the disjoint of ship and cargo, two parties should keep in touch all the time.

For small patch of cargo, booking space in a liner is enough, while for large quantities, chartering a ship is unavoidable. As soon as the cargo was shipped on board the vessel, the seller should make a shipping advice promptly to make sure the buyer could effect insurance and receive cargoes.

3. Covering cargo transportation insurance

Under FOB or CFR, the importer is responsible for cargo transportation insurance. Two common practices are usually taken by the importer. One practice is to cover specific insurance; the other is to effect the open policy.

For the first practice, after receiving "shipping advice" from the exporter, the importer will make an insurance application, fill in the "shipment notice" and send it to the insurer. The insurer then will stamp on the "shipment notice", and issue an insurance policy after the importer pays the premium.

For the second practice, the importer signs a general contract with the insurer in advance. Then the insurer is responsible for all the risks taken by the importer for a long promissory period. This practice is simple and convenient.

4. Examining documents and making the payment

As soon as the cargo is loaded on board the seller should send the draft and full set of documents (such as B/L, commercial invoice, packing list, certificate of quality, C/O, insurance policy etc.) to the opening bank. Then the opening bank will check the documents and draft carefully according to the items of L/C. The general principle adopted is that the documents should be fully in compliance with the L/C and no discrepancies should be found among documents.

Once there is any discrepancy, the opening bank is entitled to dishonor. If all documents are fully in compliance, then the opening bank should make payment immediately.

5. Quarantine-inspection declaration and customs clearance

(1)Quarantine-inspection declaration

The declarer should fill in *Declaration Form for Entry Goods* and submit relevant documents such as contract, invoice, packing list, maritime B/L or airway bill, etc. the CIQ will get a sample at random from the cargo to inspect, after inspection, Certificate of Inspection therefore will be issued to the declarer.

(2)Customs clearance

Generally, trade goods are required to pay import duties within 14 days after the declaration. The declarer should fill in the *customs declaration form* enclosed with commercial invoice, B/L, packing list, import license, sales contract, certificate of origin and other necessary documents. If the goods are statutory inspection product, the certificate of inspection is needed. Then the cargo will be released after customs' inspection and taxation.

6. Checking and handing-over of received cargo

As soon as the cargo reaches the destination port the importer need to discharge and check the cargo. If there is any short delivery, a report of shortage is needed to be signed by the shipper, and a written statement of reserving the right to claim would at the same time be presented to the shipper. If the cargo were damaged, it should be placed in a specific warehouse which was designated by the Customs. The insurer and CIQ will take measures afterward.

Those goods which are statutory inspection products are required to apply for quarantine inspection as soon as they are discharged at the destination, or nothing is allowed to do with them. Claim can be made with the certificate issued by CIQ if there is shortage or damage after inspection.

7. Disputes and claims

If there is a dispute arising from the breach of contract by either of the exporter or the importer, claim clauses are involved in contract. In the performance of the contract, various problems on poor quality, inadequacy in quantity, improper package, etc. may occur, and cause the losses of the importer. Under such cases, claims for compensation should be lodged. Generally speaking, there are three types of claims in international trade practice: a claim between the seller and the buyer, a claim against carrier, and a claim against the insurer.

The three factors should be attended when the importer claims: the necessary documents and evidence, the exact claiming amount as well as its expiry date.

16.2.2   The Filling-in of L/C Application Form

The application form for L/C, should be written in triplicate. The main contents are as follows:

①name of the issuing bank

②mode of L/C notification such as issue by airmail, swift or express delivery

③the date of application

④date and place of expiry of the credit

⑤the advising bank

⑥name and address of the applicant

⑦name and address of the beneficiary

⑧amount and currency

⑨type of the L/C

⑩documents required

⑪description of goods

⑫additional instructions

⑬price terms and country of origin

⑭shipping terms

⑮signature of the applicant

The backside part of application form is a statement to stipulate the obligations and rights between the applicant and the issuing bank.

16.3   Task Performance and Reflections

Do Task Performance

After several days' negotiation, CCIEC and Sanyong Trading Company finally signed a contract on August 3rd 2009.

(1)Issuing a Letter of Credit

After signing the contract, David made an application to Bank of China, Changzhou Branch for issuing an L/C and submitted a copy of the contract and relevant documents. After the examination of the company's financial credit and the presented documents, the clerk asked David to finish the application form.

The bank issued the L/C after David made the deposit and pay the relevant fees. Then Bank of China cabled the original L/C to the Bank of Tokyo-Mitsubishi UFJ, Ltd.

(2)Booking space

On 19 August David contacted Sunshine Trans International, and asked the agent to help coordinate the transportation of cargoes.

Sunshine Trans International arranged the transportation after accepting and examining the booking note. David then informed the Sanyong Trading Company of the shipping port, the date and the vessel name. On September the first, Sanyong Trading Company notified CCIEC that everything is ready. Later, both parties confirmed again the shipping date, port as well as the address.

(3)Insuring

On 15th September, David received a shipping advice from Sanyong Trading Company, stating that the cargoes had been shipped on VICTORIA . 0608, and the estimated time of departure is 16th September 2009. So David filled in the document —*"Commencement of International Transportation"*, and faxed it to PICC asking them to effect insurance immediately. The document was sent to the insurance company in quintuplicate. A copy was given back to David.

Shipping Advice

OSAKA, SEPT. 15th, 2009   **L/C No.** XYZSCC1223

Messr,

Dear Sirs,

Under the captioned Credit and Cover Note(or Open Policy), Please insure the goods as detailed in our **Invoice No.**   IN/SANY/09108   Enclosed, other particulars being given below:

Carry Vessel's Name: **VICTORIA . 0608**

Shipment Date: on or about **Sept. 16th, 2009**

Covering Risks (as arranged)

Kindly forward directly to the insured your Insurance Acknowledgment.

SANYONG TRADING COMPANY

---

(4)Examination of documents and payment

On 19th September, Bank of China, Changzhou Branch received the bill of exchange and full set of documents which includes commercial invoice, bill of lading, certificate of quality, packing list, and certificate of origin. After carful examination, the bank found no discrepancies between L/C and documents, and finical clerk paid the amount at once.

(5)Declaration for inspection and customs clearance

The cargo reached Shanghai port on 20th September, and then David filled in the application of import inspection and submitted it to CIQ.

(6)Delivery to the actual consumer

David checked the cargoes with other relevant clerks and found the goods in good condition, and delivered the goods to Golden Mountain Garment Factory.

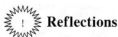 **Reflections**

After performing the FOB import contract, David has got a clearer and fuller picture of how the procedures of the contract should be conducted.

a. Opening of L/C. All the items in L/C should be in full consistence with the contract.

b. Keep in close touch with the exporter to avoid the disjoint of ship and cargo.

c. Documents should be examined carefully.

d. Quarantine-inspection declaration and customs clearance should be made properly.

e. If there is any problems on quality, quantity and packing , inspection certificate issued by the authorized government is necessary.

16. 4   Knowledge Extension

Generally speaking, it is more favorable for the importer to employ FOB trade term.

Under CIF term, it's up to the exporter to arrange the transportation. The shipping company may offer comparatively poor service to the importer, but charge higher freight. The exporter might also obtain the information of the end buyer via the shipping company, thus by passing the importer and trading with the end buyer.

Under FOB term, it is the importer who appoints the shipping company. The importer thus negotiates directly with the shipping company and the possibility of reducing the freight might be increased. The importer can also confirm via the shipping company the information provided by the exporter and get the full control of the goods, thus avoiding the exporter's deception. In international transportation, the anti-dated B/L is often employed under CIF term while it is not so under FOB term.

Workshop 5
Settlement of Disputes and Claims

Task 17

Settlement of Disputes and Claims

 Knowledge objectives: students are expected to know

◆ different laws concerning the breach of contracts and to the settlement of disputes

◆ the definition of force majeure, its components and disposal

◆ the characteristics of arbitration and contents of arbitral clauses

Skill objectives: students will be able to

◆ choose the proper methods of disputes settlement

◆ deal with the arbitration on the suffering of force majeure in contract performance

◆ simulate the arbitral procedures

17. 1　Task Description and Analysis

1. Task description

CCIEC exported for the first time garments to a French company—Golden Mountain Trading Co. LTD. The two companies are well cooperated, which satisfied the French company very much. Then the company placed a repeated order, and the time of delivery was October 30, 2010.

CCIEC and Golden Mountain Trading Co. , LTD singed a contract, the clauses of penalty, force majeure and arbitration are as follows:

Unless caused by the Force Majeure Specified in this contract, in case of delayed delivery, the seller shall pay to the buyer for every week of delay a penalty amounting to 0. 5% of the total value of the goods whose delivery has been delayed. Any fraction part of a week is to be considered a full week. The total amount of penalty shall not, however, exceed 5% of the total value of the goods involved in late delivery and is to be deducted from the amount due to the seller by the paying bank at the time of negotiation, or by the buyer directly at the time of payment. In case the period of delay exceeds ten weeks later than the time of shipment as stipulated in the contract, the buyer has the right to terminate this contract but the seller shall not thereby be exempted from payment of penalty.

The seller shall not be responsible if they fail, owing to Force Majeure cause or causes, to make delivery within the time stipulated in this Sales Contract or cannot deliver the goods. However, the seller shall inform immediately the buyer by cable. The seller shall deliver to the buyer by a registered letter, if it is requested by the buyer, a certificate issued by the China Council for the Promotion of International Trade or by any competent authorities, attesting the existence of the said cause or causes. The buyer's failure to obtain the relative Import License is not to be treated as Force Majeure.

Arbitration: All disputes arising in connection with this Sales Contract or the execution thereof shall be settled by way of amicable negotiation. In case no settlement can be reached, the case at issue shall then be submitted for arbitration to the China International Economic and Trade Arbitration Commission in accordance with the provisions of the said Commission. The award by the said Commission shall be deemed as final and binding upon both parties. .

To perform the contract promptly, David informed the factory of sending the goods to a warehouse in Shanghai Port on October 26. At 2 a. m. on October 28, the warehouse was on fire because of lightening. Although the storekeeper tried his best to put down the fire, the goods were completely burned out. As the burned goods are specially manufactured for Golden Mountain Trading Co. , LTD, and even if the company remanufactured the goods, the earliest date of production will be in late November. David promptly informed the case to Golden Mountain Trading Co. , LTD, and mailed the related certification issued by CCPIT Changzhou Branch. But Paul considered that CCIEC could not deliver the goods in time, and this was the breach of the contract, and asked CCIEC to pay the penalty. While CCIEC insisted that was the case of Force Majeure and they should not be responsible for it. The two parties had a negotiation and they did not agree with each other.

Golden Mountain Trading Co. , LTD submitted an arbitration application to International Economic and Trade Arbitration Commission, Shanghai Commission for the compensation of the loss.

2. Task analysis

In practice, disputes and claims are very common in import and export transactions. It is necessary for us to handle it seriously and carefully. It is a must to get familiar with the international trade conventions and regulations, pay more attention to investigation and study, get the truth and solve them smoothly. In claim settlement, the disputes should be settled promptly and economically, and the business relations with the partner had better be maintained. Arbitration is one of the most widely used alternatives to settling disputes.

When market conditions are changing against either the buyers or the sellers, they will find various excuses to refuse or delay the fulfillment of the contract, even practice fraud or make unreasonable demands. Force majeure is an usual excuse. It usually depends on the three compositions of a force majeure to determine whether the non-/delayed performance of a contract belongs to a force majeure or not.

17. 2　Knowledge Highlight

17. 2. 1　Disputes and Claims

1. Disputes

In international trade, there are disputes which often arise from the performance of a sales contract. When one party fails to carry out duties stipulated in the sales contract wholly or partially, the injured party may suffer from non-performance or incomplete performance of the sales contract, which very likely leads to disputes and claims. The main reasons are the followings.

Non-performance or incomplete performance of the sales contract is touched off by the buyer or the seller. For example, the seller delivers the goods which are inferior in quality or different from the stipulations of the contract in terms of quantity, packing, conformity with documents, etc.

Stipulations of the contract are vague or unclear, which may bring about different interpretations, even misunderstandings.

During the performance of the contract, force majeure events occur and result in non-performance and delayed performance of the contract.

2. Breach of contract

Breach of contract is a legal concept in which a binding agreement or bargained—for exchange is not honored by one or more of the parties to the contract by non-performance or interference with the other party's performance. If the party does not fulfill his contractual promise, or has given information to the other party that he will not perform his duty as mentioned in the contract, he is said to breach the contract. The following are different criteria to determine whether a specific failure constitutes a breach.

(1) The United Nations Convention on Contracts of International Sales of Goods

Different from British and American laws, CISG divides the breaches into fundamental breach and non-fundamental breach.

Fundamental breach refers to the violation of a contract caused by the buyer or the seller on purpose, such as the seller doesn't deliver the goods, the buyer rejects the goods or refuses to pay irrationally, which result in material injury. If one party fundamentally breached the contract, the other party might declare the invalidation of the contract and the compensation.

Non-fundamental breach of the contract refers to the violation which is not so serious and the injured party can ask for compensation instead of declaring the invalidation of the contract.

(2)Chinese Law

Chinese Contract Law stipulates that if one party breaches the stipulations of the contract and causes the injury of the other party, the injuried party can decline the contract. Meanwhile, it also stipulates that the modification, rescinding or termination of a contract shall not affect the rights of the parties to claim for damages.

3. Claim

Claim means that in international trade, when one party breaks the contract and causes the losses to the other party directly or indirectly, the party suffering the losses may ask for compensation for the losses. Settlement of claim means that the defaulting party declares that he will accept and handle the claim. In international trade, claim can be divided into the following three types.

(1) Claims against the buyer or the seller

Based on the contract, if one party breaches the stipulations, the injured party can file a claim. A claim may be filed by the buyer against the seller when the seller fails to make timely delivery or refuses to make delivery; when the goods delivered by the seller is not in conformity with the contracted quantity, quality; and the goods are damaged due to improper packing, etc. The buyer's default usually refers to the cases that the buyer doesn't accept the goods or make payment timely, or doesn't charter a ship in time.

(2) Transportation claim

The claim is based on the transport contract. If the consignee holds the clean bill of lading while the goods he has received damaged or short on weight or quantity, the consignor will not be responsible for this, the consignee can only file a claim against the carrier.

(3) Insurance claim

It is based on the insurance contract. It is a contract whereby the insurer undertaken, for a premium or assessment, to make a payment to the client or a third person if an event covered by the insurance occurs. For example, if a contract is insured against FPA, the goods are damaged in transit because of the storming; the consignee can only file a claim against the carrier.

When a claim is filed, the proofs for claim of compensation are various according to different conditions and situations. If you lodge a claim against a buyer or a seller, the sales contract is the major evidence; if you file a claim against a carrier, transport contractor B/L must be provided; if you lodge a claim against an insurance company, the insurance policy must be provided and inspection certificate(s) is (are) necessary to any claim.

Examples of Claim Clauses

There are two ways of stipulating claim clauses in the contract:

(1)Claim Clause

The clause is made concerning with the quality, quantity or the packing of the goods delivered by the seller, which are not in conformity with those of the contract.

Example: Any claim by the buyer regarding the goods shipped shall be filed within 30 days after the arrival of the goods at the port of destination specified in the relative B/L and supported by a survey report issued by a surveyor approved by the seller. If the goods have already been processed, the buyer shall thereupon lose the right to claim.

(2)Penalty

The clause in respect of penalty in a contract should stipulate that "any party who fails to perform the contract shall pay an agreed amount as penalty for compensating the other party for the losses". Penalty clause is fixed when the seller fails to make timely delivery; the buyer fails to open the relevant L/C or the buyer fails to take delivery on time, and the penalty ceiling is also included in the contract.

A claim is usually filed by the buyer against the seller who has delivered goods that does not accord with the contract.

Such as the example of claim:

Unless caused by the Force Majeure specified in Clause of this contract, in case of delayed delivery, the seller shall pay to the buyer for every week of delay a penalty amounting to 0.5% of the total value of the goods whose delivery has been delayed. Any fraction part of a week is to be considered a full week. The total amount of penalty shall not, however, exceed 5% of the total value of the goods involved in late delivery and is to be deducted from the amount due to the seller by the paying bank at the time of negotiation, or by the buyer directly at the time of payment. In case the period of delay exceeds ten weeks later than the time of shipment as stipulated in the contract, the buyer have the right to terminate this contract but the sellers shall not thereby be exempted from payment of penalty.

Notes: Laws of countries of Common Legal System only admit claims for damages, and do not admit penalty. Therefore, when signing contracts with UK, USA, Australia and New Zealand, it is necessary to care for the legitimacy of the penalty. Penalty is usually used in the contract of bulk goods or complete sets of equipment.

17. 2. 2   Force Majeure

Force majeure is called Acts of God, it means that the frustration of the contract by the party in question results from natural or social forces including flood, earthquake, typhoon, fire, war and government decrees of prohibition beyond the control of man. This party shall be free from the liabilities for performance of the contract owing to the above-mentioned event or series of events.

1. Characteristics of force majeure

Force majeure is an exemption clause, so it is vital to differentiate commercial risks and force majeure. Based on the explanation of international trade practice, the fluctuation of the price, freight and foreign exchange are commercial risks rather than force majeure events. The elements of force majeure are the followings:

a. It is after the signing of the contract that force majeure event happens.

b. The defendant must have nothing to do with the occurrence of the event.

c. If the event could be foreseen, the defendant is obliged to have prepared for it. Being unprepared for a foreseeable event leaves the defendant culpable. The consequences of the event must have been unpreventable.

2. Scope of force majeure events

Force majeure events include certain natural disasters such as fire, flood, storm, heavy snow, earthquake, etc. and social disturbances like war, strike, sanctions, etc. There are different interpretations to this term in the world. Both the buyer and the seller can stipulate force majeure events in the contract.

3. Consequences of force majeure

There are usually two consequences of force majeure: termination of the contract and postponement of the contract. Which one is suitable should be negotiated by both the buyer and the seller.

4. Notification of force majeure

After the occurrence of force majeure, the party should timely inform the other party right after the accident, usually by telegraph at first and then send the effective documentations describing the frustrating events and their consequences by airmail so that the latter is able to take necessary remedial measures.

It should be noted that the notification of force majeure should be sure to send to the counter party. Otherwise, the former will still be responsible for the loss or the extended loss caused.

5. Certificates of attesting force majeure

In international trade, when one party is entitled to invoke force majeure and asks for exemption, he should provide the effective certificates attesting force majeure issued by related bodies. In China, the CCPIT or its branches is the organization to issue such certificates.

Examples of force majeure in sales contract:

In China, in order to clarify what the terms of force majeure covers under a particular contract, different ways have been adopted.

A generalized stipulation

It means that the scope of force majeure is not specified in the contract. Such kind of stipulations is too general and when disputes occur, it is not easy to tell which party should be responsible for it.

For example:

If the fulfillment of the contract is prevented due to force majeure, the seller shall not be liable. However, the seller shall notify the buyer by cable and furnish the sufficient certificate attesting such event or events.

A listing stipulation

It means the contents of force majeure are clarified in the contract. The events that haven't been stipulated in the contract should not be invoked as force majeure.

For example:

If the shipment of the contracted goods is delayed by reasons of war, flood, fire, earthquake, heavy snow and storm, the seller can delay to fulfill, or revoke part or the whole contract.

An integrated stipulation

It is commonly used in China today, which is not only definite but also flexible.

For example:

If the fulfillment of the contract is prevented by reasons of war, flood, fire or other causes of force majeure, which exists for three months after the expiry of the contract, the non-shipment of this contract is considered to be void, for which neither the seller nor the buyer shall be liable.

Among these three ways, the last one is the best, because it is of some flexibility. If the contingency not stipulated in the contract occur, the way will be useful and helpful for the parties in question to solve the problems. It is better to use this way in the contract.

17. 2. 3　Arbitration

In international trade practice, in case of disputes, the two parties should try to settle the disputes through amicable negotiations, conciliation, arbitration or even litigation. Compared with amicable negotiation and litigation, arbitration is one of the most widely used alternatives to deal with disputes.

Arbitration means that the two parties, before or after the disputes arise, reach a written agreement that they will submit the disputes which cannot be settled through amicable negotiations to the third party for arbitration.

1. Characteristics of arbitration

a. The two parties choose the arbitration as a way of settling the disputes voluntarily. It is good to keep the proper relationship with the clients.

b. Compared with the trial which may sometimes take several years to get the disputes settled in court, there is less delay in disposing of the dispute through arbitration and the fee is low.

c. The parties concerned can choose the arbitrator.

d. The arbitration award is final and binding upon the parties concerned.

2. Arbitration agreement

Generally speaking, such agreements are generally divided into two types:

a. Agreements which provide that, if a dispute should arise, it will be resolved by arbitration. These are generally normal contracts, but they contain an arbitration clause.

b. Agreements which are signed after a dispute has arisen, agreeing that the dispute should be resolved by arbitration (sometimes called a "submission agreement").

The former is the far more prevalent type of arbitration agreement. Sometimes, legal significance attaches to the type of arbitration agreement.

The followings are the major functions of arbitration agreements:

a. It is arbitration rather than litigation that will be adopted if necessary.

b. The court is deprived of jurisdiction over the disposal.

c. The arbitration institution therefore is entitled to deal with the disposal according to the agreements.

3. Contents of the arbitration clause

The statement of the arbitration clause should be clear instead of being too vague and simple. It usually covers the place of arbitration, the arbitration institution and the payment of the arbitration fees.

An example of the arbitration clause:

All disputes arising in connection with this Sales Contract or the execution thereof shall be settled by way of amicable negotiation. In case no settlement can be reached, the case shall then be submitted for arbitration to the China International Economic and Trade

Arbitration Commission in accordance with the provisions of the said Commission. The award by the said Commission shall be deemed as final and binding upon both parties.

17.3　Task Performance and Reflections

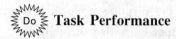 **Task Performance**

(1)To apply for arbitration

Golden Mountain Trading Co., LTD considered the delayed delivery of goods was due to the fire caused by lightening, it was not the force majeure, and submitted to the CIETAC Shanghai Sub-Commission.

(2)To establish arbitration tribunal

Based on the stipulations of Rules of Arbitration of China, CCIEC and Golden Mountain Trading Co., LTD designated one arbitrator from the arbitration committee respectively, and the chairman of the committee appointed the chief arbitrator and formed the arbitration tribunal and heard the case.

(3)To make the verdict

The arbitration tribunal heard the case and reached the decision as follows:

The fire took place after signing the contract, and it met the requirements of being "unpredictable", "unpreventable" and "irresistible", and both parties were not responsible for it, thus the fire is the event of force majeure.

After the fire, CHANGZHOU CHANGXIN IMPORT & EXPORT CORP. informed the counter party timely and provided the certificates. And since all the goods have been burned, CHANGZHOU CHANGXIN IMPORT & EXPORT CORP. was obliged to postpone or terminate the contract. CHANGZHOU CHANGXIN IMPORT & EXPORT CORP. should not make compensations for the losses of Golden Mountain Trading Co., LTD.

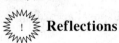 **Reflections**

(1)Obligations and liabilities of both parties should be stipulated clearly in the contract

Liabilities and obligations of both parties as well as the main transcation terms should be equally emphasized in the stipulation of the contract, which will certainly facilitate the performance of the contract.

If the clauses of the contract are too ambiguous, there might cause disputes in the fulfillment of the contract.

(2)Matters concerned in claiming force majeure

After the occurence of force majeure, the party concerned claims for force majeure should pay attention to the followings:

a. The party affected by the event of force majeure shall inform the other party of its occurrence in writing as soon as possible; and the counter party should make prompt response.

b. Both parties shall look carefully into the event to see whether it belongs to force majeure or not.

c. The party concerned shall provide the effective certificate as proofs of the occurrence of force majeure.

d. The both parties should negotiate the solution to it as stipulated in the contract and based on the reality.

17.4   Knowledge Extension

Claim period

Claim period refers to the effective period in which the claimant can make a claim against the defaulting party. Claims beyond the agreed effective period can be refused by the defaulting party. Therefore, claim period should be reasonably fixed.

Generally, a period that is too long may put the seller under heavy responsibility and a period that is too short may make it impossible for the buyer to file a claim. In practice, the claim period of common goods is until 30 to 45 days after the goods reaching the port of destination; to some foodstuffs and some agricultural goods which are easier to be spoiled, the period can not be so long. To the equipments, the claim period are different according to its stipulations about the quantity and the quality. To the quantity, the claim period usually is 60 days after the goods reaching the port of destination; to the quality, it is usually about one or more than one year as warranty period.

The Article 39 of the UNCISG stipulates that "In any event, the buyer loses the right to rely on a lack of conformity of the goods if he does not give the seller notice thereof at the latest within a period of two years from the date on which the goods were actually handed over to the buyer, unless this time-limit is inconsistent with a contractual period of guarantee."

参考文献

[1]边毅. 商务英语写作[M]. 北京：清华大学出版社，2003

[2]易露露，陈原. 国际贸易实务双语教程[M]. 北京：清华大学出版社，2006

[3]刘法公. 国际贸易实务英语[M]. 杭州：浙江大学出版社，2002

[4]诸葛霖. 外贸英文书信[M]. 北京：对外经济贸易大学出版社，2001

[5]李琪. 电子商务英语教程[M]. 西安：西安电子科技大学出版社，2002

[6]熊伟. 国际贸易实务英语[M]. 武汉：武汉大学出版社，2001

[7]张成伟. 外贸英语函电[M]. 北京：科学出版社，2008

[8]白世贞. 报关英语[M]. 北京：中国物资出版社，2004

[9]王沅沅. 国际贸易实务[M]. 北京：高等教育出版社，2004

[10]刘毅，郭琛. 国际贸易实务[M]. 哈尔滨：哈尔滨工程大学出版社，2008

[11]张素芳. 国际贸易理论与实务[M]. 北京：对外经济贸易大学出版社，2003

[12]阮绩智. 国际贸易实务[M]. 浙江：浙江大学出版社，2008

[13]丁静辉，杜国荣. 国际贸易实务[M]. 北京：北京大学出版社，2008

[14]赵立民. 进出口业务操作[M]. 北京：对外经济贸易大学出版社，2006

[15]万宁，潘维琴. 外经贸英语函电[M]. 北京：机械工业出版社，2006